ISBN 978-0-282-48461-3
PIBN 10853356

This book is a reproduction of an important historical work. Forgotten Books uses
state-of-the-art technology to digitally reconstruct the work, preserving the original format
whilst repairing imperfections present in the aged copy. In rare cases, an imperfection in
the original, such as a blemish or missing page, may be replicated in our edition. We do,
however, repair the vast majority of imperfections successfully; any imperfections that
remain are intentionally left to preserve the state of such historical works.

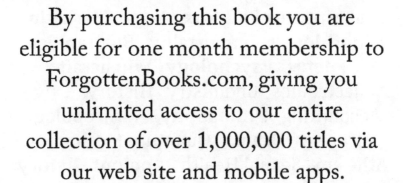

NANCY HANKS

of undistinguished families

A Genealogical, Biographical and Historical
Study of the Ancestry of

THE MOTHER OF ABRAHAM LINCOLN

———

Adin Baber

Privately Published by the Author
Kansas, Illinois
1960

Typed and Mimeographed
by
Mrs C Gerald Brann
405 Ballantine Road
Bloomington, Indiana

KINSWOMEN
(Grace Noll Crowell)

I owe a debt to all the kin of mine
Whose blood flows in my veins, exultant, free.
The things that make a commonplace day shine
Are good and gracious gifts they gave to me.
Mine were a simple folk -- they loved the soil,
They loved the land and claimed it as their right.
They knew the blessedness of honest toil,
They loved their roof, their fire, their beds at night.

These, too, I cherish, and I often see
Some dear kinswoman of the long ago
Move out across the years to come to me
To talk of precious things we love and know:
Our households, husbands, children, and the near
Good everydayness of the things we hold dear.

                    Sent by Louise Folden
                         Falls City, Nebraska

FOREWARD:

A THESIS.

This is an essay to trace the ancestry of Abraham Lincoln on his mother's side, to show her legitimacy, and to reconcile the various traditions of the southern branch of the Hanks family that seemingly are in conflict.

All that Lincoln himself wrote in the family bible and the brief autobiographies shall be accepted as basic facts, except any part that may happen to emerge as proved erroneous. The original source records of the court houses of Kentucky, Virginia, North Carolina, South Carolina, Maryland and Pennsylvania, will be taken as genuine.

All of the known family traditions will be considered, not, perhaps, to accept as wholly true, but as evidence of a possible fact to be checked. Conjectures will be stated as such. Nancy Hankses, contemporary to Nancy Hanks Lincoln, will be traced to their own elimination or disappearance from record, and lastly, it is hoped, the very Nancy who married Thomas Lincoln, June 12, 1806, shall have been certainly located and positively identified. As the mishaps of pioneer travelers left signs along the way which made plainer the trail, and followers could avoid the pitfalls, so have errors of earlier researchers in Hanksiana warned and guided this Johnny-come-lately. Inasmuch as conjecture is often a prerequisite in tracing obscure family lines to conclusion, substantiation is not always possible, and even a correct presumption may not be provable.

It is not claimed that this is to be a definitive manuscript. The evidence is cumulative and is presently briefed as it appears for future development and consideration. It is hoped to maintain such a standard of objectivity, open-mindedness, and fairness that will recommend the reasoning to fair-minded readers; and that a high degree of probability may be reached.

Be lenient, Reader! Forgive the mistakes, and help correct them.

Adin Baber
August 22, 1952.

POST SCRIPT.

Dear Reader:

     A noted historian once stated to me that the causes of
so many errors in history were superficial research and careless
writing by amateurs; that the best historians hesitate to write
about a subject until they have considered all the evidence and,
since all the evidence is seldom in, little writing is done by
them.

     The late James G. Randall, eminent historian and author
of books about Lincoln, twice suggested to this amateur, and
even advised, that as the evidence pertaining to Nancy Hanks
Lincoln was accumulated, it should be recorded for the use of
those who came after; that they may start where this thesis
leaves off.

     With respect for the two ideologies, and aware that all
the evidence is not in, and vacillating; but duty bound to
present the available evidence, I venture to deferentially
submit this thesis.

                                          Adin Baber
                                          Kansas, Illinois
                                        February 12, 1959.

ACKNOWLEDGMENTS

From my paternal grandmother, born Mary Ellen Hanks, I casually received my first knowledge of the Hanks family. I recollect that when I was of about age ten, she was reading from a little book to her sister-in-law, Mary, the widow of James Sylvester Hanks, when she suddenly stopped, and with a characteristic waving aside motion of her hand, exclaimed, "It awry!" I now think that the book was one entitled Nancy Hanks, and written by Caroline Hanks Hitchcock, as a copy was found among Grandmother's few books after her death.

From my great Aunt Nancy Jane Swango, born Hanks, and who had resided for a time in Kentucky after her marriage, I received more detailed information, although scanty, of the family.

My late wife, born Lois Shoot and in Coles County, Illinois, knew Harriett Chapman, the daughter of Dennis Hanks, when Harriett was an old lady and gave out cookies to the school girls across from her street. The first note about the Hanks family in my file, was written March, 1923, and is in her handwriting. To her I owe my initial interest in Hanksiana.

Later it was my happy privilege to help the late Dr. William E. Barton, the writer, in a very minor way and, in doing so, learned something about research, and how to decipher inscriptions from ancient weather-worn tombstones. I was invited to use his notes, and after his death did so when his papers were filed in the library of the Chicago University. For this, I am appreciative.

From them, from his books, and from the few other books on the subject of the ancestry of Lincoln, I learned that there have been several Hanks girls named Nancy, and that there is much confusion as to their identity. The Hanks family data presented in the early Lincoln Lores by Dr. Louis A. Warren, aroused my doubts as to what had been written before; and his Lincoln Kinsmen increased my interest to investigate for myself the ancestry of Nancy Hanks Lincoln. This I acknowledge. For his graciousness and generosity in making available to me all Hanks data in the famous library of which he is curator, including his own personal notes garnered from many sources, I wish to express my appreciation. In his care, the Hitchcock papers, so laboriously collected by Caroline Hanks Hitchcock, are invaluable basic material for beginning research. For this, I thank Mrs. Hitchcock. Dr. and Mrs. James G. Randall have given encouragement. Dr. Harry Pratt has been ever ready to help, and has voluntarily sent information and items he has come across.

Ralph Newman and Ruth Trantine, of that unique book shop in Chicago, where Lincoln students congregate, have kept watch for rare books with Hanks items.

My chief and ever ready and willing collaborator has been Mrs. John F. Rudolph, Sr., born Myra Hank, of New Hartford, N.Y. In preparing a genealogy of her own Hank family, she accumulated copious data of both the Hank and Hanks families; and was able to separate and sort into their respective groups the names of members of the Hank family, which were oftimes spelled in records with an "s" added, from the names of members of the Hanks family, from which names the "s" was sometimes omitted. This has been of help to me. Although physically handicapped, she has laboriously corresponded with earlier researchers, some of whom, Miss Ida M. Tarbell, Mrs. Louie D. White, Mrs. Jennie Schooley Hoffman, and others, have exchanged information with her. Her own data, and what she has received, she has made available to me. Only another researcher can know how much I appreciate this.

Mrs. Harlan H. Horner of Albany, N.Y., a student of the settlement of the Hanks family in the Northern neck of Virginia, has furnished her own hand-drawn maps of the original counties and their subsequent divisions of that part of Virginia. Her husband, Mr. Harlan Horner, has been kindly interested in this study. The Horner collection has been of use to me. For this, I am grateful.

Dr. Arthur E. Morgan, of Yellow Springs, Ohio, freely lent the notes he collected in Arkansas on the LeGrand branch of the Hanks family, and granted a personal interview to give additional information. To his early article on this subject, I owe much interest, and am pleased to report that most of what he wrote is confirmed.

ACKNOWLEDGMENTS

To Hanks Kinfolks

My greatest satisfaction comes from the way the Hanks
kinspeople have rallied to help with letters, bible records, and
family charts; and, most of all, with encouragement, interest and
moral support. I name first my first collaborator in Kentucky, Mrs.
W. E. Bach, a Hanks descendant and a genealogist in her own right,
who has diligently dug into the dusty archives of Kentucky courthouses for Hanks records for me.

Another collaborator of that state, Mrs. C. R. Galloway, of
Henderson, is a descendant of the Hardin County Hanks group, and has
freely corresponded and lent her notes to me. From these notes came
important clues. She read PART I of this Manuscript with critical
interest and made judicious suggestions for corrections and improvements, that were accepted.

Mrs. Paul Byers, Franklin, Indiana, furnished much information
pertaining to Abner Hanks, as also did Miss Nancy Hanks Salyers of
San Diego, California. Miss Emily Hanks Marshall, of Seattle, Washington, gave all she knew and had learned of Thomas and Joshua Hanks
families of Christian County, Kentucky. An article written by a
Mr. Stephen B. Hanks, a famous captain of river boats, gave a clue;
and correspondence with Mr. David W. Hanks, then aged 100, of
Davenport, Iowa, clarified that line.

Mrs. Ruth Morris Short, of Chattanooga, Tennessee, a descendant
of a rare Nancy Hanks, who married a Morris and not Tom Lincoln, has
gone to much effort to dig out data.

Mr. Alden Hanks Wyatt, of Joplin, Missouri, who had worked at
the Hanks subject for years, made a special trip to see me and to give
information which he had accumulated.

Mrs. William F. Hanks, of Lufkin, Texas, has furnished much
information about the children of Peter Hanks who was killed at the
Battle of Tippecanoe.

Miss Nancy Hanks, our contemporary cousin, has given help of
material importance.

One of the most energetic collectors of Hanks family data is
Mrs. C. G. Johnson, of Houston, Texas, a descendant of Moses Hanks of
Virginia - from her I have received information and a manuscript of
full pages of Hanks in Texas, where things are done in a big way.

So many have helped, and I must group some of their names:

Miss Marian L. Aleon, Evansville, Indiana
Mr. Charles Aler, Bellefontaine, Ohio
Mabel Thacker Allen (Mrs. William F.), Lexington, Kentucky
Mary Hanks Baggett (Mrs.), Greensburg, Indiana
Alice M. Bell (Mrs. Richard Q.), Bethesda, Maryland
Nancy Ermine Pamplin Brown (Mrs. B. B.), Fayetteville, Tennessee
Mr. Shelby Cullen Chapman, Marietta, Georgia
Coleman, Mrs. W. J. , Silsbee, Texas
Anna Aler Courtright (Mrs.), Dresdon, Ohio
Laura Hanks Dennis (Mrs. Joseph), Mansfield, Missouri
Mr. William P. Felton, Everett, Pennsylvania
Ollie Williams Faulkner (Mrs. Samuel), Carthage, Illinois
Mr. David Walter Gatlin, Madisonville, Kentucky
Edith Aler Geese (Mrs.), West Lafayette, Ohio
Miss Vinnie Gray, Madison, Indiana
Mr. Steven Hanks, Brooksville, Missouri
Mr. Harold E. Hanks, Statesville, North Carolina
Mr. David Warren Hanks (age 100), Davenport, Iowa
Jessie Eads Hanks (Mrs. Roy Robert), Bainbridge, Indiana
Helen Hersh Franklin (Mrs. E. L.), Topeka, Kansas
Miss Violet Huff, Salem, Illinois
Mr. Latt Hanks, Nortonville, Kentucky
Mr. Lee Hanks, Hardin, Illinois
Caroline Wright Hanks Hitchcock, (Mrs. Samuel M.)(age 96),
          Pepperell, Massachusetts (Collector of Hanks data)
Mrs. Bernard Hanks, Abilene, Texas
Tennessee "Tennie" Hanks Haynie (Mrs. Hugh), Avon Park, Florida
Mr. Norris Hanks, Chrisman, Illinois
Mr. L. C. Hanks, Paducah, Texas
Mr. L. V. Hightower, Billings, Montana
Beryl G. Ivy (Mrs. H.M.), Meridan, Mississippi
Edith Baker Kasper (Mrs. T.R.), Shelbyville, Kentucky
Ruth Hanks.Kamman, (Mrs. Waldo), Corbin, Kentucky
Mrs. Helen R. Kemeny, Ukiah, California
Mr. J. A. LeGrand, Perryville, Missouri
Mrs. H. H. LeGrand, Monroe, Iowa
Mr. Jesse A. LeGrand, Doe Run, Missouri
Valera Bashan Leadley (Mrs.), Chicago, Illinois
Betty M. McCroskey, (Mrs.), Wharton, Texas
Mr. A. H. Moss, Colbalt, Ontario
Sudie Hanks McHatton (Mrs. John), Port Royal, Kentucky
Mrs. Morgan Pigg (nee Brown), Fayetteville, Tennessee
Mrs. John Al Porter, Anabel, Missouri
Violet Hanks Senger (Mrs.), Rugby, North Dakota
Mrs. J. O. Franklin, Lawrenceburg, Kentucky
Mr. Bryan Hanks, Fort Worth, Texas
Miss Nancy Hanks, New York, New York

Mrs. Fred L. Steube, Danville, Illinois
Mrs. Ruth Mallow Straley, Immokalee, Florida
Miss Catherine Swiger, Paris, Illinois
Mrs. Emma Hanks Weisenberg, Cloverport, Kentucky
Mrs. C. W. Waldrop, Murray, Kentucky
Mrs. Mida Hanks Wyant, Campton, Kentucky
Mrs. Thomas Williams, Champaign, Illinois
Mrs. Guy Wright, Mattoon, Illinois

To these Hanks cousins, I display my affection and gratitude.

Acknowledgments to others who have helped:

Mr. Tish Berry, Eminence, Kentucky
Miss Hilda R. Cabaniss, Appomattox, Virginia
Mrs. Maude Johnston Drane, Eminence, Kentucky
Mrs. Price Doyle, Murray, Kentucky
Mrs. Nathaniel Gist Gee, Greenwood, South Carolina
Mrs. Nell Marion Nugent, Richmond, Virginia
Mr. R. L. Stowe, Belmont, North Carolina
Mr. T. D. Stowe, Belmont, North Carolina
Mr. Otto A. Rothert, Felson Club, Louisville, Kentucky
Mrs. Charles A. Embry, Tennessee Historical Society, Nashville, Tenn.
Mr. John Moss, Paris, Illinois
Mr. J. E. Wheat, Woodville, Texas
Miss Betty Lash, Terre Haute, Indiana
Mr. Almon E. Daniels, Arlington, Virginia

        In addition I would mention the great Historical Libraries
whose facilities I have used: Indiana, Kentucky, Tennessee, Virginia,
North Carolina, and Maryland; also, The Maryland Hall of Records, The
Congressional Library and the Archives at Washington. Studies were
made in the map rooms of the New York City Library and the American
Geographical Society. Lastly I name my own Illinois State Historical
Library, where Miss Margaret Flint and the late Dr. Harry Pratt, were
ever eager to be helpful.

        In this inadequate way I try to express my appreciation.

                        Sincerely,

                        Adin Baber

DEDICATION

I dedicate this book to

My daughter, Nancy, who is a meticulous copier of old records, and dependable, has ridden many miles to help locate some obscure Hanks place or item; and has forded deep streams to venture up Toddy Holler to the site of a former Hanks still! To her my affection, and

To my daughter, Alice, whose interest and suggestions have sustained my efforts, and who admonished me, "Pappy, stop trying to be literary, and just get it written down!"

TABLE OF CONTENTS

PART I

Chapter   Page

INTRODUCTION

PART I

PART II

ANCESTRAL QUEST

PART III

GENEALOGIES

PART IV

APPENDAGE

PART I

CHAPTER I

PRIMARY SOURCES

Lincoln's Statements

        The only fundamental sources of information pertaining to
NANCY HANKS LINCOLN seem to be what Abraham Lincoln wrote in a
bible for his step-mother, and what he vouchsafed to the reporters
for the campaign biographies. Incidentally, he told little about
his father, mentioned only one grandfather, and remarked nothing
about either grandmother. Although his information was mostly
hearsay, it was certainly first-handed, and, in ordinary cases,
would be acceptable as bona fide.

                        ***

1849. "We may be of kin," replied Lincoln to Orr, a congressman
elect from South Carolina who had mentioned his Hanks neighbors
and remarked Lincoln's resemblance to them, and Lincoln added,
"My mother was a Nancy Hanks."[1]

                        ***

1859. He prepared for Fell, the editor:

"...my parents were both born in Virginia of undistinguished families -
second families, perhaps I should say. My mother, who died in my
tenth year, was of a family of the name of Hanks."[2]

                        ***

He wrote in the family bible:

"Thomas Lincoln was born January 6, 1778, and was married June 6, 1806,
to Nancy Hanks, who was born February 5, 1784."[3]

                        ***

_____

    [1] D.J. Knotts to Barton, Aug. 30, 1919; Chicago University Library.
Barton, Paternity of Lincoln, Chap. XIV. Arthur, Western North Carolina
pp 308-326. Columbia State, Columbia S.C., 1911

    [2] Lincoln to Fell, Autobiography.

    [3] Lincoln Bible record. Clipping, St. Louis Globe-Democrat.

1859. In the autobiography he wrote for Scripps, the newspaper man, he said: "Thomas....he married Nancy Hanks, mother of the present subject, in the year 1806. She also was born in Virginia, and relatives of hers of the name of Hanks, and of other names, now reside in Coles, Macon, and Adams Counties, Illinois; and also in Iowa... He is the same John Hanks who engineers the rail enterprise at Decatur, and is a first cousin of Abraham's mother. Her maiden name was Nancy Hanks."[4]

***

1860. He answered and corrected Haycraft, of Elizabethtown, Kentucky:

"In the main you are right about my history. My father was Thomas Lincoln, and Mrs. Sallie Lincoln was his second wife. You are mistaken about my mother - her maiden name was Nancy Hanks. I was not born at Elizabethtown, but my mother's first child, a daughter, two years older than myself, was born there. I was born February 12, 1809, where Hodgenville now is, then referred to as Harden County."[5]

***

MEMORANDA

1860. He wrote with lead-pencil for Hicks, the artist:

"I was born February 12, 1809 in then called Harden County, Kentucky, at a point within the now recently formed County of Larue, a mile, or a mile and a half from where Hodgenville now is - my parents being dead and my own memory not serving, I have no means of identifying the precise location - it was on Nolin Creek, June 14, 1860. A. Lincoln."

1860. Also to Scripps he wrote:

"The present subject (Lincoln) has no brother or sister of whole or half blood. He had a sister, older than himself, who was grown and married, but died many years ago, leaving no child; also a brother, younger than himself, who died in infancy."[6]

---

[4]Lincoln to Scripps, Dec. 1859, Autobiography.

[5]Lincoln to Haycraft, May 28, 1860.

[6]Lincoln to Scripps, ibid.

SECONDARY SOURCES

Lincoln's Purported Statements

Some of Lincoln's closest associates have reported conversations with him pertaining to his ancestry; not in verbatim, but
in substance. These, also, are to be noted.

***

Charles Maltby, who knew Lincoln at New Salem, and recollected
"days and nights spent with Lincoln in the log store" where "conversation turned to our boyhood days", must have had information at first
hand. In his book he has written, "...Nancy Hanks - she was a native
of Virginia, and came to Kentucky some years previous to her marriage,
with some relatives." (underlining mine)

***

Another man who was closely associated with Lincoln on the
Circuit, seems to have missed the opportunity to learn from Lincoln,
himself, about his family, for he later tried to ascertain the
information from Lincoln relatives. These relatives thought "Nancy
Hanks Lincoln's father died in Virginia, and his widow and daughter
came to Kentucky where the widow married her second husband, Henry
Sparrow."[8]

****

1860. But a part of the above is refuted by Barrett, who had
a direct reportorial interview with Lincoln preparatory to writing
a Campaign biography, in which Lincoln would have been vitally interested in presenting only facts, and Barrett reported, "It does not
appear that the parents of Miss Hanks ever removed to Kentucky."[9]

---

[7]Maltby, Life of Lincoln, p. 11.

[8]Whitney, Life on the Circuit.

[9] Barrett, Biography, p. 16

1860. Scripps' Interview.

1865. Scripps wrote to Herndon:

"I am also very sure that Mr. Lincoln was equally sincere and conscientious in furnishing me with the facts connected with his own and his family's history."[10]

***

1895. Later Barrett wrote, "Mr. Lincoln stated to me in 1861 that his mother was born in Virginia, that she came to Kentucky with some of his (sic) (her?) relations, and not with her parents, but gave me no other clue."[11]

***

"My name should have been Abraham Abraham."[12]

****

With the exception of part of Whitney's interview with relatives, (not with Lincoln himself) all of these foregoing statements are accepted as authentic facts pertaining to Nancy Hanks Lincoln: She was of the Hanks family, and her name was Nancy; she was likely kin to Hanks families of South Carolina; she was positively kin to the Hanks families of Coles, Macon, and Adams Counties, Illinois. She had a first cousin relationship to John Hanks, the rail-splitter.

She was of particular kinship to Hankses of southern extraction, for she was born in Virginia. Her birthplace was not in North Carolina or South Carolina, or other places presented. Nor was she born in Mercer County, Kentucky, as John Hanks asserted.[13] She came to Kentucky with kinfolk, not with one or both of her parents, and

[10]Scripps to Herndon, June 24, 1865.

[11]Barrett to Hitchcock, Sept. 14, 1895: Library, Fort Wayne, Ind

[12]Gore, Boyhood of Abraham Lincoln, p. 57.

[13]John Hanks, Interview, Herndon-Weik Coll.; Hidden Lincoln, p 34

not in her mother's arms.[14] It is not reported that Lincoln said his mother was an orphan, but it is a conjecture and a concensus.

The date given by Lincoln for her marriage was later authenticated by the finding of the marriage record,[15] which proved solemnity of holy wedlock, and not mere mutual agreement to live together, as Lamon insinuated.[16]

The first child born to the union of Nancy Hanks and Thomas Lincoln was a daughter, named Sarah, and not named Nancy, as an author states. The second child born was Abraham Lincoln, who immortalized the rest of the family. The third and last child, named Thomas, "died in infancy"[17] in Kentucky, and is buried in a little grave marked T L.[18] (McM)

***

These fundamental facts, based on Lincoln's statements, confirmed by courthouse records and tombstone inscriptions, so far as they may refer to the case, leave no alternative but to search in Virginia for a record of Hankses who "may be of kin", for "some of her relations", and for the parents of Nancy Hanks who died early enough in her life to leave her an orphan.

Such an attempt is not in vain, for there are many records of reference to Hankses, and tracing their trails is not so difficult, nor unfruitful, as has been asserted.[19] The earliest record of Hankses in Virginia is the year 1618 at Jamestown. So there is the start of this search.

---

[14] Barton, Lineage of Lincoln, p. 236.

[15] Court House Record, Washington County, Kentucky.

[16] Lamon, Life of Lincoln, p. 10.

[17] Lincoln Herald, 44(2)3, June, 1942.

[18] McMurtry, Lincoln Herald, 48(1)12, Feb. 1946.

[19] Barton, Life of Lincoln, Vol. I, p. 39.

INTERPOLATION

 · The settlement of Colonial Virginia was from Jamestown -
first, the settlers moved up the James River, northerly along the
coasts, and into the navigable streams, the York, the Rappahannock,
and the Potomac Rivers. Next came the settlement of the Piedmont
and the great Shenandoah Valley.

The buffalo lumbered on the contour lines and, coming around
the mountains, grazed the grass and browsed the brush, and so cleared
a way that made natural trails for the Indian files. The white men
came, the hunters explored over these trails, and enterprising
traders blazed these ways for their packtrains to follow.[20]

On the great map of Colonial Virginia, drawn by Jefferson &
Fry,[21] the routes of the early wagon roads follow the general lines
of the earlier trails. Over these routes, from the sea coast to the
mountains, went the first frontiersmen, followed by successive waves
of settlers - herdsmen, farmers and tradespeople.

In these movements were the succeeding generations of Hankses.
They were not in the van-guard of adventurers but in the army of
artisans who came to build. They felled the trees and rived the
lumber. They were wood-workers, carpenters, coopers, and blacksmiths -
they made iron tools, cow-bells, and shod horses - wainwright and
millwright, they plied their trades.

COURTHOUSE SOURCES

Not in the history books are the Hanks names found, for they
were "undistinguished". Neither are they listed as proprietors of
the great estates, for they rate as "second families". Their names are
enrolled in court house records as ordinary citizens. The entries
indicate that they paid their humble taxes, repaired the roads, and
served on juries. Ministers' returns show that they were regularly
married, and births and deaths were sometimes registered. In wills,
they bequeathed their souls to God, always instructed executors to pay
just debts, and provided for their wives. Civil suits were rare -

[20]Hulbert, *Historic Highways*.

[21]Copy of map, Library, New York City.

one J.P. case is found where an overly enthusiastic Hanks man tangled with the law, for he "did race his horse, and on the highway, and on the Sabbath."[22]

The formal deeds, drawn up by scriveners, and entered in leather-bound books, are prolific sources of information on their premises, meets and bounds, and their signatures by name or mark. Fields and farms were transferred for Virginia currency, or for "love and affection".

GRAVEYARD SOURCES

Guided by descriptions in the old deeds, it may be possible, and has been in some cases, to locate a former Hanks homesite and, if fortunate, find an adjacent family graveyard, long since abandoned. Usually the tombstones are rude and uncarved, or worn away, but occasionally one will yield a meagre epitaph. Properly smeared with whiting to bring the lettering forth, a name or date may be deciphered that ties whole generations together, as one in Hatt Creek Cemetery.[23]

Later day graves are usually marked, but it is not unusual for a Hanks graveyard to have but few stones sketchily inscribed.

It would seem characteristic of Hanks people that, void of vanity in life, they make no show of death. They come together, sup sorrow, dig the grave, put away the departed, and return to their respective chores.

TAX LISTS AND CENSUS RECORDS

Beginning with 1782, the counties of Virginia began to keep the tax and tithe records, and many are extant. These make an informal census record, wherein are a few Hanks names. The United States census of Virginia of 1790 lists more Hanks families, but the list is not complete.[24] Court house records of both previous

---

[22] Court house record, Decatur Co., Indiana

[23] I.J. Hancs, Gravestone, Hatt Creek Cemetery, Campbell Co., Va.

[24] Missing are Hankses of Campbell Co., Va., Richmond Co., Va., and Kentucky Co., Va.

and post census of 1790 indicate there were several Hanks individuals
who were not listed. None of the lists of Heads of Families of that
part of Virginia, which is now Kentucky, can be located, although
a very complete census of Kentucky for 1800 has been compiled from the
tax records of that year.[25]

Census records are not completely reliable.

BIBLE SOURCES

It is not true, as one author has complained, that Hankses
did not keep Bible records.[26] Many references are made to old bible
records by earlier Hanks letter-writers, but those old bibles, in
which were carefully written the usual family chronicles, are long
since thumbed away at the margins,[27] broken-backed, or burned in
cabin fires.[28] Many Bibles were literally worn out by God-fearing
Hanks men who read, prayed and preached. This may astonish those
who have held the opinion (given even by a later president, Woodrow
Wilson) that the Hankses were only "white trash"[29] and illiterate.
The persevering reader of this manuscript will learn of Hanks
ministers who exhorted salvation,[30] and of others who preached
damnation.

Bible records are not copious, but there are several to confirm that the family traditions, secure in the memories of the elders,
have been passed down in the hearts and understanding of the younger
generations.

---

[25]Clift, Second Census of Kentucky, 1800.

[26]Barton, Life of Abraham Lincoln, Vol. I, p. 39

[27]William Hanks Bible, Edgar Co., Illinois

[28]Bible of William Hanks, son of Abraham Hanks, was burned
in Breckenridge Co., Kentucky about 1890.

[29]Woodrow Wilson, Division and Reunion, p. 219.

[30]Elijah Hanks, Minister, Maury County, Tennessee

TRADITIONS AND THEIR SOURCES

All history obtains first as unrecorded tradition. The birth
of a child, deeply impressed upon its parents, as a true event,
remains traditional until, nowadays, the official record is registered
by the physician, or until the parents, perhaps years later, write
name and date in the current family bible. Then it becomes evidence
that is admissable to the courts as manifest proof of an event. Thus
bible records and tombstones are only evidences of previously held
traditions.

***

So it may be necessary to revert back to traditions for some
of the sources of information. Traditions, in this case, seem to
fall into two categories - those maintained in the family, and those
that have been developed by portions of the public. Family traditions,
usually unbiased, may be relied upon as containing an inherent truth.
The Hanks family traditions are herein to be considered in detail,
not to embrace them as wholly the truth, but as the evidence and
outgrowth of things now obscured.

No family tradition will be abandoned without careful review:
"...infused into it a story so pleasant"[31] nor be summarily dismissed
if it appears that some teller of the tradition may have tried to
"hang himself onto the Lincoln family tree."[32]

Neither will a disavowal of kinship to Lincoln be a bar to
further pursuit of a clue. Extraneous traditions that have been
bandied about since Lincoln became noted will be examined, and only
those, or their parts, sustained by some evidence that was in
existence previous to his prominence, will be considered.[33]

The careful student of tradition should have no difficulty
in distinguishing the genuine from the fallacious. The sincere one
will be found to have been based on some pertinent fact - the capricious
will have no foundation in fact.

---

[31]Barton, _Life of Abraham Lincoln_, p. 55.

[32]Warren, _Lincoln Lore_

[33]Coggins, _The Eugenics of Abraham Lincoln_, Part two, Chpt. one.

An attempt will first be made to try to sort out what may have been the facts in the phantasmagoria that Herndon, the late law partner of Lincoln, put out as information, all of which he asserted and insisted was the truth.

The most eminent historian, the late James G. Randall, said of Mr. Herndon "Popular ideas of Lincoln are in a large part traceable to that picturesque but provocative individual...". "The Lincoln he has given us needs reconsideration."[34] Someone has called Herndon the great myth maker.[35] Paraphrasing, the above would read "the Hanks he has portrayed to us needs reconsideration."

***

Ever since the myth makers have tried to brand the Hanks family with the iron pen of infamy, some Hankses of southern extraction have denied their relationships, but they are unable to escape. Most Hankses are kin to each other, and all are attached to their ancestry by the umbilical cord of heritage. They are kin to many Nancy Hankses, and to Nancy Hanks Lincoln.

If this preface is overlong, it must needs be so, for this endeavor wants designing and defining, in order that what follows inspires confidence.

---

[34] Randall, Lincoln the President, Preface, p. IX

[35] Donald, Lincoln's Herndon, p. 373; Warren, The Indiana Magazine of History XII, Sept. 1945, pp. 221-244.

CHAPTER II

ALLEGED ILLEGITIMACY

Herndon, perhaps as a result of a mental quirk seems to have been obsessed with the idea that both Lincoln and his mother were illegitimates. These malignities were developed and whispered against Lincoln during the madness and bitterness of the campaigns of the Civil War times. But with the finding of the genuine records of the marriage of Lincoln's parents, anyone who now tries to maintain the fiction that Thomas Lincoln was not the real father betrays his abysmal ignorance of the proved facts pertaining to the becoming regularity of the married state of Thomas and Nancy Hanks Lincoln.

As to the alleged illegitimacy of Nancy Hanks Lincoln, those who would believe it, will inquire no further - and those who doubt it point out that there is no proof of it, even evidence; but neither is there an adequate refutation. It is a tradition that has become folklore and a myth.

The ignoble tale was first promulgated by Herndon in a letter to Hart, 1866,[1] wherein he pretended to reveal confidences about four different women who had been associated with the life of Lincoln: wife, mother, grandmother and possible sweetheart, and portrayed nothing favorable about any of them! Using his iron pen, he blurted right out, "Mr. Lincoln's mother was an illegitimate." Then he insisted that it was true and Mr. Lincoln had told him so.

A few years later, in 1870, he repeated the same sorry tale to Lamon,[2] and went into details about Hanks women, adding that Prentice[3] had "Got up some evidence on this question in 1850...", leaving the inference that they had been notorious. This was rather

---

[1] Herndon to Hart, Dec. 28, 1866, Herndon-Weik Coll. (The interested reader may find many of Herndon's letters printed by Hertz The Hidden Lincoln in which case, page numbers are given: 52)

[2] Herndon to Lamon, Feb. 25, 1870, Herndon-Weik Coll.

[3] Probably George Dennison Prentice, Louisville, Ky., journalist. See Directory of American Biography V 15, p. 186-7. "...when that silly simple Harriette Beecher Stowe accused Hon. George D. Prentice of publishing obscene literature..." See History of the Wabash Valley, p. 28.

outrageous even to Lamon's not very fastidious mind, and he said
that it would look damned ugly in print, and asked for a bill of
particulars: "You say he (Lincoln) was told certain facts...re-
garding his birth and his mother's chastity - When? By whom?
Exactly what was he told? Is this proved? When and by whom?"[4]
Lamon wanted none of Herndon's mere conjectures printed in his book.

So Herndon fired another letter and, probably aware that Lamon,
the lawyer, would want to know the occasion, began to remember the
buggy ride and to add a build-up of details, including the conversation and what Lincoln had said.

It generally has been assumed by less discriminating readers
that the buggy ride testimony could be relied upon. It was: that
as he and Lincoln, on their way to court in a buggy together, were
discussing a coming bastardy case, Lincoln apropos had told him,
among other things, that his mother was the illegitimate daughter of
Lucy Hanks and a man of Virginia. However, he added the admonition
it was not to be repeated while he (Lincoln) lived.

The salient point is, that if Lincoln alluded to such subject
matter for discussion, just what did he say? What terms did he use?
For it is simple: If Lincoln clearly said that his mother was
illegitimate, she was; if he had not been misinformed by hearsay.
If he did not so say, she may not have been. In what Lincoln may
have said is the search and the answer.

In a sentence relative to this subject, Herndon specifically
said, "In the first place, his (Lincoln's) grandmother was a halfway
prostitute, not a common one, as I understand the facts. I say this
is truth, for Mr. Lincoln told me so. Mr. Lincoln's mother was an
illegitimate. This is truth, for Mr. Lincoln told me so."[5]

There it is - Herndon said so, said Lincoln said so, and added
twice "This is truth". The reiteration of truthfulness will be discussed later. The discussion now is of the terms or words used.
The phrase 'common prostitute' may be accepted as the term in the
parlance of harlotry for a woman who promiscuously gives herself
for hire, but what Herndon meant by 'halfway' prostitute is not so
clear. When does a woman of complaisance reach the halfway point?
Are there degrees of morality in the profession? It is something
like when is a shower is a rain is a downpour? The late Samuel
Johnson, dean of nice usage of words and master of logical defini-
tions, rebuked Boswell, who had pretended to defend a woman of easy
ways, "Sir, she is a whore". Did Herndon embrace such a wholesale
definition? Was Herndon a puritan to be so uncompromising? With
his known peccadillos, was he to first cast the stone? But the
questions do not need to be answered.

---

[4] Lamon to Herndon, Feb. 18, 1870, Mar. 9, 1870, H-W Coll.

[5] Herndon to Hart, Dec. 28, 1866, H-W Coll.

Later Herndon reported the incident to Lamon, but the
wording was radically different from that which he had used in
telling Hart three years earlier. He now allegedly quoted
Lincoln as specifically saying, "My mother's mother was poor
and credulous, etc., and she was shamefully taken advantage of
by the man...."[6] Is not this an entirely different idea from the
version he first used, wherein the grandmother was described as
a 'halfway prostitute'?

Since when has a maiden, betrayed by a lover, been recognized as a prostitute, or even halfway? Of course, if by mischance,
a child is born, it is a bastard. So, even according to this latter
paraphrase and the former statement, Nancy Hanks Lincoln was a
bastard, if the tale be true. But which version is the truth to
be accepted? Just what did Lincoln exactly say, if he spoke at all?
What else did he say which is represented by the word 'etc.' that
Herndon interpolated in the letter?

Herndon was equally careless with his terms in reference to
the putative father of Nancy Lincoln. He variously used: "Well-
bred Virginia farmer; Virginia planter; Nabob; and nobleman". Did
Lincoln use any of these words, and if so, which one? Then further,
Herndon told Charles Friend that "The father of Mrs. Lincoln,
Abraham's mother, was named Henry Sparrow". If Herndon had as much
information directly from Lincoln as he claimed to have had as
early as 1851, and he inferentially had been released from the
enjoinder not to tell by the death of Lincoln, it was a form of
dissimulation to so tell Charles as much – unless it be assumed he
then thought Henry Sparrow and the Virginia planter to be one and
the same man. That he did not so think is indicated by his letters
to Hart, in which he mentions a Virginia man, but does not name
Sparrow of Kentucky.

Assuming for this argument that the story of the buggy ride
is wholly true, who told Lincoln? Herndon had surmised to Hart
that Lincoln may have heard it in Indiana, "Don't know it, have
heard so."[9]

---

[6]Herndon to Lamon, March 6, 1870, H-W Coll.

[7] Herndon to Friend, Feb. 15, 1866, Lincoln Kinsmen No. 46, p.2.

[8]Herndon to Hart, Dec. 28, 1866; Jan. 12, 1867; and Mar. 2,
1867, H-W Coll.

[9]Ibid. Dec. 28, 1866; Feb. 25, 1870.

Who, in all of Lincoln's acquaintances, in Indiana and elsewhere, was qualified to know; and who had the temerity and cruelty to tell what may have happened in Virginia many years before, and to reveal such a sorry tale to a boy or young man who had lost his mother?[10]

Of course, some such scurrility may have been thrown up to Lincoln by someone in a temper, which fastened a doubt in the boy's mind and left a scar, but he could not have had intimate details.

If such was developed in Virginia or Kentucky and retold in Indiana, it was double hearsay, and even if Lincoln repeated as he had heard, it was triple hearsay. No proper court ever accepts hearsay testimony except in certain specific cases, one of which is "the declaration of a deceased if the court finds it was made in good faith before the commencement of the action and upon the personal knowledge of the declarant".[11] This was the alleged declaration of a deceased, but it could not have been from personal knowledge.

Inasmuch as Mr. Lincoln could not have had personal knowledge of the facts in his mother's case, whatever, if anything, he told Herndon was subject to all the variations inherent in hearsay, whether the source was gossip, Dennis Hanks or himself - an example being Herndon's own failure to tell the tale twice alike.

The tale was not believed by many contemporaries of Lincoln and Herndon at the bar in Springfield. Mr. Milton Hay, a Kentuckian of the same generation as Lincoln, who came to Springfield in 1832 and knew Lincoln intimately, wrote in a letter to Vennum, "...that Lincoln confided to him (Herndon) secrets known to nobody else. It is not believed here..."

"The story of Lincoln's having told Herndon that his mother was a bastard is wholly discredited by everybody who knew Lincoln..."[12]

There is, however, a completely plausible explanation of the origin of the story, and it is found in Herndon's own words. In a letter to Lamon, and upon adverting to his previously re-taled story of the buggy ride, he wrote, "This was told me about 1852, three

10 Herndon to Lamon, Feb. 25, 1870, H-W Coll. p. 64

11 Moss to Baber, Mar. 4, 1951, Baber papers.

12 Hay to Vennum, Jan. 26, 1892, Barton, The Paternity of Abraham Lincoln, p. 360.

miles west of this city on our way to court in Petersburg, Minard
County, and State of Illinois; he told me about Dennis Hanks'
bastardy."[13]

Was it not superfluous to add more than the time and local
place? Later in the letter, he wrote, "From what Lincoln has
casually and indirectly said, I was convinced that his illegitimacy..."[13]
Isn't it possible that, twenty years later, Herndon had forgotten
much of the indirect and casual statements, and was confused as to
who was a bastard?[14]

The refutation has long since begun: One of Mr. Lincoln's
closest associates, Whitney, wrote a long letter to Mrs. Hitchcock,
in which was said, "Herndon made a mistake about what Lincoln said
about his mother and grandma: it was not Lincoln's style to talk
about those things: he has told me much of his kinfolk but nothing
of that sort. Herndon told me so but promised me he would not put
it in his book. He is an honorable man, but mistaken. You had
better go to Washington County, Kentucky, for information..."[15]

It is submitted therefore, that from the testimony of Herndon,
the charge of alleged illegitimacy of Nancy Hanks Lincoln has no
basis of fact, but is from a memory of gossip, hearsay, and fancy.

Such an infamous canard against a pioneer woman should be,
and shall be refuted.

---

[13] Herndon to Lamon, Feb. 25, 1870, H-W Coll.

[14] Horner to Baber, Sept. 3, 1959; Baber papers. "Talking of
the ride of Lincoln and Herndon to a bastardy trial at Petersburg, I
once tried to check this, using Lincoln Day by Day and the only trial
I could find was before Herndon was in the Lincoln law office and,
in addition, the County was not in the Lincoln Circuit at the date
when Herndon claims the conversation was held."

[15] Whitney to Hitchcock, Jan. 17, 1895, Hitchcock correspondence
and Papers, Library, The Lincoln National Life Foundation, auspices
of the Lincoln National Life Insurance Company, Fort Wayne, Indiana.
Hereafter shortened to "... Lincoln Lib., Fort Wayne."

CHAPTER III

DENNIS FRIEND HANKS

The reading public has an impression that Dennis Hanks was associated with Abraham Lincoln from the cradle to the grave, as it were, and is inclined to take for granted that all his statements are authentic. It is a misconception, and it is purposed to review the inferences in order to set proper values upon the observations of Dennis.

Dennis enjoyed relating how, when he was age nine, he ran all the way from his home to the Lincoln home to see the boy baby when Abraham Lincoln was born, 1809, on Nolin Creek.[1]

It may well be true, for the Thomas Sparrow couple, with whom Dennis lived, had moved from Mercer County, Kentucky, to Hardin County[2] and were neighbors of the Thomas Lincoln family.

They were not neighbors for long as Tom Lincoln moved his family to the Knob Creek farm, a good horseback ride away, and the two families were separated by a bad road over the perilous escarpment of Muldrough's Hill.

Nevertheless, Hanks people are friendly people and prone to visit and to gossip. The two Toms, Sparrow and Lincoln, had married into the Hanks family and probably went wherever the wives wished. Nancy, with two small children and expecting another, may have remained at home but the Sparrows, with Dennis, past twelve, could have ridden to call and visit overnight with the Lincolns.

It would have been a natural thing for Dennis to have been directed to look after the two younger children of the Lincolns while the elders talked. It is doubtful, if at that age, that he carried on any conversation then with Nancy about Hanks family affairs.

───────────────

[1] Eleanor Atkinson, The Boyhood of Lincoln

[2] Hardin County, Kentucky Tax List; U.S. Census, 1810, Hardin County, Kentucky.

In December, 1816 the Lincoln family moved over the Ohio
River into Indiana leaving the Sparrow family and Dennis in
Kentucky. It was a year later, 1817, that Dennis and his foster
parents followed them.[4]

There was a short interval, the spring and summer following,
1818, when Dennis and Nancy could have had conversations about her
ancestry, and Dennis could have told her, "She looked more like the
Hanks than the Sparrows".[5] Does it seem plausible that a seventeen
year old youth would have been discussing with her the ancestry of
a woman twice his age, as he asserted?

That fall, October 5, 1818, Nancy Hanks Lincoln died and
within a week's time Dennis lost his foster parents, Thomas and
Elizabeth Hanks Sparrow. These deaths removed everyone who could
have given Nancy Hanks Lincoln family information to Dennis.
Incidentally, Thomas Sparrow, by will,[6] left his property to Dennis
and Nancy Lincoln signed the will as a witness, signed by mark.[7]

Then followed a period during which Dennis did live with the
Lincoln family. As he was almost grown and able to do hard work,
besides probably having his mind on courting and attending frolics,
it is doubtful if he had much time to tutor the ten year old boy,
Abraham. Sarah Bush, who "had faculty", took over that job.

Then on June 14, 1821 Dennis married Elizabeth Johnston,[8] the
daughter of Sarah, and a very young wife she was. The couple moved

---

[3] Pratt, Lincoln, 1809-1839, p. 3.

[4] Hanks to Herndon, March 7, 1866

[5] Hanks to Herndon, February 10, 1866

[6] Probate Records, Spencer County, Indiana, Ch.

[7] Probate Records, Spencer County, Indiana, Ch.

[8] C.H. record, Spencer County, Indiana

to a farm one and one-half miles northeast of the Lincoln homestead. Dennis was again separated from close contact with Abraham.

From then on, with the exception of labors that threw them
together, such as hog driving and harvesting, Dennis and Abraham
were not closely associated. Then both families moved to Illinois
and they lived apart, more and more. It is improbable that Hanks
family relationships were much discussed by Dennis and Abraham
after they had no interest in common.[8]

---

[9]
    See Appendage for more about Dennis.

CHAPTER IV

TRADITIONS

–

PREFACE

The immediate object is to collect all the traditions pertaining to the several Nancy Hankses, in order to sort them and have left only those that give clues to information about the family of Nancy Hanks Lincoln. Ordinarily, for information pertaining to the past, recourse is had to history; and history usually consists of the accounts of the event as reported by eye witnesses or by contemporaries.

But the testimonies of witnesses of the same event often vary and, so much so, courts recognize this conflict of the versions and call upon all manner of forms of evidence to get at the truth. That from comtemporaries is considered best; but, even so, it is hearsay if it was not reduced to writing at the time of the incident.

Hearsay evidence is not admissable in most courts for the reason that the statements made were not under Oath, therefore the judge and the jury cannot observe the demeanor of the absent witness; and, for the more important reason that the accused has the right to be confronted with the witnesses against him, and to question them.

There are exceptions to the rule against the admissability of hearsay evidence. These include dying declarations, declarations against interest, ancient deeds and documents, etc. In probate proceedings for the purpose of establishing pedigrees, testimonies of hearsay and traditions may be admitted.

DECLARATIONS CONCERNING PEDIGREE

"Another exception to the rule against hearsay evidence consists of declarations as to pedigree. There are no facts of which we feel more certain than our parentage and the date of our birth.

Yet the only information which we have on these points is what comes to us from others. In other words it is hearsay. From necessity, therefore,

> hearsay evidence is everywhere admitted
> to prove what are called genealogical
> facts; such as birth, marriages, death,
> legitimacy or illegitimacy, and relation-
> ship both by blood and marriage."[1]

> "Moreover, the rule is not limited to the
> bare facts enumerated but includes the time
> and place of birth, marriages and death, and
> other facts which are essential elements of
> the primary facts mentioned."[2]

Much dependence is placed upon ancient records that were made at the time of the event; and without forethought as to the effect the record may have in the future. Such records are found in court-houses, in bibles, and in graveyards. There are also the entries in business books made in due course, and in diaries, and newspapers. These items put together in proper relationship make history.

But oftentimes, most times, there are no records made of casual events, or at best only meager ones; and only a legend of the occasion remains, which as it is passed down, tends to accumulate attributes to become a myth and a tradition. Myths tend to be of imaginary origins and of no substance; but traditions are usually based upon some fact that may be substantiated or confirmed by evidence, even circumstantial evidence.

It now seems necessary to differentiate between the properties of hearsay evidence and tradition. Hearsay evidence has been well defined at law, but a less technical meaning would seem to be: a narration of a report by a telltale that is indifferently and casually passed on by a talebearer with little regard for factual details. A hearsay may or may not be a truth, depending on its origin.

Tradition may or may not imply a lack of authentic records. Family traditions are usually passed down by word of mouth, and full credit is given by the recipient to the kinsman, that of his own knowledge and belief, he is passing on to the succeeding generations that which is true. In the memories of the elders, limited only by their interest, are the repositories of family details. This, then, is tradition.

---

[1] Shields vs. Boucher, 1 deG & Sm 40

[2] Quotation from <u>American Law & Procedure</u>, L.E. Univ. Vol. 11 p. 63-64

There are traditions pertaining to a Nancy Hanks in the several divergent branches of the Hanks family; some in agreement but others in conflict as to the identity of the particular Nancy. It is no wonder that this occurs for there were about twenty-five Nancy Hankses living at the same time, some older and some younger, of course; and of the twenty-five, at least eight, repeat 8, were born in the decade of the 1780's, and three of them in 1784!

It is no wonder that some great aunt Nancy should have lost her identity and became obscure when time had put her beyond the exact memory of those who speculated on the subject after Lincoln came into national prominance.

It is proposed to mention all the known traditions pertaining to Nancy Hanks for consideration, and possible determination. The obviously untenable ones will be eliminated forthwith. Those not inconsistent to the known facts about Nancy Hanks Lincoln, as set out by her son, will be retained and examined for clues and possible reconcilement with collateral evidence. "From necessity therefore, evidence is everywhere admitted to prove" the genealogical facts pertaining to Nancy Hanks Lincoln for the purpose of this thesis, just as a court would do.

ii

A HANK FAMILY TRADITION

The Hank family of early Chester County, Pennsylvania, which spelled the name without a final s or a final e, was from northern England, and is not to be confused with a German family that spelled their name Hanke. The first imigrant of the Hank family, Luke, purchased 500 acres of land from William Penn in now Delaware County, 1682, which transaction was the establishment of the family in America.

The early members of the family were of the Friends sect; and many of their records are found in the minutes of the meetings. John Hank of Whitemarch married Sarah Evans, of a Welsh family. This couple had children among whom was Joseph, born 1725; and the possibility has been recognized that he could have been the father of Nancy, the mother of Lincoln.[3] To further strengthen the speculation, record of members of this family have been found at the courthouse of Rockingham County, Virginia, in the county where the Lincoln family lived.[4]

---

[3] Lea & Hutchinson, _Ancestry of Abraham Lincoln_, p. 118

[4] Wayland, _Lincolns in Virginia_, p. 62.

Some of the descendants of one Williams Hank, who lived in Greenbrier County, Virginia, have tried to make a Lincoln connection in some way from the fact that he married into the Berry family, Susannah Berry.[5] This marriage was consumated two or three years after Nancy, who married Tom Lincoln, was born.

A member of this family, Myra Hank, married John F. Rudolph, Sr., and became a genealogist of no mean ability and acumen. She has rather completely traced the history of this Hank family from a beginning in England, and up into the nineteenth century; and has found no connection with the Lincoln family.

Her manuscript was published serially in the Monroe Watchman of Union, West Virginia, and concluded in the issue of May 15, 1930. A perusal of the article, with the copious references to authorative records, will convince the reader that Mrs. Rudolph's findings and conclusion is correct.[6]

Another important feature of her work is, for the Hanks family student, that the names of the several members of this Hank family are nicely catalogued in their natural niches; which is of great advantage in the separation of the members of the Hank family from the Hanks family; for careless spellings in important papers, of adding an s or leaving off an s tends to a confusion not easily resolved.

iii

A GERMAN HOUKE (SOMETIMES HANKE) FAMILY TRADITION

Incidentally, and to clear the record, there was in Rockingham County, Virginia, at about the time of the Revolutionary War, a family of the name of Hanke, spelled with a final e. In the records can be found the name of John with a wife, named Nancy. This woman was formerly Nancy Runion and she married into a family of German extraction; all the early members of it signed their names in German Script! There is no need to study this tradition further.[7]

---

[5] Fifth paragraph, Lincoln Lore, No. 692

[6] Monroe Watchman, May, 1930

[7] C.H. records, Rockingham County, Virginia.

A CULPEPPER COUNTY, VIRGINIA AND SOUTH CAROLINA TRADITION

This is an evanescent tradition that Judge Felix E. Alley recorded:

> It seems there was a report circulated in Mississippi, and Georgia, to the effect that Abraham Lincoln was the illegitimate son of Jefferson Davis' father and a woman by the name of Nancy Hanks residing at or near Culpepper, Virginia.[8]
>
> She and her father and mother were members of the Baptist Church. This church expelled Nancy on account of her condition and her parents asked for their letters, which were granted, and tradition says they went west, perhaps to Kentucky.

Another version of this tradition is nutured in South Carolina, and there the legend is that the father of Lincoln was the illustrious statesman, John C. Calhoun.[9] There was a Luke Hanks, with a wife, Ann, the daughter of Robert Dale; and they attended the Broad Run Church, had, among other children, a daughter, Nancy; and removed from Virginia to South Carolina. Their history will be discussed in the coming chapter, Nancy of Luke.

A WESTERN NORTH CAROLINA TRADITION

That this tradition pertaining to a Nancy Hanks, who lived with the Abraham Inloe family, has substance, has been avouched by testimony of witnesses of good repute. The details of it were first collected and published by Cathay;[10] it was recognized by Arthur who published it with some doubt;[11] it was twisted by Knott, and to no

---

[8] Alley, _Musings of a Mountaineer_, p. 383

[9] Coit, John C. Calhoun, pp. 49 seq.

[10] Cathay, _The Genesis of Lincoln_, 1899

[11] Arthur, _Western North Carolina_

It will be treated,hereafter, in the chapter entitled Nancy
of William.

vi

THE GASTON COUNTY, NORTH CAROLINA TRADITION

There is a tradition maintained in the Stowe family of
Gaston County to the effect that on land now owned by the family
once stood the log house of "Dicky" Hanks. A massive rock was
erected on the site with a bronze plate which read, "This stone
marks the site of the log cabin of Dicky Hanks; an uncle of Nancy
Hanks, mother of Abraham Lincoln."

This quotation and much more may be read in Chapter XIII of
the book, History of Gaston County, by Minnie Stowe Puett, and is
as has been handed down in her family from one Matthew Leeper.

The courthouse and tombstone records indicate that Hankses,
and Berrys resided in the neighborhood, and the tradition is not in
conflict with known facts; is acceptable, and will be referred to
in various coming chapters.

vii

A WESTERN ILLINOIS TRADITION

A Nancy Hanks who has been featured in a tradition pertaining
to the Lincolns was one connected with a branch of the Hanks family
of Western Illinois.[15] Mark Dellahay, the early friend and later
political helper of Lincoln in the State of Kansas married into this
family.

---

[12] Knott, Newspaper article, The State, 1911

[13] Coggins, The Eugenics of Abraham Lincoln

[14] Alley, Musings of a Mountaineer

[15] Lincoln Lore, No. 692. Seventh paragraph

He married Louisiana, daughter of Joshua, son of Richard Jr. of North Carolina. There is a suspicion that Dellahay may have taken advantage of his wife's family connections, or at least benefited from it. However, that may have been, it is certain that a friendship existed between Lincoln and Dellahay, who was really well-liked by everyone who knew him except his political enemies!

But to return to the subject of Nancy; she was the sister of Joshua and the daughter of Richard Hanks, Jr. Richard was a soldier of the Revolutionary War. His record of service is on his pension application in the Archive Building.[16]

He married Phebe Hayes, and they had nine children, of whom son John was the first-born. John later married Elizabeth Weathers[17] and lived in McMinn County, Tennessee, and reference will be made to this fact later. The youngest daughter, and sister of Joshua was the Nancy of this tradition.

A photocopy of the record in the old bible of Richard and Phebe Hanks shows she was born July 25, 1805; and this was only one year before her now famous cousin married Tom Lincoln. She, herself, later married Luke Brown, September 12, 1821[18] and her father, Richard was the bondsman. This tradition does not stand.

viii

A GRANVILLE COUNTY, NORTH CAROLINA TRADITION

In that part of older and larger Granville County, North Carolina, which is now Vance County, is a tradition of a Nancy Hanks, who was the mother of Lincoln. Inasmuch as she was born Circa 1784, and could have been married to Tom Lincoln, there shall be more about her hereafter, under the title of Nancy of Argyle.

---

[16] Richard Hanks, No. 4570

[17] Marriage records, Bonds of Tryon & Lincoln Cos. N.C., Lincoln County, C.H.

[18] Courthouse record, Lincoln County, North Carolina

ix

AN ANDERSON COUNTY, KENTUCKY TRADITION

Reuben Dale, of Colonial Virginia, who died in 1692, had
descendants who inter-married with the Hankses of the Northern
Neck. These fine people, the Dales, and the Hankses, emigrated
to the bluegrass section of Kentucky, where many of their respective
descendants live to this day; also, some went to Missouri.

To show how given Hanks names predominated in the group, and
also were applied to the negro slaves, it may be of interest to
exhibit an excerpt from the will of Alse Dale, probated 1802.[19] The
usual preamble begins, then:

"Daughter, Winny Hanks,   1 negro girl, name Nancy;
daughter, Betty Hanks,   1 negro woman, name Molly;
daughter, Molly Hanks,   1 negro woman, name Betty;
             1 negro girl, name Jane;
daughter, Viley Graddy,   1 negro boy, name Bill
Daughter, Nancy Briant,   1 riding horse and saddle
Children of my daughter Lucy Rowland; Henry $10 and
                 Nancy $10
Son, Raleigh Dale; son Fortunatus Dale.................

Witnesses: Spencer Gill and Susannah Hanks

         her
     Alse X Dale"
         mark

That the above named Hanks women were married daughters, and
not single, is shown by other records.[20] That negro slaves continued to bear Hanks names, and that some of them were very pretty
octoroons was hinted to me by an old lady of Hanks descent, whose
grandmother was a Coke.

----

[19]Will Book, Courthouse, Woodford County, Kentucky

[20]Ibid.

An outstanding individual of this Hanks family was Thomas Holman Hanks, whose biography may be read in history.[21] He was a 49'er; a confederate officer; and, for many years, connected with activities in and about the courthouse of Anderson County, Kentucky; and many of its records are in his handwriting. He was, obviously, a well informed man. It was he who gave, so it seems, the later generations of the Sparrows of Mercer County, the information that they were of kin to some of the Hankses.[22]

Another noted character of this group was Chichester Hanks; members of this family assert to know the identity of Lucy Hanks Sparrow but their knowlege is nebulous.

x

AN INDIANA TRADITION

Abner Hanks, a Revolutionary War veteran,[23] and the prolific father of some twenty-one children from five or six wives, acquired in regular and orderly sequence,[24] has been often nominated as the putative father of the famous Nancy.

From three different sources we have accumulated lists of his children and, while they vary somewhat with some of the names, all lists agree that his first and eldest child was Matilda, born December 10, 1788, from his first wife, who, by records, was Mary Dale Hanks.

Not that he could not have accomplished the procreation, for he was old enough, having been born in 1763,[25] in Richmond County, Virginia, the son of John and Susannah Hanks; but there is no evidence he had an earlier daughter than Matilda.

---

[21] History of Anderson County, Kentucky

[22] Statement of Wash Sparrow, August 26, 1922, Barton papers, Library, Chicago University.

[23] Archives, No. S31729, Washington, D.C.

[24] Wives, "Mollie", "Becky", "Frances", "Sarah", and "Sallie".

[25] Deposition, S 31729, Archives, Washington, D.C.

It would seem Abner has done right well by his descendants; some of his children intermarried with the illustrious Utterback family, and left responsible members of society. Abner hardly needs an additional honor alloted to him. The tradition does not stand.

xi

A CHRISTIAN COUNTY, KENTUCKY TRADITION

Succinctly put by Warren is the basis of this tradition:

> "Captain Stephen Beck Hanks, famous for nearly seventy-five years as captain and pilot on the upper Mississippi River, makes this statement in the Burlington, Iowa Post for April 2,.1921, with respect to a child of his grandfather; 'The girl was named Nancy and she became the wife of Thomas Lincoln and later the mother of our martyred president, Abraham Lincoln'".[26]

A later descendant,[27] a student of her own family history gave it this way:

> "Stephen Beck Hanks and his brother David, spent many hours talking about their family. They did not agree always and the rest of the family did not pay any attention to them...one of the points on which they disagreed was their relationship to President Lincoln. Uncle Stephen was of the opinion that his father, Thomas Hanks and Nancy Hanks, the mother of Lincoln, were brother and sister. David thought otherwise. I am inclined to agree with Uncle David."[28]

---

[26] Lincoln Lore, No. 692; Newspaper clipping, Lincoln Library, Fort Wayne, Indiana.

[27] Emily Hanks Marshall, Seattle, Washington

[28] Marshall to Baber, Feb. 27, 1950, Baber papers.

These two Hanks men were, in active life, steamboat captains on the Mississippi River, and of outstanding intelligence. They were noted men and in their latter days were interviewed by reporters. An article furnished by Stephen was published in the Burlington, Iowa paper[29] and gave much family data.

Much of what he gave can be verified from courthouse records but there is nothing to show that his grandfather, who was John Hanks, had a daughter, Nancy. The tradition as it now exists, in the home area in Kentucky, is more general than specific and one Hanks member expressed it, "I think Nancy Hanks some kin -- all Hankses kin -- all the old folks".[30]

Another version of the same tradition was related by a collateral member of the family, a thoughtful man of prominance in the community and of known integrity, "I know no evidence that connects Nancy with the family--just tradition. Yes, tradition is they were kin. Nancy is supposed to have gone with a brother, John I think, to visit in the Berry family."[31]

There is a further interesting phase to this tradition. Due to a misunderstanding about where the wedding was to be held, Nancy and John rode one way and Tom and his friends went another way so that they failed to meet and the wedding had to be postponed until new arrangements were made. There is even a subtle confirmation of this delay, in the incident that Tom purchased his wedding suit a month before the wedding.

Ten years before Abraham Lincoln ran for the presidency there was born at Albany, Illinois, a Hanks boy who, one hundred years later, had his son-in-law answer letters for he "had a slight palsy in his hand!" Previously, he had written to another, 1938: "My father was born in Kentucky in the vicinity of Lincoln's birthplace." The father and his brothers were aware that a kinship existed between themselves and Lincoln, but did not bother to trace it.[32]

Since no specific relationship is asserted in this tradition there are, of course, no conflicts with the known facts. If evidence shows a kinship to Nancy Hanks, the tradition will be confirmed.

[29] Burlington Press

[30] Latt Hanks, Interview, Nov. 30, 1949, Baber papers.

[31] David Walter Gatlin, Madisonville, Kentucky (Banker), Baber Papers.

[32] David Warren Hanks to T.A. Morris, 1938. Mr Hanks died November 14, 1952; aged 102.

xii

A HARDIN COUNTY, KENTUCKY TRADITION

When Lincoln furnished material for a campaign biography
in 1860, he stated, with other family information, that his mother
had kinfolks in Illinois, in Macon, Coles, and Adams counties, so
it was a natural thing for investigators to search them out to
inquire about the relationships.

They were enthusiastically willing to oblige but turned out
to be woefully ignorant of the exact connections. They were aware
that the search was for a Nancy; and that a Nancy or two had been
connected with the family back in Kentucky, but were unable to agree
which was whom.[33]

A Nancy had been named in the will of Joseph Hanks, 1793, in
which he named five sons and three daughters, the youngest, Nancy,
and born about 1785. When Mrs. Hitchcock, in her search for a Nancy
who could qualify, found this will, she made a rather natural but
erroneous conclusion that this Nancy was the mother of Lincoln.

So firmly was she convinced that, at long last, she had
identified the particular Nancy she published the little book
entitled Nancy Hanks.[34] This book, while erroneous as to the identity
of the chief character, is valuable for its collateral information;
for the Nancy she deals with was of close kin to the mother of
Lincoln; had followed her to Indiana, and is buried in an adjoining
grave.

Even if she did not marry Tom Lincoln, a chapter will be devoted here to her history under the title chapter Nancy of Joseph.

---

[33] Lincoln Lore, No. 692

[34] Hitchcock, Nancy Hanks

xiii

THE BEDFORD COUNTY, PENNSYLVANIA TRADITION

An example of descendants lacking specific knowlege of the
identity of the Nancys in their ancestral lines, and conjecturing
unto confusion, is this: "John Hanks was a brother of Nancy Hanks
Lincoln."[35] This John she refers to had a sister Nancy, all right,
but she did not marry Tom Lincoln; and her lineal descendants know
that she did not, and further, they know whom she did marry.

She was born in 1769, one of twin sisters, and in Loudoun
County, Virginia. She had a daughter, Duannah, and married Nicholas
Schooley; secondly she married Robert Akers. She died in 1835, and
all of this can be verified.

There is, however, an interesting tradition in this family.
It is that a cousin, Nancy, of the above said Nancy Akers, did
marry Thomas Lincoln. They say further that members of their family,
John and Fleetwood went to the Bedford-Campbell Virginia section;
and went on into Kentucky from there.[36] This latter tradition has
been verified from court house records. Since parts are true,
reliance should be put on the part about Nancy being a cousin. This
tradition is to be retained.

xiv

THE CAMPBELL COUNTY, VIRGINIA TRADITION

One of the strongest traditions extant pertaining to the
paternity of Nancy Hanks Lincoln is the one that obtains in Campbell
County, Virginia; and is avouched for in neighboring counties of
Pittsylvania, Charlotte, and Halifax by those interested in local
history.[37]

---

[35] Lincoln Lore, No. 692

[36] Fleetwood Hanks purchased land in Bedford County, Virginia,
1797, Deed Book 10, p. 328

[37] Lincoln Lore, No. 692

It was expressed by the late Mr. Wirt Williams thus:

> "The father of Nancy Hanks was Abraham Hanks.
> They moved from this community sometime between
> 1790 and 1800, and to Kentucky. The tradition
> that used to be circulated in this neighborhood
> claimed that Nancy Hanks married a man by the
> name of Lincoln and that she named her boy,
> Abraham, after her father.
>
> "I don't think that these facts can be verified
> by any records or historical facts."[38]

But it can be proved that an Abraham Hanks resided there for
many years; in fact, there seems to have been three Abrahams there.
One married Mary Combs and removed to Kentucky in the 1790's; another
married Lucy Jennings, 1799, and about 1830 moved to Tennessee where
he died.[39] The third one is supposed to have died in the 1890's
and, according to Campbell Chronicles by Early, is buried at Hatt
Creek. The authority for naming this place of interment is not
known but there is a Hanks burial plot there with a few graves.

This tradition has too much corroborative evidence to be
discarded, and will be taken up hereafter.

xv

THE MONTGOMERY COUNTY, KENTUCKY TRADITION

One of the chief organizers of Wolfe County, Kentucky, from
larger Montgomery, was Cuthbert Million Hanks ("Cud"), son of
Fielding, son of Abraham and Sarah Harper Hanks. Sarah was a sister
to the Harper brothers who were with Daniel Boone at Boonesborough.
Courthouse records show that this group of Hankses appeared in
Montgomery County prior to 1800.[40] Also there was a Peter Hanks
family that had originated from Loudoun County, Virginia.[41]

---

[38] Williams to Warren, Dec. 12, 1929, photo-copy, Baber papers.

[39] Various records.

[40] Tax lists, 1800, by Clift, p. 123

[41] John Hanks, interviewed for Draper.

Members of the Berry family were neighbors. Nearby resided William Calk who left the famous Calk journal.[42]

It was into this basic Hanks area that Mrs. Hitchcock first entered for her investigations in Kentucky. This quote is an extract directly from her original field notes of May 8, 1895: "Nancy Hanks lived near North Middleton...left there and went to southern part of state..." This tradition was also in an Illinois branch of the Hanks family.

An echo of this trip of Mrs. Hitchcock is found in the book, Sorrows of Nancy by Boyd (p. 40, reprint) as follows:

> "A lady who said her maiden name was Hanks and
> place of residence Massachusetts (I think),
> came to me last summer and asked me if I had
> not heard the Hanks of Montgomery say that
> Abraham Lincoln's mother was named Hanks".

The interviewed one did not so agree but the conversation indicates what the Hanks people thought.

Whereas, Mrs. Hitchcock interviewed adults who were living when Lincoln was first a candidate they must have heard his parentage discussed and recollected a reflection of the local Hanks family tradition. One tradition pertained to a James Hanks, who had been a famous hunter of eastern Kentucky.

Following her visit, a great-granddaughter of Abraham and Sarah Harper Hanks wrote, 1899, "I know from hearing my father speak of his uncles and aunts that Fielding Hanks had a sister, Nancy, and a brother, George, further I do not know."[43]

In this manner, this tradition common to the seemingly unconcerned descendants of an Abraham Hanks has been brought to light from time to time; but has never been fully developed and examined, nor considered and rejected.

---

[42] Calk Journal, The Mississippi Valley Historical Review, p.363

[43] Dora Hanks to Hitchcock, Nov. 29, 1899. Hitchcock papers, Fort Wayne, Indiana, Lincoln Library.

It is submitted, it is consistant with the Berry family
tradition, does not conflict with the affidavit of Squire Robert
Mitchell Thompson; includes an Illinois tradition; and does not
conflict with other tenable ones.

xvi

THE EDGAR COUNTY, ILLINOIS TRADITION

There are three groups of Hankses in Edgar County, Illinois:
one group came from Montgomery County, Kentucky in 1830; another
was from Loudoun County, Virginia via Ohio; and the third was from
southern Illinois, probably from the Peter Hanks family. The ones
from Kentucky were William Hanks and his mother, Sarah, and his sister,
Permelia Hanks Landsaw. His mother, Sarah, was the daughter of
Abraham and Sarah Harper Hanks of Virginia. Her second husband
was Andrew Varvell, and from this she was known in her old age as
"Granny Sallie Varvell". She lived for many years with her daughter,
Permelia, and died in 1876 at about the age of ninety. The descendants of Granny Sallie have this tradition:

It is that Granny Sallie Varvel, born Sarah Hanks in Virginia,
was a sister of Nancy Lincoln; that her son, William, and her
daughter, Permelia, were first cousins of Abraham Lincoln, and maybe
closer kin (through a marriage of cousins); that there were three
Hanks girls, Sallie, Polly and Nancy; that they were orphans and
lived with kinfolk, Sallie with a Ringo family,[44] and Nancy with the
Berrys;[45] that one man courted two of them;[46] that a cousin "Cud"
Hanks came from Kentucky to visit;[47] that Abe Lincoln visited Granny
Sallie;[48] at least once when attending court in Edgar County.

---

[44] Recollections of Mary Ellen Hanks Baber, 1920

[45] Ibid

[46] Recollections of Nancy Jane Hanks Swango, 1920

[47] Recollection of Dexter Baber of hearing his mother speak of
a "Cud" Hanks, who came from Kentucky to Illinois to visit.

[48] Recollections of the mother of Jack Hanks, Paris, Illinois,
on August 6, 1927, Baber papers.

There is no evidence that would indicate that all of this was not known before Lincoln was elevated to prominance. Certainly, it did not originate at the time of his campaign, for these Hankses were Douglas democrats, and not favorable to Lincoln, and voted against him![49] During his presidency, circumstances precipitated some of them into an affray at Charleston, Illinois, resulting in their imprisonment. At the instigation of Dennis Hanks, Lincoln leniently released them but they remained embittered. They never claimed kinship to Lincoln; but, if pressed, would admit that "Granny Sallie" was kin to Nancy. They did not visit with the Lincolns nor the Halls of Coles County, but some did fraternize with Dennis Hanks. One said regarding any kinship, "It was not discussed, just accepted as a fact."[50]

There is another portion of this tradition that does not pertain directly to the Nancy phase, but may have an indirect connection. There seems to have been some irregularity in the family back in Kentucky; it is known that William Hanks was reticent on the subject;[51] Fielding, of Milton, Illinois was non-committal;[52] Dr. LeGrand intimated as much to Morgan;[53] and Lincoln, himself, was suspected of reserve.[54]

In addition, the grandchildren of Sarah Hanks did not know the name of their grandfather. Mrs. Hitchcock lists it as James Hanks.[55] It is possible, he was a cousin who disappeared during the war of 1812.[56] He may have married Polly Hanks.[57] The case

---

[49] Coleman, Journal, Ill. State His. Soc., Mar. 1940, p. 7

[50] Dexter Baber, interview, Sept. 7, 1952, Baber papers.

[51] Ibid.

[52] Stephen Hanks, interview, August 17, 1950, Brookfield, Iowa, Baber papers.

[53] Arthur Morgan, interview, Nov. 17, 1949, Yellow Springs, Ohio, Baber papers.

[54] Herndon's Lincoln, p. 1

[55] Hitchcock papers, Ft. Wayne, Indiana.

[56] Pirtle, The Battle of Tippecanoe.

[57] Edgar County, Illinois Tradition: a vague tradition that the same man married two Hanks sisters.

is involved and is hardly to be resolved, for General John Hunt
Morgan's men burned the courthouse records at Mt. Sterling, Kentucky,
and the early marriage records were burnt.

Since this tradition survived under these adverse circumstances, it must have had an inherent quality of conformity to fact;
and those who unwelcomely acknowledged it must have had implicit
confidence in its source; or they would not have re-told it.

It is submitted that in no way does it conflict with what
Lincoln said about his mother; and that it is evidently a part of
the larger Abraham Hanks development and, as such, is entitled to
full consideration.

xvii

THE ARKANSAS TRADITION

Dr. Arthur E. Morgan,[58] the eminent civil engineer, when
working in Arkansas, 1909, interviewed Dr. James LeGrand and other
descendants of a Polly Hanks, through her daughter, Sophie, born
1809; and published a report of the family tradition that Polly
was a sister of the Nancy Hanks who married Tom Lincoln.[59]

To establish the Arkansas tradition as a part of current
Lincoln lore, it would seem necessary to qualify LeGrand as a competent witness to give testimony. To ascertain if this could be
accomplished, Dr. Morgan himself was interviewed[60] and gave the
following opinion as to the character, truthfulness and integrity
of LeGrand:

> "I met Dr. LeGrand at his hotel and was impressed
> with his talk and his earnestness...LeGrand was,
> in a way, a self-taught man but was intelligent,
> was a serious, thoughtful person, thought things
> out for himself, and was inclined to wax eloquent
> at times, was dignified, tall and straight...Dr.
> LeGrand was thoughtful, and wanted to get things
> right, was truthful, wanted to be truthful."

---

[58] Dr. A.E. Morgan, Yellow Springs, Ohio

[59] Morgan, Atlantic Monthly, p. 208; Wilson, Lincoln Among
His Friends, Chap. III.

[60] Morgan, Interview, Nov. 17, 1949, Baber papers.

Investigations made in Perry and Dubois Counties, Indiana confirmed with courthouse records much that LeGrand reported about his own mother, Sophie. This inspires confidence and, with the favorable conclusions of Dr. Morgan, established the standing of LeGrand as a competent witness whose testimony may be considered as on a par with that of Dennis Hanks and others.

To accept the Arkansas tradition that Nancy Hanks had a sister Polly does not conflict with any theory of Hanks family relationships, except that it disagrees with the opinion of those who hold that Nancy Lincoln had no sisters.

Even Dennis Hanks, whose word on the Hanks subject many accept as final, accepted Sophie as a cousin of Lincoln, and expressed wonder that she had asked for sure.[61] He later told[62] Weik that Nancy was the second daughter born of a Hanks woman. Dennis forgot his previous build-up and adherred to the facts. Thus he admitted the sister-hood.

The evidence is cumulative that Nancy had a sister: in Macon County, Missouri are descendants of Samuel Hanks, born 1820,[63] who was also a son of Polly Hanks, sister of Nancy Lincoln.

Other descendants of Polly Hanks confirm the tradition.[64]

xviii

THE MISSOURI TRADITION

Samuel H. Hanks did not know his father's name but did know, "I am an own cousin to the late Abraham Lincoln."[65] Samuel, born 1820, was a brother of Sophie Hanks, born 1809; and their mother lived until the 1850's, so they had plenty of time and opportunity to learn from her the names of her sisters. It would be strange

---

[61] Dennis Hanks to Lincoln, April 5, 1864

[62] Dennis Hanks, interview by Weik, March 26, 1885

[63] Rosy Hanks Walker to Hitchcock, March 4, 1898, Hitchcock papers, Lincoln Library, Fort Wayne, Indiana.

[64] Charles Roscoe Miles, Newspaper clipping. September 5, 1933.

[65] Samuel Hanks to Hitchcock, March 15, 1898

indeed, if she had not known.

The daughter, Sarah Rocybelle, of Samuel added to the information, "My father was Samuel Hanks, his mother was a sister to Nancy Hanks Lincoln."[66] In another letter she wrote, "My father had...2 sisters one name was Sophie."[67]

From another source the name of Sophie's sister can be had, "His (Charles Roscoe Miles) mother was Mary Amelia Peppers Miles, daughter of Mary (Polly) Hanks, who was a sister of Nancy Hanks."[68]

The obvious quiry is: if the woman known as Mary or "Polly" Hanks was a sister of Nancy Lincoln, why did her children bear the surname of Hanks; what, if any, was her married name?

It is submitted, this tradition in no way conflicts with any other tradition but tends to confirm the Edgar County, Illinois one, as to a sister Polly.

All that can be made of it is that Abraham Lincoln had an aunt who may have borne children with a common-law father and without the benefit of a legal ceremony: -- but did she? Wait and learn.

xix

THE WASHINGTON COUNTY, KENTUCKY TRADITION

When Lamon's book, with its innuendos and sinister connotations of ill births came out in 1872,[69] it caused a flurry of comment. Some-readers were in gleeful agreement; others were indignant. No marriage record of Lincoln's parents was known, but there was a small group of Nancy's kin in Kentucky that knew there had been a wedding, and that it had occurred in their community, at the Berry home.

One who had the knowledge from her grandmother, was Mrs. Charlotte Vawter, a cultured and educated woman of Indiana. The grandmother had been an associate of Nancy Hanks in the home of

---

[66] Walker to Hitchcock, Nov. 22, 1899

[67] Ibid., March 4, 1898

[68] Mibs, clipping, September 5, 1933

[69] Lamon, The Life of Abraham Lincoln, Chap. I.

Richard Berry, Sr., and had related happy memories of Nancy, including a wedding; and long before the subject became an issue.

So sure was Mrs. Vawter of this fact that she persuaded her
uncle Squire Robert Mitchell Thompson to institute a search for the
missing marriage records in the county where the family knew that
Nancy Hanks and Tom Lincoln had been married; and they were found.[70]
Later, she prepared a paper for the Louisville Courier Journal,
in which she said, "As I remember the story of Nancy Hanks, it ran
thus: Her mother's name before marriage was Shipley..."

Their uncle, who located the records, Squire Robert Mitchell
Thompson, was interviewed by a reporter for the same paper, and confirmed what Mrs. Vawter had recollected by saying, "My mother was a
Mitchell, a first cousin of President Lincoln's mother; their mothers
were Shipleys from North Carolina..."[71]

Another and last testimony of the old man, just before his
death, in 1895, was, "In the Richard and Rachel Shipley Berry home,
room was made for Lucy Hanks...she married a man whose name she took
while in Virginia and Nancy Hanks, the mother of President Lincoln,
was the off-spring."[72] The question arises: he had been previously
interviewed. Why had he never used the name "Lucy" before? Had it
been recently furnished to him? What did he mean by the redundant
phrase, "...married a man whose name she took?" Why shouldn't she
have taken a married name, even if hers was a so-called common-law
marriage?

Ordinarily a youth gives only casual attention to family
connections; later in life, of course, Mr. Thompson would have
learned about his mother's family ancestry and the several cousin
relationships, and all this information should be as trustworthy
as any such family tradition; but, when it comes to the description
of an event that allegedly occurred in Virginia and thirty years
before he was born, it was only hear-say.

It is to be noted that Mrs. Vawter never did use the name Lucy;
and Mr. Thompson used it only once and that at the last interview.
However, aside from the name, it is submitted that this family tradition from these two important reminiscences is not in conflict with
any known fact; and that the cousin relationship of whatever degree,
may be traced through a Shipley-Thompson-Mitchell connection.

---

[70] Issue, February 20, 1874

[71] Louisville Courier Journal, January 5, 1881; Lincoln
Kinsman No. 47.

[72] Louisville Courier Journal, September 11, 1895; Lincoln
Kinsman No. 4.

CHAPTER V

i

NANCY THE FIRST

The affinity of the names, Nancy and Hanks has become so
affixed in common parlance as to seem to be almost synonymous.
The earliest Nancys found were brought into the Hanks family by
marriages: the wife of James, she signed her name and left off
Hanks when they sold their farm;[1] the Nannie of Joseph, he named
in his will;[2] and the Nancy of Luke, she brought him to church.[3]

From them came the now famous name that has christianed the
long procession of ubiquitious Nancys. Their namesakes spread far
and wide with the advancing frontier of America. Within the span
of their later lives there were probably twenty-five Hanks girl
babies named Nancy, of whom at least eight were born during the
decade of the 1780's; and, of these eight then born, three were
likely born in the year 1784 as was the one who married Tom Lincoln.

It will be necessary to study the biographies of these
eight in order to determine their lots and ends, and so eliminate
all except the one who married Tom Lincoln.

The Christian names of the early God-fearing Hanks colonists
were somewhat Biblical: in Maryland was Peter;[4] in Pennsylvania were
Luke and John;[5] as were first found. Then in Virginia, these early
Bible readers called their sons Moses, Abraham, Joshua and Joseph.
There was Matthew and James and Thomas, don't doubt. There was
Raleigh and Richard with George and Chichester, and only one Argyle.

The women who came into the early family, those first
Colonial dames brought Mary, of course, and Lucretia, Lucinda,

---

[1] Amelia County, Virginia, Deed Book 10, p. 228.

[2] Nelson County, Kentucky, Will Book A, p. 107.

[3] Fauquier County, Virginia, Broad Run Church Records.

[4] Ann Arundal County, Maryland, Will Book CC #3, p. 807.

[5] Now Delaware County, Pennsylvania

Margaret and Jane. The Sarahs came from the Dorsey and Shipley
families; the Susannahs and Alices, called "Alisie" were Dale
names; Elizabeth came from their good Queen Bess in far away
England. The Hanks family, more than others, seemed to have the
happy familiarity of using pet and nicknames. Mary became "Polly",
of course; Lucretia and Lucinda were the shorter, "Lucy". Elizabeth
was "Betsey" and never Bess or Liz. Sarah was "Sally" and Nancy took
the cake with "Nan, Nance, Ann, Annie, and Nannie."

There must have been one Nancy who did not care for her own
name. Nancy married Sam Hanks[6] and, being a strong minded woman,
no doubt, abandoned the old familiar Hanks names for her children:
she broke the sequence by naming her sons, Ackland, Hannibal, and
Romulous Lycurgus. But it was the son, Rome, and not Hannibal who
became a famous officer under General Grant.[7]

For her daughters she fancied the names of Xastryra, Armina
Dye Meldeamous Torio, Laura Sudlett Zellico, Cordelia, Adelia Woodville,
Hecuba, Minerva, and Euphrasia. Four of these daughters married into
the Hon family and this researcher has often wondered what the little
Hons were named.

ii

NANCY OF LUKE

A romance of the Old South that has been preserved in tradition centers in the family of Luke Hanks of South Carolina. It
began when local gossip connected John C. Calhoun, just out of law
school, with the local Nancy Hanks, "a handsome Irish beauty"; it
was added to when Calhoun was an illustrious statesman and Abraham
Lincoln a congressman; and the fascinating tattle became sufficiently
sensational to arouse even a novice's curiosity by the time Lincoln
became of national prominence.

In after years, 1911, it was published in a newspaper, The
State, in four feature articles; and is now settled folklore with
the South Carolinians.

---

[6] Samuel Hanks married Nancy, daughter of Elisha and Nancy
Wyatt, in Mason County, Kentucky, March 16, 1802.

[7] Pennell, The History of Rome Hanks.

It appears that James L. Orr, a prominant South Carolinian, of Andersonville, who was in turn a judge, a congressman, a Governor, and an ambassador went to Washington when Lincoln was there as a congressman from Illinois; and, upon meeting him, observed the similar resemblance of Lincoln to some of the Hanks men he had known back home. It was so striking he remarked on it to Mr. Lincoln, who is alleged to have replied, "We may be of kin; my mother was a Nancy Hanks." There is no record that the subject was pursued further.

When Orr returned home he reported the incident to some of the Hankses and then learned, for the first time, of the love affair of forty years agone, between Nancy Hanks and Calhoun. The memory and the telling of the story is supposed to have come from Luke, Nancy's brother.

The story relates that Ann Hanks, a widow, operated the tavern at the famous crossroads of Craytonville. The tavern was well patronized by all who traveled the main roads, and the lawyers, riding their circuit, stopped for rest and refreshment at the establishment. Mrs. Hanks was assisted in catering to the requirements of her customers by Nancy.

Calhoun, the story continues, just out of law school, and riding the circuit, stopped with his fellow lawyers at the tavern. He was attracted to Nancy Hanks, and they became friendly. The friendship quickly developed into romance and the boundaries of propriety were apparently overwhelmed. Nancy found she was to become the mother of Calhoun's child. To the family, it seemed better to send her away; and she was sent to her Uncle John in Tennessee.

It was stated that after Luke finished telling the story he added, "...and poor girl, we don't know what finally became of her."

It is easy to believe that Mr. Orr became interested in this sensational story. Also, one can readily assume that he made some conjectures, perhaps discussed the situation with old timers -- the dust was brushed away from memories -- and conclusions reached. Mr. Orr was an attorney and no doubt of an investigating turn-of-mind. Perhaps he tried to learn more about the Hankses and, if so, this is what he could have found at the court house.

Testamentary

Luke Hanks died in 1789 and, by Will, dated May 14, 1789[1] and signed by his mark, recorded in Anderson County, South Carolina,

---

[1] Deed Book 1, p. 59, Anderson County, South Carolina, Courthouse.

left his whole estate, both real and personal "to my beloved wife, Ann Hanks." This property included a valley farm of two hundred ten acres on Hen Coop Creek, which flowed into Rocky River, not far from Craytonville.

The United States Census Record of 1790 for Pendleton, 96th District, South Carolina, shows that Ann Hanks, widow, reported ten children: 2 males, 16 years old or over, 2 males, below 16, and 6 female children whose ages were not given. These children of Luke and Ann (or Nancy Ann) Hanks traced back to the late 1700's, are shown to have been Elizabeth, Martha, Thomas, Luke, George, Susan, Lucretian, Robert, Judith, John, Scilla (Priscilla) and Nancy, the youngest, born, February 10, 1787.[2]

The tradition with these Hankses of South Carolina is that the parents and the older children, including son Luke, who was born, October 15, 1774, came from Virginia. This is borne out by courthouse records of Prince William County; and by Broad Run Church records, of across the county line, in Farquier County. More of this follows hereafter, under Luke.

When Abraham Lincoln was rapidly becoming a nationally known figure, his possible relationship to Calhoun was recalled by fellow lodge members to whom Judge Orr had commited his suspicions; and some of them were intrigued.

******

Uncle Johnny Hanks, son of Luke Hanks, Jr. was asked by Dr. W. C. Brown of Belton, South Carolina in an interview held in the presence of Brown's young wife, and she recalled the interview in later years and made a statement as follows:[3] Query: "...if there was anything to the story?" (the story of Nancy Hanks' affair with Calhoun.) The reply given by Uncle Johnny was, in substance: "I am sorry to tell you, Doctor, there is. Nancy was my father's youngest sister and I know whereof I speak. When the family found out that Nancy had sinned and gone astray, she asked to be allowed to stay until she could get away to her uncles; as best I remember, in Tennessee; that Calhoun had promised her $500.00 to take her away where it would not hurt him. This uncle was a John Hanks who came here with Nancy's father, and had moved out to Tennessee. Just at this time Thomas Lincoln appeared, with Enlow, his helper with horses, and solved the trouble. He became scape goat for Calhoun's sins."

---

[2] Knotts to Bartow, August 23. 1919, Library, Chicago, Illinois

[3] Ibid., September 1, 1919.

Whether wisdom dictates that this statement, as published, should be accepted as fact or as a mixture of memory, tradition, and gossip handed down through the generations, is debatable. The facts to be noted are that Uncle Johnny, son of Luke Hanks, Jr. (1774-1856); interviewed by Dr. Brown, in the presence of his young wife about 1860, and reported by Mr. Knotts, did have an Aunt Nancy; he did have a great Uncle John (Jonathan) Hanks who had moved to Tennessee; Aunt Nancy had removed from the Hanks community of South Carolina and it is probable that she had been lost track of, although Uncle Johnny maintains to have known more about her than his father had related to Mr. Orr.

This romance of Nancy, daughter of Luke, sweetheart of Calhoun, also intrigued the late Mr. D.J. Knotts, of Swansea, South Carolina, as it had Mr. Orr, and he worked at solving the mystery, or at least developing more leads on it.

From J. B. Lewis, a fellow lodge member of the late Judge James L. Orr, Mr. Knotts learned of Mr. Orr's conclusions and they seemed logical in view of the circumstances. Mr. Knotts knew of a Nancy Hanks who had lived in North Carolina at the home of Abraham Enloe. Mr. Enloe, following his profession of mule and slave trading and traveling to Augusta, Georgia and to Charleston, South Carolina for supplies for his community, had stopped at the Craytonville tavern. What could be more logical to assume? There might have been private consultations between Mr. Enloe and the widow Hanks, and Enloe's assistant, young Tom Lincoln, might have been hired to help Nancy to travel to Tennessee. It was safe to assume she had spent some time enroute to Tennessee at the Enloe home in North Carolina and that she had later married Tom Lincoln.

Mr. Knotts pursued this surmise to a fanciful climax to enlarge his thesis; but he learned that the Enloe clan would have none of his theory. They insisted thay had always considered Abraham Lincoln to have been Grandfather Enloe's son, born of Nancy Hanks who had lived in the Enloe home for a number of years.

This failure to identify the two Nancys as one and the same was admitted to Dr. Barton in August of 1919.[4] The evidence does seem to indicate that both Nancys had been taken through the mountains to Tennessee.

The remark, attributed to Luke, that it was not known what became of his sister, Nancy, does not seem consistent. Available information on Luke's activity in the community is that he had been "Court Crier" for many years, serving at the Anderson County, South

---

[4]See Barton, Paternity of Lincoln, p. 122.

Carolina, courthouse during the regular and special sessions of court. Men who are court attaches know something of the records and the current happenings. Even the hangers-on, the loafers on the courthouse steps can be relied upon to circulate news and gossip freely. Surely, then, Luke would have known about the final settlement of his mother's estate, in which he had shared, and that his sister, Nancy, had also been one of the heirs; that she had been publicated against under her married name of South.

Luke had the reputation of being an honest man, so much so that it was carved upon his tombstone, "God gave him an honest heart."[5] With this epitaph, the tradition as admitted by Luke, and related by Mr. Orr, the distinguished holder of high public offices, is plausable and may be believed. It is to be noted that Luke is not reported to have mentioned Tom Lincoln.

It is in what the old lady recollected of the conversation between her husband, Dr. Brown, and John Hanks, a son of Luke, that the name of Tom Lincoln appears, and in a connection with Enloe. She was reporting an incident and conversation that had happened fifty years previously. John Hanks, in turn, was contributing to the current gossip about Abraham Lincoln, alleged facts of a happening that had transpired when he was a child. The chronology of the event would place it in 1807.

Intensive research of the Hardin County, Kentucky records-- as conducted by Louis B. Warren[6] determined conclusively that Thomas Lincoln had not been out of the State of Kentucky, with the possible exception of a trip made in 1798, when he was probably with his Uncle Isaac in Tennessee; and this dating would have been too early for him to have traveled with the "Calhoun" Nancy Hanks into Tennessee, which reportedly was done after 1807; and this date would have been too late, for he was married and living in Elizabethtown, Kentucky. The date, 1807, cannot be shoved back for Calhoun did not come home from law school until June, 1806.

Then too, if the alleged "Calhoun" Nancy Hanks left South Carolina during or near the last half of the year 1806 and resided even a short while in North Carolina with the Enloe family, and was taken into Tennessee by Tom Lincoln, how could their wedding have been solemnized on June 12, 1806 by the Reverend Jesse Head? The record of date and wedding is verifiable according to a return filed at Springfield, Kentucky in the Washington County church. Other returns of the Reverend Jesse Head, for other years, and for both before and after the return of the Lincoln record, have been

---

5
Ebenizer Cemetery, Anderson Co., South Carolina.

6
Warren, Lincoln's Parentage and Childhood, p. 43.

located and found to be in the same handwriting of Jesse Head, which confirms the fact that the 1806 return on the wedding of Thomas Lincoln and Nancy Hanks is true and not spurious, as some writers have asserted.

Last, plausable and positively acceptable as evidence; the late Dr. William E. Barton had a search made in the Anderson County, South Carolina courthouse records by an attorney and a clue was found to the long-missing Nancy Hanks of South Carolina, daughter of Luke and Ann.

The court records dealing with the settlement of the estate of Ann Hanks modify the traditions relating to Nancy. The probate record[7] shows that in 1838, five years after Ann Hanks had died, the heirs of the deceased were located.

Twelve children, apparent heirs, are listed. The census of 1790 had shown Ann Hanks to have been the mother of ten children. It is probable, however, and assumed, that two had either reached their majority and left home, or had married, or had left home to seek their fortunes elsewhere. The practice was that only children under the parental roof, or the jurisdiction of the head of the household, were listed at census-taking time.

Nancy was the youngest daughter, born February 10, 1787.[8] Five of her brothers and sisters had married and left South Carolina prior to their mother's death, and it is assumed that Nancy may, also, have left the state prior to 1833. She had married a man by the name of South and was still living, long after Nancy Hanks Lincoln had died in Indiana in the Autumn of 1818.

Nancy South died between 1833 and 1838, and her heirs inherited from Ann Hanks' estate in final settlement.

In a recently published biography of John C. Calhoun, the author refers to the tradition of Nancy Hanks and states that she "...turned up again in Alabama."[9] She had removed to the area near Huntsville.

Nancy Hanks, daughter of Luke and Ann Hanks of Virginia and South Carolina--branded in infamy, redeemed by reputation. By indisputable records more surely, she did not marry Tom Lincoln, nor become the mother of Abraham Lincoln.

---

[7] Judgement Roll 286, Ordinary 964, Deed Book 1, p. 59

[8] Knotts to Barton, August 23, 1919. Library Chicago University.

[9] Coit, John C. Calhoun, p. 52 538; Coit to Baber, March 4, 1952, Baber papers.

iii

NANCY OF WILLIAM

In the beautiful Ocuna Lufta valley of the mountains of Western North Carolina, there was a tradition that associated the name of Nancy Hanks with an Abraham Enloe (Inloe, or Inlow). The time of the origin of the tale is obscure , but the legend has been preserved in the folklore[1] and when Abraham Lincoln became of national prominance and it was learned that his mother had been a Nancy Hanks, the earlier gossip was recollected by the older ones and reconstructed; and, bandied about during the period of the Civil War, it was accepted as a fact that Enloe was the putative father of Lincoln.

Another generation of time passed and the story was resurrected by a so-called "student of history" as a feature article for a newspaper.[2] Cathey, a bright young man, interviewed reputable citizens and old men, and put their memories into book form.[3] Mr. Arthur, the historian of local western Carolina annals, investigated the tradition and its ramifications.[4] One version promulgated by Mr. Knotts of South Carolina, was an endeavor to transfer this Nancy to be the Nancy of Luke, and to make Calhoun the one who fathered her child. But, when confronted with this story the Enloe family de-credited it wholeheartedly, saying that the child of Nancy was fathered, and they should have known, by their grandfather.[5]

Another and later version is an attempt to trace the origin of Nancy to Gaston, then Lincoln County.[6]

The story runs that Abraham Enloe and family, who lived near present Bostic, Rutherford County, moved westward across the mountains and settled among the Cherokees. In his household was a hired or bound girl, Nancy Hanks, who had formerly resided for a time in the home of her Uncle Dick Hanks, on the Catawba River,

---

[1] T.R. Dawley, Jr., The Child that Toileth Not, p. 271

[2] Charlotte Observer, September 17, 1893.

[3] James H. Cathey, Truth is Stranger Than Fiction, 1899

[4] John P. Arthur, History of Western North Carolina, p. 310

[5] D.J. Knotts, to Barton, in Paternity of Lincoln, p. 113 Seq.

[6] Minnie Stowe Puett, History of Gaston County, p. 175.

near present Belmont, Gaston County. She became with child, [7] which local gossip laid to Abraham; so that she was sent away. [7] One version among several is that she went back home. Another version is that she was carried away by Nancy Enloe Thompson, and this is confirmed by the tradition in the Enloe family, who of all people, ought to know what happened. Captain William A. Enloe, a grandson of Abraham Enloe, a confederate officer in the Civil War, a state representative and businessman told Cathey:

> "One Mr. Thompson married my Aunt Nancy, daughter
> of Abraham Enloe contrary to the will of my grand-
> father: to conceal the matter from my grandfather's
> knowledge, Thompson stole her away and went to
> Kentucky: On the trip they were married. Hearing
> of their marriage, my grandfather reflected and
> decided to invite them back home. On their re-
> turn they were informed of the tumult in my
> grandfather's household because of Nancy Hanks,
> who had given birth to a child; and when my
> uncle and aunt, Thompson and wife, returned
> to their Kentucky home, they took with them
> Nancy Hanks and her child. This is the family
> story as near as I can reproduce it from memory." [8]

Cathey, for his book, adduced a lot of testimony from concurrently well-known and reliable witnesses but, when it is examined and analyzed, it turns out to be mostly hearsay and the conclusions are opinions drawn from conjecture and a fanciful resemblence of Lincoln to the tall men of the Enloe family. No specific dates are given and only general times are mentioned, the presumption being that the incident occurred before the marriage of Nancy Hanks Lincoln in Kentucky. [9]

The old men he interviewed admitted that the event they were reporting happened before their time and not within their memories and not of their own personal knowledge; but, insisted that they were telling it as they had heard it, and this is not to be doubted. And younger men said they first heard the story during the Civil War days; but their stories are consistent and the local circumstances seem never to have been denied; in fact, they seem to have been con- firmed.

Certainly, it was true that an Abraham Enloe had resided in Rutherford County, near a Hanks family, and had emigrated to then Buncombe, now Swain County. [10] Certainly, it was true that Richard

---

[7] James H. Cathey, Genesis of Lincoln

[8] Ibid., pp. 60-61.

[9] June 12, 1806, Courthouse Record, Washington Co., Kentucky

[10] Courthouse Record, Rutherford County, North Carolina

Hanks, popularly known as "Uncle Dicky", an old Revolutionary War veteran[11] lived in now Gaston County, and on the Catawba River. He bought land, paid taxes, gave bond for his children to marry and is established in the county records as having been a citizen for many years.[12] He had a family of nine children, including a daughter, Nancy.

One Matthew Leeper, when an old man, is said to have told the story of Nancy Hanks to a younger man who was a member of an illustrious North Carolina family. This younger man, as he grew older, passed the story down in his family.[13] This version is merely that a niece of "Uncle Dicky" visited in his home, later was farmed or bound out, and became the mother of Abraham Lincoln.

Now, old Mr. Leeper was born in 1755, lived long and well, and had a large family; and now sleeps with many of them in the old graveyard southeast of Belmont. He, no doubt knew all about the family of Richard Hanks and the families of other Hankses in the county, but as to the maternity of Lincoln, he vouchsafed nothing--that has been added. Matthew Leeper died October 12, 1849.

Richard Hanks had several brothers: James, who lived nearby and later moved to Surry County, had children including a daughter, Nancy; Thomas, who had married Crese Hargrave, had children; Joshua, up in Grayson County, Virginia had many children, and a Nancy; David had a Nancy; and William in Rutherford County had a Nancy. Five Hanks brothers all had seen military service in the War; five Hanks brothers had daughters named Nancy. Certainly, one of these Nancys had visited her "Uncle Dickey", had lived in the household of Abraham Enloe; had removed with the family to Soco Creek; and may have supped her sorrow; may have returned "home"; and may have later removed to Tennessee. To

---

[11]
No. 4570, Archives, Washington, D.C.

[12]
Courthouse record, Lincoln County, North Carolina

[13]
Puett, History of Gaston County, North Carolina

[14]
Cathey, Genesis of Lincoln

examine the testimonies and the evidence, dependence is on Cathey.

Mr. Cathey states in his book: The North Carolina tradition does not pretend to fix the date of Nancy Hanks' leaving Abraham Enloe's.[14] This is a weakness in his arguments: It would seem that the date of the birth of the boy is of the essence of the research.

Mr. William H. Conley, who was born about 1812, gave testimony that, "when I was a lad", he had overheard some women in conversation with his mother at his father's house and "they had a great deal to say about some trouble that had once occurred between Abe Enloe and girl they called Nancy Hanks..." "I heard nothing more until the year before the War..."[15]

Mr. Philip Dills, who was born in Rutherford County, January 10, 1808, was removed with his father's family to Western North Carolina soon after his birth. According to his report, the time of the arrival of the Abraham Enloe family at Soco Creek in the Cherokee Country is established as about contemporaneously with his father's arrival—after 1808. Mr. Dills, when a very old man, testified that he had heard the story "while I was a very young man."[16]

Mr. Dills was four years older than Mr. Conley; had heard the story when he was, "a very young man." Mr. Conley had overheard the gossip, "when I was a lad." Their testimonies are in agreement and consistent and the conversations they heard must have been at about the same time of the trouble for, while such incidents cause considerable local gossip then, the interest in paternity cases quickly subsides, and is not renewed unless some later incident arouses the issue. This reasoning would seem to date the conversations as of the early 1820's; no untoward incident is mentioned that would have revived interest in any earlier event, so it is assumed the gossip and the event were then.

Cathey quotes another man, as a gentleman of the most unquestionable integrity -- Joseph A. Collins. He testified that, in 1867, he was in Texas, and met Judge Gilmore, who in turn, had told him of meeting a man named Phillip Wells, then ninety years of age. Wells narrated that he had been a salesman and trader and had called at the Enloe home, while Nancy was there and in trouble, and so he knew all about it.[17]

---

[14] Cathey, Genesis of Lincoln

[15] Ibid, p. 42

[16] Ibid., p. 39

[17] Ibid., p. 53

Arthur, who investigated this story learned that Wells did
not work for Johnston, his boss, before 1818, and rejected the Wells
story. It is obvious that Arthur based his rejection upon a pre-con-
ceived date of the birth. He might better had observed that the date
the travelling salesman called is evidence that the birth did not
occur previously to his connection with Johnston. The salesman's
report is consistent with Dill's and Conley's.

Another witness, an old lady, recollected that, when she was
a girl, she heard a neighbor woman say something to her mother about
Nancy Hanks going to Kentucky with Nancy Enloe Thompson. In a letter
that Arthur wrote to Barton[18] July 28, 1913, he says the lady was not
born before 1809; therefore, he rejects her testimony. Again, it is
apparent that Mr. Arthur's premise is that the birth-date was much
earlier; this testimony is not to be ignored; it also helps determine
the time of the birth.

The time she sets agrees with the time of Mr. Wells; if he was
at Enloe's in 1818, or after, and saw Nancy there, certainly, a girl
who was about ten years of age could have had a memory of an incident
about which neighbors had talked, perhaps mysteriously.

Confirmation of the accuracy of the testimony from the
memory of the old lady is found in its agreement with the tradition
of Nancy Thompson having taken Nancy Hanks away. It has been said
in one place that Nancy Thompson's age was about the same as Nancy
Hanks. What was Nancy Thompson's age? Abraham Enloe and Sallie
Egerton were married in 1795.[19] If it be assumed that Nancy, their
daughter, was among the earliest born of their sixteen children, as
she was said to have been, certainly she was not born prior to 1796;
consequently, she would have been only ten years of age at the time
of Nancy Hanks Lincoln's marriage in Kentucky! At what tender age
did she run off, become a child wife, return home, and leave for
Kentucky with a Nancy Hanks in time for the Kentucky wedding?

It was an impossibility for her, as a married woman, to have
conducted Nancy Hanks to Kentucky prior to June, 1806, when the
Hanks-Lincoln nuptials occurred.

One of the most positive witnesses that Nancy Hanks had
given birth to a son was Nancy Hollifield, who, when an old lady,
told her grandson, Brackston Smart, who was an intelligent man, that
she had seen Nancy and her child many times.[20] This probably was in
Rutherford County. She further stated that during her girlhood days
she was very intimately associated with the girl by the name of Nancy
Hanks at Enloes. The conclusion is that the two girls were about the
same age.

[18] Arthur to Barton, July 28, 1913, Chicago University

[19] Courthouse records, Rutherford County, North Carolina

[20] Coggins, The Eugenics of Abraham Lincoln, p. 46

Nancy Hollifield was a widow by the middle of the nineteenth century, and, as head of her household, gave her own data to the census taker. According to the census of 1850, she gave her age as 50; according to the cenus of 1860, woman-like, her age was still 50; whichever, if either is correct, it still indicates she was born at 1800, or after. This begins to determine the age of her playmate. They were born concurrently and played together after 1800, and as children!

Proof of the approximate age of this Nancy at the time of her trouble is found in the testimony of Mr. Berry H. Melton of Buncombe County, North Carolina, a man of extraordinary ability, knowledge and accomplishments. He was born at the beginning of the 19th century and lived to be 96 years of age. At about the age of 90 he was being asked how he knew so much about this Nancy Hanks.

Part of his answer was that he knew Nancy Hanks when she was a little girl. They were children together, and played together many a day.[21] This is specific information that the Nancy of Rutherford later Buncombe County, was about the same age as Mr. Melton who was born at or near the beginning of the 19th century.

It is also in agreement with the fact that Nancy Enloe Thompson, born after 1795, was older than Nancy Hanks and would have been old enough to have assisted her to leave as Nancy Enloe, a ten year old girl could not have accompanied Nancy Hanks to Kentucky.

The conclusion is inescapable that the evidence which proves that a Nancy Hanks bore a son by an Abraham Enloe, proves by its own internal evidence that the child was born after 1818; and not ten years earlier. This, therefore, is not the Nancy Hanks who married Tom Lincoln in Kentucky in 1806.

****

It may be of interest to speculate: Who was this Nancy? We know that she was a niece of Dicky Hanks and, having the name Hanks, was a daughter or granddaughter of one of his brothers. We know that each of his brothers had daughters named Nancy. William Hanks, one of his brothers, lived not too far away, in Rutherford County, and again, Mr. Berry H. Melton in his remarks about the Hanks family gives the needed assist to establish the Nancy Hanks of Enloe's. He knew her father, and knew him to be William Hanks. The Meltons came from the same community in Rutherford County where Nancy Hanks was born. Probably knew all the Hanks family well. The

---

[21]James Coggins, _Abraham Lincoln, A North Carolinian,_ p. 70

tradition is, everyone spoke of her father as "Old Bill Hanks".[22]
Further confirmation comes from the census report of 1800, which
shows William Hanks: his wife, Keziah Wright, and he were both
under 45, and he reported eight children, three children under 16;
five under 10 (four girls and four boys). The known names of the
children (some are missing) are: Thomas, Noah, born January 1, 1790;
John; Rachel; James; and Nancy, born Circa 1800.

****

There seems no doubt that the notorious Enloe-Hanks
imbroglio occured. Of course, it was recollected and re-told to
younger people at the time of the Civil War, exactly as some of the
witnesses testified to Cathey. It is submitted that it was the
origin of the scandal that named other Abraham Inloes, Enlows, and
Enloes to other Nancy Hankses, to be the parents of Abraham Lincoln.

iv

NANCY OF ARGYLE

Another traditional mother of Lincoln was a Nancy Hanks of
Granville, now Vance County, North Carolina. This story is open
and aboveboard and has no connotation of off-color as some of the
traditions have. It has persisted for years and was first put into
print by the late J. B. Watkins, from whose article it is, quote:[1]

> "The middle son, Argil, married June 20,
> 1783, the daughter of what was then and is
> today, a rich proud, aristocratic family,
> that, like most families of this border
> section, had moved from Virginia. In talking
> with his law partner, Abraham Lincoln stated
> that his mother's people were a poor and humble
> family of Virginia, but he believed there was
> some unknown ancestry that gave his great in-
> tellect, and 'all that he was he owed to his
> mother.'

[22] Ibid., p. 70

[1] Watkins, The Five Mothers of Abraham Lincoln, February 12,
1937, Baber papers.

"This family could easily have been that
'unknown ancestry'. Argil and Frances
lived on the Virginia border, the state
line being the northern boundary, 122 acres,
sixteen miles north of Henderson. Here
were born, during the next thirteen years,
nine children, Nancy the oldest, would be
in 1784 (which is generally accepted as
about the correct date for Nancy of Kentucky).

"Their log house with two large oak trees
on north, is standing today, only many years
ago it was enlarged, and all weatherboarded.

"In 1796, they moved three miles south to a
317 acre farm, which is today called 'Hanks
Place'. A negro, Ed Hanks, lives there now,
doubtless he is a descendant of the Hanks
servants. The old house was burned several
years ago.

"In 1797, Argil Hanks died and the division of
his estate gives to widow Frances and daughter,
Nancy, together, 2 negroes, 1 red heifer and
calf, 1 bull, 1 young bay horse, 11 hogs,
value 122 lbs. Then gives several more negroes
and other items to the other eight children in
pairs.

"So instead of being 'poor and humble' our Hanks
were well-off and as genteel, and Nancy had as
good an education as anyone of her time. William
Hanks, Jr. also died 1797, leaving a widow, Sarah,
and one son, so Nancy may have stayed at her Aunt
Sarah's and attended Springer College, a mile
away; which caused her to name her first child
"Sarah" in Kentucky.

"Tradition here is that around 1803, Nancy went
with some friends to Salisbury, North Carolina,
from which place she went on to Kentucky, married
Thomas Lincoln, etc...."

The foregoing excerpt is a very complete recitation of the
local Nancy Hanks tradition, as it was repeated to me by several
citizens of the community.[2] In the courthouse records at Oxford,

---

2
Interviews in Henderson, North Carolina

North Carolina, most of the above report is confirmed: Deed books
indicate that the Hanks family came from Virginia; the marriage of
Argyle Hanks and Frances Hargrave is registered;[3] the inventory
of Argil's estate is listed, and its distribution, with a part to
Nancy, just as Watkins knew.

The widow, Frances, upon the death of her husband, the same
year as his brother, Elijah, died, 1798,[4] came into court and, there
being no will, was appointed administratrix. In due, lawful manner
she petitioned the court to have the personal property divided among
"the next of kin" and guardians to be appointed to look after the
interests of the minor children.

Accordingly, a committee came into court and reported divisions
as here summarized: To Frances Hanks and Nancy Hanks, her daughter...
etc.; to Polly Hanks, Sally Hanks, and Milly Hanks; to William, to
Argil (Jr.) and to John Hanks, sons; to Green Hanks and to Willis
Hanks, sons (May 23, 1799). It is of interest that daughters, other
than Nancy, are named, viz: Polly, Sally, and Milly, for the names
of Polly and Sarah have been often given as sisters of Nancy Hanks
Lincoln.[5]

This did not end the affair of the estate of Argil Hanks,
deceased. In May court, 1802, Frances was appointed guardian for
four of the minor sons.[6] Nancy and her sisters were not named.
What had become of them? Had they become of age, or married? It
would tend to so indicate. Nancy, born 1784, was eighteen.

Here then, were the records that seemed to fulfill the
requirements for the proper Nancy Hanks: "Name of Hanks; born in
Virginia; February 5, 1784; went to Kentucky" and at about the
right time; and, by way of Salisbury, where other Hanks families
were residing, "came with kinfolk and not with her parents." This
Nancy's father was deceased, and the mother, Frances, did not go
to Kentucky. The mortises and tenons were fitting together.

I drove out to the site of one of the Hanks homesteads, and
found the landmarks. I visited the old Hargrave plantation house,
of pre-bellum days, now unkept, but grand. At the home of Ed Hanks,
colored, I found his mother, Frances Hanks, widow of James. This

---

[3]Courthouse records, Granville County, North Carolina,
Marriage Record p. 65

[4]Courthouse records, Granville County, North Carolina,
Probate Record, p. 65

[5]Courthouse records, Granville County, North Carolina, Book 5, p.1

[6]Courthouse records, Granville County, North Carolina,
Book 1790-1850, p. 12.

old colored woman had been born and reared in the neighborhood. She proudly told that her maiden name had been Hargrave.

Back of the house, under an oak tree, she pointed out two Hanks graves and said they were of "John and Ardel" who had lived alone and died "about the time of the war" (Civil). Thereupon, I asked her, "Did you ever hear of a Nancy Hanks?" "Oh, yes", she answered, "She was the mother of Abraham Lincoln and is buried up on the old place." I said, "I thought she died and is buried in Indiana." She replied, "I don't know about that, all I know is what my old grandfather told me many years ago."

With my faith in the memories of those not given to books, I was disturbed. I went back to the courthouse and began to thumb through the old probate records. Page after page, I turned and then, just at closing time, I came across it: [7]the pathetic record of the sale of goods of Nancy Hanks, deceased.

She may have gone to Salisbury to visit friends, and I rather trust that she did, but she never went to Kentucky. The half interest she had owned, with her mother, in the things she had cherished from her father, Argyle, were bid in by mother and sister Polly and Doke Prewett, who had married sister, Milly.

It is with regret that I have to report for purpose of history that a daughter of Argyle did not marry Lincoln.

NANCY OF JOSEPH

This is the Nancy who has given rise to the most confusion pertaining to the indentification of Nancy Hanks Lincoln. Herndon first thought that she was the mother of Lincoln and never quite got the matter straightened out to his own satisfaction; although Dennis Hanks told him who she was and that he, Dennis, and the Hall boys were her sons, and not Lincoln.

In many ways she qualified with what Lincoln had said. Undeniably, she was named Nancy Hanks; was born in Virginia; had come into Kentucky; was left an orphan or half orphan at an early age; went to live with relations; was of the same generation; and of about the right age to have been Nancy Lincoln. Notably, her descendants "resided in Coles County, Illinois".

Many of the descendants of her two brothers, William and Joseph of Macon and Adams counties, respectively, of Illinois, whom

_____

[7]Courthouse records, Granville County, North Carolina, February Court 1804.

Lincoln, himself, said were kin to his mother, have confused her
identity and think she was the mother of Lincoln. For this reason,
she shall be fully identified to demonstrate that she was not the
mother of Lincoln.

This is the same Nancy who was bequeathed the heifer year-
ling called "Piedy" in the now rather noted will of Joseph Hanks
of Nelson County, Kentucky.[1] This is the will that Mrs. Hitchcock
came across at Bardstown, wherein she read the name of this Nancy
and jumped to the hasty and erronious conclusion that she had
located and identified the very Nancy who had married Tom Lincoln.

This is the selfsame Nancy Hanks, who, after the death of
her father, Joseph, 1793, and the return of her mother, Nannie,
and her brother, Joseph (Jr.) to Virginia, lived at the home of
her sister, Elizabeth, who had married Thomas Sparrow. Here she
was residing when her son, Dennis Friend, was born, and was given
his mother's name of Hanks, but the two became so identified with
the Sparrow family as to be oftener called Sparrow than Hanks.

It may be that the Nancy Hanks, who married Tom Lincoln
also lived in the Sparrow home for a short while; there is tradition to that effect. Barton correctly differentiated between the
two Nancys: the one who married Levi Hall and the other, who
married Tom Lincoln.

It is of interest, however, that none of the old settlers
whom Charles Friend interviewed had any recollection of two Nancys
in the community.[2]

As has been said, a man should know his own mother, and
this is the Nancy who became the unwed mother of Dennis Friend
Hanks, 1799, and before she cast her lot with Levi Hall, the club-
foot tailor. Her early paramour was Charles Friend, the grandfather of Charles Friend, Jr., and the father of Dennis Friend
Hanks,[3] as he had testified.

From old letters extant in several archives it would be
possible to reconstruct her life as it was perhaps lived in and
about Elizabethtown.[4]

---

[1] Will Book A, p. 107, Nelson County, Kentucky, Courthouse.

[2] Friend to Herndon, August 20, 1889, Herndon-Weik Coll.

[3] Dennis Friend Hanks to Friend, March 25, 1866

[4] Helm to Herndon, Library, Chicago University

Since we now know she was not in the ancestral line of Lincoln, such an effort would be futile. Perhaps, she kept house for her brother, Joseph, the carpenter. No doubt, she knew Tom Lincoln well. Certainly she had beaux but probably no offers of marriage until Levi Hall appeared.

These two unfortunates were married by the Reverend Alexander McDougal[5] at Mrs. Cissna's home southeast of present Hodgenville, and Mrs. Middleton remembered the wedding, whereat a small boy was old enough to run around. The small boy was Dennis Friend Hanks.

Levi, perhaps to compensate for his physical handicap, was not a peaceful citizen. He was a disturber of the peace and the court records show he was arrested occasionally; and his brother-in-law, William Hanks, would go on his bond. He moved his family about quite a bit; in 1804 he paid taxes in Montgomery County; later, the Halls resided for a time southwest of Elizabethtown, at Spring Grove, on the Hartford road. In 1810 they were in Green County, and the census listed them with four children, all less than ten years of age.

Two of these were sons, Squire and William. For the record, we will digress here: Squire later married Matilda Johnston,[6] a daughter of the Sallie Bush Johnston, who had become the second wife of Tom Lincoln. Squire and Matilda had a son, John Johnston Hall, who married a Taylor and resided many years on the so-called Tom Lincoln farm in Coles County, Illinois. Here was reared a Hall family, including Nancy A.; and she was the young lady who helped entertain Mrs. Eleanor Gridley at the time of her visit to the Hall farm, formerly owned by Thomas Lincoln, and whence was moved the double log cabin to Chicago for exhibition. This Nancy A. Hall, as she is called, although married first to Mr. Thomas, and one son, Clarence, was born. He now resides near the old Lincoln farm in Coles County, Illinois.

---

[5] Brown to Durett, May 12, 1886, Lincoln Lore, Number 9.

[6] Marriage Records, September 13, 1826, Spencer County, Indiana Courthouse.

William, another son of Levi and Nancy Hanks Hall, married
more than once. One of his subsequent wives was Mary Ann Hanks,
daughter of Joseph Hanks, Jr., the carpenter of early Elizabethtown. William's son, James, also married a daughter of the same
Joseph Jr.; Caroline.[7]

To return to Levi and Nancy in Kentucky, after the Lincolns
moved to Indiana, the next to follow were the Sparrows, Thomas and
wife, Elizabeth, the sister of Nancy Hall, and Dennis Hanks, who
was almost grown, leaving the Hall family in Kentucky. It was a
most unfortunate move: the milk sickness became prevalent in
southern Indiana and took many lives.

Thomas Sparrow became seriously ill, and made his will on
the 21st of September, 1818, when it was witnessed by David Casebier
and Nancy Lincoln, who signed by mark. Thomas bequeathed his
property to his wife, Elizabeth, and at her death, to Dennis Hanks.
But, within a week both husband and wife were deceased; then on
October 5, 1818, Nancy Hanks Lincoln died. These three were all
buried on the same knoll and side by side. Within a few years
Nancy Hanks Hall died, and was placed at the side of Nancy Hanks
Lincoln. Later, her husband, Levi Hall died,[8] was buried at her
side, and with the others.

In their hallowed graves, these five lie and the site would
have remained unmarked and forgotten had it not been that the misery
of those years was left in the memory of Dennis Hanks and in after
years he was able to so exactly describe the location of the graves
that they were easily identified and marked.[9]

So, side by side, vide et crede, cloistered in the Eternal
Hills of Southern Indiana, sleep the two Nancys: the one the mother
of Dennis who lives in the light of Lincoln;[10] the other the mother
of Lincoln, who lives in the light of history.

---

[7] Joseph Hanks, Jr. chart, Baber papers.

[8] Will, January 17, 1826, Spencer County, Indiana courthouse.

[9] Barton, Lineage of Lincoln, p. 240

[10] Lincoln Lore, No. 1366, Appendix.

vi

NANCY OF MOTT

Nancy, daughter of Mott and Mary Hanks; and granddaughter of John and Mary Mott Hanks, was born at the right time and generation to have married Tom Lincoln. She was the fifth child of eight children, and her sister, just older, was Lucy Hanks. They had six brothers.1

This family lived in then Dobbs County, North Carolina, now extinct; and re-created into Lenoir, Green and Wayne counties. The courthouses having burned at the respective county seats of Kinston and Snow Hill, no early records are available; and only traces of Hanks records are at Goldsboro, at the courthouse.2

It seems that descendants of this family migrated southward and on into Texas, but no attempt has been made to trace them for this purpose. The birth dates of the eight children of this family are in orderly sequence, and the birth date of the Nancy, June 21, 1780, is so bracketed it cannot be of 1784 to qualify; so she is thereby eliminated and did not marry Tom Lincoln.

vii

NANCY OF FLEETWOOD

A Nancy Hanks, who was of the current generation to have married Tom Lincoln should be considered for her record: she "was born in Virginia and about 1784"; she "came to Kentucky and not with her parents"; she "lived with an Uncle Jonathan near Louisville."

She was born probably in Loudoun County, Virginia, the daughter of Fleetwood and Ruth Hanks, and was one of at least seven known children. In the 1790's Fleetwood moved his family southward up the Shenandoah Valley and into Bedford County, where he purchased and settled on a farm on Beaver Dam Creek. It was here that Nancy

---

1
Mott Hanks family chart. Baber papers.
2
Deed Book 5E, p. 62, Wayne County, North Carolina Courthouse.

grew up and near the Blue Ridge Mountains. The family belonged
to the Friends sect and, while a record of Nancy's marriage has
not been located in the minutes of Friends Meetings, that of her
brother, William, has been.

However, the courthouse records give her marriage license
as of October 14, 1805 to Enoch Holdron.[1] To this union at least
four children were born and two of them entered convents; namely,
Ruth and Rigenia.

Nancy married secondly, Frank DeMar (Lamar or Demar) and more
children were born.[2] The family moved to Phillips County, Arkansas,
where Nancy died in February of 1870, leaving many descendants.[3]
This record, fully authenticated, eliminates her as having married
Tom Lincoln.

viii

NANCY OF JEMIMA

There is a supposition that the Charles Hanks, son of
Joseph of Nelson County, Kentucky, and named in his will, 1793,
had sons, John and Conrad; and, daughters, Jane and Nancy.[1] No
evidence is found in affirmation nor negation of this.

It is probable that the three Hanks people inquired about
by Dennis Hanks of Charles Friend[2] were of this group; but there
is no clue in the letter as to kinship. That they were of a generation old enough to have been children of Charles, who was, himself,
an older brother of Dennis' mother, is indicated in two ways: Dennis

[1] Marriage Records, Wives, Bedford County, Virginia Courthouse

[2] Family Chart, Hitchcock papers, Lincoln Library, Fort Wayne,
Indiana.

[3] James M. Hanks to Hitchcock, March 29, 1894, Ibid

[1] Lea and Hutchinson, The Ancestry of Abraham Lincoln, p. 121

[2] Dennis Hanks to Friend, March 25, 1866, H-W Coll.

asks if they are living yet; and he refers to Jane as the sister of grandmother. The inference is that they were older than he.

It is probable, that this is the Nancy who married Peter Jones, April 16, 1804, in Henry County, Kentucky.[3] The bond at the courthouse was signed by her mother, Jemima Hanks, and by Abner Ford, and not by Abner Hanks. This fact is emphasized for the reason that when an Index of Marriages was made years ago the name Hanks was used instead of Ford; this error has been copied by those who did not refer to the original bond, and even the name 'Abner' has been slured over to Abram. This Nancy has been listed as a daughter of both Abner and Abram Hanks. It is not so: she was the daughter of Jemima Hanks and there is no indication who her father was, from the marriage records only.

By the record, this Nancy Hanks, who was certainly of the same generation as Nancy Hanks Lincoln, did not marry Tom Lincoln; she married Peter Jones.

Interestingly enough, Abner Hanks did reside for a time in Henry County, but as reported under Tradition Number X he had wives enough without Jemima.

ix

NANCY OF WILLIAM OF JOSEPH

It is to take advantage of the fact that this fine woman had the maiden name of Nancy Hanks, and use her as a "horrible example" of the unreliability of testimonies of kinship from descendants not very far removed from ancestors.

In 1926 there died near Tacoma, Washington a Hanks descendant of whom the associated press reported, "September 25,-- John B. Brown, 89, a cousin of Abraham Lincoln, and a pioneer of Washington and Oregon since they were a part of the old Oregon territory, is dead here.

"Brown was one of a family of 10 children of Sallie Hanks, sister of Nancy Hanks, mother of the martyred president."[1]

---

[3] Marriage record, Bond box, Henry County, Kentucky, Courthouse

---

[1] Clipping, Lincoln Library, Ft. Wayne, Indiana. The reporters almost invariably refer to any Hanks deceased as "cousin of A.L." or even "descendant of A.L.!"

This report was and is in conformity with some erroneous information: In 1909, the present Mrs. Arthur E. Morgan, (then Miss Lucy Griscom) at the request of Mr. Morgan, visited two old Hanks men in Oregon to interview them to get Hanks family information. One was John T. Hanks, born 1828, a son of Dennis; and the other, James Lewis Hanks, born 1829, a son of old John, the "rail splitter."

They reported that, "Nancy Hanks had a sister, Sarah, who came to Oregon in 1853 and lived with James Lewis' father (John) for seven years."[2] This was the Sallie Hanks later mentioned in the press release; and she had married J. Bosier Brown, October 23, 1828.[3] She was the daughter of William and Elizabeth Hall Hanks, and, true enough, had a sister, Nancy. But, her sister, Nancy, was born January 13, 1794 in Kentucky and married William Miller,[4] and not Tom Lincoln. But Nancy is of historic interest in her own right: She, it was, who wove the famous cloth for Lincoln.[5]

She and her husband, both born in Kentucky, pioneers to Illinois, died in Des Moines County, Iowa; she, February 17, 1873; and he, March 8, 1870.[6]

NANCY OF JOSHUA

One of the most unique of the ubiquitous Nancy Hankses was one, and about the only one, of whom some uninformed later day kinsperson does not represent as, "sister of my ancestor and who was the mother of Lincoln!" This Nancy, according to descendants, in eastern Tennessee, did not marry Tom Lincoln, but did marry Willis Morris, and had nine children.

She was the first-born, December 30, 1812, of three daughters of Joshua and Polly Renwick Hanks, and thereby hangs a tale:

---

[2] Arthur E. Morgan, interview, Yellow Springs, Ohio

[3] Marriage Records, Sangamon County, Illinois, Courthouse

[4] Davis, The Hanks Family in Macon County, Illinois. Papers in Illinois History, 1939, p. 114.

[5] Lincoln Lore, No. 70, August 11, 1930

[6] Davis, Ibid.

Joshua, the son of "Dicky" Hanks married Polly in Lincoln County, North Carolina;[7] and they moved to Scott County, Tennessee. One morning, it is alleged, he picked up his rifle-gun, whistled to his hunting dogs, went away and did not return! Eventually he married Amelia Rape, and imigrated to western Illinois[8] and reared another family.[9]

Polly, the first wife, died, and is buried in an unmarked grave at Huntsville, Tennessee. Her daughter, Nancy Hanks Morris, died March 17, 1901, and is buried on the old Morris farm, near Sunbright, Tennessee.[10]

NANCY JANE OF WILLIAM

This Nancy, with the middle name of Jane, was born September 12, 1832, in Edgar County, Illinois, the third child and first daughter of William and Mary O'Hair Hanks; she is treated of here for the reason she was the connecting link, in a way, between the traditions of the Hanks family of now Wolfe County, Kentucky, and the Illinois branch of the original Montgomery County, Kentucky stem.

She was not a pioneer but certainly her life span was from a pioneer environment to a more refined culture; from the essentials to the improvements, to even the luxuries of living and housekeeping. She had high intelligence and some schooling. She was married June 15, 1852[11] to Jesse Swango, and they went to Kentucky, whence Jesse came, to set up housekeeping. There, she came into contact with her father's people, his Uncle Fielding and his cousins; no doubt learned family history that was not known in Illinois.

---

[7] Marriage Records, Lincoln County, North Carolina, Courthouse (Bynam)

[8] Mary E. Delahay to Weik, December 23, 1913, Weik papers, Illinois Historical Society.

[9] Mrs. Ed Hanks to L.M. Morris, August 12, 190?. Baber papers.

[10] Mrs. Ruth Short, interview, Baber papers.

[11] Marriage record, Edgar County, Illinois, Courthouse.

She and her husband returned to Illinois before the Civil
War, and resided in Coles County during that troubled time. On
March 26, 1864, trouble began to brew between Union soldiers, home
on furlough, and the "butter-nuts," called "copperheads", who were
southern sympathizers. The sheriff deputized her husband to help
keep peace and order; but to no avail. An affray broke out and
several were killed in the ensuing fight. The Union forces gained
control and arrested many southern sympathizers, some guilty, and
some innocent, as was developed later.

It was this incident of the Civil War that became the
occasion for Dennis Hanks to be sent to Washington to see Lincoln
and intercede for the prisoners, who were confined in Fort Delaware.
He returned with Lincoln's watch and, later, the prisoners returned
also.[12]

Nancy Jane and her husband removed to Edgar County after the
war and resided at Swango Station, on a farm; later they retired
to South Central Avenue in Paris, Illinois where she was interviewed
in the summer of 1919, in the interest of Hanks family history, but
casually only, and with no notes taken. She had known "Granny
Varvell" for years, called her, "Granny Sallie" and stated she was
a sister to Nancy and to Polly Hanks, and to Fielding. Further data
is not recollected.

Nancy Jane had visited in the home of Dennis Hanks and knew
his daughters. She visited with Harriett Chapman and with the
Shoaffs, where Dennis lived for a time. She was not friendly to
Lincoln and Republicans. Dexter Baber, her nephew, says she also
visited once a year some Hanks people at old Livingston, Clark County,
Illinois.[13]

x

NANCY OF THE BERRY FAMILY

Since the Nancy Hanks who actually married Tom Lincoln was
living, at the time of the wedding, with members of the Berry family
of Washington County, Kentucky; and is presumed to have been a ward
of Richard Berry, Jr., it would seem reasonable to locate the kinfolk

---

[12]
    Coleman, Your Ill. His. Abraham Lincoln and Coles Co.,
March 1940, p. 226. Pamphlet, Baber papers.
[13]
    These would have been of the Elza Hanks family; some are
now buried in the local cemetery. The Patton family of that area
are descendants of Elza.

and connections of the Berry family and, from them, inquire regarding the antecedents of Nancy.

Mrs. Caroline Hanks Hitchcock,[1] an earlier researcher of Hanksiana; and the first one to make an effort to interview Hanks people and their relatives, after copious correspondence had determined the locations of several Hanks settlements, she made a journey into Virginia and Kentucky, 1895, and kept a running journal of her trip.[2]

Excerpts from the journal follow in quotation marks.

One of her first stops (she travelled by train) was at Mt. Sterling, Kentucky in Montgomery County. Here she interviewed, learned, and wrote, among other items jotted down:

"Nancy Hanks lived near North Middleton...She left there and went to Southern part of State...in Paris, Illinois have Hanks blood..."

Mrs. Hitchcock continued her journey and, stopping off at intervening points, finally arrived at Stephensport on the Ohio River, where she spent an entire day in company with, and interviewing, "Uncle Billy" Hanks, aged 90; her journal notes for that day are inexplicably missing!

Fortunately, in an unpublished MS she has written, in part, "One of the happiest days in old Kentucky was spent in a little cabin on the high banks of the Ohio River. We sat there around the big fire and sang together the old Kentucky home songs. 'Uncle Billy' led the singing and he was over ninety years old. We joined in the chorus with his stalwart sons.

---

[1] Carolin Hanks, b. September 20, 1863, N.E. His. & Gen. Reg. Jan, 1932, p. 28 to Baber on Jan. 31, 1950. Baber papers.

[2] Hitchcock papers, Lincoln Library, Fort Wayne, Indiana; facsimile copy, Baber papers.

"Everyone in the countryside calls him 'Uncle Billy.' His real name is William Hanks, and he is a grand-son of Abraham Hanks, who came to Kentucky with the Boones, and was a great friend of Daniel Boone. He had many fine children.

"Heres to you Uncle Billy...."[3]

Mrs. Hitchcock continued her journey and arrived at Springfield, the county seat of Washington County, the home county of the Berry family. Here she learned that the marriage records of Thomas Lincoln with the sustaining documents, were in the court house. From her various interviews, she was told as she wrote in her notes:

"Nancy Hanks Wedding - at one time the wedding bond was stolen from the clerks office and returned to its place again in a few weeks."

"(Squire Robert) Mitchell Thompson (at the time of the slanderers' endeavors to prove that Nancy Hanks had never been married) "caused a search for the marriage certificate to be made...found...which cleared all slanders on that score."

"Then they tried to prove that Nancy Hanks' mother had never been married."[4]

"This again is absolutely false as all the members of the Berry, Mitchell, and Shipley families know well--as they all lived close together and were as one large family."

At the courthouse she copied or at least interposed here, "Daniel Mitchell & Jane Berry--January 1, 1795."

She learned that "Sara Shipley married Robert Mitchell and had a daughter, Sarah (Mitchell)".

(Squire Robert) "Mitchell Thompson's mother was Sarah Mitchell."

---

[3] Ibid.

[4] See Chapter II

"(Squire Robert) Mitchell Thompson is dead. I saw his wife. She knew the Berry, Mitchell, and Shipley families intimately."

"She knows that Nancy Hanks was an orphan and lived with her Aunt, Mrs. Berry, as also did Sara Mitchell who was an orphan too."

"This Sarah Mitchell he ("Judge" Andrew Thompson) says was at Nancy Hanks wedding."[5]

"(Squire) Robert Mitchell Thompson was a Mitchell--Mrs. Mitchell (Sara) was captured by the Indians under the command of John Gurton--carried into Michigan--a squaw put her by a big log and hid her--was released by the army in the Northwest--she was own cousin of Nancy Hanks and lived in the same log cabin with her."

"Mrs. Charlotte Vawter [6]...knows more of the family than anyone and is the one who wrote the long article to the Springfield paper--denying all accusations."

One of the papers by Mrs. Vawter had appeared in the Louisville Courier Journal twenty years before Mrs. Hithcock gathered these notes. It said in part,
"...Thomas Lincoln and Nancy Hanks who were
married at the home of Uncle Frank Berry...as
I remember the story of Nancy Hanks...her mother's
name was Shipley...one sister married a Mr. Berry...
another married Robert Mitchell who came to
Kentucky about the year, 1780...Their only daughter;
...Sarah,...eleven years old, was captured by the
Indians. Soon after...Wayne's Treaty with the

---

[5] "Judge" Andrew Thompson was a brother of "Squire" Robert M. Thompson, and was well known by my father, Dexter Baber, born 1867, who as a young man was associated with Mr. Thompson at the Indianapolis Union Stock Yards. He, also, knew a Mr. Thompson at the Louisville Bourbon Stock Yards. My father says that the reputation of the Mitchells was, "They were honest and intelligent people." Further: "Andrew would listen carefully to a conversation without making an interruption, and later could report verbatum what had been said."

[6] Mrs. Achilles Vawter, born Charlotte Speare Hobart, October 26, 1825, at Indianapolis, Indiana, was daughter of John and Naomi Thompson Hobart. Her maternal Grandmother was Sarah Mitchell Thompson, the mother of the Thompson men, aforesaid in footnote #5.

Indians in 1792, the lost Sarah was returned
to her friends, and lived in the home of her
Uncle Richard Berry, with her cousins Frank
and Ned Berry and Nancy Hanks...[7]

"("Judge") Andrew Thompson at Bourbon Stock Yards has one
of the papers. It was written in the winter and spring of '92."

"Nancy Hanks went to Nolin on a visit and Thomas L. (Lincoln)
came to her at the same time and they passed each other on the way
and so delayed the wedding--".

Following up the clues she had obtained, Mrs. Hitchcock wrote
to Mrs. Vawter and, in a return letter, was told, among other things,

"...Nancy Hanks, who was the cousin of my
grandmother. When young they were as intimate as sisters and members of their
Uncle Richard Berry's home in Washington
County, Kentucky, until both were married...
Nancy Hanks' mother's name before marriage
was Shipley and she was a Virginian. There
were, I think, six sisters in the Shipley
family but I only remember the names of the
husbands of three: Richard Berry and Robert
Mitchell and Mr. Hanks, Nancy's father."[8]

Squire Robert Mitchell Thompson, son of the Sarah Mitchell,
who, when a girl, was captured by the Indians, and whose grandmother was, indeed, Naomi Shipley, killed by the Indians, made a
sworn statement of the facts, as he knew them, pertaining to this
case, 1891.

He deposed that he was 79 years of age, and had resided
in Washington County, Kentucky all his life except for a period
of eight years at Indianapolis. Then, among other things he
said, he made a specific statement, "The mother of Nancy (Hanks)
Lincoln, who was the mother of Abraham Lincoln, was an own cousin
of affiant's mother..."

---

[7] Courier Journal, February 20, 1874

[8] Vawter to Hitchcock, September 14, 1895; Lincoln Lore, p. 9

This affidavit was taken before Mr. James L. Wharton, clerk of Washington Circuit Court, who, in turn certified to revelant facts: He stated that Mr. Thompson was a most reputable citizen, entitled to be believed, upright, moral and creditable in every way.

Mr. Wharton says the affidavit was dictated for Mr. Thompson; and read over to him; and its contents explained to him; and that he understood the same; and did freely and voluntarily execute it. [9]

If it was dictated for Mr. Thompson, the presumption is that he first gave the information, at the request of someone interested in the subject who, in turn, dictated what was to be written from what Mr. Thompson had just stated.

This being a sworn statement, it is to be presumed that Mr. Thompson was careful what he told; and listened carefully when it was read back to him. Surely, then, there was no literary fued between Lincoln authors to have influenced his opinions.

This affidavit indicates a __difference__ __of__ __degree__ in the relationship than that expressed by Mrs. Vawter. She thought that Nancy was a cousin of Sarah Mitchell, her grandmother. Mr. Thompson thought that the __mother__ of Nancy was the first cousin of Sarah Mitchell, his mother.

Whether Nancy or Nancy's mother was "own" first cousin to Sarah Mitchell is not so important as it is to know that there was a relationship of the Shipley family to Nancy's branch of the Hanks family. Since the Shipley descendants have the impression that the kinship was through a female, the supposed Vawter relationship will be satisfied if Nancy's mother was a Shipley; and, the supposed Thompson relationship will be verified if either of Nancy's grandmothers was a Shipley.

In either alternative, it is necessary to locate the origins of the Shipley, Berry, Mitchell, and Thompson families to learn with what Hanks family they were associated. For this Nancy of that Hanks-Shipley family connection is the one who did marry Tom Lincoln.

---

[9] J. L. Wharton, Seal April 13, 1891.

All of the eight known Nancys who were born in the 1780's
and possibly could have married Tom Lincoln--all are eliminated
as candidates except one, and the nominated one fulfills all the
requirements, viz: She was born in Virginia;[10] of a family of
Hanks;[11] she was an orphan;[12] and came to Kentucky with some of
her kinfolks and not with her parents;[13] she probably had lived
with the Richard Berry Sr. family;[14] and the Richard Berry, Jr.
family.[15] She was kin to the Thompson family; and to the Mitchell
family; and a descendant of the Shipley family; and she did marry
Tom Lincoln.

xi

KITH AND KIN

The next step is to locate an area where the Berry, Mitchell,
and Thompson families resided near enough to the Shipley and the
Hanks families for members to inter-marry: and this has been made
easy by earlier researchers. In his first recorded interview in
1886, Squire Robert Mitchell Thompson informed that the Shipleys
came from North Carolina; Mrs. Vawter stated that Nancy Hanks'
mother was a Shipley and a Virginian; Mrs. Hitchcock located the
Shipley family of Virginia in what she thought was Lunenburg
County; and Dr. Warren later located the site of the Shipley farms
in what is now Campbell County. He, also, located the Mitchell
and the Thompson families in the same neighborhood; and the Richard
Berry family in the adjoining county of Charlotte.[1]

---

[10] Vawter

[11] Marriage Bond

[12] Mrs. Robert M. Thompson

[13] Barrett

[14] Robert M. Thompson

[15] R.M. Berry, obit., Lincoln Lore, No. 214

---

[1] The Lincoln Kinsman, No. 29, November, 1940

This is in the Roanoke River Country once mentioned by
Dennis Hanks and is near the James River where, according to
tradition, John Hanks of Loudoun County went on his way to
Kentucky. In the Courthouse records of Bedford, Campbell,
Charlotte, Halifax and Pittsylvania Counties are many Hanks
names. Research for this purpose has determined that, while
there are communities of Hankses in Virginia, there is no other
where are to be found the names of the cognate families together,
the kith and kin of Nancy Hanks, who married Tom Lincoln.

****

THE SHIPLEY FAMILY
IN VIRGINIA

The name of Robert Shipley II is listed in the tithe record
of Lunenburg County, Virginia for 1750 and, from other records, he
is known to be the one who acquired 314 acres of land on the north
side of Little Falling River in that part that later lay in Bedford
County, when it was cut off from Lunenburg and formed in 1754.[2] It
can be demonstrated he was from Baltimore County, Maryland by the
records of land transactions there.[3]

Robert Shipley II sold off a 150 acres, part of the 314 acres
to Robert Irvine in 1766; and he sold the remaining 164 acres to
Daniel Mitchell in 1771. His signature was made with the character
"R" and his wife, Sarah, joined in signing the deeds. One of Daniel
Mitchell's sons, Robert, had married one of Robert Shipley's daughters,
Naomi; so an inference could be that the sale was for a family
advantage. There is a tradition that Robert Shipley II then re-
moved to North Carolina.

In the meantime, in 1769, Robert Shipley, Jr. (hereafter
called III), who may have been a son or a nephew of the older
Robert, purchased 262 acres of land from Thomas Daugherty on Hatt
Creek. He sold off 30 acres, and 238 acres, and later sold 250
acres in 1777. The increase of acreage over what he had purchased
may indicate that he had acquired land by inheritance from Michael

---

[2] Pat. Book, 36, p. 872

[3] Deed of Grant, February 25, 1745; March 31, 1766.

Prewett, whose daughter, Rachel, was Robert's wife. Robert did not leave the community; he continued to reside in Campbell County, and was still there in the 1780's.[4]

James Hanks appeared in the area on March 27, 1780 by purchase of 376 acres of land on both sides of Hatt Creek, and adjoining Daugherty and Mitchell land. In 1782 both James and Thomas Hanks were taxed, and Thomas had one male tithe over sixteen. The Hankses continued in the community for fifty years, but the Shipleys seem to have disappeared. There are no indications of any Shipley-Hanks connections in the county records; it will be necessary to search the Berry family records.

****

THE BERRY FAMILY

It is easy to locate divers members of the Berry family but the interest is in the Richard Berry, Sr. family of Washington County, Kentucky; and the wife, Rachel, who was supposed to have been a Shipley, although one account names Dorsey. Both these were prominant families of Maryland, where Richard was born, July 20, 1734.

He is next located in the Roanoke River Country of the Bedford-Campbell-Charlotte Counties area; near enough to the Hanks families to have taken in an orphan girl, as the tradition is, "Nancy went to live with an Uncle, Richard Berry": but when courthouse records are examined, they show that Richard Berry Sr. sold his farm in Charlotte County[5] for the sum of "1000 Lawful money of Virginia" and removed four years before Nancy was born, and to far away Kentucky. He entered 600 acres twenty miles west of Harrodsburg, where, twenty years later, he died and left a will which was witnessed by William Brumfield, a son-in-law, and Richard Berry, his son, and James Ryan. In Maryland the Ryans had been associated with the Shipley and the Hanks families. John Ryan and William Hanks had a pew together in Christ Church in Anne Arundal County. The Thomas Hanks of Ohio married a Ryan.

---

[4] Order Book No. 1, p. 20

[5] Deed Book 4, p. 210

Richard Berry Jr., the son, and Polly (or Cally) Ewing were married in Mercer County, Kentucky in 1794. The Ewings were from then Lincoln County, North Carolina, near present Belmont. It was this Richard Berry, Jr., who signed the marriage bond for Nancy Hanks and as "Garden" (Guardian) which seems to indicate some connection. Afterward, this Richard Berry, Jr. family moved to Montgomery County, where their youngest son, Robert M., was born in 1818. Again they removed and to Calloway County, Missouri, where, later, Robert M. died at an advanced age, and his obituary mentioned the association of Nancy Hanks with his father's family.[6]

Beyond tradition and the associations of the Hanks-Shipley-Berry families in Maryland, in Virginia, and in Kentucky, there is no evidence in the form of records to indicate the relation of Nancy Hanks to the Berry family.

*****

THE MITCHELL FAMILY

At present writing, the only kinship found between the Mitchell family and the Shipley family is one link: Robert Mitchell, Jr., who was named for an Uncle, was born August 27, 1749; and he married Naomi Shipley, who was born, April 26, 1748.

The origin of the Mitchells has not been traced to earlier than the two families of Bedford and Campbell Counties of Virginia. When James Hanks purchased 376 acres of land on Hatt Creek in then Bedford County, March 29, 1780,[7] the survey named a Mitchell boundary line, which lay to the south side of his purchase.

Daniel Mitchell, made his Will June 15, 1775, and was dead by October, leaving a widow, Mary.[8] He named his brother, Robert, and Michael Pruit to be executors. It was witnessed by Charles Cobbs, young Daniel Mitchell, and Thomas McCoun. Cobbs was a local preacher. Michael Pruit, one of the executors, was the father of Rachel Pruit, who married young Robert Shipley (III). The sons, named in the will, were Daniel, James, Adam, and Robert Mitchell, the latter being the one who married Naomi Shipley; and, they removed to North Carolina. The two daughters were Molly and Sarah.

---

[6] Obit. Robert M. Berry, Newspaper Clipping, Calloway Co., Mo.
[7] Deedbook 4, p. 406
[8] Willbook A., p. 237

A few years later, April 3, 1781, the brother of the above
named testator, made his will; but it was not probated for years,
1799.[9] He, also, had a wife, Mary; his sons were Daniel, Stephen,
and Robert; Josias Campbell also received a bequest. No clue is
found to the maiden names of these two widows, Mary Mitchell,
whether they were Shipleys or not.

The Daniel Mitchell, son of old Daniel, who died in 1775,
married a wife with first name Judith; they bought out the interest
of the other heirs of old Daniel, in December of 1790; and the
transaction as recorded shows that Molly had married William
Sturman but her sister, Sarah, wasn't married. Robert, James and
Adam were all represented. Soon after acquiring this full 400
acres, Daniel and his wife, Judith, emigrated to Fayette County,
Kentucky. From there they deeded their interest in 700 acres
of land to Absolom Watkins for a ₤100; which property Judith
Pruit had been divisee of from Thomas Watkins by Will on condition
that she remain unmarried. It seems she preferred Dan to 700
acres of good Falling River Valley lands!

The other young Dan Mitchell married in Kentucky, December
29, 1791 Janne Berry, a daughter of Richard Berry, Sr., whose
wife was Rachel Shipley. Then later, John Berry, a brother of
Janne, died, 1795, and left his widow, who had been Ann Mitchell
and two daughters, Margaret and Rachel. Please note that these
names (Rachel, Robert, Adam, etc.) are Shipley names.

There were more intermarriages but this is enough to confirm the family traditions of a Shipley-Berry-Mitchell kinship.
But it was a Mrs. Vawter, and Squire Robert Mitchell Thompson who
made the narrative of it and the tradition as it pertained to Nancy
Hanks. So, now to examine the Thompson family connections.

In these Mitchell family records, no clue is found as to the
identity and kinship of Nancy Hanks.

****

9
Willbook B, p. 239

THE THOMPSON FAMILY

In the annals of the pioneer migration and settlement of
early Kentucky, nothing is more terrible than the tales of the
tragedies that befell many travelers of that weary way through
the wilderness from awful Cumberland Gap to the settlements.
Added to the commonly commitant misfortunes of trail travel were
the hazards of Indian ambush. It increased the anxiety of the
unknown for it was not a constant threat to be continually guarded
against but consisted of sporadic raids by renegade Indians to
harass and plunder the immigrants.

The well organized and better led pack-trains were seldom
molested, but the loitering maurauders would spy upon and waylay
the weaker family groups, usually along the route to the Crab
Orchard as the tired and trail-worn travelers approached their
fancied destinations and perhaps relaxed their vigilance. This
peril continued from the time of the first settlement until
Kentucky reached statehood stature; and the Wilderness Road was
surveyed, relocated, in parts, and improved.[10]

One of the last of these unfortunate incidents occurred to
the Robert Mitchell family group when it came into Kentucky from
North Carolina, 1790, and with such calamitious results that the
knowledge of it was ingrained in the memories of the descendants
of a victim as a tradition and a heritage. Nearly a hundred years
later it was vividly related by Squire Robert Mitchell Thompson to
a reporter for the Louisville Courier Journal.[11] In part he said,
"My mother was captured, when a girl in 1790, by the Indians
twenty-five miles beyond Crab Orchard at a place called Defeated
Creek[12]...Grandmother was struck down but Grandfather stood by with
a spear and carried her into the Crab Orchard Fort. She died the
next day...Mother was carried into Canada and remained in captivity
five years with the Pottuwatamies...my Grandfather went in search
of my Mother-and was drowned in the Clinch (sic) (Ohio River?)
River...my Mother was surrendered under Wayne's treaty."

Sarah Mitchell, the heroic orphan, who was surrendered,
returned and lived with the Richard Berry, Sr. family until she
was married to John Thompson, January 17, 1800;[13] and to this

---

[10] Kincaid, The Wilderness Road

[11] January 5, 1881

[12] Kentucky in Retrospect, Ardery & McChesney, p. 33.

[13] Marriage Register, Washington County, Kentucky, Courthouse

couple ten children were born. One son, Robert Mitchell, was born the year of 1812, and a contemporary of Abraham Lincoln. It was he who, after the death of Lincoln, and after the publication of Lamon's book, with its insinuations that Lincoln's parents had never been regularly married, knew and recollected from his immediate family history that a ceremony had been performed; and had a search made for the records, which were found at the Washington County, Kentucky courthouse, where they may be seen to this day.

Squire Robert Mitchell became a willing witness to the fact, and gave testimony several times pertaining to Nancy Hanks Lincoln and her family, and the traditional relationships of his own family.

Putting the Thompson Family connections together: his grandfather was Robert Mitchell, born August 27, 1742, the son of the Daniel, who died in 1775. His grandmother was Naomi Shipley, born April 26, 1748, the daughter of Robert Shipley II and his wife, Sarah.

At the time of his grandmother's death, the fall of 1790, she had a sister, Rachel, already in Kentucky, the wife of Richard Berry, Sr. There was also another Rachel in the family, a sister-in-law of Naomi and Rachel, the wife of their brother or cousin, Robert Shipley, Jr., but back in Virginia or North Carolina.

At least two other children of Robert Shipley II are known: Ann, who married David McCord and Margaret who married Robert Sloan (first)[13] and Matthew Armstrong (second).[14] These latter two resided in North Carolina then.

With respect for Squire Robert Mitchell Thompson, who knew about the Lincoln wedding, and whose search disclosed the records; and who affirmed to a Hanks-Shipley connection, this search will continue to use and depend on the information he gave.

Having exhausted the possibilities of finding records of Hanks family connections with the immediate cognate families (Shipley-Berry-Mitchell-Thompson) it now seems necessary to accumulate a list of all known Hanks men of Virginia who were living and able to procreate in the 1780's; to learn, if possible, the maiden names of their wives, for kinship with the aforesaid cognate families; to learn the names of their children, and if they

---

[13] History of Gaston County, p. 46

[14] See Genealogies, Chapter II, aaaaa-d for an Armstrong connection.

had a daughter named Nancy and, if so, the date of her birth, and her destiny.

But America had been settled a hundred and fifty years before the father of Nancy Hanks was born; longer than our mid-west and west has now been settled. Cities flourished and travel and trade moved in and across the colonies on improved wagon roads and in the coastwise sailing vessels. Nancy, herself, was Virginia born, but were her parents? They, too, may have been Virginia born, or Colonial born, or emigrants. Whence came they?

CHAPTER VI

HANKS IMMIGRATIONS

-

Preface

Having learned the hard way that there is to be no easy solution of the ancestry of Nancy Hanks Lincoln attention will now be given to the entire subject of Hanksiana in America.

There seems to have been at least five immigrations which furnished fountain-heads for the many migrations of the Hanks descendants throughout America. These were: into Virginia, the earliest; the Hank family to Pennsylvania; then Hankses appeared in New England and Maryland at the same time; and a group entered at New Bern a hundred years later.

ii

EARLIEST HANKSES OF VIRGINIA

The Hanks family in Virginia is one of the earliest in America. By records, three generations of them are indicated before the New England Hanks emigrant, Benjamin, landed in 1699. The Maryland branch of the family first became of record in 1702. Members of the Hank family, who spelled their name without the final 's', arrived in Pennsylvania in the late 17th century; but returned to Derbyshire, England on a trip, before becoming permanent settlers at Whitmarch. Some Hanks settlers at New Bern. North Carolina were "Johnny-come-latelys' via New England, about 1800.

John Hanks came to Jamestown Virginia and patented 200 acres of land as is recorded in the very first Patent Book of Virginia.[1]

---

[1]Patent Book 1 1623 to 1634, p. 450.

George Hanks a generation later became the owner of a thousand acres, as is recorded.[2]

Enoch Hanks was the looser in a law-suit in Lancaster County September 6 1653, and was ordered to pay William Clapham 930# of tobacco and costs.[3]

Robert Hanks was one of a party of five persons imported in 1661. He acquired property and died 1691 and his wife Margaret, was named to be his executrix. Later his name was used in describing a boundary line of land bequeathed in the will of George Brent of Woodstock.

Next Robert Hanks Juniors name appears on the records of the Richard County Court for judgment of his age in 1707 [4] and was thought to be fourteen. An inference is he was Robert's son; but the dates do not fit. Perhaps he was a post-humous child or the Court made only a reasonable guess close enough for our purpose. In 1727 he purchased land in Richmond County and the deed reads that he was a resident of Northumberland County.[5] Further of him or his family is not discovered.

In chronological order from 1661 to 1679 the acquisition of several farms and many acres of land is shown by Thomas Hanks, spelled Hancks.[6]

Elizabeth Hanks is named as one of sixteen persons imported by Bridges Freeman in 1635.[7] In those days a dearth of female consorts it is probable she was snapped up in the marriage mart, for, unlike the French and Spanish. who took Indian wives and concubines; the Englishmen took English wives into the ever expanding frontier.

---

[2] Patent Book 3 1652 to 1655. p. 127.

[3] Virginia Magazine of History. Lower Norfolk Co. antiquary.

[4] Order Book 4 p. 287.

[5] Deed Book 8 p. 414.

[6] Ibid. p. 159 seq.

[7] An Elizabeth Hanks deceased near Annapolis Maryland, 1702.

By 1692 present Richmond County of The Northern Neck was created from a reformation of earlier county lines. and the records were centered there. George Hanks married Mary Williams. daughter of Thomas Williams in 1700. No further record of him has been found.

The earliest Hanks man from whom a continuity of records of his descendants can be assembled. was William Hanks of Richmond County. Virginia in the Northern Neck. From courthouse records at Warsaw and the North Farnham Parish birth records several generations may be traced.

William died 1704 old time and his son William Jr. came into court and was appointed administrator February 7 1704(5). The widow Sarah petitioned for an appraisal and inventory of the estate March 7 1705 which was the first month of the new year. The appraisal was made: was accepted by the Court; then an order issued to divide the estate into four parts, which was done and reported. Richard White who had in the meantime married the Widow Hanks, obtained one fourth except he got no part of the kitchen goods; probably was already well stocked.

Then to each of the three sons was distributed in good proportions the balance of the estate. These sons were William, Luke. and John Hanks.

Inasmuch as records of descendants of many of these Hanks men of early Virginia are found in the courthouses throughout the State they will be referred to under an arbitrary but somewhat natural alphabetic order of county names, viz: Amelia, Bedford. Campbell etc.

111

EARLIEST HANKSES OF MARYLAND

The earliest Hanks records in Maryland that is found. and that anyone else has found so far as is known is of Elizabeth. who died September 17 1702; and of Peter who married August 20 1702· but who they were or whence they came is not clear.[1] Greenberry Hanks resided on the Eastern Shores in 1732; he is unplaced; no record.

This family or branch of the Hanks family is brought into consideration for the reason that descendants of Peter, the Patriarch migrated into Virginia and westward· and some southward. even unto North Carolina.

Peter died in 1733 and left a Will;[2] and his surviving son and heir. William died in Loudoun County Virginia after 1769. There are in Loudoun and adjacent county courthouse records of his presumptive children as will be treated of under the respective counties hereafter.

iv

HANKSES OF NEW BERN, NORTH CAROLINA

Time was spent and a trip made into Craven County North Carolina in trying to fit members of this family onto the branch that descended from John and Mary Mott Hanks who had long resided in nearby LeNoir County: and finally it was learned that they were Johnny-come-latelys to the south and not "chips from the Virginia block"!

Then a collaborator Mrs. William F. Hanks of Lufkin Texas happened to interview a Mrs. Jordan of Marshall Texas and learned that two Hanks brothers Elsworth and Edgar came south from New England and settled at New Bern and Little Washington North

---

[1] St. Ann's Parish records

[2] B 20 Liber CC3 Folio 807

Carolina respectively. This explained the origins of the Hankses of Craven Durham Orange and Chatham counties and since they were Yankee tar heels it took them out of this consideration.

For the record the chart is appended.[3] There is a connection of this Hanks family with the Armstrong family; also an Armstrong married a Chipley.

BENJAMIN HANKS OF NEW ENGLAND

Benjamin Hanks who died at Easton Massachusetts January 9 1755 "in the ninetieth year of his age" was born in England and according to a statement in a notebook of a friend, Richard White, "came from London October 17 1699." His wife was Abagail; to them were born twelve children one of whom William was born February 11 1703 or 1704 has no further record.[4]

---

[3]Data from: Mrs Jordan Marshall Texas--from "Jimmie" Hanks (Mrs. Wm. F. Hanks) Lufkin Texas. Five brothers came from Scotland to New York. They were Episcopalians; their occupation in Scotland: mechanical draftsmen bell manufacturers. Two of the brothers: Elsworth and Edgar moved to the South. 1. Elsworth, Mrs. Jordan's grandfather, moved to New Bern, North Carolina; 1st wife was a Bruce, 2nd wife was Clarisse Phelps. His sons were James Bruce Hanks who married Jane Edna Matthews and Robert Bruce Hanks who did not live long. 2. Edgar moved to Little Washington and Edenton. His children were Nara Carthene Georgiana. John and Edgar. John was a dentist in Jersey City Edgar a dentist in New York City.
The other brothers lived in New York and New Jersey. (Jersey City Jersey Perth Ambouy)
The other three
Mrs. Jordan's memory has suffered from an accident which has crippled her thirty years ago. A fire destroyed all family records.

[4]New England Historical and Genealogical Reg. Jan. 1932.

The usual presumption in such cases is that the subject died but, in this particular case, he was assumed by Mrs. Hitchcock to be the one who had emigrated to Virginia.[5]

It is not an impossible assumption. There was a well developed coastwide trade by the 18th century, and the boats sailed from New England to Virginia and returned.[6] It is a fact that many New England families did migrate and settled in the Northern Neck of Virginia; one family being the Richard White and whose intermarriage of some members with the local Hankses brought some Puritan names into the colony, such as Patience, Pricilla, etc..[7] The men's names, Richard and Uriah, show up in early records. In Amelia was Elijah.

But the Hankses were in Virginia long before the time of the arrival of Benjamin Hanks in New England, 1699, and before his son, William, born 1704, could have grown to manhood, left home and arrived in Virginia. If he settled "near the mouth of the Rappahannock " as is the tradition, he found other Williams nearby, so an effort will be made to account for the parentage of all of them. If such William had sons, it has been demonstrated by the late Mr. Howard M. Jenkins, they could not have reached the age of majority and been doing business so early as his supposed sons in Amelia County.[8]

Therefore, no effort will be made to trace any Hanks man of New England origin, as a possible father of Nancy Hanks Lincoln, unless one is located in Virginia, and early enough,[9] to have been an ancestor or father of Nancy Hanks Lincoln.

---

[5] Hitchcock, Nancy Hanks

[6] Barton, Lineage of Lincoln, p. 202

[7] See Chapter V.

[8] Jenkins, Pa. Mag. of History, Vol. XXIV, No. 2., July 1900

[9] This researcher would call attention to the note on page 6 of the New England Historical and Genealogical Reg., Vol. LXXXVI, January 1932: to the Chapt. II of the Lineage of Lincoln, p. 133, by Barton, for information on the origin of the Hanks family of the American Colonies.

CHAPTER VII

HANKS MEN OF VIRGINIA
ADULT 1783

It is now proposed to examine the courthouse records of counties where any possible clue of the Hanks family may be discovered, and from these records, to consider the history and family of every Hanks man of record in Virginia to possibly determine if he had a daughter, Nancy and, if not, to eliminate him. But, if so, to learn the date of her birth, and the name of her mother, and possible brothers and sisters.

To qualify as her father he must have been of procreative age in 1783; and both he and his wife (or consort) deceased while Nancy was a child; then she was farmed out or placed with her kinfolk. The death of the parents should occur during the late 1780's or the early 1790's. It was probably before Richard Berry Sr. came to Kentucky; he died there in 1798.

It is probable that her father died at middle age and before he had time to accumulate property that would have been an estate requiring administration, with the resultant probate records. It is even seldom that an active younger man makes a will that becomes of record. Therefore it is hardly to be expected that copious records of such a man will be found.

As for Bible records, an author has complained there are none, but there are many in the Hanks family. If the mother also died when Nancy was a child all the personal effects would have been distributed and scattered. Bibles are usually retained by those remaining longest at home, when the home continues intact, but this home was dissolved by two deaths. Even if Nancy received the family Bible it is doubtful it was carried into Kentucky. Only necessary articles were taken over the long Wilderness Way and foster parents would hardly have included the Bible of another.

Now, pertaining to the mother of Nancy, to qualify as such, she must have been residing in Virginia when Nancy was born, February 5 1784. She must have been the wife or consort of a Hanks man in 1783, or born Hanks. She should be a resident of the neighborhood of the Shipley-Berry area, and probably kin to them. She was deceased in the 1790's and left Nancy an orphan. In those days of sparce records, and even much later, women could be born and die without leaving a trace unless one relinquished her dower on her husband's deeds. Even in many marriage records only the name of the husband is given!

Once these parents are located and determined it may be possible to develop her family tree of ancestry, and on both sides of the house. Alas! That is the rub that has harassed the authors! With only superficial research, they have failed to find her parents and, like Herndon, have blamed the Hankses and not themselves. They have made unsubstantial implications based only on omissions.

Not omissions but records only shall now be used.

To understand more clearly:

It is necessary to keep in mind that the earlier counties of Virginia were of enormous area and extended westward almost without limit. As the frontiers moved away from the sea coast and the density of population increased in advancing areas, a new county would be created by setting a boundary line limit to the parent county and giving a new name to the newly created county.

Thus, in chronological order were counties set off, and each with respective starting dates. However, this is not indicative of locations for, while in general, all the newly formed counties lay to the west of older ones, sometimes the previously formed counties were subdivided.

If a man settled and remained in one place for the rest of his life he could without moving, be listed as an inhabitant of successively created counties.[1]

---

[1] One of the earliest counties was Charles City, created in 1634; then Prince George Co., 1703, from which a large area was lopped off in 1732, and named Brunswick. Three years later, 1735, another area was cut from Brunswick to become Amelia, Prince Edward and Nottoway Counties.

The Brunswick area had Lunenburg set off, 1746 ,and this large area embraced some nine future counties including itself; Bedford, 1754; Charlotte of Mecklenburg, 1765: Halifax ,1767; Campbell and Franklin from Bedford 1782, 1786; and Henry and Patrick from Halifax 1777 and 1791; all of which is in the so-called "Roanoke River Country".

In the same manner — old Rappahannock County was subdivided and reconstituted into newly named counties, alongside the Rappahannock River.

AMELIA COUNTY, VIRGINIA

This county, which once included the areas that are now
Prince Edward and Nottoway Counties, was itself formed from parts
of Prince George and Brunswick Counties. There are no names of
early Hankses in the later two counties. But, in Amelia County
the names of Hanks residents first appear in records of 1755-57
on the Order Books, and in 1760 in the deed Books. These dates
would seem to indicate an approximate time of their arrival in
the county.

The presumption is they came from the Rappahannock River
country; some can be identified as from Richmond County; others
cannot be traced to origins from presently known records. The
wars and fires have destroyed many courthouse records pertinent
to a search for the early Hankses.

The given names of Hanks men on the records of this county
are William, Uriah, John, Richard, James ,Thomas, and Joshua.
Also, there are the names of Abraham, Joseph and Joshua Hanks or
Hawks. There is no doubt a separate and distinct Hawks family
but on the records, the names of both Hanks and Hawks are sometimes
written so carelessly that one appears to be the other!

WILLIAM HANKS IN AMELIA

When Mrs. Hitchcock wrote her little book, entitled <u>Nancy
Hanks</u>, which was published in 1900, she stated that, according to
tradition, William Hanks, born in New England, in 1704, migrated
to Virginia and settled near the mouth of the Rappahannock River,
where he reared a large family, including sons: Abraham., Richard,
James, John and Joseph.[2] Then all migrated to Amelia County except
John. By the late 1740's Joseph Hanks was engaged in buying and
selling rather large farms. It was her conclusion that Nancy Hanks
was born here, a daughter of said Joseph.

But the late Howard M. Jenkins, an historian and a genealogist,
pointed out that there was not enough time for William, born 1704,
to grow up, court and marry, rear a family., including five sons,

---

[2]Hitchcock, <u>Nancy Hanks</u> , p. 21

with Joseph the youngest, all being of age by 1747, and trans-
acting business.[3] Thus was her theory weakened. Barton later
demonstrated that Joseph was not the father of the identical
Nancy Hanks, who married Thomas Lincoln.[4]

Whether Mrs. Hitchcock had heard a tradition that William
had five sons, or just made the conjecture from the Hanks names
listed there, cannot be determined; but there is no evidence of
such a family grouping in Amelia County. However, it does appear,
from evidence, that some of the Hanks men of this county, were
sons of a William Hanks of the Rappahannock River country. Further,
it seems assured that this is the William, born in Richmond County,
May 26, 1712, the first child of William and Hester C. Hanks, and
a grandson of William and Sarah Hanks. We designate him William III.

This William Hanks can be traced and all of his children are
known. By his father's will he inherited 100 acres in Briary Swamp
and carpenter tools, and was instructed to teach his brothers the
trade. He married Sarah Durham, January 26, 1738. Later he sold
the Swamp land to William Glascock, Junior.

William Hanks finally moved away from Richmond County and,
while all his movements cannot be traced, the evidence is, he was
in Amelia County, in Dinwiddie County, and thence he went to
Granville County, North Carolina, where he deceased in 1787. It
is from his will that the names of his children are known and the
list coincides with the records of their births in the Northfarnham
Parish register. (Copy)

The sons were Elijah, Argyle, and William IV. The daughters
were Million, Judith, Susannah, and Hannah. It is to be observed
that he had no daughter named Nancy. So this William is eliminated.
His son, Argyle, had a daughter, Nancy, born 1784, and was treated
of here before under her respective chapter V, iv.

The cases of other William Hankses will be taken up in the
respective counties where they resided.

---

[3] Pennsylvania Mag. of History. Vol. XXIV, No. 2, p. 137.

[4] Barton, Lineage, p. 222

URIAH HANKS OF AMELIA

This name appears in an Order Book of Amelia County[5] once, where he "was ordered paid 250 pound nett tobacco for ten days witness for John Wilson vs. James Gallimore." If he were of age or older then he would have been born prior to 1736. However, a witness is not necessarily of age. This is not an ordinary name of the southern branch of the Hanks family but more like that of the New Englanders. (It was also an early Shipley name).

There was a Uriah born in 1736 and aged 21 by 1757, in New England, but a family history of him under number 9 in the New England Historical and Genealogical Register of 1932 does not indicate that he may have been in Virginia.

Being unable to place this man; a mild surmise is that the name is an inadvertance for Elijah found elsewhere in the books.

JOHN HANKS IN AMELIA

The name of John Hanks appears in the Order Books for the years of 1758-69. In 1765 there was litigation between he and Joshua and George Hightower. They were sons of William Hightower, deceased. Susannah Hanks, who had married William Hightower in Richmond County, had a brother John who was born about 1715 and this John is most likely he. If so, he married Mary Mott, and it is known that they migrated southward, eventually into North Carolina; it is possible that they sojourned in Amelia County for a while. They had children of whom are discussed hereafter under the North Carolina section.

---

[5] Order Book 4, page 133.

RICHARD HANKS IN AMELIA

Richard Hanks, who resided for a time in Amelia County, was born in Richmond County, August 14 1723, the son of William II and Hester C. Mills Hanks. Richard was nine years of age when his father died and by instruction of his father's Will he was taught the carpenter trade by his older brother, William III.

Before 1753 he was married to Mary Hinds, whose dowry "was weighed out to her" according to a family tradition.[6] She joined in signing the deed when he sold 55 acres, before moving to Dinwiddie County.[7]

On March 31, 1760 his name appears as the first Hanks to own land in Amelia County:[8] probably having just arrived there for a son, James, later stated in an application for pension that he had been born 1759, in Dinwiddie County, and did not mention Amelia County.

There were probably children born earlier but certainly some later than James. A presumptive list includes William, James, born 1759; Joshua, born 1760 and in Amelia County according to a grandson, Creed L. Hanks· Richard Jr., born 1762; Thomas and David a younger son; and daughters Patience, Dicey and Kate. The 1782 census indicates nine children, which the natural presumptive list seems to fill.

If a daughter, Nancy, was born to Richard and Mary, she has not been located and, anyway, would not have been "born in Virginia" for Richard had removed to North Carolina after he sold out his 243 acres on October 4, 1770.[9] And, wife Mary, waived dower.[10]

---

[6] Ivy Correspondence, Baber papers.

[7] Deed Book 11, p. 255, Richmond County, Virginia, Courthouse

[8] Deed Book 7, p. 313, Amelia County, Virginia, Courthouse

[9] Deed Book 11, p. 208; Order Book 12, p. 138

[10] This land was on Little Creek, east side of County. Kizziah to Baber, February 1957.

He acquired land in Rowan County and he and Mary deeded it away March 1, 1788.[11] They were not the parents of Nancy Hanks Lincoln.

JAMES HANKS IN AMELIA

The name of a James Hanks appears on the records of Amelia County in 1763[12] when he first acquired a hundred acres of land, located on the east side of Irby's Rolling Road. That he had been a resident of the county previous to the purchase is evident from the wording of the deed, but how long is not determinable.

Then, in 1768 James Hanks or another James Hanks purchased 100 acres, which was located on the south side of Barebones Creek. This tract of land seems to have had no connection with the first hundred acres; they are in separate locations.[13] In fact, the neighbors, as determined in each case by the boundary lines are different. The witnesses to the two deeds are different.

The neighbors alongside Irby's road were Hutchins, Ford, Bland, and Tucker: The neighbors on the banks of Barebones were Marshall, Worsham and Stuart. The witnesses to the first hundred acres purchased, which was bought from William and James Gregg, were Mark Moore, Edward and Frances Wright; the witnesses to the second purchase, from John Appling of Barebone, were not the same group.

Ordinarily the witnesses to deeds are friends or relatives of the grantors, and different ones in these two cases would not be significant but, two sets of boundary line neighbors would seem to indicate that James was becoming the owner of lands apart or that there were two Jameses.

---

[11] Deed Book 11, p. 660, Rowan County, North Carolina, Courthouse.

[12] Deed Book 8, p. 335, Amelia County, Virginia, Courthouse.

[13] Deed Book 9, p. 357, Amelia County, Virginia, Courthouse.

It would seem to be solved, though, by a deed made by
James and his wife, Nancy, in 1769, [14] by which, according to
the record, they conveyed 200 acres, thus washing out their
land holdings, but when we examine the boundary lines of the
land sold and conveyed, it is obvious that only the Irby's Road
tract is described, which contained 100 acres. This deed, signed
by Nancy, with the supposed Hanks part of her name left off, was
witnessed by the same families, although not the same individuals,
who witnessed the purchase, six years previously--the Wrights, and
the Greggs.

In 1769 James Hanks received some funds from the "estate
of John Hamlin" with William Mumford as security. [15] One inference
is it was his wife's due from the estate, in which case Nancy's
maiden name may have been Hamlin. The Hamlins or Homlins were
from Loudoun County. An Order Book of that county has a James
Hanks listed in the index to take tithes [16] but his name is not
in the content of record; the name there is Hamilton. Which man
actually took the tithe list cannot be determined. Perhaps James
Hanks was first named but moved away?

In 1774 the 100 acres on Barebones was disposed of by
James Hanks, and no wife joined in the conveyance. [17] This land
was sold to Samuel Thompson, and one of the boundary line neighbors
was a man named Mitchell. Both these family names are significant
in our search. The witnesses to this deed were Samuel Burks,
William Gooch, and Charles X. Harrison.

With this date, all records of James Hanks and all other
Hanks are no longer found in the books of the courthouse. The
Hankses had all departed· some to North Carolina and some to
western Virginia. The history of a James Hanks will be continued
in the Bedford County and the Campbell County section of this sub
chapter, vi.

---

[14] Order Book 11, p. 103. Deed Book 10, p. 228.

[15] Order Book 12, p. 29.

[16] Order Book B, index.

[17] Deed Book 13, p. 80, Amelia County, Virginia, Courthouse.

THOMAS HANKS IN AMELIA

This Thomas Hanks must have been a mild-mannered man,
for he does not appear in any law case that is recorded in the
order books of Amelia County. His only record there is of his
will, and the probate actions, May 22, 1777. Among the assets
listed in the inventory of the estate are: books, a fiddle and
a looking glass. He apparently had no children at his death and
willed his land in Chesterford County to Thomas Draper, his
nephew. It seems unnecessary to say his death precludes his
possibility of having a daughter born in 1784, but we list him
for this record.

JOSHUA HANKS (?) OF AMELIA

It is apparent from a study of the records that the
Joshua, who died and left a will, and named several children,
including a Lewsie (Lucy) was Joshua Hawkes, not Hanks. But a
Joshua Hanks did reside in Amelia County for a time, having been
born there in 1760, but if he was a son of Richard, Sr., as seems
logical, he was removed with his father to North Carolina while
still a boy, so would not have been, and does not appear, in
Amelia records. But he would have been 24 years of age in 1784,
and will be treated hereafter under Grayson County section history
of Hanks residents.

HANKS OR HAWKS OF AMELIA

This is the name about which there has been a tempest
in a teapot between former researchers. The question resolves:
Is the name Hanks or Hawks? It may be well to observe that with
the similarity of spelling; and sometimes poor penmanship combined
with casual reading; a sharp topped 'n' may look like a 'w'; and
visa versa.

This has made for endless confusion of the records and the
endless disconcertion of those who would pursue the tenuous trails
of the two respective families. Incidentally, the same mix-up
obtains in the records of Grayson County where the Deed Index has
under Hanks heading, "See Hawks," and under Hawks, "See Hanks",
and will not be remarked on under that chapter.

This researcher has carefully examined some specific pages
of the patent books in the Archives at Richmond wherein are copies
of original land grants and has paid special attention to the
spelling of the names and formation of the letters, and is unable
to arrive at a definite conclusion; therefore, some evidence will
be presented.

For instance: the names of Joseph, Joshua, Jeffry, and
Abraham Hawks or Hanks appear. In 1733, on Patent Book 15, p. 133,
Joshua Hawks receives 172 acres, and the name is spelled with a "w",
and no doubt. In 1741, Jeffry Hauks gets 200 acres, as per Patent
Book 19, p. 1027, and the name is spelled with a "u", no doubt.

In 1747, on Patent Book 26, p. 322, Abraham gets 284 acres,
and the name is with a sharp "n", so Hanks. On page 9 of the
Amelia County Land Causes the name is actually with a combination
of a rounded "n" joined to a "u", or perhaps the little twist is
part of an unfinished "c" interpolated between the "n" and the "k".

Abraham died about 1767, and in Amelia records, the wife,
Lucy, is referred to as Lucy Hanks, widow of Abraham Hawks. In
Lunenburg County records where his will is recorded, all the
names, including two sons, John and William are written as Hawks,
no doubt.

In addition to these complexities was the use of given names
common to both families, each as Abraham, Joseph, Joshua, John,
Richard, Lucy and Nancy.

There is a theory that the name Hawkes was originally Hanks,
and this was had by Gridley from Dennis Hanks, as she reported.
However, Dennis was nearly 90 years of age, bedfast, and slightly
senile, from her testimony: and inasmuch as much of the material
he gave when he was younger cannot be confirmed, this too may not
be reliable, except as to the recognized interchanging ability.[18]

Their identities, whether Hanks or Hawks, when in doubt, may
usually be recognized by other clues, such as location of their
farms. For instance, in Amelia, the Hawkses lived in the valley of

---

[18]
From my down experience, I am often addressed as Baker, or
Barber, instead of Baber, and, in case of checks received so named,
usually just endorse them the same way they have been made out, I
surmise that this may have been the case with the Hanks and Hawks;
and that really they were two separate and distinct families; certainly each individual knew whether he was a Hanks or Hawks.

Sellers Creek, now in Nottoway County: the Hankses on or near Barebones.

Notwithstanding, these arguments, the question remains moot and even academic, for these men lived too early to have been, any one of them, the father of Nancy. Her name was clearly Hanks.

Conclusion: The history of the Hankses of Amelia County has been explored, and thoroughly, in order to show that the origin of the family in Virginia was not in that county; but that they came in from the Rappahannock River Country; and there was no Hanks of record living in Amelia County in 1784, when Nancy was born.

ii

BEDFORD COUNTY, VIRGINIA
1754

This county was formed as a large area from the still much larger area of Lunenburg County. It embraced part of the Roanoke River Valley, called Staunton River, locally, and included the James River sources. In the eastern part was the little Falling River and its Hatt Creek tributary. In this area, according to a list of the inhabitants of the community, made 1750, were Berrys, Mitchells, and Shipleys: These Shipleys had come from Maryland: Robert Shipley from Baltimore County, Maryland, first patented his land, 314 acres, 1765. Others from Maryland were the Brooks, Barnes, Hoods, and Hankses.

In 1782, the earliest year that tax records are available in Virginia, Thomas Hanks was listed as over 21, with personal property only and no real estate; and with him was a tithe listed as "over 16". It is not certain about the identity of this Thomas. He is not to be confused with another Thomas Hanks of Campbell, who, calculating from subsequent census records, was born in 1766, and so was not "over 21" in 1782 to be taxed, and, although "over 16" was not in Bedford County.

*****

There was a Thomas Hanks, born July 26, 1728, in Richmond County and died in Amelia County, leaving a Will on February 26, 1777, who is not considered.

*****

There was a Thomas Hanks who married, May 9, 1748, Sarah Hewett, in Baltimore County, Maryland, and of whom no further record has been found in that state. For the reason that the Hankses of Maryland were closely associated with the Shipleys of there, and as some of those same Shipleys came from Baltimore County, Maryland, to Bedford County, Virginia, it could be conjectured that this Thomas of Bedford was the same who married Sarah Hewett.

Another Thomas Hanks was born in Richmond County, Virginia, July 1, 1732; married Betty Lee; had a son, Joseph, born 1764, and who by these ages they could have been the pair in the tithe, one "over 21" and one "over 16". However, Thomas and his brother, Joseph, had married sisters, Betty and Nancy Lee, respectively, and daughters were born to both unions. Betty Lee Hanks named her daughter, Nancy, after her sister: Nancy Lee Hanks named her daughter, Betty. With such close connection and affection it would seem reasonable to suppose that the two families did not separate far or long. Since Joseph remained in Richmond County and was there in 1782 the presumption is, Thomas was also there and not in Bedford County. The tax rolls carry a T. Hanks who was not Turner; he was listed under his own name.

The identity of this Thomas of Bedford remains obscure.

FLEETWOOD HANKS IN BEDFORD

This Fleetwood Hanks was born in Rock Creek Parish in Frederick County, Maryland, in 1764, the son of William and Sarah Hanks. He was taxed in Loudoun County, Virginia, in 1787; continued to reside there until after 1790, when his name disappears from the records. The next record available of him is in Bedford[1] County, Virginia, where he purchased a farm of 130 acres in 1797, on the branches of Beaver Dam Creek.

Here Fleetwood and his wife, Ruth, reared at least seven children, one of whom, Nancy, was treated of herebefore.[2] Fleetwood had two brothers and six sisters; his brother, John, remained in Loudoun County but his brother Benjamin and all his sisters migrated to Bedford County, Pennsylvania, where a tradition was preserved that Fleetwood went to Kentucky.[3] This move is confirmed

---

[1] July 20, 1797, Deed Book 10, p. 327, Bedford Co., Virginia, Courthouse.

[2] Chapter V, vii.

[3] Hitchcock papers, Lincoln Library, Fort Wayne, Ind.

by courthouse records· his grandson of Helena, Arkansas wrote[4] that his grandfather "lived, died, buried on the Ohio River twelve miles above Louisville (Kentucky)". It is known that he operated a wood-yard there to furnish fuel to steam boats. This was at the mouth of Harrods Creek.

It may be of interest to note here that in the 1890's, when Mrs. Hitchcock was investigating the Hanks family records of Bedford County, the county clerk made the statement in a letter to her, that Fleetwood was the nephew of a James Hanks, who had purchased land earlier. Whether this was his conjecture or from a tradition is not stated. No evidence has been located recently to confirm or deny this. A complete list of Fleetwood's uncles on his father's side has not been compiled.

JAMES HANKS IN BEDFORD

James Hanks, whose name first appears in the courthouse records of this county, when he purchased 376 acres of land from Josias Campbell,[5] in the spring of 1780, is of special interest for the reason that his purchase was in an area where the Shipleys had resided, and the boundary line on one side corresponded with a Mitchell boundary line. The land was described as lying on both sides of Hatt Creek, and reference was had to Hatt Creek Meeting, a Friends denomination for their place of coming together, although the church house was used by other sects. This would tend to indicate that the grantor and grantee were of the Friends.

Inasmuch as James' land lay in that portion of Bedford County, that was cut off and became Campbell County, and the courthouse records at Rustville, the present county seat, show him to have been a long-time citizen: he will be further considered next under the Campbell County section.

With the creation of Campbell County, by the cut-off in 1782, there were no Hanks left, according to courthouse records, in the area that remained as Bedford County.

---

[4]Deed Book 11, p. 592; Hitchcock papers.

[5]Deed Book 6, p. 406, Bedford County, Virginia, Courthouse.

iii

CAMPBELL COUNTY, VIRGINIA

Reversing the usual practice in early Virginia of creating counties to the westward of the older counties, Campbell county was cut off and formed from the eastern part of Bedford County, which included the Hatt Creek area in 1782.

Campbell County is in the Piedmont section; the land is rolling; the rivers come down from the mountains in the West; the waters run off eastward to the sea; at evening the shadow of the Blue Ridge creeps eastward to merge with the shades of the lower hills. The uplands are clay, the valleys are fertile. The Hankses settled in the valley lands. Then, as now, the chief crops were tobacco, wheat, and corn. It is a land of timber, of pine, and oak and vines; a land of broom sedge and grasses for grazing. Here on Hatt Creek settled the Hankses and the cognate families.

This was not, then, 1784, a rough frontier country. Most of the land had been patented a generation before the Revolutionary War. The roads, such as they were, had been laid out; one went to the Hatt Creek Meeting House, which had been built. Michael Pruitt had built a grist mill. The present county line boundaries were fairly well established.

JAMES HANKS IN CAMPBELL

It was on both sides of Hatt Creek that a James Hanks purchased 376 acres of land, March 27, 1780,[1] located then in Bedford County, later in now Campbell County. It has been assumed that this is the same James Hanks who previously resided in Amelia County; but some of the Hankses arrived there from Loudoun County. Some of the Hanks neighbors were from Amelia and some from Loudoun and from Maryland.

According to Early in the Campbell Chronicles many families of the Friends from Fairfax Meeting in Loudoun County moved to the vicinity of South Meeting in Campbell County. Among these were the Barnes and the Brooks families. John Brooks established a warehouse on the river which was the start of Brookneal. His daughter, Nancy

[1]Deed Book 6, p. 406, Bedford County Courthouse.

Brooks married Thomas Hanks. Their ceremony was in accordance with the Friends Meetings.

Although the church house erected at Hatt Creek was primarily established for the Presbyterians, other sects were permitted to use the building so long as there was no interference. In the early deed records left by the Hankses, when they transferred real estate with boundaries near the church it was referred to as Hatt Creek Meeting, which seems to indicate that the Friends Meeting was held there. It also seems to indicate that the early Hankses were of that persuasion, as were some of the next generation. Therefore, it would appear that they had sojourned in the Loudoun County area where they came into the Quaker influence and connections and were not directly from Richmond County, where the Hankses were Episcopalians.

The James Hancks of Hatt Creek, formerly of Bedford County before Campbell County was created, and who spelled his name with the inclusion of a 'c' as indicated by the deed records, and proved by his genuine signature on the marriage bond of a daughter, held his 376 acres intact, until 1787 when he sold off 150 acres. The witnesses on the deed were Sarah, Thomas, and Tabeth Hancks. No wife signed the deed.

Tabeth was the daughter who married Samuel Barnes, 1793; but if Sarah was another daughter is not determined; there is no record. Of course, she could have died and without a trace. Two other Sarah Hanks are known: one was the wife of Thomas Hanks, who married Sarah Hewett in Baltimore County, Maryland; the other was the wife of the Abraham Hanks who married Sarah Harper, probably in Prince William County. This latter couple came into Campbell County, where Sarah died, and is probably buried in the old Harper Graveyard near Hatt Creek.

Associated with this James Hanks were three Hanks men who have been presumed to be his sons, viz: Abram, Thomas, and James, Jr.. No proof of their relationship has been located, save they quit-claimed land to one another; from the word of Junior on James Jr.'s name leaves the inference he was a son of James. Much can be known of Abram and Thomas but the history of James Jr. is not so clear. James Hanks, Sr., disposed of his last land holding, 150 acres, in 1799,[2] and his name does not appear again on record. James Hanks, Jr. sold out in 1800 and also disappears. But Abram continued to reside in Campbell County and Thomas in Pittsylvania County.

---

[2] Deed Book 5, p. 45.

JAMES HANKS JR. OF CAMPBELL

James Hanks Jr.'s name appears first on June 5, 1795 in a deed record[3] but James the elder Hanks began to add Sr. to his name earlier in 1793.[4] Assuming that James Jr. had become of age, 21, in the early 1790's, he was born about 1770, and after 1766, when Thomas was born. It was on the first named date that James Jr. received title to 150 acres of land from Abraham Hanks.

There is no record of the marriage of this James Jr. to be seen in Campbell County records. Although he was about the same age of a certain Lucey Hanks in Kentucky; he was not her husband, as may have been conjectured, for he was alive in Virginia when she was married in Kentucky in 1790.

There is a record of the marriage of his sister, Tabitha. She married Samuel Barnes, November 1, 1793,[5] and James Hancks Sr. signed the bond as her father; a fairly well written signature with a 'c' in the Hancks name.[6]

James Hanks, Junior disposed of his tract of land, as 145 acres, on January 15, 1800, and James Hancks Senior and Thomas Hancks were two of the witnesses of the deed.[7] There is no further record of James Jr.

It is probable that this James Hanks Jr. went to Kentucky and became "The Mighty Hunter " of whom Mrs. Hitchcock was told the tradition when she interviewed people in Montgomery County in 1895.[8] It has been conjectured that this is the James Hanks who married Sarah, the daughter of Abraham and Sarah Harper Hanks. After two children were born, William and Permelia,[9] he went off to the War of 1812 and did not return. Perhaps he was in the Battle of Tippecanoe, with Peter Hanks, November 7, 1811.[10] Further of him is not known.

---

[3] Deed Book 3, p. 560.

[4] Marriage Records 2, p. 8

[5] Ibid.

[6] Bond Box

[7] Deed Book 5, p. 137.

[8] Hitchcock Journal, Copy, Baber papers.

[9] Caroline Hanks Sizemore to Hitchcock, Lincoln Lib. Ft. Wayne, Ind.

[10] Pirtle, Battle of Tippenanoe, p. 24.

THOMAS HANCKS OF CAMPBELL

Thomas Hanks, born 1766, as calculated from several subsequent census reports, may have been the tithe "over 16" in the Bedford County tax list of 1782, but clearly was a resident of Campbell County, where he married Nancy Brooks in 1792. She was a member of the famous Brooks family from Anne Arundal County, Maryland, and from which came the name of Brooksville, Virginia. The family was of the Friends persuasion. John Brooks resided at Brooksville, where he died in the early 1790's. His future son-in-law, Thomas Hanks, was appointed administrator.

Thomas, after the administration in 1794, moved into Pittssylvania County near Sandy River, where he and Nancy reared a large family, the oldest daughter being named Sarah or Sally. She later married Dabney Clark; then Clark died soon after, all this is of record. Many records of this family are to be found at the courthouse and in the census books, but no record that Thomas had a daughter, Nancy.

He has been often named as the putative father of Nancy Hanks, and was old enough to have been but, if it is so, she was certainly born out of wedlock as her detractors have declared. This hypothesis comes nearer fitting into the traditional scandal than any other proposition but is not tenable in the light of other evidence to be adduced.

Thomas was a land holder in both Campbell and Pittsylvania Counties; in the latter he was the owner of 225 acres on Sandy River, where he was living as late as 1850, when the census was taken. The same census shows some of his sons; their descendants reside in the county to this day.

ABRM HANCKS IN CAMPBELL

Abrm Hancks (sic), as this Abraham has signed his name on papers, extant in the National Archives[11] has the most clear and consistant record of any Hanks, as shown by copious entries in the Deed and Order Books of this county; and by his own deposition in an application for pension on October 16, 1832, as a veteran of the Revolutionary War.

---

[11] Revolutionary Vet. R4569, Archives.

According to his statement, he was born April 2, 1759 in Amelia County, Virginia, and says he had the date from his father, but does not mention his father's name. He first entered military service from Bedford County in August of 1777 for a period of three months, and was properly discharged. Again, he volunteered at the Charlotte Court House on April 2, 1779 (his birthday) and served until May 1, 1781. He further stated he had resided in Campbell County, Virginia for many years, until about eighteen months previous, which indicates he arrived in Lincoln County, Tennessee, about April 1830.

He first purchased land, in partnership with Thomas Hanks, 130 acres in Charlotte County on April 16, 1788;[12] which land they disposed of June 3, 1815.[13] On June 4, 1785, there was some sort of land exchanges, or quit claims of interest between four Hanks men of Campbell County, viz: Abraham, Thomas, James Sr., and James Jr. In the deal, Abraham deeded 150 acres to James Jr., which was 100 acres more than he had received from James Sr. and Thomas, and it is not clear how he acquired the interest in the 100 acres. An abstract of all other land acquired shows a complete disposal by January 11, 1828.[14]

His wife, Lucy, went into court and relinquished dower, but not until March 28, 1831, just before leaving for Tennessee. She had been a Jennings; and their marriage record is clearly as of 1799; and not 1788; as the brother-in-law, Pamplin later claimed in order to try to get Lucy a pension! Abraham had applied for his license and given bond March 30, 1799, and they were married April 2, and on his birthday, at the age of 40, by John Chappell.[15] There is no record of an earlier marriage of this man; although earlier marriage records are so scant it would seem some are missing. Nor are there records of any unplaced Hanks children who, if born of Abrm earlier should have shown up somewhere, we think.

---

[12] Deed book 6, p. 20.

[13] Deed book 13, p. 119.

[14] Deed book 20, p. 108.

[15] Register of Marriage, p. 25.

The reason for relating the history of this man so much in detail is that he has been named as the father of Nancy. He could have been a father in 1784, the year of her birth, for he was then 25 years of age, but there is no evidence or even clues that he was.

Abrm did have children born of Lucy. By census 1810 he had two sons. One of them, I. J. Hancs (sic), born January 19, 1800 (nine months after marriage) died May 12, 1811, and is buried in the Hanks plot at Hatt Creek cemetery; and a tradition is the mother carved the stone, or had it carved, before going to Tennessee.

The other son, John, lived to maturity, and went to Tennessee and descendants of his live there and in Missouri.[16] They have a tradition that their ancestors were related to Nancy Hanks Lincoln but they do not know the alleged relationship.

In Campbell County Order Books, the name of Abrm Hanks appears from No. 4, 1791 to No. 15, 1824, inclusive, as he was given various duties as juryman, road supervisor, witness, etc., so it appears he resided continuously in the Hatt Creek neighborhood and did not go to Tennessee, until later.

Neither is he the Abraham Hanks who accompanied William Calk into Boonesborough, 1775, as per the Calk Journal. This was determined by a handwriting expert of National reputation,[17] who compared photo copies of signatures of Abraham Hanks and determined them to be the writing of two different men.

Therefore, this man did not go to Kentucky; he did not marry Lucy in 1788 and die to leave her a widow by 1790; he did not have a daughter, Nancy; and, he did not die until 1833.

The date of his death precludes his having left an orphan; and, he is eliminated as a putative father of Nancy Hanks Lincoln.

16
 Baber papers.

17
 Herbert C. Walker, Chicago, Illinois.

ABRAHAM HANKS, THE TRADITIONAL

An Abraham Hanks is supposed to have resided in Campbell
County, Virginia, at an early day; died there and was buried in
the Hanks plot at Hatt Creek churchyard cemetery. This tradition
is so well and consistently established that Early recorded it as
a fact in her book, Campbell Chronicles, from which is quoted,

> "...a tradition prevails in the county that Abraham
> Lincoln owed his ancestry to this Campbell County
> family on the maternal side and that he inherited
> his name from Abraham Hanks." 18

The late Mr. Wirt Williams of Brookneal, a local historian
of the county annals, wrote in 1929 to the effect that,

> "The father of Nancy Hanks was Abraham Hanks. They
> moved from this community sometime between 1790 and
> 1800 to Kentucky. The tradition that used to be
> circulated in this neighborhood claimed that Nancy
> Hanks married a man by the name of Lincoln, and that
> she named her boy after her father." 19

At present the tradition remains afresh:

> "...My mother is 78 years old (1949), and she heard
> the story from her father who was told it by his father...
> they moved away when Nancy was 12 years of age, probably
> to Kentucky." 20

Frustratingly, no records are apparent to verify this tradition; but there is ample presumptive evidence. The records confirm
that there was a Hanks settlement of several families and their
allied and cognate families at and nearby Hatt Creek.

---

18 Early, Campbell Chronicles, pp. 422, 423; 45, 46, 47, 48.

19 Williams to Warren, December 12, 1929, photo-copy Baber papers.
(See Appendix)

20 Miss Hilda R. Cabaniss to Mrs. W. E. Bach, December 4, 1949
(See Appendix) Original in Baber papers.

The names, Abraham Hanks and AbrM Hancks, sometimes spelled
out in full, and other times shortened, are on several records.
Hanks is spelled both with and without the 'c' before k. There is
no way to differentiate the names; although all of the real estate
holdings seem to be by the Abrm Hancks, for when he moved to Tennessee
in his old age, the last deeds he gave washed out the number of acres
previously acquired.

In the Hatt Creek cemetery there is a Hanks plot, indicated by
one stone, and the surrounding small area lacks markers; which could
be unmarked grave spaces. A short distance away is an old abandoned
Harper graveyard on land formerly owned by a Hanks; this place is
also likely to have been used for Hanks interments.

The Friends' records prove that some of these Campbell County
Hanks were of that sect; as were some of the Loudoun County Hanks.
The Quaker settlement was about South River; to this area came thirty
Quaker families from Fairfax Meeting in Loudoun County. Many of the
Hiatt family of near Winchester were Friends and some went to Camp-
bell County. Perhaps that is the origin of the Hatt Creek name?
The Hatt Creek church was organized by a colony of Presbyterians from
Pennsylvania. They permitted other sects to use the building. The
Friends held indulged Meetings there.

So far, records have been found of only two Abraham Hanks,
adult in 1780's; the Revolutionary War veteran of Campbell County,
and the apparently foot-loose Abraham, who went to Kentucky with
William Calk, helped Calk survey Boonesborough, 1775, then returned
to Prince William County, Virginia. The next record in Prince
William is in 1782 when he was taxed for one horse. Where he was
in the interum is not known; no tax records were kept prior to then.
In Breckenridge County, Kentucky is a tradition he was in the Revolutionary War[21] but, if so, he died before pension applications were
made so his service record is missing. He left Prince William County
in 1783 and, for lack of any other Abraham Hanks, just has to be
this evanescent Abraham of Campbell County.

Having knowledge that this traditional Abraham of Campbell
was a real person in Virginia, further consideration of his case
hereafter in the Fauquier section.

_____

[21]Rev. Jno. Hanks to Hitchcock, Lincoln Library, Fort Wayne, Ind.

iv

DINWIDDIE COUNTY, VIRGINIA

There is quite a bit of evidence that Hankses once lived
in Dinwiddie County. William Hanks III, who married Sarah·Durham
removed from Dinwiddie to Granville County, North Carolina, as
indicated on his first deed of purchase in Carolina. Thomas Hanks,
who was listed as over 21·and for taxation in 1785, with one tithe,
one horse, and one cattle, probably was the son of Elijah and the
grandson of the above William·Hanks III. This is likely the Thomas
who married Margaret Clements, but the wedding was after the date
of the license application, December 23, 1784, which was the same
year that Nancy Hanks Lincoln was born, but later in the year.
Thomas is eliminated.

FAUQUIER COUNTY, VIRGINIA

ABRAHAM AND LUKE HANKS

In·the earlier courthouse records of this county, in the
year 1773, are to be found the names of two Hanks men, probably
brothers: Abraham and Luke. In the old records of Broad Run
Church, Nancy Hanks is named as joining on June 13, 1778; Luke,
her husband tardily came into the membership the following year,
on August 25, 1779. The organization of this church is still
intact and active.

The church house itself is a well proportioned frame
structure, painted white. It is located alongside the speed-lined
highway that outgrew the ancient road. Serenely and chaste, it sets
at the eastern end of the little village of New Baltimore. Whence
the name of this town? Was it first settled by people from Baltimore?
It would seem so. Some of the Hankses were from Anne Arundal County,
Maryland, originally and some of them had come up from the lower
Northern Neck.

To the east of the church and not far away the Broad Run
stream flows southeastwardly into the bay; further east, and parallel,
is the Bull Run stream of the famous Civil War history. Between
the streams lies the boundary line of Fauquier and Prince William
counties. The land is level, but rolling save near the streams. It
was here the Hanks men lived.

How long they had resided in the county prior to their records is not known. Luke had been there long enough to get in debt and be sued.[1] He must have been "Hard-Up" or he would have paid the debt for he acknowledged that he owed "by a note in writing" as the clerk of the court recorded. However, the court reduced the amount the plaintiff claimed. It is of interest that years later, when a son of Luke died in South Carolina, also named Luke, his epitaph reads, "Here lies an honest man."

Luke's kinsman, Robert Dale, lived across the line in Prince William County. Luke moved to that County, and will be discussed further.

In the same year, 1773, in the August court, Abraham Hanks was sued by Rueben Payne for a small amount, and lost to the plaintiff. Since Abraham was the defendant; it indicates he was a resident of the county; by legal procedure, suit would have been brought in the county of his residence where subpeona service was had on him.[2]

Both of these Hanks men, Luke and Abraham, were old enough to have had families by 1784, and did have. Both of them later removed to Prince William County; they will be further considered under that county.

vi

GRAYSON COUNTY, VIRGINIA

JOSHUA HANKS

Joshua Hanks, according to a grandson, Creed L. Hanks, was born in 1760 in Amelia County and resided, before going to Grayson County; in North Carolina. He married Ruth Bryan in 1784, in Surry County, North Carolina, and they reared a large family of children, among whom was a Nancy. Her father, Joshua, lived to a ripe age of 94, dying in 1854.

Some statements made by the above mentioned Creed L. Hanks, are of interest in trying to identify Joshua and through him, others. From his letters and from his reputation around Galax, Creed was an

---

[1] Order Book 1768-72, p. 474.

[2] Order Book 1773-1780, p. 82.

intelligent man. He stated that his grandfather, Joshua had a
brother, or uncle, he did not know which, named Joseph, who went
to Kentucky. There are records of two Josephs in Kentucky: One
of Nelson County in the 1790's, and one of Christian County listed
in 1810 census. By ages, the first could have been an uncle, and
the second, a brother of Joshua. But Richard Hanks, Sr., the presumptive father of Joshua had no brother, Joseph; according to the
birth record of North Farnham Parrish; he had a cousin Joseph. It
would follow that, if Joshua did have an Uncle Joseph, he was not
a son of Richard, as Mrs. Hitchcock has listed him, and as presumptive evidence appears to place him. This slight conflict is
not resolved.

If Joshua had a brother, Joseph, it could have been the
Joseph of Christian County; with children born after 1800, and
not of our notice, for this search.

There are two solutions: One, Creed L. Hanks may have
thought that the Nancy, daughter of William of Western North
Carolina, and niece of Joshua, was the one who married Tom
Lincoln, as is a tradition. This tradition is erroneous, as
previously proved herein;[1] or, Creed L. Hanks was not mistaken
and Joshua was a younger brother of Abraham and Joseph Hanks.

But, any solution is rather academic: Joshua had a
daughter Nancy, among other daughters, and she married George
Moore and not Tom Lincoln.

vii

HAMPSHIRE COUNTY, (WEST) VIRGINIA

JOSEPH HANKS

After the Northern Neck of Virginia was settled, and that
part of Maryland west of the Chesapeake Bay, the tide of migration
moved up the Potomac River Valley, and into the mountains. By
1754 the area of Patterson Creek and its tributaries had sufficient
inhabitants to warrant the creation of Hampshire County, which was
set off from both Frederick and Augusta Counties, Virginia. At
about the same time it became necessary to establish a line of
frontier forts, for the protection of settlers.

---

[1] Chapter V, ii.

Customarily, the pioneer roads followed the trader's trails, and, widened for wagons and tobacco rolling, the increased traffic developed the highways. From the Northern Neck of Virginia and from the Rock Creek Crossing at the big stone, two main lines of travel roughly paralleled the river on both sides as far as Fort Cumberland. It was over these two parallel routes that Braddock marched his army from Alexandria to the fort; beyond this he opened a new road, up Wills Creek and over the mountains to the site of his defeat at near the present location of Pittsburgh.

At the end of the French and Indian War and with the Indians uneasily placated, the settlers again surged westward over these roads; some on into western Pennsylvania, and some eventually went down the Ohio River and into Kentucky.

According to a tradition that was preserved by a descendant of the Hanks family, and who was born in 1832, and had it from his aunts: there were three Hanks brothers who went up the Potomac River and acquired an interest in land. Two sold out to the third and went to Kentucky and the one who remained went to Bedford County, Pennsylvania. This last can be confirmed from Courthouse records, and his name was William. The other two were John or Jonathan and Joseph. No record of John or Jonathan has been located in this area but the tradition is probable. There is a record of a Joseph Hanks in the Patterson Creek valley, which is across the Potomac River from Bedford County, but there is no evidence he is the brother, although his kinship is not known. The courthouse records show that he was a resident of this large Hampshire County, then in Virginia.

This much is known: by order of the Court, John Wilson took a census of the county and, as of November 14, 1782, Joseph Hanks had a family of eleven Souls and no blacks.[1] On the list his nearest neighbors were William Lee, William Sage and Richard Wood. There was another list taken by Abram Johnson, Gent., who listed Joseph Wood and Peter Jones. The significance of these names of neighbors will come up later.

Joseph Hanks had acquired an option or interest in 108 acres of land, with a bond from George Tooey to convey title. This was part of a survey made for Peter Hardman, a land owner. Nearby was Peter Putnam, who became an owner of much land. On March 9, 1784, Joseph mortgaged only his interest for ₤21:9s to said Putnam, and the following Autumn the document of the deal was proved before the Court, November 9, 1784.[2]

---

[1] Census, Virginia, 1782.

[2] Deed Book No. 6, p. 168-9, Hampshire County, Courthouse.

Thus, in due course of law, the title was transferred, which was a way of transferring title then in Virginia. No further record is shown of Joseph Hanks in Hampshire County.

Next in point of time at which the name Joseph Hanks appears is in the Nelson County courthouse at Bardstown, Kentucky. On February 28, 1787, this Joseph Hanks of Nelson County made a contract with John Lee to purchase 150 acres of land from a larger grant Lee had purchased from Joseph Barnett; just as soon as Lee could obtain a deed, in order to re-deed and pass title to Joseph. Lee was retaining the upper end of the tract whereon he lived. This made Lee a neighbor; possibly he was a kinsman of the William Lee with whom Joseph had been a neighbor back in Hampshire County. It has been stated that Joseph's wife was a Lee and she well may have been; but the statement itself is now known to have been based upon an erroneous assumption.

Joseph Barnett, the dealer in this land transaction, is of particular notice. According to Thelma M. Murphy[3] he was a minister of the Baptist church; helped organize the Severns Valley Baptist Church in Kentucky, 1781. Two years later, 1783, he entered 1000 acres of land, and, from then on, was dabbling in real estate; so much so it seems he neglected his church affairs.

Due either to his amateur efforts or to the entanglements of the early Kentucky land titles, he failed to give title to Lee, to pass on the Hanks. Barnett died, 1797, and the uncleared title and ownership of the land, the 150 acres, was in question for many years.[4]

Barnett was from Hampshire County, Virginia and came to now Ohio County, Kentucky in 1779; previously had been a member and moderator of the Patterson Creek Church back in Virginia. William Wood was also a member. It is evident that the associations and acquaintanceships of Barnett with men he had known in Hampshire County were of use to him in his adopted business. It is possible, and would even seem probable, and likely, he may have promoted the emigration of a group of farmers from Hampshire County to Kentucky County, Virginia, including the Hanks, the Lee and the Wood families.

Joseph Hanks of Nelson County was about fifty years of age when he made the deal to purchase the land but he did not live long to enjoy the use of it. In January of 1793 he felt "Weak in body" but "sound of mind" and dictated his will. He died come Spring and

---

[3] Kentucky Reg. No. 174, p. 81.

[4] Chancery Bundle, 1819, Nelson County, Kentucky, courthouse.

his Will was probated May 14th.[5] It enumerated eight children and
the wife. These with himself made a family of ten prior to his
decease. This is almost the same number of souls, lacking one,
enumerated in the house of Joseph of Hampshire. This similarity
has been taken as a clue that both Josephs were one. The association
with the same group of neighbors and with Barnett in both places
would seem to strengthen the assumption.

Barton thought that Joseph of Hampshire was the father of
Lucy Hanks, who was the mother of Nancy Hanks Lincoln. Mrs. Hitchcock thought that Joseph of Nelson was the father of Nancy Hanks
Lincoln;. Warren seems to think that James Hanks was the husband
of Lucy, the son of Joseph of Nelson. With these divergant view-
points it may be in order to go into detail and explain more about
the family of Joseph. In fact: two or three of his oldest sons
would have been old enough to be the father of Nancy Hanks Lincoln,
and so need to be considered, also, for this purpose.

In his will he named first five sons, probably in the order
of their ages: Thomas, Joshua, William, Charles, and Joseph, (Jr.).
He gave a horse to each and the farm to Joseph in addition. He
did not list any children of a supposed deceased son, James. He
named specifically only three daughters: Elizabeth, Polly and
Nancy. He gave a heifer to each one of them; the balance of his
estate he left to his wife, Nannie, "during her life, afterwards
to be divided among all my children." An inference is all the
children are named in the will.

It is to be noted that he did not name Lucy Hanks in his
will either as a daughter or a daughter-in-law; nor did he make
any provision for any children or daughter of Lucy. Barton's
theory that Joseph disinherited a daughter, Lucy, is a fantasy;
his arguments are chimerical; anyone who knows the characteristics
of Hanks people would recognize his reasonings as fallacious.

Thomas Hanks, the first named son, has never been positively
identified; but as he was born early enough to have had children by
1784 his case will be considered later.

The son, Joshua, probably born about 1763, is known to have
been in Kentucky. He went on an expedition against the Indians in
Ohio and received a certificate for service, 1787. There is a clue
that he later located in Ohio. There is no clue he had a Nancy.

---

[5] Will Book A, Nelson County, Kentucky, Courthouse.

The son, William, born in 1766, according to the 1850
census, can be traced from The Rappahannock River country to the
Sangamon River Country, and to his grave. He did-have a daughter,
Nancy, who was born in 1794 and married William Miller; so is
eliminated by the lateness of her birth.

Charles seems to have been a missing son for no record of
him has ever been found.

Joseph Jr., the youngest son, like his brother, William,
can be traced through his lifetime. His and William's families
in Illinois were referred to by Lincoln as kin to his mother.

Of the daughters, Polly married Jesse Friend, and they
moved to Edgar County, Illinois, with other Hankses, where she
died.

Elizabeth married Thomas Sparrow. She remained a loyal
friend to Nancy Hanks Lincoln. All three of them are buried
together.

Nancy, the youngest child of Joseph. is treated of herebefore in Chapter V, v. She was born in Hampshire County, now
West Virginia. She did not marry Tom Lincoln.

THOMAS HANKS IN OHIO

Thomas Hanks of Ross County, Ohio, was born, according to
his pension application as a Revolutionary War veteran, in Hampshire
County, Virginia in 1759. Therefore, he was an adult by 1784 and
is to be considered as the father of children including a Nancy.
He moved from Hampshire County about 1800 to High Bank, Ohio; thence
to Ross; to Clark; and to Logan Counties, the last where he died.
Matter of fact, he had a daughter, Nancy, among some six known other
children; but she married or deceased and disappears from any record.
Her tracing is not important for she was born after 1800.

This Thomas Hanks was placed by Hitchcock as a son of Joseph
Hanks of Nelson County, Kentucky; Lea & Hutchinson accepted her
conclusion; Barton followed suit, although doubting his authorities.
As Warren said, "There is no positive evidence he is the same Thomas
whose name appears on the will of Joseph Hanks."

There is, however, evidence to the effect that he was kin to
the aforesaid Joseph Hanks of Nelson County. A granddaughter of
Joseph Jr., son of Joseph, once wrote, "The Hanks family at Vienna
Cross Roads, Clark County, Ohio, are the descendants of Joshua Hanks,

brother of Joseph. We found a grandson of Joshua Hanks in the hospital at Quincy during the war and he told us the story of his family in such a way, that we knew he was a relative."[6]

Another grandson wrote, "...Absalem, a son of this same Joshua settled at Vienna Cross Roads, Clark County, Ohio in 1832." This would place two Absaloms there, for Thomas had a son, Absalom and, so far, the two Absaloms have not been located in the same area at the same time; the Absalom at the Vienna Cross Roads appears to have been the son of Thomas. This Absalom had two sons who went to Illinois and lived at Fairbury. It is not too important for the case is academic so far as Nancy Hanks is concerned.

viii

LANCASTER COUNTY, VIRGINIA

LUKE HANKS IN LANCASTER

In the scanty records of the Hanks family in this county the names of Luke, Dawson and Alexander appear. By 1757 Luke was deceased and Henry Tapscott came into Court to so report and was appointed administrator to settle the estate, and did so.[1] At the appraisal most of the items were listed as "old" and of little value. There was no livestock, not one horse nor cow. The sale brought small returns; and the estate was insolvent. The widow, Sarah, bid in a bed; Dawson Hanks acquired a barrell of corn as his "due".[2] His relationship is not apparent; but probably a son. Sarah, the second wife, had a daughter, Martha, then five years of age.

Luke, by a first wife, Elizabeth, had two children of record, who would have been past thirty-five years old at the time of his death, of whom there is no notice; he also had a son, Turner, aged twenty then, who resided in adjoining Richmond County, where he reared a family. But, due to the spaces of time between these several births, it is to be supposed that Luke had other children, who, like Turner, would have been of the same generation as the parents of Nancy; so his case requires further consideration.

---

[6]Wilson to Hitchcock, March 13, 1895, Lincoln Library, Ft.Wayne.

---

[1]Order Book, 11, p. 42.

[2]Volume 11, p. 52.

WILLIAM HANKS

This William Hanks, from the elimination of the other known Williams, is presumed to have been the brother of Joseph, who settled Catharine Hanks' estate in 1782, and received his share. He was born in Richmond County; his wife was Winifred; his only-known child was Mary Ann, born in the North Farnham Parish, April 16, 1737. It is obvious that he could have had other children, not of record but, there are no unplaced Hanks men nearby, so probably he had no more.

ix

LOUDOUN COUTY, VIRGINIA

In the last half of the eighteenth century, from about 1760 to its end, the records in the old Order Books, from Book A to Book O, indicate there was a family of Hanks resident there, and with several members who were of age to appear on the tithe and tax lists of the county. If they were farmers they must have rented land from others or the propriators of the Fairfax estate.

It is known and confirmed that some of these Hanks families migrated westward into Pennsylvania; and some southward in Virginia. It is probable that the Hankses of Bedford and Campbell Counties were part of them, at least those of the Quaker sect, from Loudoun County.[1]

WILLIAM HANKS
(William the Quaker)

In the year of 1763, the records of the Friends Meeting of West River near Annapolis, Maryland, indicate that William Hanks applied for a certificate of transfer to be admitted to the meeting at Fairfax in the colony of Virginia.[2] This was at Waterford where the old Meeting House stands. Further evidence of this William's origin and identity is his name on a quit claim deed with Sam'l

---

[1] Early, *Campbell Chronicles*, p. 47

[2] Friends Records, Stoney Run Meeting, Baltimore

Musgrave's name in Anne Arundel County, Maryland which recites that
"William Hanks of Lowden County of Province of Virginia" and dated
November 3, 1766.[3] His name appears on the tithe list for 1764 and
each succeeding year including 1769, and not thereafter. It is presumed he had deceased, as he was an elderly man, then. He had
children, and his family will be discussed in the following. (For
identity, this William will be referred to hereafter as William the
Quaker.)

WILLIAM HANKS
(William of Bedford)

The name, William Hanks, again appears on the earliest tax
list extant, 1782, of Loudoun County, and this man is known to be a
son of William the Quaker, and was born April 27, 1739 near the
Patapsco River in Anne Arundel County, Maryland. Quoting from a
letter of one of his descendants, Mrs. Jennie Schooley Hoffman,
it reads:

> "This William Hanks settled in Loudoun
> County, Virginia, near where Leesburg
> now is. His wife was Sarah, born 1754,
> died in May 1804. William Hanks died
> 1814. They had nine children, all born
> in Virginia. Three sons: John, Fleet-
> wood, and Benjamin. ...six daughters,
> Rachel, Leah, Nancy, and Rosanna, twins,
> born October 4, 1770, Mary and Sarah."[4]

This William had previously resided in Frederick County,
Maryland, where his son, Fleetwood was born, and where William
mortgaged his personal property to secure a loan in 1768.[5]

---

[3] Chidsey, Hanks Family of Maryland, p. 13

[4] Hoffman to Rudolph, April 18, 1927, Baber Papers.

[6] Deed Book No. L, p. 219, Frederick County, Maryland, C.H.

It was his daughter, Nancy, who has been thought by some to have married Tom Lincoln; but she did not. She had a daughter, Duannah, and then married Nicholas Schooley, by whom she had two children, a son and a daughter; then she married secondly Robert Akers, and by him there were six more children. The tradition is that she was a fine woman. The daughter, Duannah, became a noted and beloved school teacher and, at her death, left by will, considerable property to her half-brother and half-sister.

The tradition in this family is not that their Nancy married Thomas Lincoln, for they know differently, and as courthouse records confirm; but that their Nancy was a cousin to the Nancy who did marry Tom. The tradition still obtains among the present descendants of William of Bedford, who reside in Pennsylvania, in Ohio, and in Edgar County, Illinois. This tradition of kinship could explain the coming together of the descendants of Peter and Abraham Hanks in North Carolina, in Kentucky, and in Edgar County, Illinois.

This family will be discussed further, hereafter, in Part II, Ancestral Quest.

JOHN HANKS

(Jno. Hanks)

In the 1770 tithe list of Loudoun County, the name of John Hanks appears. By the evidence, he was a son of William the Quaker; the points are proximity; tradition in the Bedford County, Pennsylvania family of three brothers; and the knowledge that Fleetwood Hanks, a son of William of Bedford want to Kentucky to join his Uncle John.

That this John was not the son of William of Bedford, who had a son John, is the fact the latter was born, 1764, and was only six years of age, and not tithable when the older John was listed.

The January court of 1777, "Ordered that Thomas Bird serve his master John Hanks until he discharge ₤ 3 and sixpence and eighty three days absence as per account, according to law...[6]"

John Hanks was born in Anne Arundal County, Maryland, and about 1754   He was first mentioned by Dr. William Jacob Lodge in

---

6
Order Book G., 1776.1783, p. 7.

family notes in the 1880's; and subsequently by Mr. A. D. Chidsey.[7]

As the family tradition relates, "he went South to the James River Country." And further the tradition continues, "he went later to Western Kentucky, where Fleetwood joined his uncle John." Just what part of Kentucky was meant by the designation of "western" is not now clear. Nor is the time of Uncle John's arrival in the western part known. Before about 1800 Louisville was on the frontier and the county seat of Jefferson County, which was created by Virginia in 1780. The next year Abraham Lincoln was spying out land on Long Creek east of Louisville, which he patented,[8] so that area was being settled then.

Fleetwood did not leave Virginia until after 1802 and went to Harrods' Creek a few miles above Louisville in what was then Henry County. There is in Henry County a tradition of a John Hanks who died there southeast of New Castle. It is probable that the Jamima Hanks, widow, whose daughter, Nancy, married in 1804, was John's family. She was treated of here before under Chapter V, ix.

RACHEL HANKS

There was also a daughter of William the Quaker, Rachel, and she wished to join the Friends Meeting at Fairfax. and was received, as per their records, "6 mo. 26 da. 1782".[9] (Friends New Year began with March, so 6 mo. was August.)

She married Joseph Wilkinson. who "was outside" and where she "had lived before marriage" and was dropped by the Friends, 5 mo 26 da. 1792.[10]

Wilkinson made his Will, March 25,1795 and died the Spring of 1800.[11]

---

[7] Chidsey, Hanks Family of Maryland, p. 26.

[8] Coleman, Lincoln's Lincoln Grandmother, Journal Ill. St. His. Soc., Spring 1959.

[9] Friends Meeting, Fairfax, Book B. p. 222

[10] Ibid., p. 526.

[11] Book O., p. 82, Loudoun County Courthouse.

These three: William of Bedford, Jno., and Rachel are the
known children of William the Quaker, as was determined by the research
of A. V. Chidsey. In addition, the family tradition, as reported by a
grandson of William of Bedford, Dr. William Jacob Lodge, who was born,
1832, names Joseph; and further that Joseph and Jno. went to Kentucky.
Of all these more, hereafter, and in this chapter.

PETER HANKS

The name of Peter Hanks, (Sr.) first appears of record in
Loudoun County,Virginia; last in Gibson County, Indiana; and, in the
interim,in Western Pennsylvania and in Salisbury District, North
Carolina. This old Revolutionary War Veteran had a varied career and
lived in several places and will be written up here where his father
and mother,William and Ruth, lived.

This is the Peter Hanks, who was the father of John (Jno) Hanks,
who was interviewed by Schane for Dr. Draper. The interview was
held in 1832 in Montgomery County, Kentucky. John Hanks then stated he was
born in 1767, so Peter Hanks' wife was living in Loudoun County,
Virginia as early as that date.

The earliest reference to him, in the county records seems
to be April 17, 1772 when he was sued by Christopher Snyder, and the
suit dismissed by agreement.[12] Two years later, April 14, 1774,
Thomas Wyatt, an assignee of Peter, sued Ruth Hanks, upon a Petition
but, "the defendant being reported by the Sheriff a non-resident,
the Petition is abated."[13]

But, before this, in 1769, he had been in Western Pennsylvania,
and entered land on the Monongahela River.[14] Then, later, 1773, he
was taxed in Rosstraven township of Bedford County. Ten years later
he served with the Rangers on the western Frontier of around Wheeling
in 1782. With him was William Hanks, probably his brother.[15] At
the close of the Revolutionary War he emigrated to North Carolina. It
is now determined that he was a son of William the Quaker, as was suspected by Chidsey.[16] t

---

[12] Order Book E, 1770--1773, p. 293

[13] Order Book F, 1773--1776, p. 380

[14] 204 1/4 acres, called "Carol" surveyed Oct. 2, 1769,
on Order No. 33 -- dated June 13, 1769 for Peter Hanks.

[15] Pa. Archives: 5 Ser. Vol IV, p. 771; 6 Ser. Vol. 11, p. 7, 11;
3 Ser. Vol. XXIII, p. 205.

[16] Chidsey, The Hanks Family of Maryland, p. 34.

On March 15, 1785, Peter and William Hanks were sued for a
debt by William Reeder. On the same day, the Commonwealth brought
suit against Peter and on a complaint of the same William Reeder.
He did not appear to complain so the suit was dismissed.[17] Then the
attorney for both Peter and William came into Court and bound himself
to "surrender their bodies to prison" if they were convicted, "in
failure thereof he the said James (McKensie) will do it for them."[18]
It seems the attorney had faith in his clients! These men are probably
the sons of old Peter, for he is supposed to be in North Carolina at
this date, where his daughter, Ruth, was born, June 13, 1782, and named
for her grandmother, Ruth Ryan Hanks.   Peter had a son, Peter, who
was _____ _____ _____ later census records, and would have
bee_____   '85, so this defendant is
pro_____   Carolina, where he was listed
in_____   ford County; thence he removed
to_____   le of Tippecanoe. It is doubt-
fu_____   n, embraced the Friends religion
of_____

f_____   s son, John, made to Schane,
s_____   ived in Kentucky in 1787. They
s_____   ry County. Here, also, came

C_____   a minister, and later of Gibson
v_____   ounty, Indiana and who, as pre-
I_____   Battle of Tippecanoe; Absalom,
n_____   and whose grandson, Absalom Hanks
                                        Grants armies;[20] Samuel, who
                                        Bath County, Kentucky; and John,
                                        n the Draper papers.[21]

                                        and probably, Savilla. (Savilla
                                        There is now a tradition of a
                                        family.

                                        p. 456.

[19] John Hanks interview, Draper papers, Madison, Wisconsin.

[20] Reminiscenses of Abraham Lincoln, p. 629

[21] Wisconsin Historical Society, Madison, Wisconsin

These three: William of Bedford, Jno., and Rachel are the
known children of William the Quaker, as was determined by the research
of A. V. Chidsey. In addition, the family tradition, as reported by a
grandson of William of Bedford, Dr. William Jacob Lodge, who was born,
1832, names Joseph; and further that Joseph and Jno. went to Kentucky.
Of all these more, hereafter, and in this chapter.

PETER HANKS

The name of Peter Hanks, (Sr.) fi
Loudoun County,Virginia; last in Gibson C
interim,in Western Pennsylvania and in Sa
Carolina. This old Revolutionary War Vet
lived in several places and will be writt
and mother,William and Ruth, lived.

This is the Peter Hanks, who was
who was interviewed by Schane for Dr. Dra
in 1832 in Montgomery County, Kentucky.
born in 1767, so Peter Hanks' wife was 1
Virginia as early as that date.

The earliest reference to him, in
to be April 17, 1772 when he was sued by
suit dismissed by agreement.[12] Two years
Thomas Wyatt, an assignee of Peter, sued
but, "the defendant being reported by th
the Petition is abated."[13]

But, before this, in 1769, he ha
and entered land on the Monongahela River
was taxed in Rosstraven township of Bedfc
he served with the Rangers on the western
in 1782. With him was William Hanks, prc
the close of the Revolutionary War he emi
is now determined tha, he was a son of William the Quaker, as was suspected by Chidsey.[16] t

---

[12]Order Book E, 1770--1773, p. 293

[13]Order Book F, 1773--1776, p. 380

[14]204 1/4 acres, called "Carol" surveyed Oct. 2, 1769,
on Order No. 33 -- dated June 13, 1769 for Peter Hanks.

[15]Pa. Archives: 5 Ser. Vol IV, p. 771; 6 Ser. Vol. 11, p. 7, 11;
3 Ser. Vol. XXIII, p. 205.

[16]Chidsey, The Hanks Family of Maryland, p. 34.

On March 15, 1785, Peter and William Hanks were sued for a debt by William Reeder. On the same day, the Commonwealth brought suit against Peter and on a complaint of the same William Reeder. He did not appear to complain so the suit was dismissed.[17] Then the attorney for both Peter and William came into Court and bound himself to "surrender their bodies to prison" if they were convicted, "in failure thereof he the said James (McKensie) will do it for them."[18] It seems the attorney had faith in his clients! These men are probably the sons of old Peter, for he is supposed to be in North Carolina at this date, where his daughter, Ruth, was born, June 13, 1782, and named for her grandmother, Ruth Ryan Hanks.   Peter had a son, Peter, who was born by 1765, according to later census records, and would have been old enough to have been sued by 1785, so this defendant is probably he. He too, removed to North Carolina, where he was listed in the 1810 census as living in Rutherford County; thence he removed to Kentucky and was killed at the Battle of Tippecanoe. It is doubtful if these two Peters, father and son, embraced the Friends religion of old William the Quaker.

According to a statement of his son, John, made to Schane, for Draper, 1832, the Hanks family arrived in Kentucky in 1787. They settled on Slate Creek in now Montgomery County. Here, also, came some, perhaps all, of his children.[19]

The known ones were William, a minister, and later of Gibson County, Indiana; Peter Jr., of Knox County, Indiana and who, as previously was stated, was killed at the Battle of Tippecanoe; Absalom, who resided at Winchester, Kentucky, and whose grandson, Absalom Hanks Markland, was Post Master General of Grants armies;[20] Samuel, who married Nancy Wyatt, March 16, 1802, Bath County, Kentucky; and John, the blind man, whose deposition is in the Draper papers.[21]

One daughter is known, Ruth, and probably, Savilla. (Savilla may have been a daughter of John.) There is now a tradition of a daughter, Nancy, connected with the family.

---

[17]
Order Book H, 1783, 1785, p. 456.

[18]
Ibid., p. 456

[19]
John Hanks interview, Draper papers, Madison, Wisconsin.

[20]
Reminiscenses of Abraham Lincoln, p. 629

[21]
Wisconsin Historical Society, Madison, Wisconsin

She has not been located and identified as a daughter, but Mrs. Hitchcock did hear, and in Montgomery County, Kentucky, and recorded it in her Journal, of a "Nancy who went south."[22] If Savilla was a daughter and born January 18, 1787; and Ruth, known to have been a daughter, born June '3, 1782, it leaves an interval of 1784 when a daughter, Nancy, could have been born.

From family data it is learned that Peter died in Gibson County, Indiana in 1830, aged 93; so was born 1737 which would have been in Anne Arundal County, Maryland.

For the time being or until such contradictory evidence may be adduced, Peter Hanks will have to be considered to be one of the possible candidates as the father of Nancy Hanks Lincoln.

ELIZABETH HANKS

The name of Elizabeth Hanks appears in Loudoun County Courthouse records as one of three daughters of a Thomas Wyatt, whose Will was probated in November court of 1772. The other daughters were named, Mary Lynn and Sarah Cooper.[23]

It is obvious these women were adult, so Elizabeth must have been the wife of a Hanks born 1750 or earlier.

On the supposition that only members of the family of William the Quaker were in and about Loudoun County, she may have been the wife of one of William II sons, but of which one, no evidence is found.

GEORGE HANKS

The name, George Hanks, appears once only on the tax records of Loudoun County for the year of 1787. He is listed as, "over 16, owning one horse." No other record of George has been located in this county and further of him is not known.

---

[22] Hitchcock Journal, Lincoln Library, Fort Wayne, Indiana.

[23] Wells, 1757-1800, Loudoun County Courthouse.

FLEETWOOD HANKS

Fleetwood Hanks, a son of William of Bedford and Sarah Hanks, was born in Rock Creek Parish of then Frederick County, Maryland, January 19, 1764, according to the record in the old book of Prince George's Parish. He bagan to pay taxes in Loudoun County, Virginia, when of age and his name is not on the list after 1790. He next purchased a farm in Bedford County in 1797[24] and where he had been in the interim is not known. He sold the farm in 1802[25] and removed to Kentucky where, according to family tradition, "He joined his uncle John." He lived in Henry, now Oldham County, Kentucky at Harrod's Creek, twelve miles upriver from Louisville, where he operated a woodyard for the steamboats. This is where he died and was buried.[26]

Fleetwood and his wife, Ruth, had at least six children, one of whom, Nancy, is treated in a preceeding chapter V, vii, under the title, Nancy of Fleetwood. It was learned there she did not marry Tom Lincoln.

x

MIDDLESEX COUNTY, VIRGINIA

GEORGE HANKS

George Hanks of Middlesex County was born about 1750, and he married Mary Tuggle, July 2, 1774. By the time the Virginia census of 1782 and 1785 were taken, they had a family of five. The identity of this man is not positively verified, but he probably was a nephew of Turner Hanks of Richmond County. The sons of Turner lived in Kentucky, and had a tradition of a kinsman, George, who was killed at Yorktown in the Revolutionary War.

It is a conjecture that the heroic George may have been the father of this George, who married Mary.

However, in Will Book F, is a record that Tabitha Fox leaves to the children of George and Mary Hanks, and names three: Catharine, William and Jack. No Nancy is named.

---

[24] Deed Book No. 10, p. 328.

[25] Deed Book No. 11, p. 592.

[26] James M. Hanks, Helena, Arkansas to Hitchcock.

xi

PITTSYLVANIA COUNTY, VIRGINIA

MOSES HANKS

The earliest Hanks record to be found in Pittsylvania County is of Moses Hanks and his family of eight, there being six children then, as listed in the 1782 census of Virginia; whence he came is not known, but since his wife, Aggatha, is supposed to have been a Dodson, and that family source was centered in Richmond County, it is probable that he was from there.

He died in Maury County, Tennessee, August 19, 1831, and the epitaph says age 85 which makes him born in 1746, but a record in a Bible of his son, Thomas, who lived in Texas, gives the birth of Moses as July 15, 1748. From that same Bible is had a list of Moses and Aggatha's children, and they number eleven, from Joicy, born 1769, to Mary Gwynn, born 1796--no Nancy is listed.

There is, however, an interesting tradition pertaining to Nancy Hanks Lincoln: A Mr. Witherspoon of Nashville has asserted[1] that Elder Elijah said "Nancy Hanks was the daughter of an Uncle of his." The man who reports the statement was only three years old when Elijah died in 1871. Moses Hanks has been conjectured to be a brother of Mott, Epiphroditus, and John Hanks of eastern North Carolina. Mott had a daughter, Nancy, born 1780; although she did not marry Tom Lincoln. The statement does seem to place Moses in a family tree, but he, himself, is eliminated as the father of Nancy Hanks Lincoln.

His grandson, Thomas Hanks, of Missouri, was born March 15, 1816; he corresponded with Mrs. Hitchcock in 1895 and, since he omitted citing any kinship to Lincoln, it is significant. He was an educated man, a minister of the Gospels, and father of a large family. Certainly, he was aware of the passing historical incidents and, had his family been close kin to Lincoln, he would have said so.

---

[1] Baber Papers.

PRINCE EDWARD COUNTY, VIRGINIA

LEWIS HANKS

There was a Lewis Hanks who married Elizabeth Blanton in
1786 in Prince Edward County, Virginia, according to a notation in
Weik papers.[1] But, from an examination by Mrs. E. L. Gibbon, researcher,
this name seems to be Hawks. Either way, the late marriage date obviates
further consideration.

In Mercer County, Kentucky, Lewis Hanks or Hawks, with a wife,
Betsey, deeded land to Nelson Matthews in 1807.[2]

There was a Lewis B. Hanks, who received a deed from Elizabeth
Hanks, in Gaston County, North Carolina.[3]

For the reason it has been doubted that two Joseph Hanks
would have had wives named Ann or Nannie, these items, which do not
pertain to Nancy are listed in order to demonstrate the point: that
men with the same names may marry wives with the same given names!

PRINCE WILLIAM COUNTY, VIRGINIA

William Calk, of this County, is brought into this writing
for the reason that Abraham Hanks of Fauquier County was associated
with him in some capacity, and accompanied him into Kentucky and before the Revolutionary War. Calk was born in 1740; married Sarah
Catlett of the family that furnished the name Catlett in Fauquier
County. He became a very ambitious and enterprizing person; went
in 1765 to settle in Orange County, North Carolina, but returned
to Virginia the following year. It seems that his restlessness
remained with him.

---

[1] Weik, Illinois State Historical Society Library, Springfield, Ill.

[2] Deed Book 6, p. 366.

[3] Deed Book 2, p. 386.

In the Spring of 1775 Calk gathered a small company of companions, including Abraham Hanks and set out for an exploratory trip into Kentucky. He kept a diary of the adventurous trip which has become a rather famous historical journal.1 Several entries refer to Abraham Hanks. Hanks returned to Virginia in Autumn of the same year he went out, and Calk also came back. This is evidenced by a document on record2 wherein one William Brown indentured himself to Calk for seven years, and it is signed by Brown and Calk with Abraham as one of the witnesses, November 8, 1775.

There is a tradition in the Calk family that Abraham Hanks continued to be with Calk for several years, and this is borne out by the characteristic ABraham hanks (sic) signature on papers of subsequent dates. In 1782, Abraham is listed as a tax-payer . of this Prince William County and, in the same year, Luke Hanks, formerly of the adjoining Fauquier County has moved into this county and is on the tax record.

This Luke Hanks is the father of Nancy of Luke of Chapter V, ii. His wife, was Nancy Dale, kinswoman, probable neice, possible daughter of Robert and Elizabeth Dale. In his Will, dated, 1770, and probated in 1779, Dale said, "I give 160 acres in Prince William County where I now live unto Luke Hanks and his heirs after my wife's decease, and not before.3." Luke also shared in other property, including eight negroes.3

The widow Dale married again and Luke, the remainder-man, probably impatient, and doubting whether he would ever own the 160 acres, deeded his interest to the second husband in 1784, and Luke's name disappears from further record in the county. It has already been shown that his daughter Nancy did not marry Tom Lincoln; but further consideration will be given to his family. His name, also, disappears from the tax list; he, like Abraham, is supposed to have moved to Campbell County; thence to South Carolina, where records of him appear.

1In possession of a descendant, Mrs. Charles W. Harrmann, Mt. Sterling, Kentucky. Read and copied from for this purpose.

2Deed Book T, p. 183, Prince William County Courthouse.

3 Book G., pp. 44-55.

RICHMOND COUNTY, VIRGINIA

The most copious and clear records of the Hanks family in
Virginia, from the earliest times to the present, are to be found
in the courthouse, parish and church records of Richmond County.
From them it is possible to compile fairly complete genealogies from
the founders even unto the fourth and fifth generations. There are
exceptions: the names of Robert and George Hanks appear in the courthouse records of early seventeen hundreds but there are no records of
their wives or children, if any, or unplaced Hankses who could have
been their children.

Then, there is Luke Hanks Ist, whose death is mentioned
previously under Lancaster County, who has a gap or hiatus in the
birth records of his children, and it is not satisfactorily explained.
There are unplaced Hankses who seem to belong to his family. His
son, Turner, has a clear record of birth and of his children. There
are at this writing, 1955, some three or four unplaced Hanks men of
the right generations to be sons of Luke I and brothers of Turner.

Although their parentage is unkown there are lists of their
children to show the Nancys or the lack of Nancys.

ROBERT HANKS

Robert Hanks was estimated by the Court in 1707 to be 14 years
of age. In 1727 he purchased 55 acres of land from John Hammond, at
which time he was a resident of Northumberland County and had the word
"Junr." attached to his name. Further of him is not known.

ALEXANDER HANKS

This Alexander Hanks was born October 31, 1719, the son of
Luke I and Elizabeth Hanks. In the 1740's he was in business in
Lancaster County. In 1750 Henry Tapscott got a claim allowed against
the estate of Alexander Hanks. Presumable he was deceased. There is
no record of a wife nor children; nor unplaced children who could have
been his.

ALEXANDER HANKS

Alexander Hanks, born December 2, 1734, the son of John and Catharine Hanks, was likely the Alexander who served in the Revolutionary War. He was not then a young man; most wars are fought by younger men than he.

The record states: "Alexander Hanks, private, Capt Burgess Ball's Company of the 5th Virginia Regiment of Foot commanded by Lieutenant Colonel Josiah Parker." His name appears on the company roll for the period from August 1776 to May 31, 1777; but with the notation "died 16 September, 1776."

When his brother, Joseph Hanks, settled their mother, Catharine's, estate in 1782 no distributions were made to the deceased Alexander's heirs; so presumable he had left none or had no children.

JOHN HANKS

John Hanks, born May 4, 1728, the son of John Hanks, seems to have married late; at least there is no record of children born before the late 1750's. The four known ones were sons and inasmuch as these sons were themselves old enough to have been the fathers of daughters by 1784 they are to be considered forthwith.

It is of interest to note, though, that this then old-like man became a Revolutionary soldier. (The service record attached to him in a DAR record belongs to John Hank, not Hanks, of Pennsylvania and later Virginia.) But, John Hanks has his own good Revolutionary War record as does also his son, Abner.

GEORGE HANKS

George Hanks, son of John, above, was born before 1762, according to the date he first paid taxes; but may have been born a little earlier. He married Elizabeth Dale, daughter of Thomas and Alse Dale and their first child, a daughter, Winnie, was born October 27, 1781, followed by Alse and Fannie; but there is no record of a Nancy.

ABNER HANKS

Abner Hanks, named herein in tradition number two[1] was born in this county, 1763, the son of John and Susannah Hanks. He served in the Revolutionary War. The Order Books contain his name: Once he received pay for driving cattle; another time he was put into gaol for debt. He leased a small farm but gave it up and migrated to Kentucky with his brothers. Thence, he removed to Indiana where he died in Johnson County about 1846.

The date of his birth qualifies him for the chance to be named as a possible father of Nancy. The fact that he had some half-dozen wives, in sequence of course, indicates his virility and the possibility. But from three different sources, the lists of his children by his first wife, Mary Dale, agree that his first and oldest child was Matilda, born 1788. No Nancy can be found as a child of Abner.

ELIJAH HANKS

Elijah Hanks was born October 19, 1766, son of John and Susannah Hanks; probably was unmarried by 1784 as there is no record of such. He married a widow, Winnie Bryant, March 4, 1792, who was the daughter of Thomas and Alse Dale. His wife is named in the Alse Dale will, probated 1802 in Woodford County, Kentucky. In 1808, in that county, they donated land for the New Hope church site. This church was established two years previously on the premise that slavery was contrary to the gospels.

In 1821 Elijah took a flat-boat load of produce to New Orleans, and his death occured there. No money was located from the proceeds of the sale of the produce; the tradition is that he was killed and robbed. There is no record that he had any children other than the step-children, the children of Winnie Bryant. Later, Sydnor Dale Hanks quit-claimed his interest in the church property.

JOHN HANKS

John Hanks, son of John Hanks of Richmond County, and brother of Abner and Elijah, was born October 20, 1765. According to papers in possession of Alden Hanks Wyatt, a descendant, John married Susannah Dale and to this union only one child, a son, Sydnor Dale, was born

---

[1]Chapter IV.

possible daughter, Nancy, born 1784, and eliminates John.

ABRAHAM HANKS

Abraham Hanks is listed in the index of Order Book 15 of Richmond County as "Abraham Hanks to be bound," and refers to the term of Court held June 6, 1763.

> "Ordered that the churchwardens of Northfarnham
> Parish for the time being bind Abraham Hanks to
> Turner Hanks according to Law he being now dis-
> charged from his former master William Glascock
> Junr.
>   John Woodbridge"

So far no clue to the identity of this Abraham Hanks has been located, beyond the implication that both Glascock and Turner Hanks had some connection or responsibility with him.

The use of the word 'bind' seems to connote an apprenticeship, in which case he was probably in his teens past twelve years of age. Had the Court act been by reason of minority of Abraham a guardian would have been appointed for the ward.

TURNER HANKS OF RICHMOND COUNTY.

Turner Hanks was born June 18, 1737, the son of Luke and Elizabeth Hanks and, married twice, lived and died in this county. The records of this family are perfectly clear. Turner had two daughters by his first wife, Million Durham; he had six sons by the second wife, Sarah. These were all born in an age bracket to have included a daughter, Nancy, but the Parish and Bible records show only two girls, neither named Nancy, and six sons.

However, for the record, five of these sons went to near the Lincoln locale in Kentucky and one went on to Missouri. After 1782 the name of Turner appears regularly on the tax list; alongside a man listed as "T. Hanks" who probably was Thomas. The son of Turner, Luke, who remained in Richmond County, became the ancestor of descendants who reside there today. There is no Nancy in this line, born 1784.

JOSEPH HANKS OF RICHMOND COUNTY

"Born Joseph, son of John and Catharine Hanks, December 20, 1725" was an entry casually and routinely made in the North Farnham Parish Register that has been examined and scutinized by many researchers; for some think he was the father of Nancy Hanks Lincoln; others think he may have been a grandfather. Also, it has been stated by a rather eminant author, not a genealogist, that this Joseph of Richmond was the Joseph of Hampshire and, in turn, the Joseph of Nelson.[1]

Let the evidence be examined: In the settlement of the estate of William Lee, deceased 1764, the provisions of his will, dated May 11, 1747, were carried out. An entry of final accounting, April 3, 1769, reads, "To Joseph Hanks for his legacy bequeathed to his wife by Elizabeth Taylor Dec'd, 2-2-6"[2]. The name of the wife of Joseph was Ann; she had been Ann Lee. These are courthouse records.

Two years after the settlement of the estate of Lee, and with no connection whatever to court affairs, an entry was again made, in the North Farnham Parish register, along with many others, "Born Betty, daughter of Joseph and Ann Hanks, March 4, 1771." This is the only record of births in the Parish to this couple, although Joseph and Ann had been residing in the Parish and continued to live there for at least fifteen years more, according to various entries in the Order Books. Joseph had been born into the Church; all his brothers and sisters had been registered there many years before; the fact that Betty was registered indicates that Joseph and Ann were still communicants; if there were other children, why were they not registered? Or, if there had been a failure to register ones earlier than Betty why were not the entries made when Betty's birth was recorded, as was often the practice as seen in the old Registers?

On October 4, 1773, the Court for Richmond County sat with four Justices present. Along with regular and routine business they took action and the clerk recorded, "Joseph Hanks is appointed Surveyor of the highway in Room of LeRoy Peachey."[3] Members of those early Courts were recognized as men of discretion and ability. No doubt Joseph Hanks had been well investigated and found favorably qualified before the appointment. To have established such a reputation he must have long been a resident.

---

[1] Barton, _Lineage of Lincoln._

[2] Deed Book 5, p. 531——42, 2s, 6p.

[3] Order Book 19, p. 40.

In 1779, Catharine Hanks, widow of John Hanks, long
deceased, and mother of Joseph, died. Her oldest son, William
was living but, for some reason or other, he was not appointed as
administrator. A younger son, John, was living in the county; had
been a soldier in the Revolutionary War or maybe was serving then
and he was not appointed. Joseph was available and appointed for
the job. He carried it through in orderly manner, wound it up, and
made his final distribution and report, 1782.[4] The record shows that
brother John, who received his share, was living right at hand;[5] the
brother, William, who received his share was living just across the
line in Lancaster County.[6] Brother Thomas received his portion.
Also, Joseph had two brothers-in-law, Woolard and Dodson, right at
home, either one could have acted administrator. Would the Court
have appointed a man living so far away as Hampshire County to serve?

Then, again on April 5, 1785, Joseph Hanks brought suit against
Richard Beale for a debt of ₤25 and damages ₤5.[7] Now the question of
the identity of Joseph comes up; for there was a Joseph, his nephew,
just turned 21, who could have brought the suit; but it hardly seems
likely that a young man would have such a then relative large sum
owing to him? Surely it was the older Joseph; further the Order Books
do not give.

As remarked, the wife of Joseph of Richmond was Ann Lee; the
wife of Joseph of Nelson was Nannie, and it has been suggested that
she was a Lee. This could very well be but, if it proves anything,
it is that two of the several Joseph Hanks married Lee girls named
Ann or Nan. That this is not improbable and that anything is possible
in the Hanks family, this instance is given: Three Hanks brothers
married three Dale sisters, and one of the sisters was named Ann,
sometimes called Nan.[8] Luke Hanks, later of South Carolina, also

[4]Order Book 18, p. 75.

[5]Census, Virginia 1782-5 into U.S. 1790.

[6] Tithe List, Lane Co., 1782.

[7] Order Book 19, p. 239, 241.

[8]Alse Dale Will, Courthouse, Woodford County, Kentucky.

married an Ann Dale, who was sometimes called Nancy. Luke's wife, Ann, was not one of the three sisters. Is not this just a coincidence that both Josephs married Anns?

Another coincidence is that both Josephs had daughters, Elizabeth or Betty; but here a difference appears. The Betty who was the daughter of Joseph of Richmond was born March 4, 1771;[9] the Elizabeth, daughter of Joseph of Nelson, and who seems to never have been called Betty, was born in 1776. She gave her age when her license to marry was applied for.[10]

Joseph of Hampshire had eleven in his family and if Thomas Hanks of Ohio was a son, born 1759; then his father, or mother at least, was not back in Richmond County.

It does not seem that Joseph of Richmond ever had enough children of record to become a man with a household of eleven souls in Hampshire County. Unfortunately, this leaves the identity of the Joseph of Hampshire obscure. But it does seem that Joseph of Richmond had no daughter, Nancy.

Joseph Hanks of Richmond County, whose wife was Ann Lee, had a brother, Thomas, who married a sister of Joseph's wife, Betty, and that brought another Lee into the family. This couple had, by record of the Parish, two children, Joseph, born February 21, 1764, and Nancy, born September 15, 1766. No other births are recorded and it is thought that Thomas continued to reside in the area; the tax and tithe records list a 'T' Hanks for several years, it is not Turner, for his full name is written.

This son of Thomas would have been old enough by 1784 to have been the father of Nancy but there is no record of his marriage nor of any children, either before or after that date. Ordinarily any Hanks man, in due course, as they seemed to do, would have married and had a family by say 1790; but no such record. The 1790 census list of Virginia and her Kentucky County are missing; also the 1800 for Virginia but one for Kentucky, which had become a state, has been compiled from tax lists of that year. No Joseph Hanks name appears.

There is listed in 1810, in Christian County, Kentucky, a Joseph Hanks with a family; in Ohio in 1820 is the name also; but the presumption is these men belong to the family groups that were located there, and were not from the Richmond County, Virginia ones.

---

[9] Parish Records, Northfarnham Parish Register.

[10] Marriage Register, Nelson County, Kentucky Courthouse.

In ordinary genealogical searches if a subjects name
disappears after his birth record from subsequent records it is
presumed he was deceased; but, in this case, there is no ordinary
search, so nothing is to be taken for granted. However, there is
no record of Joseph Hanks (Jr.) having a daughter born in 1784; he
is out.

WILLIAM HANKS

William Hanks, who married Sarah Durham, had a family of
children, including Elijah, Argyle, and William, all of them were
born early enough to have children by 1784, and did. William and
Sarah eventually arrived, after several moves, in Granville County,
North Carolina, where their children with their families followed
and settled. Therefore, his sons will be treated of under the title
of that State, except Argyle, who was written of herein under
Chapter V, iv.

JOHN HANKS

John Hanks married Mary Mott of Northumberland County and
they moved by successive steps through Hanover and Amelia Counties
southwardly to Halifax County, North Carolina. At least three of
their sons are known: Mott, Epiphroditus, and John. All had children.
These three will be treated under the Carolina title; although none
were residing in Virginia in 1784, when Nancy Hanks Lincoln was born
there.

RICHARD HANKS

Richard Hanks received quite a dowry when he married Mary
Hinds. They too, soon after their marriage moved south to Dinwiddie
County, thence to Amelia County, and finally over into North Carolina.
According to the census they had nine children. From presumptive
evidence it has been determined that there were at least six and
maybe seven sons. Their names were remarked under the Amelia County
title; William was treated of here in before in Chapter V, iii. The
other sons, of them more hereafter.

HANKS MEN OF NORTH CAROLINA, ADULT, 1783.

ELIJAH HANKS

Elijah Hanks, the oldest child and son of William and Sarah Durham Hanks, was born December 17, 1740, in Richmond County, Virginia. He married Ann Craft; they lived in Granville County, North Carolina, where he died in 1798 and by his will, named his children: Samuel, David, William, Thomas, John, and Betsey. It is apparent that he had no daughter, Nancy.

ARGYLE HANKS

A younger brother of Elijah Hanks, was Argyle. He married Million Hargrave for his first wife and they had a daughter, Nancy, born in Virginia, in 1784; and is alleged to have married Tom Lincoln. Her biography was treated here before in this manuscript under the name of Nancy of Argyle, of Chapter V, iv.

WILLIAM HANKS IV

William Hanks, the youngest brother of Elijah and Argyle, probably was born about 1755, at least after his sister, Hannah, born, 1752. His name is not recorded in the parish records as are those of his brothers and sisters; but he is named in his father's will. He married Sally and they resided in Granville County, North Carolina. William died early, 1795, left only one child, a son, William Haney. He had made his will a short time before his death so it was not unexpected. There was no daughter, Nancy, named in his will.

WILLIAM HANKS

William Hanks, probably the oldest son of Richard and Mary Hinds Hanks was born circa 1755. He married Keziah Wright and they resided for a time in South Carolina; but after 1790 and before 1800 they moved to Rutherford County, North Carolina. The census of 1800 shows that he had four sons and four daughters in his family. One of the daughters was Nancy, born about 1800, and treated heretofore in Chapter V, iii, p. 47.

MOTT HANKS

Mott, son of John and Mary Mott Hanks, was born April 23, 1742, in North Farnham Parish and his second wife was Susanna. He had at least eight children but the Census of 1790 for North Carolina shows only five at home. This was in Dobbs County to which his father had come years earlier.

The first child and son of Mott, was born 1774, named Nathan, and became a surveyor General of North Carolina. The fourth child was Lucy, born 1778; and the fifth child a daughter Nancy, was born June 21, 1780. Since she was, therefore, four years older than the Nancy who is the object of our search, and not born in Virginia, she may be dismissed. All early courthouse records of Dobbs County are burned, so nothing further is known of this Nancy.

It is known that part of Mott's family removed into Alabama.

EPIPHRODITUS HANKS

Epiphroditus, called "Epi" for short, was born January 25, 1747 in Hanover County, Virginia, the son of John and Mary Mott Hanks; while he was still a child his family moved to Dobbs County, North Carolina.[1] Epi was a Revolutionary Soldier, and when his service ended he went to Halifax County, North Carolina.

He was twice married; and William and James are known to have been children of the first wife; and Stephen was the only child of the second wife; so obviously Epi had no daughter, Nancy.

Epi, was in some ways, a remarkable man. He resided later in Sumpter District, South Carolina, and when past ninety years of age, travelled alone by stage to visit his descendants in Wilcox County, Georgia. He died July 4, 1838.

----

[1] Dobbs County, North Carolina, census, 1790.

JOHN HANKS

John, son of John and Mary Mott Hanks, was born C. 1750, moved with his parents to North Carolina, resided in Wayne County[2], purchased his father's (John) farm land on Pond Creek in Christian County, Kentucky after 1800. His wife, Mary, was probably a Dawson.

Their children were of the same generation as Nancy Hanks Lincoln; five sons and one daughter; the traditional name of the lone daughter has been given as Nancy; but not so, she was Betsey.

However, John's brother Mott, did have a daughter, Nancy, born 1780, and she is probably the origin of this family's tradition of a Nancy in the family.

The children's names as given by Stephen Beck Hanks and other cumulative evidence are: Thomas, born January 24, 1777 m. Catharine Beck; Joshua, born February 17, 1787; Nathan; Joseph; and Betsey, married Russell Gray, August 16, 1809.

RICHARD HANKS

Richard Hanks of Lincoln County, North Carolina, whose name appears in the 1790 census was a veteran of the Revolutionary War and old enough in 1784 to have been the father of a daughter, Nancy; but according to the record of his own Bible, his first child was John, born August 31, 1786; so he is eliminated. He was, most likely, the son of the Richard Hanks, who, with wife, Mary, immigrated to North Carolina into Rowan County. He was the father of Joshua Hanks, treated of here before in Chapter IV, vii.

JAMES HANKS

James Hanks, also of Lincoln County, North Carolina, at the time of the 1790 census had, besides his wife, three females in his family. He had married August 26, 1779, to Mary Starrett, so they could have had a daughter, Nancy, born 1784; maybe did have; but James continued to live in North Carolina, where all of his children most likely were born, and did not remove to Virginia by 1784 or thereafter,

---

[2]Wayne County, North Carolina Census, 1790.

so a daughter, Nancy, does not qualify as having been "Born in Virginia."
It is of interest, thought, that there was a Nancy Hanks of Wilkes
County, where James later resided, and she married Lambeth Blackburn,
November 29, 1822. She, probably, was a daughter or granddaughter of
James, and James, himself, was likely a presumptive son of Richard and
Mary Hinds Hanks.

DAVID HANKS

David Hanks, a presumptive son of Richard and Mary Hinds Hanks,
resided in Lincoln County, North Carolina, where he was married to
Elizabeth Hoyle, of a rather well known family, on October 31, 1783.
Their bond was signed by Frederick Bess, his brother-in-law, who had
married his sister, Patience. The children of this couple are not
known to this research. But, any daughter, Nancy, would have been
born too late and in North Carolina to qualify.

THOMAS HANKS

The 1790 census of Mecklenburg County, North Carolina, lists
a Thomas Hanks with only three in the family, which includes the wife
and a male under 16. This record is a confirmation of his marriage.
On March 2, 1789, Thomas took out license to marry Crese (Lucretia?)
Hargrave of Rowan County. On her tombstone at old Goshen the name
is spelled as Croseie. By 1800 the couple had five children. At the
entrance to the cemetery, in now Gaston County, a placque lists the
names of Revolutionary soldiers buried within, and included is the
name of Thomas Hanks. This item connected with his proximity to both
James and Richard Hanks of nearby, and to the fact that their father,
Richard Hanks resided in the adjoining county of Rowan, would seem to
indicate that he was a son of the older Richard; although another
record has Thomas, son of Richard, deceased much earlier. Another
confirmation is that Joshua Hanks is presumed to have been a son of
Richard, and is known to have had four or five brothers in the War.

Thomas' stone reads that he died November 4, 1851 in his
88th year; so he was born about 1763. No doubt, Crese was his first
and only wife, so he had no wife and no Nancy, a daughter, in 1784.

Near his grave is a long row of Berry and Barry graves, also,
several graves of the Ewing family. In Kentucky, Richard Berry married
Polly Ewing, which seemingly makes a connection here.

ABRAHAM HANKS

The earliest record of this Abraham Hanks of North Carolina
is in Caswell County in 1790 where he was listed as a taxable in
Gloucester District, and near John Hightower. The next year, he was
taxed on 258 acres of land; but on only 100 acres in 1792. However,
there seems to be no record of his real estate in the Deed Records,
neither as a Grantee nor Grantor.

He married January 12, 1792, to Mary Combs of Caswell County;
of her there is no earlier information but later: it seems to be she
who is listed as Polly Hanks, head of the family, in the 1810 census
of Montgomery County, Kentucky. She later moved to Edgar County,
Illinois; but what became of her husband is not so clear. He was
in Montgomery County, Kentucky by 1799 where various courthouse records
of his name so indicate. He operated a tavern in 1804. Subsequently,
he becomes traditional.[3] He may have gone to Hardin County where he
had a brother, William.[4] He was a blacksmith or worked in iron for
there are two traditions that he made cow-bells.[5]

OTHER ABRAHAM HANKSES

To recapitulate for this record and to avoid confusion all the
known Abrahams will be here listed:

There was the Abraham Hanks or Hawks, who owned a large farm
in Amelia County, Virginia, and died 1767, leaving a widow, Lucy.

In Richmond County, Virginia, on June 6, 1763, the Court
ordered that Abraham Hanks be bound out to Turner Hanks. If this child
or teen-ager survived until the 1780's he could have become the father
of children and Nancy.

---

[3]Mrs. Hitchcock, when interviewing people at Mt. Sterling, Ky.,
in 1895, was told that Fielding Hanks had a brother, Abraham.

[4]James Hanks of Tobasco, Ohio, wrote to Mrs. C.R. Galloway in
1930 that: "Abraham Hanks lived in Hardin County...was father's uncle."
(The father of said James was a son of William Hanks of formerly Hardin
County.)

[5]Mrs. W.E.Bach has learned about: "An Abraham Hanks who came
to Martins Station in Kentucky at an early date with the Berrys."

There is the Abraham, who was with Luke Hanks in Fauquier County, Virginia in 1773, and who later accompanied William Calk to Kentucky.

The one of Caswell, North Carolina, who married Mary Combs.

An Abraham Hanks who purchased a chip axe at the sale of the estate of George Hanks, deceased, in Montgomery County, Kentucky, on January 3, 1814. A conjecture is he was the Abraham who came into the county about 1800; or his son.

In Mecklenburg County, North Carolina, on October 12, 1825, an Abraham Hanks obtained a license to marry Judy Rodin. In 1838 he mortgaged chattels, including a blind horse to secure a debt. His name is not on the Bible page record of Richard Hanks of nearby, now Belmont, as a son. He could have been a son of Thomas and Lucretia Hargrave Hanks who are buried at Old Goshen, near Belmont.

In Greenup County, Kentucky, on January 24, 1827, Abraham Hanks received a license to marry Polly Ann Wigglesworth, and James Wigglesworth signed the bond.

In Nottoway County, Virginia, on December 28, 1867, Abraham Hanks married Margaret Jackson. His place of birth was Charlotte County and his father's name was, also, Abraham.

There is the Abram Hancks, the Revolutionary War veteran of Campbell County, Virginia, who went to Lincoln County, Tennessee, where he died in 1833, and left a wife, Lucy.

Abram Hanks, who died in Lincoln County, Tennessee, had a grandson, born 1837, who was named Abraham. He, later, was taken to Wright County, Missouri, where he died in 1916.

From the foregoing it is learned that Abraham has been a rather common given Hanks name for two centuries. It is supposed to have originated with the Dale family of Virginia, whose members intermarried with those of the Hanks family.

THOMAS HANKS

In the St. George's and St. John's Parish records, copies of which are at the Maryland Historical Library, Baltimore, is the record of Thomas Hanks and Sarah Hewitt, March 9, 1748. It is doubtful if this couple had children so late as 1784, but they could have.

It is possible that he is the Thomas Hanks listed as taxed in Bedford County, Virginia in 1782, and with a tithe over 16, who could have been a son, Thomas, born 1763. This is speculative.

GREENVILLE HANKS

In the St. Lukes Parish record of Church Hill, Maryland, Greenville Hanks and wife, Mary, had a baby boy, John, who was born and died in 1739.

There are at this time, Hanks families on the Eastern Shores of Maryland.

ORANGE COUNTY, VIRGINIA

REUBEN HANKS

A record in this Orange County indicates that one Rodney Hanks obtained a license to marry Alice Chandler, May 26, 1803. Assuming that Rodney was aged twenty or twenty-five years, then he would have been born of parents who had themselves been born not later than 1760. This couple could have had other children, including a Nancy; but there are no further records nor clues to be located. The parents of Rodney were Reuben and Elizabeth Hanks. Thomas Wyatt of Loudoun County, by will in 1772, named a daughter, Elizabeth Hanks, who seems to have been by his first wife. Thomas' second wife was

Margaret Hanks by whom there were five children, including Reuben
Wyatt. There seems to be some significance in all this, but the
connections are obscure; there is no record of a Nancy.

※※※※※

       The Ivy family, of whom the famous Dr. Andrew C. Ivy of
Chicago is one, are descendants in one line of a Susan Hanks, who
was born, 1769, the daughter of a William Hanks, and she married
Charles Tankersley. He was born in 1765 the son of William and
Margaret Nelson Tankersley. The Tankersleys seem to have been in
and about Charlotte County, Virginia and it is thought that Charles
went to Caswell County, North Carolina. William Hanks, who had a
daughter born in 1769, could have had other children born later but
the Ivy family historians do not know anything further about William
and neither does this researcher.

       Paddock's History of Central and West Texas gives a James
Hanks, who was born in South Carolina, in 1770, the son of William
Hanks. This line is unplaced.

       This research has located some other individual Hanks, and only
a very few, whose identity cannot now be placed but, fortunately, of
such late dates that they are precluded from having any connection
with the ancestry of Nancy Hanks Lincoln.

       In Lancaster County, Virginia, in 1756, one John Hanks petitioned
the Court to be apprenticed and stated that he was an orphan of William
Hanks, deceased. This William Hanks is unknown to this researcher;
if the son, John, had children is not known.

       In order to make this work as definitive as possible, every
Hanks name discovered in the records has been noted.

CHAPTER VIII

THREE POSSIBLE CANDIDATES

Having developed a Census of adult Hanks men of the 1780's
from material collected from all known and suspected original sources,
and not from secondary copies, these brief biographies of those men
of procreative age in 1783 were assembled and considered to determine
which one, if any, could have been the father of Nancy Hanks Lincoln;
each one and all have been definitely eliminated as "possible father"
except three, viz: James, of Campbell County, Virginia; Peter, the
Revolutionary Soldier; and the Abraham, who came to Boonesborough,
Kentucky, with William Calk.

JAMES HANKS

From a single descendant of the Shipley family is a tradition
that the father of Nancy was a James Hanks. A notable Lincoln student
has accepted this and incorporated it in his writings.[1]

Parish records show a James Hanks born in Richmond County,
Virginia, February 12, 1732--no further records of him have been
located in that county. A James Hanks, with a wife, Nancy, sold
land in Amelia County, March 19, 1769.[2] A James Hanks, without a
wife, sold a farm in the same county October 26, 1774,[3] on Barebones
Creek. These transactions were witnessed by different sets of
neighbors; so, whether, the tracts were owned by one man and separated
widely or the sale was by two individuals cannot be determined. Considering one James or two James of Amelia County, it is obvious the

---

[1] Warren, Lincoln Kinsmen, No. 4, p. 6.

[2] Deed Book 10, p. 228.

[3] Deed Book 13, p. 80.

wife, Nancy, had died or disappeared before 1784, for her signature is not on the later deed. It never appears again on any record located for this investigation.

A James Hanks purchased land in Bedford County, March 27, 1780, in the Hatt Creek area that became a part of Campbell County.[4] He is presumed to have come in from Amelia County. This is based on the fact that all the Hankses had left Amelia; according to records his supposed son, Abram, later deposed that he was born in Amelia County in 1759; neighbors of James were from Amelia. The point is that if this James came from Amelia his wife, Nancy, had deceased and before 1784. There is no evidence that James had a wife in 1784 nor that he did not have. The record is wanting. But, it is clear that he had no wife in 1787.

When he sold a part of his Hatt Creek land in Campbell County to Daniel Walker, July 17, 1787,[5] there were two women in his household, or at least associated with him, who witnessed the deed. They were Sarah and Tabitha Hanks. That Sarah did not join in executing the deed eliminates her as a wife. She may have been a daughter but no further record is located to learn if she were so. Tabitha was a daughter; her marriage record shows that James Hanks, Sr., signed as her father.

It has been conjectured that this James Hanks, Sr., of Campbell County was a son, an older son, of Joseph Hanks of Nelson County, Kentucky. This is not plausible for he is not named in the will of Joseph Hanks, and James was living and survived many years after the decease of said Joseph. James and Joseph were of the same generation; more likely brothers or cousins.

It has been further conjectured that this James Hanks, Sr. had been the first husband of the Lucey Hanks of Kentucky, and who married Henry Sparrow in 1790 in Mercer County. This conjecture is not tenable because James Hanks, Sr. was living when Lucey married in Kentucky and he survived for many years after, as evidenced by his signature on deeds and by subsequent census records.

There is no evidence, neither clue, to support the theory that James Hanks, Sr., was the father of Nancy Hanks Lincoln.

There is, however, a tradition in Campbell County that Nancy Hanks was born in the house and home or on the farm of James Hanks, Sr. This is possible and plausible and can be supported with evidence to be adduced later in this.

---

[4] Deed Book 6, p. 406, Bedford County, Virginia.

[5] Deed Book 2, p. 252, Campbell County, Virginia.

To continue with the subject of James Hanks as a possible
father: in all the many records searched in Virginia and in North
Carolina, only one more James is located, who would have been old
enough to have fathered Nancy. He is the James of Lincoln County,
North Carolina, the son of Richard; he was born in Virginia but
moved with his father to his adopted state and never returned to
Virginia; nor to have a daughter born in 1784.

No records are found, no evidence, no clues, and no traditions
save the single one mentioned, that any James Hanks was the father of
Nancy Hanks Lincoln.

11

PETER HANKS

Peter Hanks, the Revolutionary War veteran (of Chap. VI,iii)
inasmuch of presumptive kinship to the Joseph Hanks family of Nelson
County, Kentucky, the proved kin of Nancy Hanks Lincoln, is a very
likely candidate to be her father. Such tradition does now exist
among some of the later generations of his descendants.[6]

His qualifications are: he and his wife, at one time, resided
in Virginia; they had children, born in Virginia, some of whom were
born in the 1780's; they migrated to North Carolina and resided in the
Salisbury District, where they were in proximity to the Berry family,
whose name figures in these traditions; later they removed to Montgomery
County, Kentucky, where is a tradition that Nancy Hanks once lived;
there also resided the John Berry family on Slate Creek; thence came
Richard Berry, Jr., to live near his kinsfolk; he had signed Nancy's
bond.

A fact of significant importance is there is an interval between the known birth dates of two of his daughters, Ruth and Savilla,
when another daughter could have been, possibly was. Ruth was born
June 13, 1782; Savilla, was born January 8, 1787.

It is also of interest that Peter and all of his children,
except John, emigrated to southern Indiana shortly before the Lincoln
family moved there. (John, who remained in Kentucky was later interviewed by Schane for Draper, the historian.)

---

[6] Helen Hersh Franklin, correspondence, 1954, Baber papers.

For sometime during this research and investigation it
appeared that Peter Hanks was the putative father of Nancy Hanks
Lincoln; but finally and only after long and earnest consideration
the theory was discarded and for the following reasons.

Peter Hanks was living in North Carolina in 1784, the year of
Nancy's birth and not in Virginia where she was born. When John Hanks
was interviewed by Schane for Draper he mentioned only one sister who
was Ruth. In the 1890's there was correspondence between descendants
of Ruth Hanks Marshall, the daughter of Peter, pertaining to their
family relationships. One was a minister at Franklin, Indiana; the
other was a judge at Howard, Kansas. From copies of their letters
it is apparent these men were of high intelligence. They mention
Humphrey Marshall, grandparents, and great grandparents clear back
to Salisbury, North Carolina. One of them, the minister was born
before Lincoln became prominant and was living long after his death.
Inferentially, it would seem that a kinship would have been remarked;
had one existed.

For this purpose, people around Princeton and in Gibson County,
Indiana, have been interviewed, where Peter lived out his last years,
and no tradition has been uncovered there. Six miles east of Princeton,
an old graveyard is pointed out where Peter Hanks and a few other
Revolutionary soldiers are supposed to be buried; but never a word
about any connection of a Hanks-Lincoln is vouchsafed.

Both this Hanks family and the Lincoln family lived in Southern
Indiana at the same time. An early trail that passed through the
Lincoln country northwestwardly to Vincennes had a left fork to Princeton.
It is known that the Lincolns went to Princeton to mill. It would seem
that if Peter Hanks had been the father of Nancy Hanks Lincoln, her
son would have known all about it and mentioned it as he did mention
her kinfolk in Illinois. It seems that, as a politician, he would have
been proud to proclaim himself the grandson of a Revolutionary soldier.

Finally and conclusively: Peter did not die until 1830 and so
left no daughter, Nancy, who was an orphan in 1806. The tradition
that Peter Hanks was the father of Nancy Hanks Lincoln fails.

iii

ABRAHAM HANKS

     The elimination of two of three possible candidates to be the father of Nancy Hanks Lincoln leaves only Abraham Hanks to be considered. These are his qualifications: like Peter Hanks and other adult Hanks men, Abraham was a resident of Virginia, was married, and the couple had children born to them in the 1780's. Also, like seven other Hanks fathers, Abraham had a daughter, Nancy, born in the 1780 decade. Along with three other Hanks men, he was residing in 1784 in Campbell County, Virginia, the location of the Berry, the Shipley, the Mitchell, and the Thompson families. But here his points of similarity with other Hanks men cease and this is important.

     In the identifications of persons it is known that mathamatically the facts of similarity with others decrease rapidly to a point of improbability, and with only seven attributes. But we need to identify and differentiate Abraham from a relative few Hanks men. It is known by descendants of Abraham, through his daughter, Sarah, that he died when she was small, and about the 1790's. The three other Hanks men of Campbell County lived beyond then. Also, it is known that Sarah Harper, his wife was deceased about early 1790. Thus their children became orphans.

     The younger children were "farmed out". Two of the boys were placed with the Harper family; the daughter, Sarah, went with the Ringo family; Polly seems to have been associated with the Lynch family; the daughter, Nancy, lived with the Shipley family and later became a ward of the Berry family. Eventually these children came into Kentucky, some into Montgomery County and some into Hardin County. The daughters came respectively, "with their relations and not with their parents." Of these, Nancy, came first to Montgomery County, then went to Hardin County and from there to Washington County. Here she lived with the Richard Berry family. Here, she married Thomas Lincoln.

     By cumulative elimination of probabilities; by presumptive and by associate evidence; by logical and by reasonable deductions; and by mathamatics, ABRAHAM HANKS has the most qualifications to be the father of Nancy Hanks Lincoln.

CHAPTER IX

ABRAHAM HANKS

The Qualified Father

It is obvious that Herndon, the author of Herndon's Lincoln, and Weik, the writer who did the final arranging and transcribing of Herndon's material, were fully aware of a close connection between Abraham Hanks and Nancy Hanks Lincoln, the mother of the president. This recognition is evident from the fact that in their presentation of the book to the public it was found that they had devoted a whole page in Chapter one to the young Abraham Hanks, who, with others, had accompanied William Calk into Kentucky in 1775.[1]

The late Archer Butler Hulbert, in his work on the location of the early trails and roads, describes travel on the trail that Boone blazed through the wilderness into Kentucky and states without reservation, although he gives no authority, that Abraham Hanks was the maternal grandfather of Abraham Lincoln.[2]

The late Samuel C. Williams, the eminent Tennesseean, a Justice of the Supreme Court of Tennessee and Chairman of that State's Historical Commission for many years, made researches and reports. He wrote of Henderson's Purchase and that part of it that became Tennessee; he, also, was the author of The Lincolns of Tennessee. He made the flat statement, as if it needed no affirmation, that, "Abraham Hanks, the father of Nancy, and maternal grandfather of President Lincoln, was of this party (Calk's) which joined the Henderson party."[3]

Mrs. Caroline Hanks Hitchcock, who collected an enormous amount of information pertaining to the Hanks family of New England, and investigated records of Hanks in Virginia and Kentucky, and then wrote the little book, Nancy Hanks, learned that an Abraham Hanks was of close kin to Nancy Hanks Lincoln.[4] In 1895 she interviewed Hanks

---

[1] Herndon's Lincoln; Chapter I, p. 8.

[2] Hulbert, Historic Highways; Vol. VI, p. 107.

[3] Tennessee Historical Magazine, Vol. 5, April 1919. No. 1, p. 14.

[3] Williams, Lincoln Herald, 43. (XLII) 3. Oct. 1941., P. 3.

[4] Hitchcock, Nancy Hanks.

people in Kentucky, and one of member of the family who lived in
Stephensport, she left this record: "Everyone in the countryside
calls him 'Uncle Billy.' His real name is William Hanks, and he
is a grandson of Abraham Hanks, who came to Kentucky with the
Boones, and was a great friend of Daniel Boone."[5]

The William Hanks to whom she refers was born in Hardin
County, Kentucky, January 1, 1804; he was of the same generation
as Abraham Lincoln, and about the same age as Dennis and John Hanks.
Inasmuch as he was born and reared in the same locality as they, he
should have known, as much as they did, what he was talking about,
and, so far as his own grandfather was concerned, known more. He
had resided for a time, with other Hankses, in Decatur County,
Indiana; had removed to Iowa where he entered the real estate business;
and, in his old age had returned to Kentucky, to Breckenridge County,
where he lived around with kinfolk. He was noted locally as a great
singer and would sit on his porch at eventime and sing; and his neighbors would come to listen. Mrs. Hitchcock sang with him on her visit.[6]
He died in 1900 and is buried at Stephensport.

Another William Hanks, born 1807, and also of the same generation as Abraham Lincoln, migrated to Edgar County, Illinois. In 1895,
Mrs. Hitchcock corresponded with two of his daughters, about the
Hanks family there, and in one of the letters she received, is the
following statement, "My great grandfather, on my father's side, was
Abraham Hanks. His wife's maiden name was Sarah Harper, both natives
of Virginia.[7]

Also, in the Hitchcock papers at the Lincoln Library at Fort
Wayne, Indiana, is a letter from the Rev. Jno. Hanks, of La Dora, Iowa,
in which he wrote, "The Revolutionary soldier was named Abraham Hanks.
His sons were Luke, John and William. He, also, had a daughter who
was the mother of Abraham Lincoln. The three sons migrated; Luke to
Tennessee, William and John to Kentucky; where John settled in Henry
County, near New Castle." The Reverand Mr. Hanks was a descendant of
an Abner Hanks, and not of the Abraham referred to, so his statement

---

[5]Nitchcock, M.S., Lincoln Library, Fort Wayne, Indiana

[6]Hanks Singers; See Herdon's Lincoln; n.P. 4.

[7]Sizemore to Hitchcock; 1895, Lincoln Library, Ft. Wayne, Ind.

so far as it pertains to the connnection between Abraham and the mother of Lincoln, should have been unbiased.

Dennis Friend Hanks, born 1799, who professed to know everything pertaining to the Hanks family, (but more safely should be quoted only from what he may have known from his own experience and observations) was ten years old when the baby boy, Abraham Lincoln, was born to Nancy in February of 1809. It is possible that Dennis may have been present, as he affirmed,[8] when the child was named, "Abraham,". He told Eleanor Atkinson, as she reported in her book, that Abraham was named, "...after his grandfather, that came out to Kentucky with Daniel Boone...."[9]

This statement has been interpreted by some researchers and writers as referring to the President's paternal Grandfather, Abraham Lincoln. But, Grandfather Lincoln did not come to Kentucky with Daniel Boone at Boonesborough. It was grandfather Abraham Hanks who was at Boonesborough with Daniel Boone the Spring of 1775. Grandfather Lincoln did not arrive in Kentucky until 1781 or 1782, according to his grandson.[10] He made a preliminary trip the year before, 1780, to spy out the land he wanted to enter.[11]

Thus, it would seem that when Nancy said she was naming the baby "...after his grandfather," she was referring to the grandfather Hanks and not to grandfather Lincoln. Surely though she must have known and remarked the happy incident of two grandfathers Abraham.

Colonel Theodore Roosevelt, author of _Winning of the West_, once remarked to Major A. T. Wood, who was serving as congressman from Montgomery County, Kentucky, that he considered the Calk Journal to be the most important record extant of pioneer Kentucky. From the original in the Calk home near Mt. Sterling, Kentucky, is quoted the first entry:[12]

---

[8] Weik, _The Real Lincoln_; p. 44.

[9] Atkinson, _The Boyhood of Lincoln_, p. 8.

[10] Lincoln to Fell, Dec. 1859, Autobiography, "My paternal grandfather, Abraham Lincoln, emigrated from Rockingham County, Virginia, to Kentucky, about 1781 or 1782..."

[11] Coleman, Lincoln's Lincoln Grandmother, Journal Ill. St. His. Soc., Vol. LII No. 1, Spring, 1959, pp. 69, 70, 71.

[12] By courtesy of Mrs. Charles Harrmann.

William Calk;...his Journal[13]............
  "1775 March 13th mond I set out from
prince Wm. to travel to caintuck on Tuesday
Night our company all Got together at Mr.
Prises on Rapdan Which was ABraham hanks
philip Drake Eanoch Smith Robert Whitledge
my self thear abrams Dogs leg got broke by
Drake's Dog.............[14]

Together the party journeyed southwestward through Virginia,
towards the awful Cumberland Gap; the passage found by Dr. Thomas
Walker, which gave entry into what was to become Kentucky and
Tennessee. At Martin's Station in Powell Valley, they came upon
Richard Henderson and his party, camped on the trail, and joined
up with them. This was the trail blazed by Daniel Boone, called
the Wilderness Way, and destined to become the epic way to the
land of the Western Waters.[15]

The two parties, each reinforced by the other, together
passed on through the Gap and, wandering with the Wilderness Way,
came to camp at the Rock Castle River. Here they were met by refugees,
fleeing the Indians, and Abraham and some others, being men of discretion, "turned back," as Calk so succiently reported in his journal.
However, Abraham did not retreat far; he joined one of Henderson's
work crews in Powell Valley and helped clear the way of the trail;[16]
then he followed on in to Boonesborough, in time to help Calk survey
the town, and to plant corn.[17]

---

[13]
  A true copy of William Calk's Journal may be had in the
Mississippi Valley Historical Review; Vol. 7, No. 4, March 1921.

[14]
References: Kentucky Papers; Wis. His. Soc.
             Philip Drake, p. 482; Enock. Smith, p. 495;
             Whitledge, p. 456.

[15]
  Pusey; The Wilderness Road To Kentucky; Kincaid, The Wilderness Road.

[16]
  John Floyd, to William Preston; April 21, 1775. Ky. Papers.

[17]
  A plat of Boonesborough, and surveying instruments are in
possession of Mrs. Charles Harrmann, Mt. Sterling, Kentucky.

"ABraham hanks,"as he wrote his name with the Big A, and B, and
the little h, signed as a witness to a note given by John Coppage
of Fauquier County, Virginia, to William Calk, and in amount of
"Twenty eight shillings & Six Pense." This was on June 1st, 1775,
and at Boonesborough. It is noted that Coppage was from that part
of Virginia whence came Calk's party. Coppage probably remained in
Kentucky.[18]

In the days when signed their names by mark, the more careful
clerks at the courthouses, when important papers were recorded, such
as deeds, tried to make a facsimile of the signers mark. Abraham Hanks
did not sign by mark--he could write his name, and did with a unique
signature.

So it was, that when Calk and Abraham returned to Virginia,
in the fall of 1775, and Abraham was, with two other men, witness to
an Indenture, whereby one Andrew Brown indentured himself to Calk,
and the paper was brought before the Court for proof and recording, a
meticulous clerk copied Abraham's signature exactly as he wrote it,
with the characteristic 'A' and the minor 'h' on hanks.[19]

"ABraham hanks" spelled his name the same way, with the capitals
AB and the small h, two years later on a bond he gave William Calk,
February 10, 1777, and for ₤68. It[20]has been conjectured that this
was for the purchase of land on Slate Creek, in now Montgomery County,
where Calk had acquired a large acreage. This bond had a payment made
on it; but it has not yet been completely liquidated, and is still in
the hands of the Calk heirs![21]

There is no further account of Abraham in Kentucky. His name
subsequently appears on the Tax list of Prince William County, Virginia,
for the year 1782. His name is not on the 1783 list, nor thereafter.
It is presumed that Abraham Hanks moved with his family to Campbell
County, Virginia, before 1784, in accordance with the tradition that
he was there then.[22]

---

[18] Coppage memo; Kentucky Papers, p. 33.

[19] Deed Book No. 7, p. 103, Prince William Co., Va. Courthouse.

[20] Harrman to Baber, October 9, 1949.

[21] Photostat; Kentucky University.

[22] Campbell Chronicles by Early, Chapter XIV, p. 422.

The tradition is further that he died there in the early 1790's, and is buried in the Hanks plot of the Hatt Creek Cemetery. Since his wife was a Harper, and is presumed to have died also in the late 1780's, in accordance with a tradition in Edgar County, Illinois,[23] it is more reasonable to assume that he is buried in an old Harper Graveyard on land near the Hankses of Campbell County.[24]

Later entries of the name, Abraham Hanks, in the Montgomery County, Kentucky, courthouse records of about 1800 are probably those of the son, Abraham (Jr.), who is known to have been there with two of his brothers, Fielding and George. In fact, when Fielding Hanks died, the statement was made for Vital Statistics, that his parents were Abraham and Sarah Harper Hanks.[25] This record is priceless and is the last known record of Abraham Hanks to have been made in Kentucky.

Peter Harper, a kinsman of Sarah Harper, made a will in 1785, in Prince William County, Virginia; he named only his mother, Betty, as legatee, which gives no clue.[26]

The foregoing comprises a meagre record of the Abraham Hanks, who qualifies as the only Hanks man who could have been the father of Nancy Hanks Lincoln. The Courthouse records of Fauquier and Prince William Counties, Virginia; the Calk papers; the Vital Statistics; and a Hanks family chart, all prove that such a man existed, and was living, at the precise time of the birth of Nancy, at the identical place where there is a strong tradition that an Abraham Hanks was the father of Nancy Lincoln, as he was, indeed. Of this singular man, yet more hereafter.[27]

---

[23] Steube to Baber, Interview at Danville, Illinois, January 21, 1949, Baber papers.

[24] Harper Graveyard is about 2 miles Southeast of Hatt Creek cemetery; and about ¼ acre in area. Faucett to Baber, September 14, 1955, Baber papers. "The Harper graveyard is about two miles from Hatt Creek, in a southwardly direction. It has been used continuously and the last interment was in 1925." Photos of Harper gravestones by Baber, Baber papers.

[25] Fielding Hanks; D. Aug. 13, 1861; Vital Statistics of Kentucky.

[26] Will Book B, p. 66; Fayette County, Kentucky, Courthouse.

[27] Ancestral Quest of this manuscript.

CHAPTER X

SARAH HARPER

Whereas, Abraham Hanks was the father of Nancy Hanks Lincoln, it follows that the wife he had in 1784 was the mother, and no other. By the Vital Statistics of Kentucky, Fielding Hanks, a son of Abraham was born in 1783 (although a census calculation makes it 1785) of a mother, Sarah; by family knowledge of descendants of Abraham's daughter, Sarah,[1] who was born in about 1788, her mother was Sarah Harper. The obvious conclusion is, with lack of any other marriage record, that the wife of Abraham in 1784 was Sarah Harper, and Sarah Harper Hanks is nominated to be and was the mother of Nancy Hanks Lincoln.

A certain Lucey Hanks has not been identified as the first or second wife of Abraham Hanks. There was a Lucy Jennings married an Abraham Hanks, but he was another Abraham, and the wedding occured in 1799. There was a Lucy or Lucretia Hargrave married Thomas Hanks, but that was in North Carolina and took place in 1788. Lucy M. Mitchell married George Hanks in Kentucky in 1791. Sarah Harper is the only woman who can qualify as the wife of Abraham Hanks in 1784 and the mother of Nancy Hanks Lincoln.

She, probably, was the sister of Peter and Isaac Harper of Prince William County, Virginia; probably John, Thomas, Charles and Nicholas Harper were her brothers or half-brothers. It is proved by various courthouse records that the parents of Peter and Isaac Harper were George and Elizabeth Harper. Fielding and his brother, George Hanks, both married daughters of John Harper, supposedly their cousins or half-cousins, so it would follow that John and his brothers were children of George also; but the evidence is not so clear. What is clear and of record, all these Harpers were associated together at Ft. Boonesborough, Kentucky, and fought in the Indian warfare.

It is of record that John and Peter Harper, were with Daniel Boone at Boonesborough, the Spring of 1775, and, with others, signed the rules adopted by the settlers for raising a crop of corn.[2]

---

[1] Mrs. Steube, Danville, Illinois to Baber. Baber papers.

[2] Draper papers 29, c.c. 59

In fact, Nicholas Harper was killed at the Battle of Blue Licks, August 19, 1782, with some sixty-five others.

In 1787, John Harper received a Military Certificate for his service in an expedition against the Wabash Indians, as also did his son-in-law, Fielding Hanks, the son of Sarah Harper Hanks. They were, also, in the War of 1812.

These Harper brothers and their kinsman later resided on Slate Creek at or near Harper's Station. The Draper papers locate Harper's Station as "3 miles southeast of Mount Sterling. On a Cross road that runs from the Spencer to the Mud Lick Road. Both these roads lead from Mount Sterling to the Olympian Springs--and this cross road is on the ridge that lies between them."

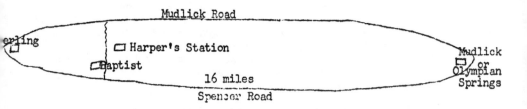

Peter Harper had 400 acres there, near the lands of Peter Hanks and his sons; and sons of Abraham Hanks. Old deed records describe boundary lines between their farms.[3]

Morgan County, Kentucky was created from Bath and Floyd Counties in 1822; and Bath had been part of Montgomery. Olympian Springs is now in Bath County. When Thomas Harper died, his residence was in Morgan County. A sale of his personal property was held at his late residence, and only his kinsmen bid and bought.[4]

---

[3] Courthouse records, Montgomery County, Kentucky.

[4] Will Book, D., p. 256, Montgomery County, Kentucky, Courthouse.

Fielding Hanks, a nephew of Thomas, purchased twenty articles including a Bible. William Hanks, a grandson of Sarah Harper Hanks, and who had not been married long, bought a smoothing iron, for his wife; a parcell of upper leather, sweat pad and an iron drag.

William O'Hair, whose sister Mary "Polly" who had married the aforesaid William Hanks, made purchases, as did Jesse Ogden, another brother-in-law of O'Hair and William Hanks. Another buyer, James Miller, who could have been he who married into the O'Hair family; but he is more likely to have been another James Miller, who had married Sibby Harper Hanks, a widow of George Hanks, deceased, 1814.

William Calk had spied out much fertile land on Hinkston, Stoner, and Slate Creeks; and had located a never failing spring. In June, 1779 John Harper helped Calk erect a cabin at the spring. This is near present Mt. Sterling. Calk at one time had claims of 58,000 acres of land, and in a suit to protect title John Harper made a deposition to help Calk keep his land.

Some of this land, on Slate Creek, was acquired by the Harper and the Hanks men. Peter Harper had 400 acres.

When John Harper died, his Will, February 4, 1838,[5] read, "Whereas, John Harper has eight children..." He named Lydia, wife of Fielding Hanks, and Sibby's son, Stephen England by her first husband, George.

Peter Harper had died much earlier than the others. It is not known if he were older or anticipated death; his will was made, 1785. It would seem he wrote it preparatory to leaving Prince William County, for the far west--then it was probated in Fayette County, Kentucky.[6]

_____

[5] Deed Book 18, p. 293

[6] Book B, p. 66, Fayette County, Kentucky, Courthouse.

"I do will unto my mother, Betty Harper the half of my lands
after my deceas and if I _died_ without heir, then she is to have all
I possess, but if I have any heir than the whole is to be left to my
heir after my mothers _desceas_ this I acknowledge to be my hand and
seal this 10th day of October, 1785."

Signed
Peter Harper

Witness
    Isaac Harper
    Sarah Harper X
              her
              mark

> Fayette County, March Court, 1790
> This Will was produced in Court, proven by Oathes
> of Sarah Harper a subscribing witness thereto and
> ordered to_be recorded.
>
> Teste-Thomas Arnold, D.C.F.C.

Another legal item of interest is in the record[7] at the
Montgomery County Courthouse between Elijah Green of County of Prince
William in Virginia and Rachel his wife (formerly Rachel Harper)
daughter of George Harper and sister to Pater Harper, now deceased,
of one part and Charles White of County of Montgomery, State of
Kentucky of the other part.

> "Whereas, Peter Harper hath departed this life
> possessed of a tract of land in the county and
> state last mentioned containing 400 acres, grant-
> ed to said Peter Harper by the Government of
> Virginia X Treasury Preemption Warrant No. 139
> issued 16th of March 1780 X on waters of Slate
> Creek X consideration £ 40 current money of Virginia.

his
Elijah X   Green
mark
her
Rachel X   Green"
mark

---

[7] Deed Book 3, p. 13

Later, it seems there was some question about the title to
the land, and a writ was sent by Levi Todd, clerk of the County Court
of Fayette County to Thomas Ferguson, Justice of the Peace of the
County of Randolph in the Illinois territory, requesting him to take
deposition and examination of Isaac Harper as a witness to the Will of
Pete Harper, deceased...and "send to our said court for record."

"This 14th day of July, 1806."

It is from this procedure that much information was gained:

> "This day came Isaac Harper personally" saith
> "That in Prince William County, Virginia that he
> was present and saw his brother Peter Harper write
> and sign a will to his mother and he the said Isaac
> Harper was one of the subscribing witnesses with
> Sarah Harper to the said Will."[8]

This brings up a question: Who was the Sarah Harper, who
signed as witness to the Will? Why was her oath sufficient? Was
she a sister of Peter and Isaac? Certainly, she was of the family.

If she were the Sarah Harper who married Abraham Hanks, then
she was not the mother of a Nancy born February 5, 1784, being then
unmarried; but, she could have been the wife of Abraham after September
10, 1785, and become the mother of Sarah Hanks Varvell, who died 1876
"aged about ninety."

On the other hand: The mother of Sarah Varvel is supposed
to have died at the birth of a child or shortly thereafter, and
probably in Campbell County, Virginia.

From this meagre evidence it would seem there were other
Sarah Harpers, and more information is needed, to develop the Harper
family relationships.

---

[8]Book B, p. 66, Fayette County Courthouse at Lexington, Kentucky.

The thought occurs: If Sarah was not the mother of Nancy
Hanks Lincoln, would Nancy have named her daughter "Sarah"[9] for a
step-mother? We doubt it.

HARPER FAMILY (TENTATIVE)

GEORGE HARPER AND WIFE, ELIZABETH---"BETTY"

(George named as the
father of Peter and
Rachel in Deed Book
3, p. 13, Montgomery
County, Kentucky Courthouse.)

("Betty" named as mother
of Peter in his will, 1785,
Book B, p. 66 in Fayette
County, Kentucky, courthouse.)

Peter, b.
d. after 1785,before 1790
Isaac, later resic `. in Randolph County, Illinois
Rachel, married Elijah Green, resided in Prince William
County, Virginia
Sarah, married Abraham Hanks, and died in Campbell County,
Virginia, about 1790-92.

If John and Peter were brothers, then it follows:

John m. Mary Ann — eight children
daughter Lydia m. Fielding Hanks
daughter Sibby m. George Hanks

Thomas
d.
Charles

Nicholas - killed at Battle Blue Licks

The sworn statement of Isaac Harper, made in Randolph County
in the Territory of Illinois affirming that he was present in Prince
William County, Virginia and saw his brother, Peter Harper, write and
sign a Will to his mother, almost certainly places the Harper family,
and Sarah Harper as residents of Prince William County, Virginia, prior
to their migration to Kentucky.[10]

---

[9] Sarah Lincoln, born February 10, 1807.

[10] Courthouse records place George Harper in Prince William County,Va

Prince William County is adjacent to Loudoun and Fauquier Counties, the locale of the Hankses and the home of Abraham Hanks, when he was a young man. It is entirely consistent that he met and married his wife there.

The precedent assumption, based upon the tradition in the Vawter family, that Nancy's mother was of Shipley descent, and more specifically: from the sworn statement of Squire Robert Mitchell Thompson[11] that the mother of Nancy Hanks Lincoln was the daughter of a Shipley woman, it would indicate that Elizabeth Harper, wife of George Harper, was born, Elizabeth Shipley, of whom more in the chapter on the Shipley family of Maryland.

This Harper family of the Northern Neck seems to have lived originally in Richmond County; about the earliest record of them there is of Abraham Harper, born December 21, 1708. A later record is of his marriage to Cathrine Carroll, January 8, 1729/30.

In the next generation, the records indicate w William Harper, but he would not have been a son of Abraham. He was inclined to get into "hot water" occasionly and would be summoned before the Court for appropriate penalties, which put his name on record in the Order Books.

When he died his will was brought into Court, June 1, 1761, accepted and properly probated. His wife was Elizabeth, to whom he left his estate for her life; also, made her an executrix with his son, Joshua, who received a bequest. Other children were: Mary, who had married a Caventer, Susannah and Hannah Harper, and sons, William, Daniel, Wilmouth and George Harper.

Some of this family is supposed by this researcher to have moved to Prince William County; at least, the same names are found there. Elizabeth married a Canterbury; she went there; she and George Harper had business connections. This George Harper had a wife, Elizabeth, and is thought to be the same George Harper, who was the father of Sarah Harper, who married Abraham Hanks.[12]

---

[11] Confer Chapter V, xi, Kith and Kin.

[12] This researcher has not done a thorough examination along this line; but sufficient for a "working theory". It is to be hoped that more will be accomplished as this is by no means a definitive work.

159

CHAPTER XI

CONFIRMATIONS OF FAMILY TRADITIONS

Notwithstanding the lack of documentary and direct evidence
to prove that Abraham and Sarah Harper Hanks were the parents of Nancy
Hanks Lincoln it is submitted: that from a preponderance of indirect
and from circumstantial evidence; from presumptive and from associated
evidence; there should be no doubt that they were the parents.

It is further submitted that most all the phases of the many
family traditions are confirmed and sustained by courthouse records;
family relationships, as alleged by the immediate family traditions
are verified and proven, even unto the relationship of Dennis Hanks
and his cousin, John Hanks, to Nancy Hanks Lincoln.

Lincoln said of John Hanks, "...who engineers the rail enter-
prize at Decatur...(he is) first cousin to Abraham's mother." John
Hanks' father, William, was a son of Joseph Hanks of Nelson County,
Kentucky; Lincoln's mother, Nancy, was the daughter of Abraham Hanks,
who was a brother of Joseph. Thus, William was Nancy's first cousin,
while his son, John, the Rail-splitter, was Nancy's first cousin, once
removed. Lincoln used the old method of reckoning relationships; he
knew that John and Nancy were "close kin" though not brother and sister,
so he called them first cousins, which kept them within the bounds of
close kinship. No doubt, he thought of John as his second cousin which
is exactly what they were - that is, children of first cousins.

Dennis Hanks, the illegitimate son of Charles Friend and Nancy
Hanks (daughter of Joseph Hanks of Nelson County and she,who became
Mrs. Levi Hall in 1801), was also a second cousin to Lincoln. This is
exactly the degree of relationship that Harriett Chapman, a daughter of
Dennis Hanks and recognized as an intelligent woman, made affidavit.
(she) "...the affiant further states that she is related to Abraham
Lincoln this way: that her father (Dennis Hanks) was a second cousin
to Abraham Lincoln."[1] Dennis Hanks and John Hanks, the rail-splitter,
were first cousins. Harriett could have as well said of John, "He,
(like Dennis) was a second cousin of Abraham Lincoln." This relationship would have placed him, as he was, the first cousin once removed of
Abraham's mother.

This relationship was, also, confirmed by Harriett's sister,
Sarah Jane Dowling in her conversation with Mrs. Eleanor Atkinson at
the occasion of her interview with Dennis Hanks in 1889. Mrs. Dowling
said, "...and we called him Uncle Abe, though he was only father's
(Dennis's) second cousin."

------

[1]Harriett Hanks Chapman, Charleston, Illinois. Affidavit pertaining to the Lincoln Way, etc., November 2, 1912.

When Congressman Orr remarked that Lincoln looked like some Hanks men whom he knew in South Carolina, Lincoln replied, "We may be of kin, my mother was a Nancy Hanks." Nancy's father, Abraham Hanks, and Luke Hanks, Sr., father of the South Carolina Hanks men, were brothers. Luke Hanks, Jr., born 1774, and Nancy Hanks Lincoln, born 1784, were first cousins. Lincoln himself, was a first cousin, once removed of Luke Hanks, Jr., and second cousin of Luke Hanks III and his eight brothers and their sister, Rachel. It is universally recognized that family characteristics continue to crop out in succeeding generations, so no doubt Orr was correct in his observation.

The twin daughters of William Hanks of Bedford County, Pennsylvania were, through intermarriage between their respective Akers and Lodge descendants, both grandmothers of William Jacob Lodge (1832-1905), the eminant physician, a Lodge family historian. From 1880 until the time of his death, Dr. Lodge spent a great deal of time collecting family records and, while from them, he never quite convinced himself that the Bedford County Hanks family was closely related to Lincoln, he left just such records as to have enabled modern researchers to determine several new relationships and to confirm that his Hanks family is kin to the other Southern Hanks families.

Descendants of the Ohio family of Thomas Hanks, who is said to have been a son of Joseph Hanks, state that their ancestor and Lincoln's grandfather were brothers. This tends to confirm that Joseph and Abraham were brothers, as is the tradition elsewhere.

There is no reason, whatsoever, to doubt the tradition in Campbell County, Virginia, that Nancy Hanks Lincoln was the daughter of an Abraham Hanks and was born in that county and in the Hatt Creek community and that her parents are buried in a local graveyard, probably at Hatt Creek or in the nearby Harper graveyard.

The tradition of the Edgar County, Illinois Hanks family that Nancy had brothers and sisters seems to be confirmed by the proved fact that Abraham and Sarah Harper Hanks had a family of eight children, five sons and three daughters, including a Nancy.

The testimony of Dr. Arthur E. Morgan that Dr. James LaGrand of Arkansas was a truthful man is seconded by the finding of many courthouse records that verify LeGrand's statements.

Dr. LeGrand's statement that names Samuel Hanks as one in the list of the children of Polly Hanks is proved by the locating of the descendants of Samuel in Macon County, Missouri, and their own knowledge of their descent from a Polly Hanks through Samuel.

There is no conflict whatever between these long established
traditions and the proved family relationships. These traditions
collected over a period of nearly eighty years and slowly and laboriously
proven one after another and by one searcher after another by evidence
from original source records of the counties of Maryland, Virginia,
North Carolina, Tennessee, Kentucky, Indiana, Illinois, Missouri, and
Arkansas --- these traditions, now stripped down to facts, confirm
the ancestry of Nancy Hanks, the mother of Lincoln.

Nancy Hanks, mother of Lincoln, was born in Virginia,"...was
of a family of the name of Hanks," was left an orphan, removed to
North Carolina, lived in the Richard Hanks home there, went to Kentucky
with some of her relations, lived with the Berry families, and
married Tom Lincoln.

Paraphrasing what Lincoln said in his "House Divided" speech
to fit the House of Hanks, is: "...we cannot exactly know that all
these exact adaptations are the result of...but when we see a lot of
framed timbers, different portions of which we know have been gotten
out at different times and places and by different workmen...and when
we see these timbers joined together, and see they exactly make the
frame of a house or mill, all the tenons and mortises exactly fitting...
in such a case we find it impossible not to believe."[2]

---

[2] Speech at Springfield, Illinois, June 16, 1858.

CHAPTER XII

CHILDREN OF ABRAHAM AND SARAH HARPER HANKS

For a complete and verified correct list of the children of
Abraham and Sarah Harper Hanks, including their Nancy, no authority
has been found, except secondary and associate records. If this
couple made a Bible record of their marriage and the births of their
children, it has not been seen recently enough to be recollected by
descendants now living; although, it may have been the old Hanks Bible
that is known to have burned in a cabin fire in Breckenridge County,
Kentucky, many years ago.[1] No will has been found nor record of a
Probate proceeding in which children are named, nor a quit-claim deed
to which brothers and sisters, together with wives and husbands, would
ordinarily subscribe, in the settlement of an estate.

Since Abraham died at middle age, and had been more or less a
wanderer, at least moved a few times, and is reported to have been a
soldier in the Revolutionary War, and would have lacked opportunity
to accumulate, and was probably a blacksmith and iron monger, it is
doubtful he had much property to be administered. Certainly, there
was not enough to support the children and to have a guardian appointed
for them, -- they had to be "farmed out."

Because this paucity exists, and in order to substitute other
evidence, present descendants of Abraham have been located and, from
them and their sources, gathered from each a partial list of the
children of Abraham, in an attempt to piece out the whole list. However,
there are many traditions, previously presented, of the family relationships, - surely one can be depended upon to know his own first cousins,
especially so, if he has never fallen victim to the power of suggestion,
exercised by a would-be genealogist, with "pet theories" to exercise
and prove. These family traditions, carefully collected from different
sources, and studied; associate records, such as vital statistics,
order books, diaries, historic collections of pioneers' memories;
usually associate records, to support and confirm the family relationships, will answer the question.

Sons and daughters of this couple immigrated to Kentucky, where
they lived apart and reared families; but seem to have visited back
and forth and maintained family contacts for a time.[2] From this circumstance there was retained in the memories of the grandchildren of

[1]Mrs. Fife, Interview, Stephensport, Kentucky. Baber Papers.

[2]"Cud" Hanks from Kentucky visited his aunt Sarah and his cousin,
William in Illinois in the 1850's, as was recollected by Mary Ellen Hanks.
A.J. Hanks corresponded in the 1860's; so did John Berry. Baber papers.

Abraham, and passed down, the name of their own Hanks parent, of course, and names of aunts and uncles and cousins. These incidents of family histories now connect the divergent family groups. These groups have been apart and isolated since their respective forebears emigrated from Kentucky over a hundred years ago. These some six or seven groups of Hankses have had no connections or contacts or correspondence with each other since then, until visited and interviewed by this researcher for this purpose. The evidence as adduced will be presented in about the order it was received from the respective source.

In the locale of one of the earlist Hanks settlements of Kentucky, in present Montgomery County and the counties formed from it, Morgan, Wolfe and Powell, are many Hanks and cognate families. From these may be had the name of their Kentucky ancestor, Fielding,[3] and the names of a brother and sister. The brother was George and the sister was Nancy. George has records in the courthouse; and the record of Nancy is the tradition that "She went south." From another source it was learned that the parents of Fielding were Abraham Hanks and Sarah Harper.[4] A more specific information was given to Mrs. Hitc-cock by a granddaughter of Fielding, and who wrote, "...that Fielden Hanks had a sister Nancy and a brother George..."[5]

One of the two sons of George Hanks, who was Stephen England, moved to Putnam County, Indiana, and left descendants there, who were able to name their Kentucky ancestor, George, and in addition they name Fielding and Nancy as brother and sister to their George.[6] Stephen England was born in 1813 and, while he could not have had information from his father, George, who died when Stephen was a child, certainly he had known his father's people in Kentucky, for he did not go to Indiana until 1851,[7] and was accompanied by his mother, who had been born Sibby Harper, the daughter of John Harper. John Harper,

---

[3] Fielding's name was given by Mrs. Mida Wyant, Campton, Kentucky, who also named Nancy as a sister of Fielding.

[4] Mrs. W. E. Bach, Lexington, Kentucky, quotes V.S. at Frankfort to prove that Abraham and Sarah Harper Hanks were parents of her ancestor, Fielding.

[5] Miss Dora Hanks, Campton, Kentucky, to Hitchcock, November 20, 1899.

[6] George's name was given by Mrs. Roy Hanks, Bainbridge, Indiana. That he was a son of Abraham comes from the fact he was known to be a brother of Fielding. They married sisters. After the death of George, 1813, Fielding attended the sale of the estate and bid in many items.

[7] Adin B. Hanks, interview, August 25, 1957. Adin is an old man and new personally his grandfather, Stephen E. Hanks.

probably was a brother-in-law of Abraham Hanks.

The other son of George Hanks, Fielding II, named for his uncle, of course, went to Pike County, Illinois, and reared a family there, and left descendants. One of his grandsons, Stephen Hanks of Brookfield, Missouri,[8] stated that when young he was associated with his grandfather quite a bit and he well recollected of often hearing his grandfather tell of never knowing his own father, George, who had died, but that he well knew his uncle Fielding and all of Fielding's family; and knew that his father, George, had had the sister, Nancy, and later in life, he learned that she was the one who married Tom Lincoln. He knew that he and Abe Lincoln were first cousins. The epitaph on the tombstone of Fielding II, at Milton, Illinois, gives his birth as 1812 and his death as 1890, so he was born early enough and lived long enough to know of his own knowledge, and to pass it on. His grandson, Stephen Hanks, bore a reputation for truth and veracity.

Edgar County, Illinois descendants of William Hanks, who came to the state in 1830, and was a grandson of Abraham and Sarah, are able to name the mother of William as Sarah ("Granny Sallie" Varvell), and name her sisters as Polly and Nancy; and her brother as Fielding. When Mrs. Hitchcock was gathering Hanks family information in the 1890's, one of William Hanks' daughters, Caroline Hanks Sizemore, wrote, "...My great grandfather on my father's side was Abraham Hanks, his wife's maiden name was Sarah Harper, both natives of Virginia..."[9] Another daughter, Nancy Jane Hanks Swango stated, in 1919, that her father had had the two aunts, Nancy and Polly.[10] Thus, is had two more names.

The Hanks families and their kinfolks of other surnames presently residing in Breckenridge County, Kentucky and elsewhere,[11]

---

[8]Stephen Hanks, interview, August 17, 1950. Baber papers.

[9] Caroline Hanks Sizemore to Hitchcock, 1895; F.G. Hanks to Hitchcock, September 15, 1894. Hitchcock papers, Lincoln Library, Fort Wayne, Indiana.

[10] Baber papers.

[11] Information is from Mrs. C.R. Galloway, Henderson, Kentucky; Mrs. Emma Weinenburg, Cloverport, Kentucky; Mrs. Valera Leadley, Chicago; and letters from James Hanks, Tobasco, Ohio.

know themselves to be descendants of William Hanks of Hardin County, and who later moved to Dorrett's Creek north of present Hardinsburg. They all know that William had a brother, Luke and a sister, Nancy. One of them knew that William had a brother Abraham in Hardin County.[12] William Hanks had a son, William, who was born in 1804 and lived until 1900. In later life he lived at Stephensport and was known to be a very bright and keen old man. (Mrs. Hitchcock interviewed him but got his father confused with a William of Joseph) No doubt, this man who lived almost the entire nineteenth century knew much family information which he gave to his children and grandchildren. Thus, are added the names William, Luke, Abraham, and Nancy.

Descendants of Luke Hanks seem to have held themselves apart from other Hanks families but they know their kinfolk and are able to name their Kentucky ancestor as Luke and say that he was born in 1771 in Virginia; resided in Eastern Tennessee and came to Kentucky to join his brother, William in Breckenridge County.[13] In addition, they know from John Wesley Hanks, a son of Luke, and who survived until 1891, that Luke Hanks had the sister, Nancy. Also, from James Taylor Hanks, a grandson of Luke, and who was born in 1844, came information to the same effect.[14] Luke died in the 1850's and is buried at Union Star Cemetery, Breckenridge County, Kentucky.

Among the early settlers of Edgar County, Illinois, were Polly Hanks and some of her children from Montgomery County, Kentucky.[15] She was the widow of Abraham Hanks, Jr., and there was such a disparity in the ages of their children that it is hard to know them from grandchildren. One of her daughters or granddaughter was Sarah Ann Hanks, who married William Guyman in 1834 and the couple then moved to Hancock County. They were followed by Andrew Jackson Hanks, her brother or uncle who took the name of Ringo. Polly Hanks, the widow, married Cornelious Ringo, and moved to Clark County.

[12]James Hanks to Galloway, January 22, 1930.

[13]Miss Ada Hanks, interview, Louisville, Kentucky, November 19, 1949. Baber Papers.

[14]That William was a son of Abraham was well known for in 1895 the Rev. Jno. Hanks of Ladora, Ia. wrote to Mrs. Hitchcock. "The Revolutionary Soldier was named Abraham Hanks. His sons were Luke, John and William. He also had a daughter, who was the mother of Abraham Lincoln." Hitchcock papers, Lincoln Library, Fort Wayne, Indiana.

[15]Entry Book, Edgar County, Illinois, Courthouse; Montgomery County, Kentucky census 1810, 1820.

Over a hundred years later, when contact was made with their descendants, one wrote, "They came from Paris (Illinois) locality. ...I have always felt she (Sarah Ann) was a relative of Lincoln's mother."[16] While this is not a direct and positive statement it does indicate that a tradition existed, probably about as much as could be expected since Polly was a daughter-in-law of Abraham Hanks, the Senior, and had remarried. As for her first husband it is not known what became of him nor when or where he died.

There are only a few descendants of Polly Hanks in Edgar County, Illinois, and recently the last one bearing the Hanks name died. She was Martha Ann, a maiden lady.[17]

Descendants of another Polly Hanks in Missouri, after called "Sarah" and in Arkansas stated to Dr. Arthur E. Morgan in 1909 that their grandmother, Polly, was a sister to Nancy Hanks Lincoln.[18] This relationship would make Polly a daughter of Abraham Hanks. That it has the color of truth is indicated in an exchange of letters between Sophie Hanks Lynch LeGrand and Dennis Friend Hanks.[19] Also, there is evidence of connection in a letter of Dennis to Lincoln, wherein Dennis reports his correspondence with Sophie and expresses his astonishment that she was not quite sure of her cousin relationship to Lincoln. He even adds a family touch and writes, "Her boys all in the Army, Yunion boys at Knoxburg." (sic)[20] It is further formed as truth by a letter from Samuel Hanks of Macon County, Missouri, in which he states he was a son of Polly Hanks and a cousin of Lincoln.[21] Certainly, cousins ought to know their own cousins! The evidence seems to include Polly as a sister or half-sister of Nancy; so, she was a daughter of Abraham Hanks.

---

[16] Mrs. Sam Faulkner, Carthage, Illinois to Baber, February 23, 1955. Baber letters and papers.

[17] Newspaper clipping, Baber papers.

[18] Dr. Arthur E. Morgan, ATLANTIC MONTHLY, February 1920, p. 208; Wilson, Lincoln Among His Friends, p. 40; Dr. Morgan interviewed, Nov. 17, 1949, Baber papers. Letters, Dr. James LeGrand to Barton, Lincoln Room, Chicago University Library.

[19] Sophie LeGrand to Dennis Hanks, February 21, 1864, Photo-copy, Baber papers.

[20] Dennis Hanks to Lincoln, April 5, 1864; to Sophie LeGrand, February 5, 1889.

[21] Samuel H. Hanks to Hitchcock, March 15, 1898.

These Abraham Hanks family traditions have been garnered from old letters and from new letters and from personal interviews and from casual conversations of his descendants. They have been carefully collected and brought together without bias or preconceived ideas from seven different and widely separated sources and tell the same story, clearly, simply, and precisely. It is submitted that they are in accord and not in conflict. All agree that Nancy Hanks was a sister of their respective ancestor.

From the foregoing information, most of which is confirmed by courthouse records, as will be brought out in the next chapter, it is possible to list the known children of Abraham Hanks.[22]

---

[22] This list differs somewhat but in general coincides agreeably with a list that Mrs. Hitchcock has made in an unpublished manuscript at the Lincoln Foundation Library, Fort Wayne, Indiana. She lists as the daughter of Abraham, the Polly Hanks, who married Richard Rogers, May 24, 1813, at Elizabethtown, Kentucky. She is more likely to be the daughter of Abraham (Jr.) who is reported to have lived in Hardin County.

She lists as the daughter of Abraham, the Nancy Hanks, who married Peter Jones, April 16, 1804, in Henry County, Kentucky. But the mother of this Nancy was Jamima and not Sarah. She is more likely to be the daughter of a John or Jonathan Hanks who resided in Henry County, Kentucky at an early day. As her mother was a widow, and Abner Ford signed the marriage bond, the John Hanks who was taxed in the County in 1807-8-9 probably was her brother. He married Amy Swift, November 21, 1814, and they left descendants in the county.

Mrs. Hitchcock lists this early John Hanks of Henry County, as the father of the older Abraham Hanks but it is an impossibility by chronology. He could have been the son, John, she lists, and whom I have not found but, if so, he would have been older than Abraham (Jr) to have had the daughter, Nancy born and reared in time to marry by 1804, unless both he and she were married at very young ages. It hardly seems probable that Abraham would have named his first son, John unless he, himself, was the son of an unknown John?

It is to be noted there is a gap in the birth dates of his children between the first boys and the next group. This may indicate that Abraham was away at the Revolutionary War, as tradition asserts, according to a History of Kentucky or it could be there were two wives.

NAME	BIRTH	AUTHORITY
Abraham (Jr.)	1769 circa	Estimated from his marriage date and as supposedly oldest child.
Luke	1771	Ada Hanks, a great granddaughter.
William	1772	From 1850 census Breckenridge Co., Kentucky.
George	1782	His first known tax record, 1804.
Fielding	1783	From Vital Statistics, probably furnished by his son, Cuthbert M.
Nancy	1784, Feb. 5	Bible
John	1786	From Hitchcock list but not confirmed. Taxed, 1807.
Sarah	1787-8	From Mrs. Steube, Danville, Illinois, a granddaughter who attended the funeral of Sarah.
Polly	1790-2	Dr. James LeGrand; 1850 census of St. Francois County, Missouri

If it seems strange that the descendants of Abraham and Sarah Hanks are now willing to come forward and admit their kinship to Lincoln let it be known that they have always admitted it but only to the others of the family. The Hankses are a casual people and not prone to assert themselves; for with chagrin at the indignities, that have been intimated by the sensational writers their attitude has been to stand mute; but when they are approached and questioned by a sympathetic examiner, they all tell the same family tradition. All agree that they are descendants from Abraham Hanks. All assert that he had a daughter, Nancy, and that she married Thomas Lincoln.

CHAPTER XIII

SKETCHES OF ABRAHAM HANKS' CHILDREN

Abraham Hanks, Jr. was born circa 1769 and probably in
Fauquier County, Virginia; at least, his father and Luke Hanks were
there a few years later. After his father died in Campbell County,
Abraham seems to have drifted over into Caswell County, North Carolina.
There he was taxed on one horse in 1790; the next year he had two
horses and was assessed on 258 acres of land, but the deed records do
not show his land ownership. The next year he was taxed on only 100
acres. The same year, 1792, he married Mary Combs, on January 12th
and signed his bond with a clear bold hand. Thereafter, he is not
listed on the records of the county.[1]

In Campbell County, Virginia, there are traditions of three
Abraham Hankses, or three phases of one tradition, depending on the
narrator's version: there is an Abraham who died there; an Abrm who
married Lucy Jennings and later went to Tennessee; and an Abraham who
moved with his family to Kentucky sometime in the 1790's.

By August 22, 1800, Abraham Hanks, Jr. was in Montgomery County,
Kentucky, with other Hankses, where he was taxed on a horse.[2] His
name remained on the tax lists following. In 1805 he signed as witness
to a deed when Peter Hanks, Jr. purchased 100 acres of land. By 1806
he was in business and taxed on a tavern license. That same year,
Fielding, his brother, who had reached the age of 21, had his name
added to the Tithe list. The 1810 census does not have his name but,
oddly enough, when Mrs. Hitchcock visited there, many years later, his
name was recollected as a brother of Fielding, as it was told to her.[3]
Perhaps he had removed to Hardin County where a tradition places him,
as reported many years afterward, in a letter by James Hanks of Ohio,
in which he stated, "Abraham Hanks lived in Hardin County...came from

[1] Courthouse records, Caswell County, North Carolina.

[2] Tax lists; also "census" 1800, Clift.

[3] Hitchcock Journal; copy; Baber papers.

Virginia there...Abraham was father's uncle."[4]   The father of James was
William, who was born in 1804, and his father was the older William of
Hardin County.   Therefore, "Father's uncle" was the brother of William
of Hardin County.   In 1813, Polly Hanks in Hardin County, married
Richard Rogers, and she was supposedly Abraham's daughter, but where
was the rest of his family?   Did he leave them in Montgomery County?

In the 1810 census of Montgomery County the name of one Polly
Hanks appears as "Head of Family" with 2 males and 3 females under 10.
If this is the same woman as Polly whose name appears in the 1820 census
with older children; and as Mary in the 1830 census with still older
ones in her family; it is supposed she is the widow of Abraham.   An
Abraham purchased a "chip axe" at the sale of the George Hanks estate
in 1814 and he is unplaced, unless it is Abraham returned; for two more
sons were born to Polly then.

A partial list of her children would include Polly, Thomas
Jefferson, Dulcena, Caroline, Andrew Jackson, and Elza Hanks.   The
widow, Polly, removed to Edgar County, Illinois in 1830 and took up
land.   Some of the children and grandchildren accompanied her.   She
later lived in Clark County with a son for a while; then, probably,
went to Hancock County about 1840 to be with her daughter or granddaughter, Sarah Ann Hanks, who had married William Guymen.

Two of the sons, Thomas Jefferson and Elza, remained in Clark
County, where they are listed in the census of 1850.   The son, Andrew
Jackson, moved to Hancock County, and changed his name from Hanks to
Ringo.   The records of the family of Abraham, Jr. are bbscure.

ii

LUKE HANKS
1771--1855

Luke, a son of Abraham Hanks, was born in 1771 in Greenbrier
County, Virginia, according to a great granddaughter, Ada, who had
the information from her grandfather.   There was no such named county
at that time but the date does fit into a proper sequence of Hanks
children births so it is probably correct; the place of birth being
Virginia, perhaps that part that later became Greenbrier County.

4
   Hanks to Mrs. C. R. Galloway, correspondence, 1930.

Luke resided in North Carolina for a time and where his daughter, Nancy, was born from his first wife. He married, second, Celia and lived in Knox County, Tennessee, where were born Henry, Winifred, and John Wesley. In 1833, he sold his farm;[1] thence, he removed with his family to be near his brother, William, in Breckenridge County, Kentucky. In 1838 he purchased 280 acres of land on Dorret's Creek.

Luke was a wagon maker and farmer, and his daughter, Nancy, married Peter French, a blacksmith, which was perhaps a happy way and arrangement to keep the mechanician business in the family. There is a reference to Luke's family in a History of Kentucky, wherein is mentioned the Revolutionar War service of his father, Abraham.

Luke died about 1855 and is buried in the graveyard at Union Star, Kentucky, with some members of his family alongside.

iii

WILLIAM HANKS

William, son of Abraham Hanks, was born in 1772, according to his age given in the 1850 census of Breckenridge County, Kentucky, where he was then residing with a son-in-law, Absolem Robins. It is probable he was born in Fauquier County, Virginia, at least his father was in that county by 1773; near present New Baltimore.

The first record of William appears in Madison County, Kentucky, when he married Margaret Wilson, December 28, 1797. To them were born Polly, John, William (Jr.), Elizabeth, Margaret and Permelia.

About 1804 he located in then Hardin County, now Hart County, on a farm one mile east of Mumford's Ferry, and on the north bank of Green River. Some time after the 1810 census his wife was drowned in the river.

William married the second time to Elizabeth Loyd, July 9, 1811, and of the same county where he got his first wife. A few years later his son, John, married Elizabeth's sister. To William and Elizabeth, two children were born: James and Jamima.

---

[1]93 3/4 acres to Isaiah Wilson, Deed Book Y, Vol. 1, p. 14, Knox County, Tennessee, courthouse.

Pay attention: This William Hanks, son of Abraham, whose
second wife was Elizabeth, has been much confused with another William
Hanks, his cousin, who was a son of Joseph of Nelson County, and who,
also, had a wife named Elizabeth. Her maiden name was Hall.

William of Abraham later moved westward into Breckenridge
County to settle on Dorrett's Creek, a few miles north of Hardinsburg;
William of Joseph moved westward into Grayson County to settle on
Rough Creek, a few miles south of Hardinsburg. With them, both Williams
took large families of children of about the same ages. Both had sons
named William, John, and James; and both had a daughter Elizabeth.

Them, believe it or not, to further baffle mental separation,
both Williams removed to two Decatur destinations: William of Abraham
went to Decatur County, Indiana; William of Joseph went to Decatur,
Illinois. Both migrations were in the years of the late 1820's.

William of Abraham finally went back to Breckenridge County,
Kentucky, where he died about 1855; William of Joseph lived southwest
of Decatur, Illinois, about six miles, where he died about 1855, and
was buried in the Gouge graveyard.

In 1895, when Mrs. Hitchcock interviewed at Stephensport,
Kentucky, William Hanks, age 90, son of William of Abraham, and spent
a whole day with him, according to her report in an unpublished
manuscript at the Fort Wayne Library, she no doubt got much of this
Hanks information; so much, she got mixed!

iv

GEORGE HANKS

George, the son of Abraham and Sarah Harper Hanks, was born
circa 1782, and probably in Prince William County, Virginia; his
father was taxed there then. The first official record of George
appears in Montgomery County, Kentucky, where he, himself, was taxed
as being over 21 in 1804; on land of 120 acres and 3 horses.

George married Sibby Harper, a daughter of John Harper, and a
sister to Lydia Harper, the wife of his brother, Fielding Hanks. To
them at least three children were born: Fielden & Fidelia, twins,
born January 16, 1812, and Stephen England, born August 27, 1813.

George Hanks died in the Autumn of the year that his son, Stephen England was born, and a sale of his effects was held on January 3rd following. His brother, Fielding, purchased a sorrell horse, and the widow, Sibby, bought a bay mare and colt at thirty-one dollars. Abraham Hanks got a chip axe for two dollars.

The widow, afterwards, married James Miller, and they moved to Putnam County, Indiana, where Stephen England Hanks followed. There he reared a family of seven children; died in 1883, and is buried at Brick Chapel, Putnam County, Indiana.

The other son of George, Fielden, emigrated to Pike County, Illinois, and settled at Milton, where he operated a tanyard and sold leather to the Mormans at Nauvoo. He married Martha A. Bagby, and they had one son, George, who in turn had four sons and no daughters. Fielden and Martha died after 1890, and both are buried in the French cemetery just north of Milton.

The twin, sister of Fielden, Fidelia, married a Mr. McClelland, and they are supposed to have gone to Western Illinois.

FIELDING HANKS

Fielding, son of Abraham and Sarah Harper Hanks, was born in 1783, according to calculations made from Vital Statistics; and 1785 from the census records, and in Virginia, according to the 1850 census report; probably in Campbell County. It is tradition in the family that he later lived in North Carolina. He may have lived with his Uncle, John Harper, for Fielding was an orphan.

He married Lydia Harper, a daughter of John Harper; she was born in the fort at Boonesborough, Kentucky; she was probably his cousin. They reared a large family, the children were, in order of births: Jordan, William, Lucinda, Annie, Cuthbert Million, Andrew Jackson, Nancy, George S., Louisa, and Lydia.

Fielding paid his first taxes in 1806, listed as 'over 21' and in Montgomery County, Kentucky, where he resided on Slate Creek. At that time he owned only a horse; later, he acquired more property. It is from an entry made by Mrs. Hitchcock in her Journal, May 8, 1895, we can know more about Fielding. Some of the personal items read,

"Fielding was a great hand for hunting in the mountains.
   "Fielden had a brother, Abram.
   "Fielden drank himself to death.
   "Fielden died of cancer.

The son of Fielding, who was given the name, Cuthbert Million, had the nick-name "Cud" by which he was known far and wide. He was a successful business operator; organized Wolfe County, Kentucky, and became its first sheriff. He married Millie Ann Garrett, and they had a large family.

vi

JOHN HANKS

Since Mrs. Hitchcock listed a John Hanks as a brother of William and Luke Hanks of Breckenridge County, it is highly probable that she had the information from old Uncle "Billy" Hanks of Stephens-port, Kentucky. He was born in 1804; his information is acceptable, although the relationships of the Hanks people in Henry County are not quite clear. It would seem that there were two families: one of Jonathan Hanks, a son of William the Quaker; the other, John Hanks, a son of Abraham.

The children of Jonathan were probably the ones that Dennis Hanks inquired about in his letter to Charles Friend[1] and the Nancy,[2] the daughter of the widow, Jemima Hanks. All this is discussed in a previous chapter.[3]

John Hanks, the more probable son of Abraham, married, November 21, 1814, to Any or Amy Swift, the daughter of Thomas Swift, and Clarris Swift joined in signing the bond. By census and courthouse records they had five children: Marion, Thomas, Louisa, Elizabeth, and Mary. Amy Hanks seems to have been a widow by 1839. Her son, Marion, who had married Elizabeth Berry, December 6, 1845, died suddenly August 24, 1852, and left one son, William Thomas Hanks. He married Bettie Berry, July 6, 1875, and they had seven children, all daughters but one son, who died in infancy.

---

[1] Dennis Hanks to Friend, March 25, 1866.

[2] Married Peter Jones.

[3] See ante.

Thomas Hanks, son of John and Amy, was born February 27, 1822, and he married Sarah E. Grimes, September 6, 1873; they had Luther and Sudie, who married a McHattan.

Louise Hanks married Will I. Baugh, July 11, 1845; Mary Hanks married David Harris, son of W.J. Harris, October 24, 1849; Elizabeth Hanks, born December 5, 1828, married Thomas Harris, October 16, 1851, and they had seven children, including a Nancy, who died in infancy.

vii

SARAH HANKS

Sarah, daughter of Abraham and Sarah Harper Hanks, died in 1876 in Edgar County, Illinois, and is buried in the Hanks row in the Ogden graveyard, south of Paris, Illinois. According to her descendants she was aged about ninety. In the census of 1850, for Edgar County, her age is put as 50, a palpable error, for her son, William Hanks, was born April 30, 1807, and her daughter, Permelia, was born two years later.

The family tradition is that the mother of Sarah died at childbirth, either at the birth of Sarah or a later baby. It is known that Sarah was an orphan and put out with the Ringo family. That the Ringos were of some connection is evidenced by the fact that Sarah's family and the Ringo family continued to be associated together in Illinois. Sarah was born in Virginia or in North Carolina; she came to Montgomery County, Kentucky, where her two children were born, both surnamed Hanks. The explanation is: she married a Hanks cousin, and his first name was, probably, James; the marriage records of that county were destroyed in a fire at the courthouse that burned a part of the records at the time of a battle during the Civil War when Union soldiers and General John Hunt Morgan's men were engaged. No associate nor secondary clue has been found. Nor, is it known what became of James; he was in the Battle of Tippecanoe and disappeared.

When Mrs. Hitchcock was in Mt. Sterling in 1895 she heard a tradition of a James Hanks, who was a "Mighty Hunter" but whether he hunted before or after the War of 1812 is not known. There is, however, an unburned record at the Montgomery County, Kentucky courthouse which confirms that Sarah did reside in that county, for on June 15, 1814, she transferred the title to her little personal property to her son, William; probably, preparatory to marriage to (2) Andrew Varvell. She and "Old Andy" as one of her granddaughters used to term him, went to

Edgar County, Illinois, and lived on land owned by her son, William
Hanks, who, by then, had married Mary O'Hair of Hazel Green, Kentucky,
and had named his first child, James.

In addition to the census record, it is here again in the
courthouse Deed Books that her name appears, with that of her husband,
Andrew, when they deeded 80 acres of land they had entered from the
Government to her son, William. For many years the couple lived in a
log house about a half mile north of her son's house, and not far from
her daughter, Permelia, who married John Landsaw, and reared a large
family.

In her last years she lived with the daughter, Permelia, and
one of her Landsaw grandsons recollected collecting driftwood from
the nearby creek for them to burn in the fireplace. Sarah outlived
her son, William, by one year, and upon her death was buried the next
grave, but one, south of his grave, leaving a space for Polly Hanks,
the widow of William. These graves, including Permelia's are in the
old Ogden Cemetery.

This is the aunt of Lincoln about whom Herndon queried Dennis,
who denied that Lincoln had an aunt in Edgar County.

viii

POLLY HANKS

Mary or Polly Hanks, an alleged sister or half-sister of
Nancy Hanks Lincoln, and if so, and the evidence is not to the
contrary, was a daughter of Abraham Hanks. If her mother was Sarah
Harper is not indicated, but her grandson, Dr. James E. LeGrand of
Jasper, Arkansas, stated that her mother was Sarah Hanks, and in
answer to a question put to him in a letter by Barton, "What were the
names of the parents of Nancy Hanks Lincoln?" he wrote the answer,
"Sarah Hanks".[1] It is of interest that Polly, after her first child
was born, took the name of Sarah or Sally for herself, although she
had a sister, Sarah Hanks.

The first historical reference to Polly Hanks was written by
Dr. Arthur E. Morgan in the Atlantic Monthly, February 1920; which
article is included in the book by Wilson, Lincoln Among His Friends.

---

[1] LeGrand to Barton, July 31, 1920. Barton papers, Chicago
University.

Dr. Barton makes a reference to Polly or Sarah in his book, The Paternity of Abraham Lincoln (p. 406), but ignores her existance further; although he had carried on a copious correspondence with LeGrand about her.[2]

Polly Hanks was born, according to LeGrand, about 1791 in Virginia; the 1850 census gives her age as 58, making her born in 1792, which is near enough for this purpose. Certainly, she was not born before 1790 which fact becomes pertinent. Dennis Hanks thought that Polly Hanks was a daughter of Lucey Hanks Sparrow, as he wrote in a letter to her daughter, Sophia.[3] But Lucey was married to Henry Sparrow in 1790 and before the birth of Polly; besides her children had the surname of Sparrow. Lucey had a daughter, Polly, but she married Benjamin Whitehouse, July 9, 1808, in Mercer County, and continued to reside there.

Dennis also thought that Lucey Hanks Sparrow had a daughter, Nancy Sparrow, and would include the names of both Nancy and Sally among Lucey's children; but a correct list of the children of Henry and Lucey Hanks Sparrow, as furnished by Amanda Pilcher, their grand-daughter, to Barton,[4] and which list may be confirmed by courthouse records, does not list either a Nancy or Sallie, nor are they mentioned as pre-marriage children. The list of Sparrow children that Dennis made for Herndon does not agree with the list he sent to Sophia, and neither list agrees with the correct list. Dennis told Weik[5] that Nancy was the second child of Lucey Sparrow, thus, inferentially making Polly older than Nancy; but LeGrand definitely stated that Polly was a few years younger than Nancy, which is correct, for Nancy was born, 1784, and there was their sister, Sarah, born between their births. Dennis seems to have been unaware that they had this sister, Sarah, living in Edgar County, Illinois, for he denied to Herndon that Lincoln had an aunt there;[6] although he had stated to Charles Friend that an alleged Aunt, Polly Hanks Friend, had died there.

---

[2] Barton papers

[3] Dennis Hanks to Sophia LeGrand, Feb. 5, 1887. See Appendix.

[4] Statement, Pilcher, August 6, 1922, Barton papers, Chicago Univ.

[5] Interview, Paris, Illinois, March 26, 1885.

[6] Dennis Hanks to Herndon, January 26, 1866.

But Dennis was in full knowledge of the kinship of Nancy and Polly and confirmed the relationship in his correspondence with Sophia Hanks LeGrand[7] and with Lincoln.[8] Dennis thought it "strange" that Sophia did not recognize Lincoln as the cousin she had lived with in the Lincoln home in Indiana. In a later letter to Sophia[9] he reminded her of several incidents that occured when she lived with the Lincolns. This is confirmed by LeGrand who stated that his mother, Sophia, lived with the Lincolns and attended school with Abe, also with Dennis, and it was a long walk to the schoolhouse, about three and a half miles. Sophia was the same age as Abe.

Polly Hanks was living in Hardin County, now Larue County, when her daughter, Sophia, was born, and near the other Hanks families there. There were William and Luke Hanks, both sons of Abraham Hanks; there were William and Joseph Hanks, both sons of Joseph Hanks, Sr.; there was Nancy Hanks Lincoln and Nancy Hanks Hall, cousins, both married. Nearby was the Thomas Sparrow family with the boy, Dennis Hanks. There was a Mary or Polly Hanks, who married Richard Rogers, May 24, 1813, and Mrs. Hitchcock lists her as a daughter of Abraham Hanks, but, if so, she kept her Hanks name. By 1820 Polly Hanks was in Mercer County, in that part that later became Boyle County, and here other children were born to her. They bore the surname of Hanks, same as their mother, but whether they were of whole or half blood is not known.

It is family tradition that Polly Hanks was a character, a woman of forceful character, and her record bears it out. She was a prolific reader of books, especially history, and all subjects she could find in print, and so educated herself. It was a common practice for people to come to hear her read orally; this was one of the forms of entertainment in the early times. She had a good memory for what she read and could recollect most of the dates of historical events. She also taught school for a number of years and in later life when

----

[7]Dennis Hanks to Sophia LeGrand, Feb. 5, 1887.

[8]Dennis Hanks to Lincoln, April 5, 1864.

[9]February 5, 1887

crippled with rheumatism the parents of her pupils would volunteer
to take her to the schoolhouse and back home.

By 1844 most of Polly's children had removed to near Gentryville,
Indiana, so she was fetched there by her son, Samuel. Later, she
removed with her daughter, Sophia and with Sophia's family to St.
Francois County, Missouri. Here, she was living with her daughter,
Margaret in 1850 when the census was taken. She died September 9, 1854,
and is buried about three miles southwest of Bismark, Missouri.

The daughter and first child of Polly Hanks was Sophia, who was
born in Hardin County, Kentucky, March 12, 1809, one month later than
Lincoln was born. She seems to have lived with the Thomas Sparrow
family, or at least went to Indiana with them; later, after their
deaths, she lived for a time in the Thomas Lincoln home. Sophia first
married, June 13, 1827, Dillings Lynch; and second, October 4, 1842,
to John LeGrand, both men of DuBois County, Indiana. The Lynch
children were, as known: Sarah, b. 1833; John, b. 1835; Nancy, b.
1838; and Elizabeth, b. 1839. John LeGrand was a widower with children:
Elizabeth, b. 1828; John, b. 1833; William, b. 1835; Matilda, b. 1837;
and Talitha, b. 1839. After he and Sophia married they had a son,
James LeGrand,[10] who later became a practicing physician, delivered
over thirteen hundred babies, and supplied much of the Polly Hanks
family history to Dr. Morgan. Almost everything that LeGrand related
as pertaining to his family has been verified by this researcher.

Samuel Hanks, a son of Polly, was born in Mercer, now Boyle County,
Kentucky, January 1, 1820. As a young man he went to near Gentryville,
Indiana, where he married Pauline Overstreet, February 8, 1842, to
whom the following children were born: Moses, James W., Silas E.,
Laura Ann, Alice, Amanda, Sarah Rocybelle. In 1844 Samuel went to
Kentucky to fetch his mother to Indiana. Later, he removed his family
to Macon County, Missouri, where he died, August 30, 1898. A descendant
is presently John Al Porter.[11]

Greenberry Hanks, another son, lived in DuBois County, Indiana,
and where he married, and was killed by falling from a shade tree,
which he was trimming at his home at DuBois. There is a record that
he held the office of Justice of the Peace. His wife may have been
named Rebecca for a Rebecca Hanks, widow, married Phillip Sumner in
1844.[12]

---

[10]Census, 1850.

[11]John Al Porter, the grandson of Sara Rocybelle Hanks.

[12]DuBois County, Indiana records.

James Anderson Hanks, another son, also lived in DuBois
County, Indiana and south pf present Holland. He married Nancy
LeGrand, May 17, 1845.[13] They removed to Mississippi, where he
became an officer in the Confederate Army. Before a battle a
commanding officer addressed the men saying that their coming work
would be very easy, as the northern army was made up of flop-eared
Dutchmen who could not fight except by pulling ears. Later James
Anderson addressed his men and told them that he had lived in Indiana
and near the Dutchmen and knew what sort of men they would have to
meet. He predicted that they would have hard work ahead of them to
win. For this so-called insubordination he was court-martialed and
reduced in rank. But, his warning was full-filled. Holland, Indiana
was settled by Germans at an early day; one old cemetery there has
many epitaphs written in the German language. Further of James
Anderson is not known but this researcher corresponded with Mr. L.C.
Hanks of Paducah, Texas, who was a son of LeGrand Gary Hanks, a
probable descendant.[14]

Creed Harris Hanks, a son, married Mary A. Bebee, October 1,
1857, and in DuBois County, Indiana. She was probably the daughter
of Benjamin H. and Nancy Beebe. Creed went to California and became
a cattleman at which business he is said to have prospered and made
a fortune. In 1853 he was back and visited his mother and sisters
in St. Francois County, Missouri. Upon his return to his home he was
not heard from again.

Margaret Hanks, the youngest child of Polly, was born, according to the 1850 census about 1826 and in Indiana; if so, Polly must
have gone to Indiana and returned to Kentucky, to go again to Indiana
at a later date. Margaret married Jackson LeGrand, April 25, 1845, in
DuBois County. They removed to St. Francois County, Missouri, where
Polly Hanks lived with them in 1850. The children of Margaret LeGrand
were, in 1850, Sophia, age 9; Winifre, age 3; and Horace, a baby.[15]
Margaret died September 8, 1877.

---

[13] Ibid.

[14] Baber papers.

[15] 1850 Census.

After consideration of all the evidence at hand it is the opinion of this researcher that Polly Hanks was a sister of Nancy Hanks Lincoln and a daughter of Abraham and Sarah Harper Hanks. From the fact that most of the statements made by Dr. James E. LeGrand have been verified, it is submitted that full faith and credit should be and have been given to them. If Abraham Lincoln was reticent about his Hanks family connections, as Herndon alleged, it may be surmised it was because he had an aunt who continued through life with her maiden name?[16]

---

[16]Dennis Hanks to Lincoln, April 5, 1864. (See Appendix for letter). On March 26, 1885, Jessie W. Weik interviewed Dennis F. Hanks at Paris, Illinois, the copy of which is in the handwriting of Weik, and at the Library of Illinois State Historical Society. It consists of phrases separated with dashes, which seems to indicate each phrase was in answer to a question. Here follows,

"....Lincoln's mother born of a Hanks woman who had come from Va. and in Ky. married a Sparrow – but always bore the Hanks name – had 8 children – Nancy was 2nd child but was called Hanks – was not illegitimate – ..."

It was Lucey Hanks who married a Sparrow.
Whence she came is not known.
She had eight children; none of the eight named Nancy.
She went by the Sparrow name, not Hanks.
The woman, who always bore the Hanks name, was Polly "Sarah" Hanks.
Polly Hanks had two daughters; but neither was named Nancy.
Polly Hanks was the daughter of Abraham Hanks.

CHAPTER XIV

NANCY HANKS LINCOLN

The commonplace, the epic, and the tragic history of the
mother of Lincoln is universally known; little is to be added. She
was born, February 5, 1784, the daughter of Abraham and Sarah Harper
Hanks, in the home of, or on the farm of James Hanks, her kinsman,
and probably her uncle, in Campbell County, Virginia. Her birthdate
fits becomingly into a regular sequence of the births of her brothers
and sisters, some older, some younger, which bracketing gives to her
a positive legitimacy of birth.

****

It is an accepted tradition that Nancy became an orphan early
in life. The dates of the death of her parents are unknown; but if
the Sarah Hanks, who signed as witness to a deed for James Hanks in
1787 was the wife of Abraham, as is supposed, Nancy's mother survived
until past 1790.

****

Nancy, for whom Tom Lincoln,on June 10, 1806, obtained a
license to marry, and did marry June 12; becomes of historic interest
and courthouse records take over; although in the meagre manner and
paucity of detail that is of people without property; dedicated to
labors of service only.

So Tom Lincoln,accompanied by Richard Berry,Junior, rode to
the courthouse of Washington County, Kentucky, to get the license and
arrange for a minister, and not a mere Justice of the Peace, to solemnize
the marriage ceremony. Thomas, of whom his son said, could only
bunglingly write his name, did sign his name in full and not by mark;
Richard Berry, Junior and John H. Parrott signed as bondsman and
witness respectively.

The day after Tom's trip to the courthouse was spent, no doubt,
by the Berry family and all the nearby friends and neighbors in helping
prepare for the wedding and the infare and all the usual festivities

that went with such a pioneer occasion. There was food to be prepared
and plenty of it as has been described by one who was there and from
his long memory described the happy incident many years later.

Came the wedding day and the minister and all the friends and
acquaintances from up and down the valley. Some rode out from the
county seat; even Mr. Parrott, the Clerk of the Court and, probably
the members of the Court for the records show that there was no court
sat on that now historic day.

So, Nancy and Tom were married and, in course of time, when he
got around to do it, the minister, Jesse Head, filed the marriage return,
and with others, "...this 22nd Day of April 1807." This report of the
wedding was belatedly deposited with the clerk after the date of the
first child, a daughter, Sarah, was born to Nancy; but the return
lists the marriages of others both before and after the Lincoln-Hanks
date of marriage, which fact brackets the date of June 12, 1806.

The original return is now properly and carefully preserved
in a glass case upon the wall of the vault of the clerk's office at
the courthouse, where those who wish may loyally read.

Happily and cheerfully, of course, the young couple set up
their house-keeping and in keeping with the social and economic levels
of the time and the settlements. Tom, who had spent the wages of his
recent flat-boat trip to New Orleans for his wedding clothes and other
items, returned to his job as a woodsman and began to learn the carpenter
trade and cabinet making. Nancy took up the usual and ordinary chores
of housekeeping that are never done. the cooking, the cleaning, the
spinning, the weaving, and the gardening. With all of this she took
up the immemorial ritual of the woman who lovingly prepares the swaddling
clothes.

It is true, that in Kentucky, she lived in log houses, and
after her marriage, she lived in log cabins, but what of it? The early
homes in Kentucky were properly built from the material at hand, logs and
clay. The thick log walls, chinked with flitches, and daubed with wet
clay that dried hard, gave protection from possible Indian arrows. Wood
is one of the best insulating materials, a non-conductor of heat and
cold, and a well-built log house is a very comfortable place in which
to live. It is true that a fireplace tends to create a draft, but its
radiant heat warms the fresh air in the room, and its draft draws away
the bad air - certainly an essential condition for health in a crowded
cabin. It is true that some log cabins had earthen floors, and have
been scorned, but the packed clay was dry and warm, and there was no
draft coming up through floor board cracks. Then, too, if the fire

popped out when the family was away, there was slight chance that
the house would burn. As for puncheon floors, which some have dis-
dained, an expert adzer could smooth the surface until a hickory broom
would leave no dust, and after a scrubbing with soft soap and water,
the suds drained away through the cracks, and the white floor was a
pride for the housewife to behold.

As for the supposed hardship of cooking at an open fireplace,
there was none. The habits of the mothers descend to the daughters,
and from all time past, until most recently, cooking was done at the
hearth, each mother teaching each daughter in turn. The simplest
utensils were of the highest utility - a pot, a kettle, a spit and a
spider - with trammel and crane, and a noggin of water, Nancy was
ready to prepare a meal. It was not always a meagre diet of corn-pone
and side meat, as John Hanks described, but had to be more satisfying
for men who worked out in the open at hewing timbers, building mills,
and splitting rails for fences, corn cribs and pig pens.

Nancy put the kettle on with a gourdful of spring water. Then,
in went the beans, green or dry - depending upon the season - then a
piece of meat, a red pepper pod and a dash of salt, and the crane was
swung back over the fire where the contents of the pot could simmer
and bubble into a savory stew by next mealtime.

There was no dearth of crockery and mixing bowls. Into a wooden
bread bowl, put some flour, add the soda, dry - soda made from the special
wood ashes kept for the purpose. Add a smidgen of salt, and a dab of
shortening (butter, if the cows aren't dry) and last, clabber milk or
buttermilk, and stir furiously. When the bubbles appear, spoon the
dabs into the dutch oven and set to bake. Do not put it on the live
coals - the food will burn - set it near and heap the hot ashes over
it, lid, and all around.

After a while, and usually a short while, take up the turkey
wing feathers and brush away the ashes from the lid and peep in. When
nice and brown, set the oven aside until the men folks come to eat.
No, Nancy did not get all hot and bothered at getting a meal, whirring
up a cake, spinning, or weaving. All this she did "with cheerful dis-
position and active habits."[1]

A personal description of Nancy Hanks Lincoln can hardly be
had from the hearsay and divergent descriptions of her. There are
clues, though, to her personality, mental faculties and intelligence.

[1] Vawter, Courier-Journal, Louisville, Kentucky, Feb. 20, 1874.

It may not be quite apt to imagine her as a rude and crude
and illiterate woman brought up on the frontier, for her girlhood
had been in Virginia and North Carolina, in parts long settled and
not on the western fringe where the more boisterous people resided.
Certainly, during her orphanage in the homes of the Berry family,
she was with more prosperous people of culture and refinement.

Herndon may have had a description of her physical appearance
from ones who remembered her in Indiana. He described her as of
above medium stature, but does not say she was tall. In fact, he
reports that she was slenderly built, and of weight about 130 pounds.
She had dark brown hair and gray eyes. Lamon, who may have had his
information from Herndon, put it in this way: she was slender,
symmetrical, and of medium stature, a brunette with dark hair, regular
features and sparkling eyes. John Hanks had noticed her high fore-
head, and remarked about it, but his description varied some from
what others said. He did stress that she was an intellectual woman,
above the ordinary, "rather extra ordinary."

Herndon reported that "Mr. Lincoln, himself, said to me in 1851
on receiving the news of his fathers death... His mother was highly
intellectual by nature,[2] had a strong memory, acute judgment and
was cool and heroic."[3]

About her, Scripps, the reporter, put:

> "Facts in the possession of the writer have impressed
> him with the belief that, altho of but limited education
> she was a woman of great native strength of intellect
> and force of character. She, as well as her husband,
> was a devout member of the Baptist Church. It was her
> custom on the Sabbath, when there was no religious
> worship in the neighborhood - a thing of frequent
> occurrence - to employ a portion of the day in reading
> the scriptures aloud to her family."[4]

This habit of bible reading to the family seems to have been a
practice of other members of the family, of which there have been
several ministers of the gospel.[5] There is one old Hanks bible that
has the margins of the pages literally worn away by thumbing.[6]

---

[2] See appendix for a description of Rosanna Hanks, a cousin of Nancy

[3] Herndon, Herndon's Lincoln, Vol. I, p. 13.

[4] Scripps, Jacobs Peoria Reprint, pp. 11 and 12.

[5] Baber papers.

[6] William Hanks Bible, Paris Illinois, in possession of
Catharine Swiger.

A granddaughter of the one who thumbed his way through the bible, has related it was the grandfather's practice to read aloud. While doing so, he would sit bolt upright in a straight-backed chair, with both feet flat on the floor and the bible on his knees - and woe betide the one who was not attentive - he would rue the omission!

Just so, in this humble home, was inculcated the mighty cadence and the diction of the King James Version to be echoed down the literary corridors of time.

The daughter, the first child, and there is no record what-soever of an earlier child, was born February 10, 1807; was named Sarah for Nancy's mother, Sarah Harper, deceased. So was fulfilled what Lincoln later stated, "I was not born in Elizabethtown but my mother's first child, a daughter, two years older than myself, now long deceased, was."

To Nancy were born two more children, sons, but the third child, named Thomas for his father, died in infancy. In the old Redmon family graveyard, six or seven miles northeast of Hodginville is or was a stone marked T L, which is presumed to be his grave.[7] "He had a sister..., also a brother, younger than himself, who died in infancy."

The second child of Nancy, whose birth is bracketed by the birth of the sister, older, and a brother, younger, was born February 12, 1809. Dennis Hanks, a boy of nine, ran to see, and recollected in his old age that he asked Nancy what she was going to name the baby. She answered, "Abraham, after his grandfather, who came out to Kaintuck with Dan'l Boon."

This second child, of humble and auspicious birth was the grandson of both Abraham Lincoln and of Abraham Hanks. He, it is whom Austin Gollaher quoted, "My name should have been Abraham Abraham."[8]

---

[7] McMurtry, *Lincoln Herald*, 48 (1), 17.

[8] Chapter IX, note 9.

A HANKS GRAVE

A wooded hill - a low sunk grave
    Upon the hilltop hoary;
The Oak tree's branches o'er it waves
Devoid of slab - no record save
    Traditions' Story.

And who the humble dead that here
    So lonely sleeps
And who, as year rolls after year,
In summer green or Autumn sere,
    Comes here and weeps.

           Wm. Q. Corbin.

APPENDIX
FOR
PART I

36   BOONE'S WILDERNESS ROAD

". . . . . A little later in this
narrative we shall read of one "Abraham
Hanks" who went, an unknown pioneer, with
Daniel Boone through Cumberland Gap at the
very van of all western immigration!
Atwater was not referring to his grandson
--the immortal son of Nancy Hanks."*

*Archer Butler Hulbert, HISTORIC HIGHWAYS, p. 36.

TENNESSEE HISTORICAL MAGAZINE, Vol. 5, April, 1919, No. 1.
by
Samuel C. Williams*

Henderson and Company's Purchase in Tennessee   13

........fled ecept Daniel Boone and a party of about fifteen who
stayed to take care of the wounded;....

....A third party under Capt. Hart followed in the wake of   14
Boone towards the promised land, and William Calk, one of the
number, kept a journal. Abraham Hanks, the father of Nancy and
maternal grandfather of President Lincoln, was of this party,
which joined with Henderson's party at the home of Col. Joseph
Martin in Powell's valley in which is Cumberland Gap.

* Nashville, Tennessee, March 9, 1950.

I have just asked Mrs. Embry,** "Was Mr. Sam Williams a careful
writer?"

She answered and said, "Yes, we have confidence in what he wrote,
he was a careful investigator, but, of course, he could make mistakes.
His notes are in the library but not available. They have not been
indexed. Have you ever tried to read his writing? It is, almost,
impossible to decipher some that he wrote towards the last."

**Mrs. Charles Akin Embry, Librarian, TENNESSEE HISTORICAL SOCIETY.

EXCERPTS FROM THE WILLIAM CALK JOURNAL*

1775 March 13th mond I set out (from prince wm.)
to travel to Caintuck on tuesday Night our company all Got
together at Mr. Prises on Rapadan Which was ABraham hanks
philip Drake Enoch Smith Robert Whitledge & my Self....

Satrd 25 ...Eanock ABram & I got lost tuesday...

thursd 30th ...ABrams flask Burst open a walet of corn & lost a
good Deal

mond 3rd (Apr.) ...ABrams saddle turned & the load all
fell in (Indian Creek)....

tuesday 11th ...abrams mair Ran into the River with Her load
and Swam over he followd her and got on her and made her Swim
back again. ...Mr. Drake Bakes Bread woth out Washing his hands...

Wednesday 12th ...We meet another Company going Back they tell Such
news ABram & Drake is afraid to go aney further there we camp this
night --

thursday 13th this morning the weather Seems to Brake & Be fair
ABram & Drake turn back** ...we meet about 20 more turning Back...

        *Excerpts from the Mississippi Valley Historical Review and
checked with the original Journal, now in the possession of Mrs.
Sarah Harmann, Mt. Sterling, Kentucky.

        **ABram and Drake went to work with a labor party in Powell's
Valley. John Floyd to Wm. Preston, April 21, 1775. Kentucky papers
Draper Coll.

THE MISSISSIPPI VALLEY HISTORICAL REVIEW

Vol. VII, No. 4   March, 1921

370 Notes and Documents (Journal of William Calk   371)

..."Abraham Hanks, however, was a greater favorite. Calk refers to him frequently and intimately.

Hanks and Drake had not gone far back over the Wilderness road, after quitting their companions, when they met another band of pioneers going to Kentucky. The two Virginians regained courage, joined this band, and reached Boone's Fort shortly after Colonel Henderson and his followers.

No further mention of Philip Drake is found in the Calk papers. But there are several documents bearing upon Abraham Hanks. He was an uncle of Nancy Hanks, the mother of Abraham Lincoln. "While a well meaning and likeable fellow, no doubt, he appears to have fared badly in Kentucky." His friend William came to his assistance on more than one occasion. Among the Calk papers is a note stating that "I ABraham hanks Am held and firmly Bound unto William Calk in the just and full Sum of Sixty Eight pounds Virginia Currency." On the back of the note is the acknowledgment: "1777 March ye 17th Received of ABraham hanks ten pounds currency in part of the Within Bond." The balance, it seems, remained unpaid, for the note was never surrendered.

THE BOYHOOD OF LINCOLN

by

Elinor Atkinson

page 9

Dennis Friend Hanks, who was interviewed by Elinor Atkinson, was
reported as stating, that Abraham Lincoln was named:

> "...after his grandfather that came
> out to Kentucky with Daniel Boone."

It has been assumed by the writers and even some of the historians
that the statement referred to the president's paternal Grandfather,
Abraham Lincoln. But, Grandfather Abraham Lincoln did not, so far
as is known, come out to Kentucky with Daniel Boone.

While it is probable that he came to Kentucky to spy out the land
and conditions previous to settling there; he did not become a
resident until after 1780. That was the year he sold his farm in
Virginia and began to acquire land in Kentucky.

So,it seems more likely, that Dennis in his statement to Elinor
Atkinson, was repeating a reference that Nancy had made to the
baby boy's Grandfather Hanks and not to Grandfather Lincoln.
Surely, though, she must have remarked the happy incident of two
Grandfather Abrahams.

Brookneal Va.
Dec 12th 1929

Mr. Louis A. Warren
Fort Wayne Indiana

My Dear Mr Warren

        Your letter in regard to the Hanks
family was duly received.
The father of Nancy Hanks was Abraham
Hanks. They moved from this community
some time between 1790 and 1800, and
to Kentucky
The tradition that used to be circulated in
this neighborhood claimed that Nancy
Hanks married a man by the name of
Lincoln, and that she mamed her boy
Abraham after her father.
I dony think that these facts can be
verified by any records or historical
facts,
The grave stone that you photograf d is the
brother of Nancy Hanks and died 1800.
This is all that understood on account of the
ravige of time
The slab covered graves you asked about are
the graves of the Irvins who were among the

first citizens of this community. They came
from Pennsylvania some time about 1738
or 1740.
I will be glad to add any thing I can
to help you solve this matter
        With best wishes I am
        Yours truly
                Wirt Williams

Miss Hilda R. Cabaniss to Mrs. W. E. Bach, Dec. 4, 1949.*

"At my mother's request I am answering your letter of November 22. My mother is 78 years old, and she heard the story from her father. The Hanks family lived about ¼ mile from the Hat Creek church in a little house no longer in existence. They lived in this community only a few years. It is not known where they came from. They moved away when Nancy was 12 years of age, probably to Kentucky. Abraham Hanks, Nancy's brother, is the only one buried at Hat Creek. When the family decided to move away, the father made a tablet of soapstone and carved the child's name, date of birth and death upon it. I went to the cemetery and tried to read the inscription. This is all that I could decipher:

Born Jan, 9, (?) 1800
Died May   1811

The stone had been covered in moss and in removing this, someone had evidentially partially obliterated the letters in the soft soapstone. I shall try to get a snapshot of the tablet and send it to you.

My great grandfather said the Hanks family were very poor, but good people. There are Harpers in this community, but I do not know if any of them married into the Hanks family.

I am sorry I cannot give you more information. My mother is the oldest living member of the Hat Creek church and this is all she knows about the family.

Sincerely yours,
Hilda R. Cabanis
Appomattix, Virginia

*Original letter, Baber papers.

James Hanks to Mrs. C. R. Galloway, Henderson, Ky.

"Tobasco O Clermont Co
Jan 22nd - 1930
Dear Mrs. Galloway   I will try
and do the Best I can in tracing
the Hanks family you wanted
to now wher Uncle John Hanks lived
and died He was Born in Hart Co Ky
He moved from there to Breckenridg Co
while quite a lad they Settled near
Hardinsburg lived there til his death

Abraham Hanks lived in Hardin Co*
Came from Virginia

Abraham was father's uncle...
that is the Best that I can do
hope that will help some

I close
        James & jennie Hanks

*This was Abraham Hanks, Jr., as confirmed
by the next line, and by other evidence.

From her Aunt, E.M.* to Mrs. C. R. Galloway, Henderson, Ky.

                    May 27: 1930 Glendean Ky
                        Dear Grace
                            Recon you think
            by this time that I am awfully Slow about
            answering your letter.

                                    Well Grace
            about the Lincons you Said in your letter that
            If Grandfather Hanks was the William that you
            thought he was he was an uncle of Nancy H.
            It has always been my understanding that our gran
            Father Hanks was Nancy Hanks brother & that was
            why Grandmother Meador & A Lincon were
            first cousins.

            Grandfather Meador was Born in the
            year of 18 hundred In the month of February

                                This William Hanks
            you Speak of Is certainly our Grandfather.
                            Lovingly
                                Aunt E M

        *Aunt E. M. was a descendant of William Hanks through his
    daughter, Elizabeth Hanks, who was born c 1804, and married Juble
    Meador (Meadow) June 10, 1821.

Miss Ada Hanks to Mrs. Caroline Hanks Hitchcock.[*]

Stephensport, Ky.
Oct. 27, 1894

"The information I sent to Rev. John Hanks of Iowa
was obtained from a relative of ours -- William
Hanks by name who is a son of William Hanks the
son of Abraham Hanks, according to his own account.
He is now about 90 years of age. In giving the
names of Abraham Hanks children he mentions the
name of Nancy and said she is the mother of
Abraham Lincoln.

My 21st Birthday "That touch of Nature which
makes us all akin
Breckenridge Co Ky   Ada Hanks

Rev. Jno. Hanks to Mrs. Caroline Hanks Hitchcock.[*]

Ladora Iowa Co Ia

"The Rev soldier was named
Abraham Hanks. His sons
were Luke John & William
He also had a daughter
who was the mother of
Abraham Lincoln. The
three sons Luke to Tenn
Wm. to Ky John to Ky
who settled in Henry Co
near New Castle.
                Rev. Jno. Hanks

[*]Original letters are in the Library of the Lincoln National
Life Insurance Company, Fort Wayne, Indiana, in the Hitchcock papers;
photo copies in Baber papers.

Mrs. Caroline Hanks Sizemore to Mrs. Caroline Hanks Hitchcock.

"My father was borned (sic) in
Morgan Co. Ky. Came to Ills 58 yrs
ago Entered the Homestead where he
lived continuously until he died.
My mother was borned in Wolf
Co Ky
Was borned unto them 14 children
seven boys & seven girls
All lived to be grown except youngest
girl.

My great grandfather on my father's side, was
Abraham Hanks, his wife's maiden name was Sarah
Harper, both natives of Virginia.
My father.

          Respectfully
            Mrs. Caroline Sizemore

Paris, Illinois
March 4, 1951

Mr. Adin Baber
Kansas, Illinois

Dear Adin:

    In looking for a rather concise definition of "hearsay evidence",
I find one made by the Supreme Court of North Carolina in the case entitled, In re Nelson's Will, 210 N. C. 398, 1936, which covers the
definition about as well as any I have encountered. The statement
follows: "Evidence, whether oral or written, is called hearsay when
it depends, either wholly or in part, upon the competency or credibility
of some person other than the witness who is testifying. Such evidence
is inadmissible for the reason that the statements made were not under
oath, the judge and jury can not observe the demeanor of the absent
witness, and for the further and more important reason that the con-
stitutional guaranty, that the accused shall be confronted with the
witnesses against him so as to allow opportunity for cross examination,
is not complied with."

    The North Carolina Court continues and points out the more
common exceptions to the hearsay rule in the same case. These exceptions
follow: "The exceptions are admissions, confessions, dying declarations,
declarations against interest, ancient deeds and documents, declarations
concerning matters of public interest, boundary, matters of pedigree,
the res gestae (meaning part of the natural sequence of events), and
perhaps some others."

    To the foregoing I would add the following types of evidence
generally considered admissible in most jurisdictions, including Illinois,
and considered exceptions to the hearsay rule; spontaneous statements,
records to refresh past recollection, regular entries in business,
official written statements, standard treatises, recitals in ancient
writings, general reputation, and the declaration of a deceased if the
court finds it was made in good faith before the commencement of the
action and upon the personal knowledge of the declarant.

    Should you be interested in pursuing the definition of hear say
evidence and its admissibility to a greater degree of detail, I refer
you to the classical statements of Wigmore in his treatise on Evidence.

Sincerely,

(signed)   John R. Moss

From Jimmie Hanks (Mrs. Wm. F.) Lufkin, Texas to Adin Baber

Data from: Mrs. Jordan, Marshall, Texas

Five brothers came from Scotland to New York.
They were Episcopalians; their occupation in
    Scotland: mechanical draftsmen,
    bell manufacturers.
Two of the brothers: Elsworth & Edgar
moved to the South

    1. Elsworth (Mrs. Jordan's grandfather) moved to New Bern, N.C.
        1st wife was a Bruce
        2nd wife was Clarisse Phelps
        His sons were James Bruce Hanks
                who married Jane Edna Matthews
          and Robert Bruce Hanks
                who did not live long.

    2. Edgar moved to Little Washington and Edenton
       His children were: Nora, Carthene, Georgiana, <u>John</u> & <u>Edgar</u>.
       (<u>John</u> was a dentist in Jersey City)
       (<u>Edgar</u> " " " " New York City)

The other three brothers lived in New York and New Jersey.
    (Jersey City, Jersey, Perth Amboy)

Mrs. Jordan's memory has suffered from an accident which crippled her
thirty years ago. A fire destroyed all family records.

202

Feb 21th 1864

Dent Station Mo

St francois County

Dear Cosin

I take the present oppertunity
of informing you of our health
which is Good at present
hoping when this few
lines comes to hand they
may find you enjoying
the Same Good Blefsing
well being as I never wrote
any to you and not knowing
whether you will get this letter
or not I wont say but
a few words to you. I heard
where you was living at
and I thought I would
write you a few lines
and I want you to write

To me as quick as you get
this letter as I would have
wrote to you Sooner if I
had knowned where to write
or to Send my letters
I want you to write as
quick as you get this letter
and let me know how
meny of my friend is yet
living for I have not heard
from them since tha all
went to Illinois
So I will quet noing
whether you get this letter
or not
        I Will Come To Close
            But Remaine
Your Affectionate
            Cosen Until
                Death

Direct Your

Letter Like this

        Dent Station
St francois County Mo

        Sophia Legrand
To
    Dennis Hanks

April 5, 1864[1]

Dear Abe:-
   I received your check for $50.00 I showed it to
Mother. She cried like a child Abe, she is Mity childish.
Heap of trouble to us.

Abe, I received a letter from <u>Sophia Lynch</u>. (Underlining mine)
Now, John LaGrand is her last husband. She wants to
know whether you are Abe Lincoln, her cousin or not.
Is that not strange to you. It was to me. Her boys
all in the Army, Yunion boys at Noxburg.

        Yours Respectfully
         D. F. Hanks

[1]
 It is apparent that there was correspondence other than
these two letters between Sophia Legrand and Dennis Hanks, and
from Feb. 21st to Apr. 5th, 1864.

   Their correspondence may have been desultry for on
Feb. 5, 1887, Dennis wrote to Sophia saying he had received her
letter which surprised him very much.

AUTHOR'S COLLECTION OF HANKS BIBLIOGRAPHY

THOSE WITH SPECIAL REFERENCE TO THE PARENTAGE OF LINCOLN.

TITLE	AUTHOR	DATE PUB.[*]
The Pioneer Boy	William M. Thayer	1864
The Life of Lincoln	Ward H. Lamon	1872
The New England Historical and Genealogical Register	Samuel Shackford	1887
Herndon's Lincoln, Vol. I	William H. Herndon	1890
The Sorrows of Nancy	Lucinda Boyd	1899
The Genesis of Lincoln	James H. Cathay	1899
Truth is Stranger than Fiction	James H. Cathay	1899
Nancy Hanks	Caroline Hanks Hitchcock	1900
The Ancestry of Abraham Lincoln	Lea & Hutchinson	1909
Pennsylvania Magazine of History: The Mother of Lincoln	Howard M. Jenkins	1920
The Matrix	Maria Thompson Daviess	1920
Atlantic Monthly: New Light on Lincoln's Boyhood	Arthur E. Morgan	1920
Abe Lincoln & Nancy Hanks	Elbert Hubbard	1920
The Paternity of Abraham Lincoln	William E. Barton	1920
The Boyhood of Lincoln	J. Rogers Gore	1921
A Story of Nancy Hanks	Ethel Calvert Phillips	1923
Abraham Lincoln, A North Carolinian	James Caswell Coggins	1925
Lincoln's Parentage & Childhood	Louis E. Warren	1926
The Lineage of Lincoln	William E. Barton	1929
Lincoln Lore, Vol. I	Louis E. Warren	1929-33
The Lincoln Kinsman	Louis E. Warren	1938-42
The Eugenics of Abraham Lincoln	James Caswell Coggins	1940
Random Thoughts & The Musings of a Mountaineer	Judge Felix E. Alley	1941
Lincoln Among His Friends, Coll.	Rufas Rockwell Wilson	1942
Nancy Hanks Lincoln	Harold E. & Ernestine Briggs	1953
The Buffalo Trace	Virginia S. Eifert	1955
In Freedom's Dawn	Alice Shelbourne	1957
Transactions of the Illinois State Historical Society The Ancestry of Abraham Lincoln	William E. Barton	1924
Journal of Illinois State Historical Society The Hankses	William E. Barton	1928
Journal of Illinois State Historical Society Is Lincoln Among the Aristocrats	William E. Barton	1929

THOSE WITH SPECIAL REFERENCE TO THE LINCOLN FAMILY

TITLE	AUTHOR	DATE PUB[*]
Abraham Lincoln, an American Migration	Marion Dexter Learned	1909
Indiana Magazine of History	J. Edward Murr	1918
History of the Lincoln Family	Waldo Lincoln	1923
In the Footsteps of the Lincolns	Ida M. Tarbell	1924
Lincoln and the Lincolns	Harvey H. Smith	1931
The Lincolns and Tennessee	Samuel C. Williams	1942
The Lincolns in Virginia	John W. Wayland	1946
Mary Lincoln	Ruth Painter Randall	1953
Lincoln Herald		1937-58

BOOKS WHOLLY ABOUT HANKSES

A Rambling Discourse on the Hanks Family of Maryland	A.V. Chidsey (MS)	1930
The Monroe Watchman (Newspaper)		
The Hank (sic) Family	Myra Hank Rudolph	1930
The Northeast Historical and	Genealogical Register	1932
The History of Rome Hanks	Joseph Stanley Pennell	1944
Founders of the Gatlin Family	David Walter Gatlin(MS)	1955
Moses Hanks	Gladys Hanks Johnson (MS)	1956

BOOKS WITH PERTINENT REFERENCES

Lincoln	Charles Maltby	1884
Reminiscences of Abraham Lincoln	Allem Thorndike Rice	1888
Lincoln Memorial Album	Osborn H. Oldroyd	1890
Behold He Cometh in the Clouds	George Washington Noble	1912
History of Elizabethtown, Kentucky	Samuel Haycraft,1869;Print 1921	
The Real Lincoln	Jesse W. Weik	1922
Campbell Chronicles	R. H. Early	1927
Origins of Clements-Spaulding and Allied Families	J. W. S. Clements	1928
A Raft Pilot's Log	Walter A. Blair	1929
Two Centuries in Texas	G. L. Crockett	1932
Transactions of the Illinois State Historical Society		1934
The Hidden Lincoln	Emanuel Hertz	1938
Life of Abraham Lincoln, as was Corrected by Abraham Lincoln	W.D. Howells, 1860; reprint 1938	
Papers in Illinois History, The Hanks Family in Macon County	Edwin David Davis	1939
History of Gaston County (N.C.)	Minnie Stowe Puett	1941

Abe Lincoln's Other Mother	Bernadine Bailey	1941
John C. Calhoun	Margaret L. Coit	1950
Life of Abraham Lincoln, 1860	John Locke Scripps, reprint	1951
Its Dogwood Time in Tyler County, Texas	J. E. Wheat, Pres.	1952
Abraham Lincoln and Coles County, Illinois	Charles H. Coleman	1955
The Oliver R. Barrett Lincoln Collection, Catalogue 1315	Parke-Bernet Galleries	1952

* Arrangement in chronological order to show when facts and fancies
first became available to the reading public.

PART II

ANCESTRAL QUEST

PART II

ANCESTRAL QUEST OF ABRAHAM HANKS

CHAPTER I

FOREWORD

Now that we have definitely reached the conclusion, for
the reason there is no alternative, that the father of Nancy Hanks
Lincoln, was, as the early historians stated, the Abraham Hanks,
who accompanied William Calk to Kentucky, in 1775; and her mother
was his wife, Sarah Harper; the natural inquiry is: who were they?

For nearly a century, in spite of the clear statement of
the earlier historians and due to the sensationalism "created" by
Herndon there has been no ready answer to this question. Because
of the reluctance of genealogists, unconsciously influenced by
Herndon, to reopen a supposed unsavory subject, only one attempt
was made to trace Hanks family lines; it ended abortively.[1] In the
specific case of Abraham and Sarah, few of the records, which one
usually finds,when tracing members of a family, have been found.

The Colonial origin of the ancestry of Abraham Hanks was
likely in Virginia, for the Hanks family was among the first there,
and the names of its members are to be seen in the early records and
more than one hundred years before they appear in the Colonies of
New England and Maryland.

Shortly after Lincoln's death, when John Hanks, the "Rail-
splitter" of Macon County, Illinois, was interviewed by Herndon,
at the Sanitary Fair in Chicago, he, in a rather ambiguous statement, or the way that Herndon wrote it, mentioned the Rappahannock
River country, as the locale of the "founders" as he called them,
of the family. That country had been the seat of much recent
Civil War news. This is a definite area but a large territory. The
Rappahannock is one of several streams flowing through the Piedmont
section of Virginia. It is hardly to be remarked about without
previous knowledge by one born on the western waters, as was old
"Rail-splitter John."

---

[1] Hitchcock, Nancy Hanks, The story of Abraham Lincoln's
Mother, pub. New York, 1900.

John Hanks was, from all accounts, an illiterate but not an ignorant man. Certainly, he could not read so his use of the word, "founder" and in connection with the Rappahannock River would indicate he had it from a family source, perhaps his father, William, who was born in the east in 1766. Considering Herndon's abyssmal ignorance of the Hanks family connections, and the reputation for truthfulness that old John Hanks bore, it seems likely that this information was communicated by John and was not an interpolation by Herndon; so it is to be accepted as plausable.

The Rappahannock River arises in the foot-hills of the Blue Ridge Mountains and, flowing southeastwardly, forms the southwest boundary of Fauquier County and, a hundred miles or more downstream, forms the southwest boundary of Richmond County. It flowed through two communities of Hanks families: that of the Fauquier-Loudoun section and, downstream, that of the Richmond-Lancaster group. John's information is not specific enough to be of much help.

Dennis Hanks, who always tried to be helpful, once told Weik that the Hankses came from "The Roanoke River country in Virginia..." He was not certain as to what county but thought it may have been Halifax. This statement is not in conflict with the information that John gave when it is known that Hankses from both the Richmond and the Loudoun Counties areas migrated to the Roanoke River valley. Inasmuch as the records of the Hanks family are found in Richmond County a hundred years earlier than those of Loudoun and Fauquier counties, and even earlier than any Hanks family records are to be located in Maryland, it would seem logical to presume that the fountain head of the southern branch of the Hanks family was in the lower Rappahannock River country.

So to start the search for the ancestry of Abraham Hanks his trail is back-tracked from Kentucky to Virginia where, at the crossing of the Rapidan River, he met William Calk and the other companions, he was to accompany. It is obvious the meeting had been previously arranged, for all arrived with accoutrement, for a long trail trip of the times. They were on horseback and with pack horses, armed, provisioned, and accompanied by a slave or two and hunting dogs. Calk wrote, "Our company all Got together..." and the implication is they had known each other and probably resided not more than a days horseback ride apart; and northward, not southward of the meeting place. Calk was from Prince William County, and since he mentions no companion on his way to meet the others, it would seem that their respective homes were in nearby and the adjacent counties. The nearest were Fauquier and Loudoun in which to look for Abraham Hanks.

It is known from previous reading of this thesis that an
Abraham Hanks did reside in Fauquier County, which undoubtedly
identifies him as the one who accompanied William Calk to Kentucky.
Up to this point all has been factual but here we enter into the
conjectural, even speculative, until more evidence is discovered
and revealed. It is hoped that eventually all doubts as to the
ancestry of this Abraham Hanks shall have been resolved.

To this end consideration will now be given to the notice
of all known Hanks patriarchs who were old enough to have been his
father, if he was born, as is supposed, about 1750, and by elimination
leave only one, as his possible father. If the search is confined
to the "Rappahannock River Country" it forwith eliminates the members
of the New England Hanks family and the early Hankees of North Carolina,
who went there, but rather lately, from New England. The consideration
will include the three sons of William Hanks I, and their oldest sons
in turn; the one known son of Robert Hanks; the one son of Peter Hanks
of Maryland and who came into Loudoun County of the Rappahannock River
section, and called herein "William the Quaker."

The three sons of William Hanks I were William II, Luke I,
and John. William II had five sons, all born early enough to have
fathered Abraham; but all the sons of the five sons are known, and
there is no Abraham among them. John Hanks had five sons and all
the sons of the five sons are known, and there is no Abraham. All
the sons of Luke I are not known so he will have to be considered
further. It is probable that all the sons of William the Quaker are
not known, so his case will have to be examined. A study will be made
of the possible descendants of Robert Hanks, Junior.

This is no new line of endeavor, many researchers have gone
before. Herndon may be said to have made the first attempt but his
efforts were so desultory they were a smear. Hitchcock collected an
enormous amount of Hanks family charts in the 1890's and made a
natural but abortive conclusion. Barton followed in the footsteps of
Herndon and added little. Warren was an assiduous student of Hanksiana
for years but more important intrrests caused him to leave off. Mention
will now be made of some minor investigators whose works have been of
help for this purpose.

CHAPTER II

EARLIER RESEARCHERS

The eminant historian, Dr. Lyman C. Draper, had a collaborator, John D. Schane, who interviewed many early settlers of Kentucky; and recorded the historic incidents, personal experiences, and family items of many. These papers are now with the Wisconsin Historical Society.[1] In 1832, John Hanks of Montgomery County, Kentucky was one of these interviewed. He stated for the record, that he was born November 29, 1767, in Loudoun County, Maryland (sic). This was a palpable error, for there is no such county in Maryland and, no doubt, he intended it to read, Loudoun County, Virginia; for the records, and his own statement, indicate that his father's family resided there. This error, on his part, is of significance; for it seems to show some connection with Maryland.

(For identity, this John Hanks will be referred to, hereafter, as Draper's John Hanks.)

Draper's John Hanks further narrated that, "In May 1786, we came to Kentucky." He mentions his father, Peter Hanks, and his brother, William, and indirectly, a sister but does not name her.[2] They settled on Slate Creek, near Morgan's Station[3] in what is now Montgomery County, where they planted corn, but the turkeys ate the first planting and the frost got the second planting! He tells of his father's war experiences on the western Frontier of Pennsylvania, all of which may be confirmed in Pennsylvania Archives.[4]

Another brother of John's arrived, Peter Hanks (Jr.) with wife, Isabella, and later moved to Knox County, Indiana and was killed at the Battle of Tippecanoe.[5] Peter, Sr. moved away but Draper's John continued to live on Spence Fork of Slate Creek where he was interviewed.

The same year that Draper's John Hanks was being interviewed in Kentucky, there was born in Bedford County, Pennsylvania, March 29, 1832, a boy named William Jacob Lodge. In Loudoun County, Virginia, his grandmother on his mother's side was born Nancy Hanks, (the twin of Rosannah), and who had married first, Nicholas Schooley, in Loudoun County.[6] Young Lodge grew up in a Hanks

---

[1] Kentucky Papers, Wisconsin Historical Society

[2] o Hanks, Interview; 12 cc, 138-44

[3] John Morgan's Station, on Slate Creek, near now Howard's Mill, Montgomery County, Kentucky.

[4] 3rd Series, Vol. 22, p. 39; Vol. 23, p. 205; 5th Series Vol. IV; 6th Series Vol. II; etc.

[5] Pertle, Battle of Tippecanoe, p. 122.

[6] Lodge Family History.

community, was given a good education, and became a Doctor of
Medicine, and practiced for many years.

In the early 1880's, Dr. Lodge conceived the idea of writing
a Lodge family history for his son, Dr. Gonzalos Lodge, once on the
staff of Columbia University. He did so, and of course, his family
tree included some genealogy of his Hanks ancestors, so far as he
knew. This was long before the genealogy of the Hanks family was
impugnly botched by Herndon; and long before the mention of a Joseph
Hanks by Mrs. Hitchcock; and the rehash of Herndoniana by Barton.
Later, in 1895, he furnished much of his Hanks information to Mrs.
Hitchcock and his letters are available to students at the Lincoln
Library at Fort Wayne, Indiana.

The Hanks family to which Dr. Lodge belonged were descendants
of the William Hanks (called heretofore, William of Bedford) who,
after the death of his parents, and about 1800, he and his wife,
Sarah, and their grown children, with the exception of Fleetwood,and John
moved at intervals from Loudoun County to Bedford County, Pennsylvania,
where William's brother, as will be shown, preceded him and had
"scouted out", in the Brush Creek section, the land William was to
own. With William and his sons and daughters, went many Loudoun County
neighbors,---the Akers, the Schooleys, the Jacksons, the James, and
etc., whose sons had married William's daughters. William's sister,
Rachel, married the widower, Joseph Wilkinson, and remained in Virginia,
These families continued to live in a common community, where Dr. Lodge
could have, as a boy, known most of them. One of his grandmothers,
and some of his great aunts and uncles survived several years after
his birth, in 1832.

From them he could have gained much family history, that was
well known to the earlier members from Virginia, and handed down to
the grandchildren in Pennsylvania. Also, he had access to the family
Bible of William Hanks; which has not been located recently. Thus
qualified, his information may be, and is, accepted with full faith;
of most singular import are his references to the Hanks family of
Loudoun County, Virginia.

He has written that his great grandfather, "William Hanks, my
ancestor, lived near the Patapoco River in Maryland, about fourteen
miles from Baltimore... from there he moved to Loudoun County, Virginia,
and subsequently to Brush Creek Valley, Pennsylvania; where his remains
rest." Although they were not in his 'Lodge' line of ancestry, he
supplied incidental information, that his great grandfather William.
had two brothers, Joseph and Jno who had, at one time, been associated
with William in ownership of land; the interest in which, they sold,
to go live in Kentucky.

This information identifies the William of Bedford County,
Pennsylvania; who came from Loudoun County, and whose name appears
earlier in Ann Arundal County, Maryland.

In the 1920's Mrs. John F. Rudolph, Sr., who was born Myra
Hank, became interested in tracing the family tree of her Hank family,
at about the same time that Miss Ida M. Tarbell was preparing to
write her book, In The Footsteps of The Lincolns.

Miss Tarbell was, of course, interested in anything pertaining
to the Hanks family and the common interest of these two women brought
on a copious correspondence.

Mrs. Louie D. White, a genealogist of Boston, was working at
learning the connection of the Hanks or Hank family with the Shipley
family of Virginia, which line she had traced back to Anne Arundal
County, Maryland, where she also located some Hanks names in the
records. Mrs. Tarbell suggested to Mrs. White that Mrs. Rudolph could
help her. These three women then worked together and garnered much
information from the early records of Maryland, including some of the
data that Dr. Lodge had given to Mrs. Hitchcock, that pertained to
the Bedford County, Pennsylvania Hankses, his ancestors.

Another descendant of the Bedford County Hanks family was
Mrs. Jennie Schooley Hoffman, and through the Schooley line of descent,
in which she was interested. She worked assiduously at tracing it
and its connection with the Hanks family. She obtained from Dr.
Gonzalos Lodge, the son of Dr. Lodge, that part of the Lodge history
that dealt with the Hanks ancestors, and which his father had collected
in the 1880's. This she incorporated in her own line of descent from
them.

Then, Mr. A. D. Chidsey of Easton, Pennsylvania, and Mr. A. E.
Ewing of Grand Rapids, Michigan, became interested in the Hanks and
Hank subject and the mutual concern of all these people resulted in
a file of correspondence with Mrs. Rudolph, who had become a sort of
"clearing house" for it.

Mrs. Rudolph has worked for a long time at both Hank and
Hanks family records in Pennsylvania, Maryland, and Virginia, and in
order to separate the Hanks members from the Hank members, and build
a Hank family genealogy. This she was able to accomplish, and it was
printed in the Monroe Watchman, a newspaper of Monroe County, Virginia,
in 1930.[7]

---

[7] Photo-copy, Baber papers.

The early Hank ancestors of Mrs. Rudolph were of the Friends persuasion and, in searching for them, she investigated the old Friends' records. In doing this she learned that a Hanks family of Loudoun County, Virginia, also were Friends. This turned out to be the family of William the Quaker, the ancestor of Dr. Lodge.

Also, in the Friends' records of the Fairfax Meeting of Loudoun County, she located a Rachel Hanks, whom the Quakers had disowned for "marrying out" and she was identified as a daughter of William the Quaker. Thus, the chips from the Hanks family tree began to fit back into the trunk. She gave all this information to Mr. Chidsey.

Mr. Chidsey then began some investigation of records for himself and what he found new he added to what he had received and wrote it up in a manuscript entitled, A Rambling Discourse on the Hanks Family of Maryland. From it we learn that he has visited the Hall of Records at Annapolis, Maryland; the courthouse of Loudoun County at Leesburg, Virginia; and the Hanks area of Bedford, now Fulton County, Pennsylvania. He follows the trail of this Hanks family migration from Anne Arundal County, Maryland through Loudoun County, Virginia, and up the Potomac River Valley into Brush Creek Valley of Bedford County, Pennsylvania, and verifies many family traditions from records. A copy of this report was presented by Mrs. Rudolph for use in preparing this thesis.

But, before the Chidsey Report was reseived and studied, there was had from the Hall of Records at Annapolis; from copies of Parish records at the Diocosan Library; the Maryland Historical Society Libraries, at Baltimore; and from courthouse records, some of the same information that Chidsey had had. A comparison of the two sets of notes confirms that his data are correct, and that both sets of notes are in agreement. In addition, information has been collected that Mr. Chidsey seems not to have had.

In his manuscript his facts are authenticated and combined into logical sequence so well, that his reasonings make clear his conclusions. His doubts are so frankly expressed, and the want of additional evidence recognized, that no errors of conjecture are found. His report can be, and is, accepted as correct, aa are those previous reports that went into it.

It is to be noted that the information furnished by Draper's John Hanks; by Dr. William Jacob Lodge; confirmed by the findings of Mrs. Rudolph; supplemented by Mrs. Hoffman; and briefed by Mr. Chidsey; completely dove-tail to make a continuity of Hanks family history spanning almost two centuries, from 1767 to now.

The combination of the information from those who have
chronicled before, with the knowledge from the latest research[8]
produces a reasonable family genealogy or orderly sequence and
natural connections. There are no incongruities, no straining
kinships, and no impossible dates. This line of descent is from
the Peter Hanks who lived near Annapolis, Maryland, and who shall
for identification be called Peter the First. Upon this Rock the
House of Peter shall be established. This shall be for the record
and for future genealogists and to possibly help determine if
Abraham Hanks, the one sought, is of this line.

---

[8] Baber papers.

CHAPTER III

THE HANKS FAMILY OF MARYLAND

In the minutes of the original records of old St. Anne's Parish, of Anne Arundal County, Maryland; appears the record of the marriage of Peter (the First) Hanks and Mary Beez, August 20, 1702. In the same records are the names of four of their children: Lydia, born September 25, 1704; William, born July 25, 1707; Ellinor, born July 10, 1709; and Peter, born 1711. These children were baptized the same day, the 20th of September, 1713.[1]

Peter the First acquired an option or interest in a tract of 100 acres of land lying in the Great Fork of the Patuxent River; he named it "Beyond Far Enugh" and no doubt it seemed far enough from Annapolis; at least he did not get the children baptized soon after their births. This farm was located not far from where Fort Meade is now located.

Later, Christ Church of Queen Caroline Parish was organized and a site selected for the church structure not far from present Guilford. There were two "wading places"[2] where Peter's family could cross the river to get to church.[3] A second building was erected on the site, in 1804 and still stands. The nearby cemetery is not an old burial ground and no Hanks graves are to be seen there.

Whence came Peter, nor the date of his birth has not been found. There were, of course, Hankses in Virginia earlier, but there is no record of any of them settling in Providence (now Annapolis) in 1649, when a group of settlers came from Virginia. There was an early Greenville Hanks on the Eastern Shore. Did they come out of Virginia after the Bacon Rebellion? It would seem so. Hankses came together again in Virginia, as Hanks cousins did, and Peter the First made his will, April 1, 1733; and in it instructed, "That my dear wife may be

---

[1] Original record, Hall of Records, Annapolis.

[2] Record, Diocesan Library, Baltimore.

[3] Ibid.

under the care of my two sons, Will and Peter Hanks," He named
Elinor Nelson, but did not mention Lydia, only her husband's name,
John Martin. John's name appears on record, on later land deals.
The Will was probated three months after the date;[4] the copy is
shown as signed by Peter Hanks and without mark. One witness to
the Will was Robert Nelson, a son-in-law, and the other witness to
the Will was James Brooks. The name, James Brooks will again appear
with Hanks names in other records and in other states, and is to
be noted.

The inventory of Peter Hanks' estate lists the usual items
of a farm, and includes, "1 woman servant, 15." "Parcel of old books."
"Parcel Carpenter and Cooper tools." It is of interest that the early
Hankses of Virginia also were carpenters, ooopers, and wood-workers.
The witnesses of this document and the appraisers of the estate
included Adam Barnes and Phil Hammond, and these names are to be
noted for future reference.[5]

The son, Peter (Jr.) did not receive his share of the estate
so it is presumed he deceased between the time of making the Will and
its final settlement. In his stead, Robert Nelson therefore received
a patent on the 100 acres, named "Beyond Far Enough" on[6] June 10, 1734.
The son, William, acquired a patent on 100 acres of land called it,
"Far Enough." William and the two brothers-in-law continued to acquire
land and, traded among themselves until, by 1761, William owned four
tracts of land, 321 acres.

Queen Caroline Parish was erected, 1728; ten years later,
Richard Davis, Abell Brown, John Dorsey, Richard Shipley, and Adam
Barnes, vestrymen for Christ Church, received a deed for two acres
of land for a site for building.[7] Upon the erection of the house and
the assignment of pews, July 6, 1736, William Hanks and John Ryan were
assigned pew number 28 together; Robert Shipley[8] was given all of pew
number 11; and Adam, Richard, and Samuel Shipley had pew number 15.

---

[4] Wills, 1730-1734; CC #3; p. 807, Hall of Records, Annapolis, Md.

[5] Liber 18, folio 185, Hall of Records.

[6] Liber EI #1, folio 444, ibid.

[7] These names to be noted for future references.

[8] The Robert Shipley name is to be noted especially.

It is alleged that William Hanks married Ruth Shipley, a daughter of Robert and Elizabeth Shipley;[9] but if so she was a first wife for when John Ryan Sr. made his will in 1762, he named Ruth Hanks as a daughter.[10] But the Ryans, Shipleys and the Dorseys intermarried. Robert Shipley (Jr.) has as wife, Sarah Dorsey, who was, of course, of the family of John Dorsey, the Vestryman. The inference is that John Ryan's family was kin to the Dorsey family. The Ryan name is to be noted for reference.

That the William and Ruth Ryan Hanks family had children born into it is known from tradition and from evidence but, inexplicably enough, no record of their births is found in the Parish records of the contemporary time. What makes the omission more an oddity is the fact that William Hanks was a Vestryman just after the probable period of the births; it would seem he would have attended to the recording of the births of his own children. There is one probable explanation.

The names and birthdates of the children of Robert and Elizabeth Shipley, including their daughter, Ruth, are entered upon the record and all upon one page. This is understandable for the names were transferred from the St. Ann's church records of earlier dates, into the Register of the Queen Caroline Parish after the formation of the new Parish. Also, transferred and put onto the first pages of the new Register were the names of other members of the new congregation, with the given names of their wives, and the names and birth dates of their children; all on a single page for the respective family.

There are two of the old Record books: the aforesaid Register and a larger book of the business transactions of the Vestry. The larger book has always been intact, but an examination of the Register shows that it has been rebound sometime in the past and not recently. It starts with the original Index, and lists some of the first families of membership but, apparently, not all; the Index was not added to when new members came in.

The first page after the Index ends, starts with the number 34, on which is written the data of the family of Greenberry Griffiths. The pagination then runs in order up to include page number 45, comes page 2, upon which is listed the family data of Joshua Dotsey. On page 4 is the record of Robert Shipley's family. Page 8, originally, had but one entry, leaving blank below almost the entire page.

---

[9] Shipley Family History, Public Library, Annapolis, Md.

[10] Will Book 36, p. 205, Hall of Records.

Someone has written a heading thusly:

---
copy

Hereon, someone, long ago, has tried to preserve the record of
John Martin's family by copying off scraps of a mutilated page,
the remnants of which are pasted onto a following page 11. These
vestiges are parts of old page 29. The wife of John Martin is named as
Liddia; she was a sister of the William Hanks, whose records we search
What may have been on the obverse side of page 29, it is now impossible
to tell, for the relics are pasted securely.

The upper part of page 11, onto which these fragments were
attached, contains references to the John Ryon (Ryan?) family. This
may have some significance; it is apparent from other entries in the
Vestry book that kinspeople shared pews. The Ryan family shared a
pew with the Hanks family. The Ryan name occurs later, and in other
states as associated with the Hanks family; as, also, does other names
of these early families. Viz: Shipley, Howard, Dorsey, Hammond, etc.

The following page 12, has pasted thereon a large triangular
piece of the Martin entries, and one entry is dated August 2, 1732,
which dates the era of these records, in a way. The sheet, which
evidently contained pages 30 and 31, is missing. The page, 32, is
intact, with page 33; then the numbers jump to 46, which follows the
page 33.

If the family of William and Ruth Ryan Hanks had a record
of the names and births of their children, they were probably on one
of the missing pages; it would follow that the records of William's
other sister, Eleanor Nelson, were on the other missing page. On the
other hand, if the births of the Hanks children were after the formation
of Christ Church, and the acquiring of the new record book, they
would not have been transcribed from an earlier record, but should
have been entered in this record. But the records of births of
children of other members of the church seem to not have been recorded
either. It is a frustration. Perhaps William and his family did not
reside in the area so early, and records of his family are elsewhere.
It is hoped so.

William Hanks was elected to the office of Vestryman, May 5,
1747, and served three years, during which interim he attended many
business meetings of the Vestrymen, as is recorded in the minutes.
Then his allegiance must have weakened, for on April 16, 1715, notice

was given to choose Vestryman, "...in place of Lance Todd and William Hanks." Did some untoward incident effect this vacancy? Is it the reason that the records of Hanks children are not located?

*****

By "ye 25 of ye 6 Mo 1756" it is recorded in the minutes of the West River Meeting of the Friends[11] that "William Hanks hath attended our meetings" and James Brooks was "sent to Enquire" and reported that William appeared "to be a man of orderly life" so he was accepted into the Friend's sect.[12] William Hanks had definitely left the Church of England and the church of his wife's people.

In the year of 1761, William Hanks, the Planter, and his wife, Ruth, deeded the four tracts of land, 321 acres, to "Josiah, son of Cornelious Howard of Baltimore."[13] William signed the deed, and Ruth gave written consent, and both without mark.[14] William Hanks then moved to Loudoun County, Virginia, as is shown by the records kept by the Friends: "8 mo 26 da 1763 William Hanks granted Certificate to Friends at Fairfax in Colony of Virginia."[15]

Later, "27 da 10 mo 1764" he was received into the Fairfax Meeting,[16] which was then at Waterford in Loudoun County, Virginia. An old stone Friend's Meeting House still stands there, being used as a private residence, and adjacent is a large cemetery. From an older part of the cemetery many stones have been broken and are now piled in the northwest corner. It is said that cavalry horses were tethered there during a campaign of the Civil War and broke the stones. This is the same William Hanks referred to in the Loudoun County chapter as William the Quaker.

---

[11] 6 mo was August; O.S. Friend's New Year began March 1st, before 1752

[12] Later, Dennis Hanks denied that any Hanks were Quakers.

[13] Members of the Howard family accompanied Hanskses into Virginia, and into Kentucky, where now, Howard's Creek, Howard's Mill, etc., in Montgomery County, Kentucky.

[14] Liber BB #2, Folio 510

[15] West River Meeting minutes.

[16] Fairfax Monthly Meeting Records.

His name is on the Tithe list of Loudoun County from 1764 to 1769, inclusive, and not thereafter.[17] By the usual surmise, he moved away or died. A search of the standing stones in the old grave yard at Waterford fails to locate a Hanks grave, but his marker may be in the pile.[18] There is no record that he owned real estate in Loudoun County, but as this territory was in the hands of the Proprietors, it may be he only rented or leased land.

The foregoing information, as collected by Rudolph, collected by Chidsey, and verified by notes from original records[19] makes clear the origin and identity of the branch of Hankses of Loudoun County, Virginia, as from Maryland. Incidentally, there were other Hankses in Maryland who were contemporary with William the Quaker.[20]

The other brother of William of Bedford who was mentioned by his great grandson, Dr. Lodge, was John or Jonathan. It is shown by the tithe records that John was for a time a citizen of Loudoun County. From two family sources the tradition is that he "went south" and "to the James River country;"[21] also, that "Jonathan was in Western Kentucky," where, "Fleetwood joined him." Courthouse records of the respective counties in the two states do confirm that Fleetwood went south into Bedford County, Virginia; thence into Henry County, Kentucky, where tradition places a Jonathan Hanks.

There was a John or Jonathan Hanks residing for a time in Nelson County, Kentucky, and just three fourths of a mile from Joseph Hanks.[22] Probably the John, Jane, Conrad, and Nancy Hanks mentioned by Dennis Hanks in his letter to Charles Friend were the children of Jonathan for they were not the children of Joseph. Nancy married Peter Jones.[23]

---

[17]Gibbon's report, Baber papers.

[18]
The pile should be searched.

[19]
The Baber Papers.

[20]
Thomas Hanks married Sarah Hewitt, May 9, 1748.

[21]
Baber Papers.

[22]
John W. Kerrick, affidavit, Warren papers, Lincoln Library, Fort Wayne, Indiana.

[23]
Marriage records, Henry County, Kentucky, Courthouse.

There was, also, a John Hanks who entered land in Henderson
County, Kentucky, in that part that later became Hopkins County,
and this area would have been considered "western Kentucky" then.
The census of 1810 shows also a Peter Hanks and a Joseph Hanks
residing in this same area. The question is whether the Nelson
County John or the Hopkins County John Hanks was the son of William
the Quaker?

Both Johns removed from their respective areas; the one from
Hopkins County went to Tennessee; the one from Nelson County went to
Henry County. Since Fleetwood was later located in Oldham County and
not far from Henry County it is presumed that Jonathan of Henry was
the son of William the Quaker.

The name, Peter Hanks, being, also, in the records of Loudoun
County, contemporary with William the Quaker, Joseph and Jonathan Hanks;
he is nominated to be another brother, and a son of William the Quaker;
and for the following reasons: First, the name, "Peter" was used in
the Maryland family of Hankses, and is not found in the earlier Hanks
names of Richmond County, Virginia. Second, the names that Peter
gave to his children indicates his ancestry. These were: William,
for his father; Peter IV, for himself and after his deceased uncle and
his grandfather; and he named a daughter, Ruth, for his mother, who was
Ruth Ryan. Other names he gave were Absalom and Samuel. Third, Peter's
family was living in Loudoun County in 1767, where other members of
the Maryland family were when his son Draper's John was born. Fourth,
in 1769, Peter was granted land on the Monongahala River[24] where
William of Bedford joined him. Fifth, Peter was taxed in Rosstraven
Township of Bedford County, Pennsylvania, in 1772, which became the
future home county of William of Bedford, indicating knowledge of it
on William's part, probably from Peter. This is the location of
Friend's Cove whence came Jonathan Hanks of Nelson and Henry Counties,
Kentucky. Sixth, both Peter and William served in the War on the
Frontier of Western Pennsylvania in 1782, from later area of Washington
County. Peter was in Stockley's Rangers and William was in Captain
William Scott's Company of Militia.[25] The presumption is that this

[24]204 3/4 acres, named "Carol" surveyed October 2, 1769.

[25]Pennsylvania Archives 6th Ser. Vol. II, p. 38.

[26]Order Book H, p. 456, Loudoun County, courthouse.

William was Peter's brother but, it is admitted, that the positive
identities of the several Williams and Johns Hanks cannot always be
verified.

Seventh, Peter and William Hanks were made joint defendants
in a suit filed in Loudoun County, Virginia, for debt,[26] and their
answer was made for each by the same attorney. This action would
seem to indicate a close association in business or that one had gone
on the other's bond. More likely, it indicates close kinship.

However, from the date of the suit, it may have been the sons
of Peter and William, who were sued, for by then, Peter, the Revolutionary War veteran, was supposed to be in North Carolina; at least
his daughter, Ruth, was born there that year. Nevertheless, whether
the suit was against fathers or sons, there was a close connection.

It is submitted that the evidence sustains the argument that
Peter Hanks, the Revolutionary soldier was a brother of William of
Bedford, and both of them were sons of William the Quaker.

After the end of the Revolutionary War, Peter Hanks took his
family and followed the great migration southward, and settled them
near the Yadkin River in the Salisbury District of North Carolina.
There his daughter, Ruth, was born June 13, 1782. At the same time
he was assessed for land in Fayette County, Virginia, which was in
the part that later became the State of Kentucky. In 1786 he removed
to what became, later, Montgomery County, Kentucky, and settled on
Slate Creek.[27]

With him were his sons, Peter Jr., William, and Draper's John;
also, the daughter, Ruth. Peter Jr., later brought his family from
Rutherford County, North Carolina;[28] then removed to Knox County,
Indiana. He was killed at the Battle of Tippecanoe; his wife, Isabella,
and her children moved to Texas, and settled in now San Augustine County.
William, the son, was a minister and established some of the first
churches in Gibson County, Indiana. The son, Samuel, married Nancy
Wyatt,[29] of Mason County; they gave their children Romish names.

---

[27] Draper's John Hanks, Interview.

[28] U.S. Census, Rutherford County, North Carolina, L 810

[29] Marriage Records, Mason County, Kentucky, Courthouse.

Absalom, another son, resided near present Winchester, and one of his grandsons, Absalom Hanks Markland, became the Post Master General of Grant's Army; was, also, a confidente of Lincoln.[30] The daughter, Ruth, married Hubbard Marshall, a son of Humphrey Marshall. Their descendants became ministers[31] and lawyers.[32]

In the 1790's all members of this family were settled in and about the Slate Creek area; the courthouse records indicate they were engaged more or less in the business of farming and related occupations. At the same time, and near them, and on Slate Creek, were other Hankses. They, also, had come from Virginia and through North Carolina. Slate Creek drains a considerable area, and carries its waters northward to empty into Licking River. It's chief tributaries are Spence Creek, Harper Creek, and Howard Creek.

Nearby Morgan's Station was settled in 1789, which became the scene of an Indian massacre, and a woman, who hid in the spring cave smothered her little baby trying to keep it from crying. She was the only one who escaped. Within this community and near Morgan's Station all these Hankses lived on neighboring farms; at least the tax assessor listed the names close together on the pages as he rode the trails, which indicates they were nearby neighbors.

The names of Hankses other than the listings of members of Peter's family are on the tax lists, and upon other records at the courthouse at Mt. Sterling, Kentucky. These are: Abraham Hanks (Jr.), Fielding and George; there is Sarah with a son, William. These families also resided near Slate Creek near Morgan's Station, and on Harper Ridge, and near Howard's Mill on Howard's Creek. They are known to have been the children of Abraham Hanks who came to Kentucky with William Calk in 1775.

From the common origin of both families in the Rappahannock River country of Virginia; from their continued proximity in North Carolina; from their association in Kentucky; and from circumstantial evidence: it is submitted that the two family groups were kin.

The exact relationship has not been determined but, whatever it was, it indicates that the families of Loudoun County, Virginia and of Fauquier and Prince William Counties, were of a cousinship; and migrating side by side and coming together; as they later emigrated in to Indiana and into Illinois and westward. They had ambitions, and characteristics alike and in common. They were of the same root stock!

_____

[30]Reminiscenses of Abraham Lincoln, p. 629.

[31]The Rev. Leon P. Marshall, Bowling Green, Indiana

[32]Judge John Marshall, State of Kansas.

CHAPTER IV

LINES OF DESCENT

-

THE PETER HANKS I LINE

To sum up the previous chapter, there is no direct evidence that Peter Hanks I,who married Mary Beez in Maryland, 1702, was a son of Thomas Hanks of Virginia; but from the association of his descendants with the descendants of Thomas in Virginia, and the continual coming together of all of them, it would seem they were at least close kin. There was continuous coastwise trade along the shores of Chesapeake Bay; Virginians settled Annapolis; there is no evidence that Peter I did not, also, come up from Virginia.

Peter Hanks I had a son Peter, who deceased without issue; but he had another son, William, who had a son Peter. This grandson of old Peter I became a rather famous Revolutinnary War soldier on the western frontier of Pennsylvania. His own son, Peter, went to the War of 1812 and was killed at the Battle of Tippecanoe. Thomas Hanks of Ohio also had a son, Peter; further the line has not been traced.

Old Peter I's son, William, joined the Quakers, and moved over into Loudoun County, Virginia. Thence some of his descendants went south and eventually into Kentucky. Others went westward up the Potomac River valley and into Ohio and Kentucky. Then, those in Kentucky removed to Indiana and to Illinois; those of Ohio came on west to Indiana and to Illinois.

After Peter Hanks was killed at Tippecanoe, his family went to Texas. At the same time, the descendants of Moses Hanks went to Texas to join the Austin Colony. Everywhere the Peter Hankses went the Virginia origin Hankses went: to Carolina, to Kentucky, to Illinois, and to Texas. So it seems certain to this researcher that the Peter Hanks family was a part of the Southern branch of the Hanks family; but there seems to be no place in this line of descent to place Abraham Hanks.

CHART TO SHOW DESCENT FROM PETER HANKS I, THROUGH HIS SON,

WILLIAM, TO HANKS MEN LIVING IN 1784, IM VIRGINIA

ELIZABETH HANKS
b. ?; d. 1702

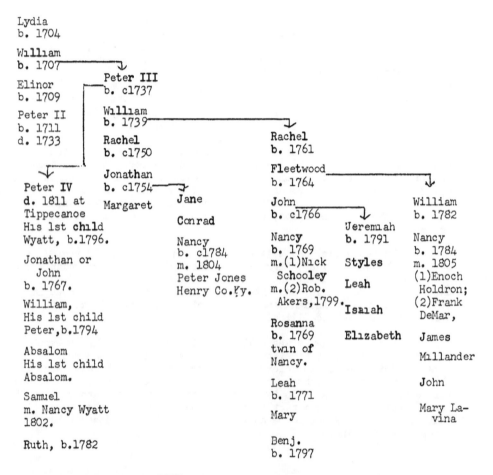

PETER I
d. 1733

Lydia
b. 1704

William
b. 1707

Elinor   Peter III
b. 1709   b. c1737

Peter II   William
b. 1711   b. 1739   Rachel
d. 1733   b. 1761
      Rachel
      b. c1750   Fleetwood
            b. 1764
      Jonathan
Peter IV   b. c1754   John   William
d. 1811 at Margaret Jane b. c1766   b. 1782
Tippecanoe   Jeremiah
His 1st child   Conrad Nancy b. 1791 Nancy
Wyatt, b.1796.   b. 1769   b. 1784
      Nancy m.(1)Nick Styles m. 1805
Jonathan or b. c1784 Schooley   (1)Enoch
 John   m. 1804 m.(2)Rob. Leah Holdron;
b. 1767.   Peter Jones Akers,1799.   (2)Frank
      Henry Co.Ky.   Isaiah DeMar,
William,   Rosanna
His 1st child   b. 1769 Elizabeth James
Peter,b.1794   twin of
        Nancy.   Millander
Absalom
His 1st child   Leah   John
Absalom.   b. 1771

Samuel   Mary   Mary La-
m. Nancy Wyatt   vina
1802.   Benj.
         b. 1797
Ruth, b.1782

Traditional Nancy, b. 1784; no records, evidence, or clues located to
confirm the tradition.
Savilla, b. 1787; m. James Craig, 1803.
(May have been a daughter of John, b. 1767.

ii

THE WILLIAM HANKS II LINE OF DESCENT

In a search for the ancestry of Abraham Hanks of Richmond County, Virginia, to one who has become somewhat acquainted with the characteristics of this Hanks family, some of their peculiar traits and practices may be guides. One is their propensity to use the same given names in each succeeding generation; another proclivity is their going apart in their successive migrations and the coming together again in the several Hanks family settlements.

So, it is no wonder to learn that William succeeded William in a long line of descent; the trace of the line becomes the sign of the route of their exodus from the Northern Neck; their heirs southward through Virginia, the Carolinas, to settlements in the deep South. Happily, one of the emigrants, old Epiphroditus, became a character in his own right and escaped anonymity; for without an occasional unique given name the identification of the accompanying Williams, Johns, and Thomases, would be more difficult.

This latest research has discovered and identified early William Hankses of Richmond County, Virginia, and has developed the line and lists of the children of William I, of William II, and of William III, even unto the fourth generation, William Henry Hanks, of Granville County, North Carolina. This branch of the family that wended its way southward apparently left no male member of the branch in Richmond County. In the subsequent generations of this family from William Hanks I, through William II, several girls named Nancy were born, and, from various records, are placed; but there is no Abraham Hanks in this line to have been a father of one, and obviously no place for him to be fitted into it.[1]

Since these three Williams are placed, the exceptional William is, by the elimination, known to be the son of John and Catharine Hanks, and born March 9, 1715. He was old enough to have been the father of Abraham Hanks, and the possibility will be discussed under the following sub-chapter iii, of John.

There is one indirect reference to a fifth William Hanks of the Northern Neck area, who could not have been one of the above four;

---

[1]
cf: chart, end of this sub-chapter ii.

for he was lately dead before a poll of Freeholders was taken in
Richmond County,[2] and the identity of the two listed thereon are known.
Then too, he may have been a resident of Lancaster County; at least his
son, John was. The Lancaster County Court met on March 19, 1756, and
this is the record.[3]

> "On the prayer of John Hanks orphan of
> William Hanks dec'd he is by the Court
> bound to Joseph Blakemore til the age of
> twenty-one years his said Master is to
> Learn him to Read and Write and the Trade
> of Taylor and to find and provide him with
> sufficient Wholesome and Cleanly diet Lodging
> and apparrell and at the Expiration of his
> Servitude to pay and allow him as appointed
> for servants by use or customs."

The fact that this young John Hanks, who was bound, has his
record in Lancaster and not in Richmond County where Abraham likely
resided, is not material, for all the Hankses resided in the area
where the three counties, Richmond, Lancaster and Northumberland
come together. But, it does seem that if Abraham Hanks, of Richmond
County, had been a son of this William Hanks deceased, he too, would
have been bound out at about the same time and the record of his binding out ought to appear on the Order Books of one of the three counties.
The Books of the counties are extant, and have been carefully examined
for this purpose, but no such record has been discovered. In addition,
in Lancaster County are a set of books called Account Books and a
search of them uncovers no name of Abraham Hanks.

This deceased William Hanks has not been identified for this
purpose. If we assume for the sake of speculation that John, bound,
was aged twelve, the minimum age for apprenticeship, his father,
William, could have been born as late as the early 1720's . Considering
dates and ages this William could have been a son of Robert Hanks,
Junior, but there is no clue. An equal inference could be that he was

---

2
Order Book 14, p. 262, Richmond County, Virginia.

3
Order Book K #10, p. 415, Lancaster County, Virginia.

a son of Luke I, if he died in Lancaster County, where John was
bound, for Luke I and some of his children finally congregated
there; but the place of his death is not known. Then too, since
both William II and John named their first born sons William for
their father, William, it may be that Luke I also did so; if this
theory is correct this William would have been born about 1712.[4]

But, the more important question is: did he have children
other than son, John, and was _Abraham_ a son? The question remains
moot.

---

[4] Could this man be the William Hanks who, according to
tradition, as mentioned by Mrs. Hitchcock, went from New England to
settle near the mouth of the Rappahannock River in Virginia?

CHART TO SHOW DESCENT FROM WILLIAM HANKS I, THROUGH HIS SON,
WILLIAM II, TO HANKS MEN LIVING IN 1784, IN VIRGINA

WILLIAM HANKS I
Born c 1650; died 1704

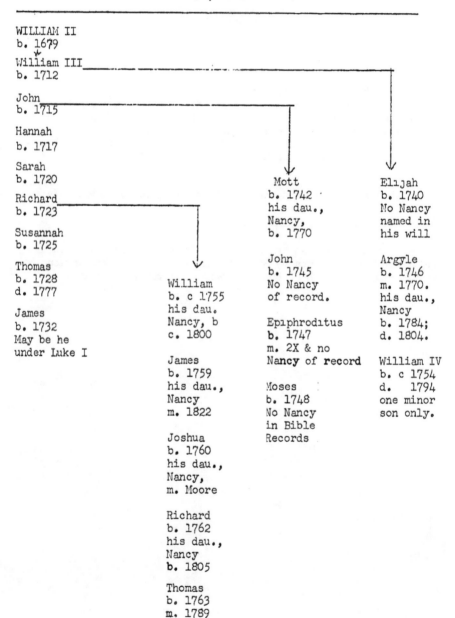

WILLIAM II
b. 1679

William III
b. 1712

John
b. 1715

Hannah
b. 1717

Sarah
b. 1720

Richard
b. 1723

Susannah
b. 1725

Thomas
b. 1728
d. 1777

James
b. 1732
May be he
under Luke I

William
b. c 1755
his dau.
Nancy, b
c. 1800

James
b. 1759
his dau.,
Nancy
m. 1822

Joshua
b. 1760
his dau.,
Nancy,
m. Moore

Richard
b. 1762
his dau.,
Nancy
b. 1805

Thomas
b. 1763
m. 1789

Mott
b. 1742
his dau.,
Nancy,
b. 1770

John
b. 1745
No Nancy
of record.

Epiphroditus
b. 1747
m. 2X & no
Nancy of record

Moses
b. 1748
No Nancy
in Bible
Records

Elijah
b. 1740
No Nancy
named in
his will

Argyle
b. 1746
m. 1770.
his dau.,
Nancy
b. 1784;
d. 1804.

William IV
b. c 1754
d. 1794
one minor
son only.

iii

THE JOHN HANKS LINE OF DESCENT

The dates of births of the known children of John and
Catharine Hanks, from 1715 to 1734, as recorded in the North
Farnham Parish Register indicate such orderly sequence and becoming intervals as to leave no doubt that all the births of
their children were recorded. It is true that after the death
of John, the widow, Catharine was cited by the Court to show
cause why her younger children should not be bound out.[1] Three
years earlier, John himself, had been so cited.[2] Perhaps the
family was indigent and John in ill health. He died just past
middle age. From these circumstances, and Abraham Hanks being
a bound boy, an inference could be that he was a son of John.
But, John was deceased by 1740 and as Abraham was born after 1743
he could not have been even a posthumous child of John; so that
theory is out.

But, John had sons born early enough to have been the father
of Abraham. His oldest son was William, born 1715 or 16, and he was
mentioned in the preceeding sub-chapter under the title of William
Hanks II, in order to identify and differentiate him from the other
Williams. The Parish record of North Farnham shows that a daughter,
Mary Ann was born April 16, 1737, to William and Winifred Hanks. An
assumption is that this William was the son of John, but, of course,
he could have been the William, who died before 1756 and left a son
John, to be bound in Lancaster County.

In either event; there are no later records of births of
children to William and Winifred, although a William continued to
reside in North Farnham parish. In July of 1757 when the poll list
of Freeholders in Richmond County was taken and two William Hanks
names appeared. One of them was William, who married Sarah Durham;
the other was the William, son of John. He was only twenty-one or
two years of age, and if he was married to Winifred, when Mary Ann
was born, naturally other children would be expected. There are a
few unplaced Hankses of Mary Ann's generation but the evidence does
not seem to place them with William and Winifred. In 1782 William

---

[1] Order Book 11, p. 100, August 4, 1740.

[2] Order Book 10, p. 512, April 4, 1737.

son of John, received his distributive share of his mother, Catharine's estate. Had he not been living the probate record should have shown the names of his children, if any, as his heirs. The presumption is he was not the father of Abraham.

Joseph Hanks, the second son of John, was born 1725 and apparently late in life married Ann Lee.* He is the Joseph Hanks who was adopted by Barton to be the father of an unplaced Lucey (sic) Hanks of Kentucky, and who was alleged to be the mother of Nancy Hanks Lincoln. It can be demonstrated that Barton based his theory upon an erroneous premise.[3] He thought that a census of 1782 listed only one Joseph Hanks. Therefore, he deduced that the Joseph born 1725 just had to be the Joseph on the 1782 list and also, the late Joseph of Nelson County, Kentucky. But, this poll was the local tithe list required by the Court of Hampshire County. A national census, properly taken, that year would have shown four or five other Joseph Hankses. From several records, this Joseph, son of John, seems to have always resided in Richmond County, Virginia. The parish register shows that he and his wife, Ann, had a daughter, Betty, born March 4, 1771. Since this couple had Betty's name recorded does it not seem reasonable to presume that if other children had been born to them the names would have been recorded? No other names are recorded, included the absence of the name of Abraham as a son.

John Hanks, the third son, was born 1728, and his wife of family record was Sussannah. If the couple had daughters, it is not known, but at least four sons are attributed to them and, of these, George, the oldest, was born in the late 1750's; the others, in the 1760's. The subsequent tax records of Richmond County confirm these birth dates and show no other probable sons, nor an Abraham.

Thomas Hanks, the fourth son, was born in 1732, and married Betty Lee, a sister of the wife of his brother, Joseph. The couple had two children, born in the 1760's. It is obvious that Thomas was rather young to have fathered Abraham, born in the late 1740's.

Alexander Hanks, the last and youngest son, was born in 1734; there is no record of his marriage; he went to the Revolutionary War and died during his service, 1776, leaving no heirs, for when his mother's estate was settled in 1782 he was deceased and no heirs were listed as his children to receive what would have been his distributive share.

---

* CF: Chapter VII, xiv.

[3] Daniel Fish to Barton, Correspondence, Barton papers, Library Chicago University.

Although there is a tradition among the descendants in the
John Hanks line that their more immediate ancestors were close kin
to Lincoln; and the mother of Alden Hanks Wyatt, a descendant,
mentioned Abraham Hanks as connected in some way; there does not seem
to be any place in this line of descent to put him.

CHART **TO** SHOW DESCENT FROM WILLIAM HANKS I, THROUGH HIS SON
JOHN TO HANKS MEN **LIVING** IN 1784, IN VIRGINIA

WILLIAM HANKS **I.**
Born c 1650; died 1704

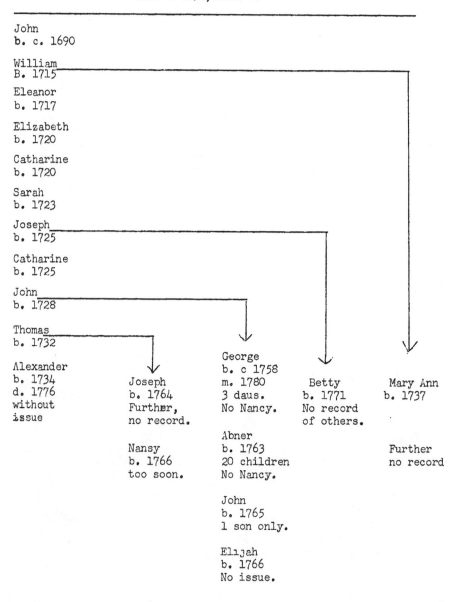

John
b. c. 1690

William
B. 1715

Eleanor
b. 1717

Elizabeth
b. 1720

Catharine
b. 1720

Sarah
b. 1723

Joseph
b. 1725

Catharine
b. 1725

John
b. 1728

Thomas
b. 1732

Alexander
b. 1734
d. 1776
without
issue

Joseph
b. 1764
Further,
no record.

Nansy
b. 1766
too soon.

George
b. c 1758
m. 1780
3 daus.
No Nancy.

Abner
b. 1763
20 children
No Nancy.

John
b. 1765
1 son only.

Elijah
b. 1766
No issue.

Betty
b. 1771
No record
of others.

Mary Ann
b. 1737

Further
no record

iv

THE LUKE HANKS I LINE OF DESCENT

We are confronted with the irrefutable fact that an
Abraham Hanks lived and died in Virginia and was a boy in Richmond
County. It has been demonstrated that he cannot be placed in the
family lines of descent of Peter Hanks I, of William Hanks II, or of
John Hanks. There are no records extant, if any ever existed, to
show that Robert Hanks Junior[1] had a wife or family or descendants.
It follows, therefore, that only Luke Hanks I, or one of his sons, is
left to be presumed as the father of Abraham Hanks.

From these same demonstrations of constituted families the
presumption is that Luke Hanks I and his two wives were the parents
of other unplaced Hanks children of the next generation. Since Luke I
is the only one of the Hanks men of his generation, who is known to
have had children and whose children are not all known, it is necessary
to try to develop a list of them and to explore the possibility that
Abraham may be included without disturbing the chronological order
of their births. Of all the groups of Hanks children, the determination
of those of Luke I is the most difficult and is probably the most important for the present purpose.

Luke Hanks I became the ancestor of a long line of successive
generations with members bearing the given name of Luke. The name
occurred not only in the straight line of descent from Luke Hanks,
father to son, but also among the sons of the brothers and sisters of
the several Lukes. It is to be observed that, while the name of Luke
prevails in this branch, it was not used one single time in any of the
other three branches.

Another thing to be noted is that the descendants of Peter
Hanks I moved mostly westward through Pennsylvania to Ohio, Indiana
and Iowa. Every branch of the William Hanks II line worked southward
and thence westward. The descendants of John continued in the Northern
Neck except some grandsons, who married daughters in the famous Dale
family and followed the Dales into Kentucky. Luke's sons and descendants
were the restless ones: they went up the Rappahannock River valley;
they wandered southward; and, eventually, most of his grandsons
settled in Kentucky. Some of the sons of Luke II, who migrated to
South Carolina, even joined their uncles in Kentucky and in Tennessee.

---

[1] cf: Chapt. VII, xiv.

Luke Hanks I, who was born after 1679 and before 1687, did not need a guardian in 1708 when his step-father died, as did his younger brother John. Luke probably married at the usual age of twenty-five and his first children should have been born in due course. His children of record in the parish register were Alexander, Lucretia, and Turner. The known unplaced Hankses of his children's generation are: William, deceased by 1756; Dawson, George, Ann and Sarah; Joseph; James of Campbell County; lastly, the Abraham, whose identity we seek.

As was suggested in sub-chapter ii, it is possible that the unplaced William Hanks, who died prior to 1756, leaving a son John, may have been the first child of Luke I, in which case he was born about 1712. It is not known whether Abraham was his son as was stated before.

The name Luke Hanks, Junr., appears in an Order Book in 1736. The natural inference is that he was a son of Luke I and then aged twenty-one or past, with a birth date of about 1715. For identification, he will be referred to as Luke II. His life history can be easily traced to his death in South Carolina in 1789, where he left a will. The records there indicate he had twelve children; but no Abraham was among them.

Years later, some grandsons of Luke Hanks II, including the Rev. Matthew E. Hanks, a remarkable and intelligent man, set down the family traditions[2] that their grandfather had had brothers and named a "James, with wife Nancy, John and George or Robert." Before adding these sons to the family of Luke I, these clues must be examined with the other evidence.

The name of Dawson Hanks appears several times in the Order Books in civil cases, either suing or being sued. He was in the same locality as Luke Hanks I, in Richmond County and later in Lancaster County. In Lancaster County, he attended the sale of assets of the estate of Luke Hanks I, deceased, and was awarded a "Barrell of corn as his due." The earliest dates, pertaining to him, begin in the 1740's. He was probably born at least twenty-one years earlier, or prior to 1720. Therefore, we place his birth at about 1717. (Incidentally, the name Dawson, being the surname of a local family, may indicate that Luke I's first wife was a Dawson. This is only a surmise based on the assumption that Luke I named his first son William for his father, the second son, Luke for himself, and the third for his wife's people.)

---

[2] D. J. Knotts to Barton, Correspondence, Lib. Chicago University, Barton papers.

On solid ground, we come to the entry in the parish
register: "Born, Alexr, son of Luke and Elizabeth Hanks, Oct. 31,
1719." Later in life, this son, like Dawson, has his name in the
old Order Books, in the same years and the same localities as his
father. As with Dawson there is no record, evidence, or clue that
he had a wife and children. But his name scattered through the
records gives evidence that ALEXANDER HANKS with known birth date
survived to maturity.

Next in the copy of the births of the North Farnham Parish
is, "Born, LUCRETIA, dau. of Luke & Elizabeth Hanks, June 1, 1722."

Following this birth there is an interval of fifteen years
when no births are recorded for the family of Luke and his wife
Elizabeth. Then, "Born Turner, son of Luke & Elizabeth Hanks, June
18, 1737." These are three important dates: they show that Elizabeth
was a childbearing woman over a period of years and probably not
barren between the births as recorded. It is obvious that the date
of birth of Turner is too late for him to have been the father of
Abraham, born as late even as 1750.

Again comes an hiatus of several years before there is
recorded, "Born, MARTHA, dau. of Luke & Sarah Hanks, May 26, 1752."
This is a different wife but undoubtedly the same Luke; for Luke, who
died in Lancaster County in early 1756, had a wife Sarah. His property
and furniture were listed by the appraisers as "old" as would be the
case if the items had been owned by an old man who had worn them out
by use.

It would seam natural and fitting that other births occurred
in the family; but, if so, the birth records are missing, as is the
record of birth of Luke Hanks Junr., who is almost certainly the
son of Luke I. If such other supposed births were recorded, careful
search has not revealed them. Unfortunately registers of neighboring
parishes are no longer extant.

Luke Hanks I was a member of the Church and not a dissenter,
but he was hardly in good standing. His home was many miles away
from the church in North Farnham and he was not a regular attendant.
At the June term of Court, 1717, it was,

> "Ordered that the Sheriff Sumons to next Court
> Luke Hanks John Hanks (13 others named) to answer
> presentment of the Grandjury....for not going to
> Church."

So the omission of the birth records may mean that Luke I was not
co-operative or that he was out of the parish for a time. He lived
near the county line and was a tenant farmer. He evidently moved
over into Lancaster County and into a different parish. It is of
interest to note, three years after Luke's death, a record on page 54:

> "At a Vestry Held for the upper precinct of
> Christ parish in Lancaster County on Tuesday
> the 2 of Aprell 1759 for Distributing the fines ---
>
> * * *
>
> To Luke Hanks   00 - 5 - - "

The absence of records of birth dates for the unplaced Hanks
children necessitates their estimation from other sources. In an
Order Book is the name, ANN HANKS, and under circumstances that indicate
she was born about 1725. This fits so well in order after the birth
of Lucretia that we list Ann as a presumptive child.

In a History of Kentucky, with reference to the Hanks family
of Anderson County, is the statement that their ancestor, George Hanks,
was killed at the Battle of Yorktown. But, by irrefutable evidence
and proof, their ancestor in Virginia was Turner Hanks, the son of
record of Luke Hanks I. Goerge Hanks, however, did exist and the
memory of him has been kept in the family traditions of Kentucky and
South Carolina, for his name appears once as a witness to a will made
in 1767, along with Rawleigh Gibson and George Glascock, Jr..[3] There
are no records in the old Order Books that he was ever summoned before
the Grandjury, or put under peace bond, or fined for not attending
Church, or sued for debts or tobacco, as were some of his Hanks
cousins, whose misdemeanors we forgive, for their more undesirable
records add items which permit us to trace them more readily.

George seems to have been a man of peace who went to war.
Very likely he was killed at the Battle of Yorktown, as is the tradition. Perhaps it was in his honour that so many future George
Hankses were given his name. The gratifying conclusion is that he was
a son of Luke I.

It is a conjecture that the George Hanks, who married Mary
Tuggle in Middlesex County in 1775 was a son of this George of Luke I;
but there is no evidence. If he were a son of George and born about
twenty-five years before his wedding, it would make his father born

---

[3] Will of Alice (Goad) Dodson Fowler, Will Book 6, 1753-1757,
p. 420.

about 1728, which date fits into the supposed sequence of births.

Considering this birth date for George, Abraham Hanks could have been his son; but this is hardly feasible in consideration of evidence to be adduced.

There has been much speculation pertaining to the origin of Joseph Hanks of Nelson County, Kentucky. It seems well settled that he once resided in Hampshire County, (then in) Virginia, in Amelia County, and, according to Dennis Hanks, in Halifax County. In all this there is no conflict; the sons of Luke Hanks I were rovers, and he is presumed to be one of them.[4] Calculating from the known birth dates of some of his younger children and from the supposed dates of birth of his older ones, a marriage date in the late 1750's seems probable as does a birth date in the 1730's. In his will he names five sons and three daughters but no Abraham. By tradition, not confirmed and not refuted, he was a brother of Abraham Hanks.[5] By a tradition in South Carolina, he was a brother of Luke Hanks II.[6] This latter relationship makes him another son of Luke Hanks I.

The name of Sarah Hanks is in an Order Book, connected with an incident that would place her birth as, also, in the 1730's say, about 1735. She has not been identified and, being unplaced, may have been a daughter of Luke I.

The fulfillment of the interim between the births of Lucretia and Turner with dates, not entirely arbitrary, but in orderly sequence and inferentially from known facts, seems reasonable. This brings the proposition up to the birth of Turner Hanks and to the consideration of the next gap to "Born Martha, dau. of Luke & Sarah Hanks, May 26, 1752." There are only two unplaced Hanks people left to fill out this space: James Hanks of Campbell County and, of course, Abraham, whose father we seek. But, there is possibly Moses Hanks of Pittsylvania County, Virginia, to be considered. Previous presumption pertaining to Moses has placed him as a son of another than Luke I, but without positive evidence.

---

[4] cf: VII, vii.

[5] Hitchcock, Nancy Hanks, p. 28.

[6] Knotts to Barton, Correspondence, Barton papers, Chicago University Library.

James Hanks of Campbell County, Virginia, named his first son Abraham. There is no evidence to connect him with Luke Hanks I but there is much circumstantial evidence that connects him with our subject, Abraham Hanks. He had previously resided in Amelia County where his wife Nancy died. In Campbell County, where he later resided, Abraham Hanks came to be near him. The Sarah Hanks, who signed as a witness to a deed for James may have been the wife of Abraham. James had a third son, James Junr. There is a family tradition, unconfirmed, that Sarah Hanks, a daughter of Abraham Hanks, married a cousin, James Hanks. If the James she married was the son of James of Campbell, then he and Abraham were brothers, if the term "cousin" was used precisely, with the same parentage or, at least, the same father. The determination must wait.

It was, of course, after the birth of Turner and before the birth of Martha Hanks that Elizabeth, first wife of Luke I, died and he married Sarah. So far, no record of their marriage has been located. Sarah may have been the mother of James and Abraham but in the absence of proof it is assumed that Martha was the only child of Luke and Sarah Hanks. It is of interest that Luke Hanks II named a daughter Martha after his half-sister. This is another clue that tends to confirm his relationship to Luke Hanks I.

It has been remarked that it was the practice of many Hanks parents to name their children for their own parents or their brothers and sisters. A comparison of the names of their children shows that Turner, Luke II, Abraham and Moses, had sons named George. Again, Turner, Luke II, and Abraham, had sons named Luke. It may be significant that Abraham called his second son Luke after his first son was named Abraham for himself. James named his first son Abraham, followed by Thomas and James. Joseph had sons Thomas and James.

The first daughters of Luke II and Joseph Hanks were named Elizabeth, for their grandmother, Elizabeth. Luke II, Joseph, and Abraham all three had daughters named Nancy, for the wife Nancy of Luke II or Nancy of James. They were the first Nancys known in the Virginia Hanks families. James wife was probably Nancy Hamlin of Loudoun County.

It is submitted that if this were an ordinary genealogy the foregoing placements would be acceptable but, considering that it may be of more historical import to place Abraham Hanks, the father of Nancy Hanks Lincoln, the proposition that he may have been a son of Luke Hanks I, will be taken up next.

John Hanks, the younger brother of Luke I, died between
1737 and 1740, and left his wife, Catharine, a widow with nine
children, the youngest having been born in 1734. The members of
the Richmond County Court were concerned about their welfare and
cited Catharine, the widow, to come into Court and show cause why
some of her children should not be bound out. This was the legal
custom then with the cases of indigent children. There is no
further record of what was done; but there is, years later, the
record of another case, in an old Order Book, that is pertinent to
this investigation.

On June 6, 1763, the Court of the same county, Richmond, as
was its practice, gave consideration to certain circumstances of
another case and, after deliberation:[7]

> "Ordered the churchwardens of Northfarnham Parish
> for the time being bind Abraham Hanks to Turner Hanks
> According to Law he being now discharged from his
> former master William Glascock Junr.
>
> John Woodbridge."

This very first record, so far discovered, of Abraham Hanks,
places him with the Hanks family in Richmond County, Virginia. His
given name of Abraham probably indicates kinship with the Dale family
in which the name was often used.

The fact that Abraham was a bound boy in 1763 indicates he
was under twenty-one so he was not born prior to 1742. From other
records, it is known that his first child was born about 1770, so it
is likely that he was not born after 1750. His birth date may be
assumed as approximately 1745. His earliest possible birth date
eliminates him as a possible posthumous son of the deceased John Hanks
and widow Catharine. But he was born before the death of Luke I, and
the commitment to William Glascock Junr. may have followed. No record
of this act has been located. If one was made it was probably in the
North Farnham Parish Vestry book and it is missing.[8]

---

[7] Order Book 15, p. 119, Richmond County, Virginia.

[8] Northern Neck of Virginia Historical Magazine, Richmond County,
p. 712.

In other records of minors "bound out" a reason is usually given in the entry which will state that, "WHEREAS ... the child is an orphan, or an afflicted child, or the bastard child of .....etc." as the case may be. In cases of apprenticeship "until the age of twenty-one" the duties of the Master are fully set out; like the list of instructions when John Hanks of Lancaster County was bound.[9] It is to be noted that there is no explanation for the binding "for the time being" in Abraham's case and no duties laid upon Turner to fulfill, to teach him to read and write or to see that he has a good start in life at the age of twenty-one. In fact, no age limit is set.

This very state of being a ward would seem to indicate that Abraham was an orphan or half orphan, or the child of indigent parents, or of a helpless widow. Perhaps Abraham was only a step-child of Sarah, the widow of Luke I. After his decease, when Henry Tapscott settled his estate, the proceeds of the sale of personal property did not bring enough to pay all the debts; the estate was insolvent. There were no funds left for the widow and her family. Abraham Hanks may have been doubly destitute and devoid of a home until William Glascock Junior took him up.

The Glascock Neighbors

William Glascock Junior is first known by this name in the will dated November 5, 1747, of his grandmother, Million (Downman) Glascock.[10] She was the widow of George Glascock who had pre-deceased her as early as 1714. He left a will in which he named sons William, George, Thomas, and John. In 1740 Thomas died and left all his property to his mother. In her will she mentions her sons George and John and several grandchildren by name, including both William and William, Junior. Another son, not named in her will, was William, the father of William Glascock Junior. When he died years later, he left, "...son William (Junior) 150 pounds and forgiveness of all accounts against him."

Million's son, George Glascock, died February 27, 1752. His will[11] dated, June 2, 1749, was witnessed by William Hanks, Richard Hanks and Thomas Hanks. The Hanks witnesses were evidentially brothers, three of the sons of William Hanks II and his wife, Hester C. Mills. William Hanks III had married January 26, 1738, Sarah Durham, daughter of Thomas and Mary (Smoot) Durham. Richard Hanks married before September 25, 1753, to Mary Hinds, daughter of James and Patience Hinds.

---

[9] cf: IV, ii, p. 228

[10] Will Book 5, p. 644, Richmond County, Virginia.

[11] Will Book 5, p. 710, Richmond County, Virginia.

The connection of these Hanks brothers with the Glascock family has not been determined.[12]

Richard Chichester married on July 3, 1734, Ellen Ball, a sister of Judith (Ball) Glascock, who was the wife of George Glascock, (Jr.). Richard died in 1743 or 1744, leaving six children: Richard, J[O]hn, Elizabeth, Ellen, Mary and Hannah. His widow, Ellen, married on June 12, 1747 William Downman, a nephew of Million (Downman) Glascock. One of the daughters, Elizabeth, was born about 1737; she married at the early age of fifteen, on January 20, 1752, William Glascock, Junior.

William Glascock, Junior and his young bride had a bright future. She had inherited a fortune from her father, Richard Chichester, and it was being administered under the trusteeship of careful William Downman, her step-father and guardian. The father of William Glascock Junior deeded to him a gift of 200 acres of farm land in the Autumn of the year of his wedding,[13] and he could start his farming operations and tobacco growing the coming Spring. The farm lay on Marsh Landing Creek, one of the entry ports for shipping out tobacco. The Glascocks were of an important and influential family; the Court often appointed a member to some serious service; young William, Junior was appointed Captain of the Militia. Yes, his prospects were favorable.

But William, Junior could not leave well enough alone. William Downman wrote to his brother,

> "......that Mr. Glascock would not let me rest until I gave him 'Betty's' fortune...but before I gave it to him I got a bond from him exonerating me from any further charges on her estate."

The next year, no doubt using his wife's money, he purchased from William III and Sarah Hanks, the tract of land called "Briary Swamp" of 95 acres that William had inherited from his father, William II. The cost was £50, in hand paid, a tidy sum but, no doubt, William felt affluent!

Happily on July 4, 1754, a baby boy was born to the couple and named William Chichester Glascock. His birth is recorded in the North Farnham Parish Register. Then tragedy struck; the little boy at the cute age of two years died, and the bereft mother was not yet twenty.

---

[12] All the names, dates, and relationships are set out for future searchers.

[13] Deed Book 11, p. 139, Richmond County, Virginia.

If the parish records may be accepted, no other babies came to take
his place. Luke Hanks I died a poor man in 1757. His sons were not
too prosperous and some were still single and not capable of caring
properly for a younger relative. It would seem the natural thing
for the prosperous local merchant, William Glascock, Junior, to take
Abraham Hanks, the boy, especially since he and Elizabeth had lately
lost their two year old son. It was especially fitting if Glascock
or his wife was kin to the Hankses.

William Glascock, Junior began to sell off his farmland and
go into business as a merchant. From the names of some of his customers
that he had to sue to collect his accounts, he apparently operated in
the area where Richmond, Lancaster and Northumberland Counties meet.
In this vicinity many members of the Hanks family resided, including
Luke I and his sons, Luke II, Dawson and Alexander. There was also
John Hanks who married Mary Mott, and the younger John Hanks, who was
bound to Joseph Blakemore. Henry Tapscott, an important business man,
was here. James Gordon, Gent., another noted business man had to sue
John Hanks for some Ł 66. William Glascock, Junior finally sued even
William Downman and his wife, Elizabeth's mother!

Due to the lack of direct evidence, these antecedent events,
so far as they are relevant, including the death of Luke Hanks in 1757
and the six year interval to the transfer of responsibility for
Abraham Hanks from William Glascock, Junior to Turner Hanks is important
for the purpose of this research. Abraham Hanks is by this record,
above noted, located in Richmond County, Virginia, under the super-
vision of the Court, and for a time, previous to the transfer, in the
care of William Glascock, Junior. Abraham Hanks was presumably by this
time within a few years of his majority. The inference is he was an
orphan.

But by 1763 conditions had changed and Glascock was in
financial and domestic difficulties. His creditors were bringing suits,
obtaining judgments and attachments against his properties and even
garnishments of his debtor's accounts. One man wrote in his diary,
"I was summoned to declare what I owed Capt. Glascock, who is run
away." Another entry reads, "This day we had it confirmed that Capt.
Glascock ran away last week and took a young woman with him and left
his wife." The diarist continued to be interested in the sad affair,
"Mr. Chichester went to see his sister Glascock, who must be in great
distress."[14]

_____

[14]William & Mary College Quarterly Mag., 1st Ser., Vol. 12,
p. 1 Journal of Colonel James Gordon of Lancaster County for 1763.

Indeed, the distress of the abandoned young wife must
have been great due not only to humiliation but impending destitution
and actual want of victuals for herself and for the bound boy,
Abraham Hanks. Becoming aware of the situation, the Richmond County
Court took action and they did transfer Abraham Hanks to the custody
and care of Turner Hanks and without restrictions and without the
usual instructions pertaining to apprenticeships. From this fact, the
inference is that the Court had full faith and confidence and expecta-
tion that Turner would treat Abraham as a member of his immediate
family, even as a brother.

Abraham was in his teens when he went with Turner Hanks and
Turner was only twenty-five years old, newly married and with a baby
just two years old. It was asking quite a bit for the young wife to
take on another burden, the care of a boy, but the Hankses have always
looked after their own. Of course, Abraham was then old enough to be
helpful around the house and on the farm of 105 acres that Turner
purchased from Thomas Durham the following year. Turner continued to
live on this farm until his death, after which his heirs owned it a
long time.

Abraham Hanks was not growing up in the border country; the
Virginia frontier had been pushed back to the Blue Ridge and beyond,
where a line of forts, both to the north and to the south of Fort
Cumberland on the Potomac River, was established in an attempt to
keep back the French and Indians. In fact, county courts had been
functioning in the lower counties of the Northern Neck for a hundred
years. The Courts made a practice of binding young men out to learn
the trades of carpenter, cooper, candlestick maker, and all the other
necessary service trades.

Many of the Hanks men were carpenters: William I, and his
sons and grandchildren followed the trade for three generations.
Peter Hanks I was a carepenter and cooper. As noted, John Hanks
was apprenticed to be a "Taylor". It is thought that Abraham became
a blacksmith. There is a vague tradition to that effect; but whether
he learned it under the tutelege of Turner or under the direction of
William Calk is not known. His son, Abraham, Jr., was said to be a
blacksmith and a maker of cow-bells. Descendants of the Hanks family
own one he made.[15] Another son of Abraham, Luke, was a worker in iron
and a wagon maker in Breckenridge County, Kentucky. Luke's daughter,
Nancy, married Peter French, a blacksmith, and kept the trade in the
family.

[15]Mrs. Valera Leadley to Baber, Correspondence, Baber papers.

Some one taught Abraham to write, and it may well have been William Calk. It has been remarked before that ABraham hanks (sic), who accompanied William Calk into Kentucky had a characteristic signature, as noted. This is exactly the same way that Calk wrote Abraham's name in his journal a few times. There is more to be said: his genuine signature on an original bond, not a copy,[16] has been examined for this purpose, and it indicates the writing of one with little practice; such as one bound out would lack opportunity to learn to write well. His son, Abraham, Jr., it is of interest, signed his marriage papers with a good hand.[17] Abram Haniks (sic), the Revolutionary War veteran of Campbell County and later of Lincoln County, Tennessee, signed his pension application papers with a bold hand.[18]

After the end of the French and Indian War, many inhabitants of the lower counties of the Northern Neck pushed up the ridge road, between the Rappahannock and the Potomac Rivers, to settle in the upper counties. These included, by the new names that began to appear in the courthouse records of the respective counties between the rivers, members of the Dale, the Dodson, the Sydnor, the Wyatt, the Harper, and the Hanks families. There was Robert Dale, whose niece or daughter, Nancy, had married Luke Hanks II. There was Thomas Wyatt, whose daughter, Elizabeth by his first wife, married a Hanks. Thomas, himself, married second, Margaret Hanks, the daughter of William Hanks the Quaker; their son, Abner Wyatt, was bound out at the age of fourteen to be taught the trade of tailor. William the Quaker had come into Loudoun County from Maryland. George and James Hanks were there in Loudoun County and they have not been identified. The Hamlin family lived there; James Hanks of Amelia County had a wife, probably a Hamlin whom he may have met here. Joseph Hanks, whose wife was a Shipley or a Lee, went further up the valley to Hampshire County. Also, up the ridge road came George and Elizabeth Harper to settle in Prince William County; it was their daughter, Sarah, who later married Abraham Hanks.

Knowing that Turner and Luke Hanks II were brothers, and with Abraham associated with Turner, it is not surprising to learn that when Luke II removed from Lancaster to Fauquier County, he was accompanied or joined later by Abraham. All this area was in the Fairfax proprietorship. The land was leased and not owned by the

---

[16] Calk papers, Mt. Sterling, Kentucky, Photo-copy, Baber papers.

[17] Marriage records, Caswell County, North Carolina, Photo-copy, Baber papers.

[18] Revolutionary War Records, Archives Building, Washington, D.C., Photo-copy, Baber papers.

tenants, so it is difficult to know where some of them lived, except when some church records indicate the parish of residence. The Broad Run Baptist church was in Fauquier County near the Prince William County line; the Friends Meeting was in Waterford in Loudoun County.

Later there was a large migration of the Quakers from this area southward into Bedford and Campbell Counties. It was then that some of the Hanks families removed southward to settle in the Hatt Creek section of Bedford, later Campbell County. James Hanks purchased land and settled near the Hatt Creek Meeting and with children: Abram, Thomas, James Jr., and Tabitha. Moses Hanks lived across the county line in Pittsylvania County and his daughter Frances married Fortunatus Dodson in Halifax County. Thomas Hanks, probably a son of Joseph Hanks, married Nancy Hammock in Lunenburg County. A local tradition in Campbell County points out the farm where Joseph Hanks resided.[19] Abraham and Sarah (Harper) Hanks arrived in this area of the Hatt Creek neighborhood in 1783.

This places this group of Hanks families, most of whom were of the Friends' persuasion, exactly in the section where lived the Shipley, the Berry, the Mitchell, and the Thompson families, some of whom were also Quakers. In this County of Campbell and in the Hatt Creek locality prevails the strongest tradition that Abraham Hanks was the father of Nancy.

CONCLUSION: Evidence presented to support the following facts: 1.) that Abraham Hanks was a boy in Richmond County, Virginia, where resided members of the family of Luke Hanks I.; 2.) that Abraham was not a son or descendant of William II or John Hanks; 3.) that Abraham was placed with Turner Hanks, a son of Luke I and a brother of Luke Hanks II; 4.) that when Luke Hanks II went to Fauquier County he was joined there by Abraham; 5.) that Abraham and Luke Hanks II lived in Fauquier County for several years at the same time; 6.) that both moved to Prince William County at the same time; 7.) that both were taxed the same two years in that county; 8.) that both their names appear on the same page of the tithe records, indicating they were close neighbors; 9.) that both of them left the county at the same time; 10.) that both migrated southward the same year; 11.) that the tradition is strong in Campbell County that Abraham arrived there; and 12.) that Abraham died and is buried there: these factual events, so concurrent and so related, so numerous as to be impossible to be coincidences, all point to the conclusion that Abraham, like Turner, was a brother of Luke II, - all sons of Luke I.

19
    Mrs. Marian A. Faucett, Interview and Correspondence, Baber papers.

FINALITY: The father of Nancy Hanks Lincoln was Abraham Hanks, one of the earliest pioneers to Boonesborough, Kentucky. It would seem from the available evidence, as herein presented, that her grandfather was Luke I, that her great-grandfather was William I, that her great-great -grandfather was Thomas Hanks, the Virginia Planter.

One year after writing the above:

I, Adin Baber, hereby certify that the following is a true and exact copy of the names on an old yellowing sheet of paper, that was received in the mail by me February 19, 1960, and from Melda (Mrs. C.W.) Waldrop of Murray, Kentucky. For further reference see page 316.

	J John	
Luke		Thomas
Allexander		Abraham
Abraham		Thomas
Moses		Samuel
Josepeh		John
James		James
Luke		Joseph
Thomas		Reubin Gen 29
		Daniel
		Jonathin
Sarah J Gen 17		
		Reubin Gen 29

The above described paper is $6\frac{1}{4}$ x $7\frac{1}{2}$ inches.

CHART TO SHOW DESCENT FROM WILLIAM HANKS I, THROUGH HIS SON,
LUKE I, TO HANKS MEN LIVING IN 1784, IN VIRGINIA

WILLIAM HANKS I.
Born c 1650; died 1704

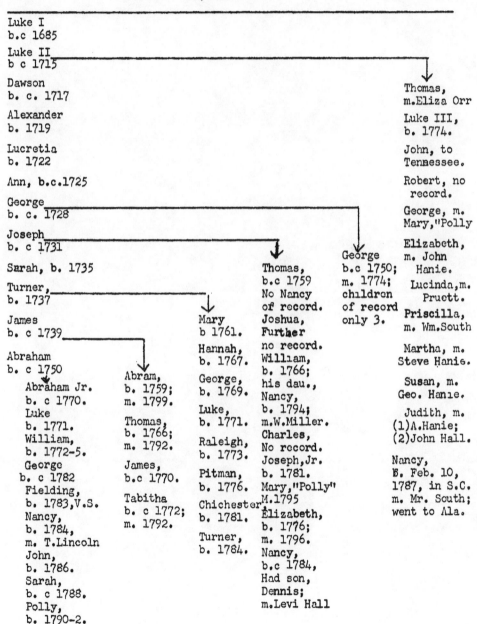

Luke I
b.c 1685

Luke II
b c 1715

Dawson
b. c. 1717

Alexander
b. 1719

Lucretia
b. 1722

Ann, b.c.1725

George
b. c. 1728

Joseph
b. c 1731

Sarah, b. 1735

Turner,
b. 1737

James
b. c 1739

Abraham
b. c 1750

Abraham Jr.
b. c 1770.
Luke
b. 1771.
William,
b. 1772-5.
George
b. c 1782
Fielding,
b. 1783,V.S.
Nancy,
b. 1784,
m. T.Lincoln
John,
b. 1786.
Sarah,
b. c 1788.
Polly,
b. 1790-2.

Abram,
b. 1759;
m. 1799.

Thomas,
b. 1766;
m. 1792.

James,
b.c 1770.

Tabitha
b. c 1772;
m. 1792.

Mary
b 1761.
Hannah,
b. 1767.
George,
b. 1769.
Luke,
b. 1771.
Raleigh,
b. 1773.
Pitman,
b. 1776.
Chichester
b. 1781.
Turner,
b. 1784.

Thomas,
b.c 1759
No Nancy
of record.
Joshua,
Further
no record.
William,
b. 1766;
his dau.,
Nancy,
b. 1794;
m.W.Miller.
Charles,
No record.
Joseph,Jr.
b. 1781.
Mary,"Polly"
M.1795
Elizabeth,
b. 1776;
m. 1796.
Nancy,
b.c 1784,
Had son,
Dennis;
m.Levi Hall

George
b.c 1750;
m. 1774;
children
of record
only 3.

Thomas,
m.Eliza Orr

Luke III,
b. 1774.

John, to
Tennessee.

Robert, no
record.

George, m.
Mary,"Polly

Elizabeth,
m. John
Hanie.

Lucinda,m.
Pruett.

Priscilla,
m. Wm.South

Martha, m.
Steve Hanie.

Susan, m.
Geo. Hanie.

Judith, m.
(1)A.Hanie;
(2)John Hall.

Nancy,
B. Feb. 10,
1787, in S.C.
m. Mr. South;
went to Ala.

CHAPTER V

THE SHIPLEY FAMILY

The clue to the earliest Shipley family in America was con-
tributed by a Mrs. Walthall to Mrs. Hitchcock, who was gathering [1]
the material preparatory to writing her little book, Nancy Hanks.

According to this information, one Robert Shipley of
Londonderry, Ireland, married Mary Tunis of Edinburgh, emigrated to
Pennsylvania, and settled at Pequa in now Lancaster County. They
had thirteen children, of whom, one became the great-grandfather
of Mrs. Walthall, which fact was the origin of her knowledge.

When Lea and Hutchinson prepared their book, The Ancestry
of Abraham Lincoln, they incorporated much of Mrs. Hitchcock's findings
into it, including that about a Robert Shipley and five daughters.
Mrs. Hitchcock had information also from a Mr. J. L. Nall of Missouri,
who told her that the Shipley family of Kentucky came from the Boone
region in North Carolina;[2] but much of Mr. Nall's information has
proved to be woefully unreliable; and records of Shipleys in North
Carolina are scarce.

The late Mrs. Louis D. White of Brookline, Massachusetts,
an able and experienced genealogist did research pertaining to the
Shipley family, and collected data, much of which she communicated
to Mrs. Myra Hank Rudolph, then of Warren County, Ohio, who was
developing the genealogy of her own Hank family. Mrs. Rudolph has,
in turn, made all her Shipley material available for this research.
A study and examination of it indicated that there are many records
of members of the family in the archives and court houses of eastern
Maryland. The early families seem to have resided in Baltimore
County, perhaps in the area south of Baltimore; in fact there was a
small railroad station and post office, of the name, Shipley, just
south of the city and in Carroll County.[3]

---

[1] February 24, 1895, Lea & Hutchinson, N. p. 107.

[2] Nall to Hitchcock, September 27, 1895, Lincoln Library,
Fort Wayne, Indiana.

[3] Postal Guide, 1892, p. 220.

Adam was the first man: Adam Shipley, listed in "Early Settlers, 1668,[4] and of other records in Ann Arundal and Baltimore Counties, Maryland. One source reads he settled on the Severn River. Records show he acquired 200 acres of land March 30, 1681, and named it "Shipley's Choice". Then again in 1687, under the name "Adam the First" he received 500 acres.[5]

His wife was Lois Howard, of a prominant family, whose family name, Howard, is perpetuated in the name of a County, created from Ann Arundal. According to tradition they had a large family of nine sons and two daughters. A partial list of the children includes the daughter Lois, who married Basil Poole; and two sons, Richard and Robert. The name, Katura is a figure, probably a daughter or daughter-in-law. Katura married James Barnes; they had a son, Nathan, and a daughter, Katura. This Barnes name is associated with the Shipley and Hanks names, alongside in records, for a century following.

Richard Shipley, son of Adam, in his Will[6] named his wife, Susannah; she is supposed to have been a Stevens. Four sons were named, viz: Adam, Richard, Samuel, and Peter; who were not "comes to the age of twenty-one". It is obvious that Richard died when a comparatively young man. There was named one daughter, Lois; there had been a daughter Katurah, born March 25, 1717; a friend was named, Benj. Stevens. The will was witnessed by two members of the Dorsey family, and by his brother, Robert Shipley, who used the letter "R" for his mark.[7]

The son Peter of Richard did not live long after his father. He was a young man when he prepared his Will.[8] And, he left everything to his brother, Richard. The Will was probated in 1737.[9] It is evident he was a sick man for when pews were assigned in Christ Church, only his three brothers were named, Adam, Rich, and Sam, to share pew 15.

4
Liber 13, Folio 17

5
Hall of Records, Annapolis

6
Will dated October 5, 1724.

7
The Hall of Records, Annapolis.

8
January 11, 1736

9
January 11, 1736, Liber 21, Folio 769.

The son Richard, of Richard, married Katurah Barnes, October 27, 1728. His family has not been traced for this record.

Samuel Shipley, another son of Richard, lived to a proverbial old age; he was born about 1710, and died in early 1780.[10] He named a wife, Martha; his sons were: Greenberry, Peter, and Simon; and the daughters were: Hannah, Rachel, Susannah, Jean and Chloe.

Robert Shipley, son of Adam, the First, was born prior to 1700. He died in 1763, and had a Will, dated December 6, 1761, which was probated March 9, 1763. From it is had much Shipley information. Robert, during his lifetime, was a prominent man and active in church affairs.

Queen Caroline Parish was erected in 1728 by an Act of the Assembly, and when a site for the building of Christ Church was supplied by Caleb and John Dorsey, ten years later, and a building erected, a brand new book was acquired for the Parish records. The names of the charter members were entered under the proper letters, A to Z in the index; then vital records of their families were transferred and transcribed from other and earlier records. In this manner and due to the fortunate circumstance, the names and birth dates of the children of Robert Shipley are on record.

The list is as follows:

"Charles Shipley, son of Robert Shipley and Elizabeth was borne on the 27th day of March in the year of our Lord, 1711." (The rest are abbreviated.)
    Robert II, born Oct. 19, 1711
    Ruth, born Aug. 14, 1715
    Keturah, born Nov. 22, 1717
    Elizabeth, born March 7, 1718
    Sarah, born June 3, 1721
    Lois, born June 1, 1723
    George, born Sept. 25, 1726
    William, born May 1, 1729[11]

---

[10] Will, probated March, 1780; Baltimore Reg. Probate, Folio 396-3.

[11] P. 4, Christ Church records, as copied, p. 195 at Baltimore Historical Society.

Upon the completion of the erection of the building the
pews were assigned: Robert Shipley's family was large enough
that they had all of pew number 11; three sons of Richard Shipley,
Robert's brother, were given pew number 15; the families of William
Hanks and John Ryan were small enough they shared pew number 28.

Robert Shipley was a vestryman in Christ Church for many
years. If he continued to reside on his farm of 240 acres, on the
Patapsco River, and south of the Great Falls, he had a good horseback ride to attend the vestry meetings. Robert sold off 140 acres
of his farm in 1742 to Nathan Barnes, probably his nephew. Two years
later he sold the balance to Peter Porter, and moved to near now
Sykesville, Maryland. At his death, 1767, he left a Will,[12] signed
with his "R".

No wife is named in the Will, the inference is that she was
deceased. The two youngest sons, George and William were named as
executors, and not Charles the oldest, as was customary, and not
Robert II. However, it is known from other records that Robert II
had migrated to Virginia; it is presumed that Charles was not available.

Robert gave his youngest son, William, 190 acres of land in
addition to the 100 acres of "whats left" he had previously received.
Robert gave to his grandson and namesake, Robert, the son of William,
240 acres, and another tract called "Shipleys Search" and plantation
houses and orchards. It seems a generous bequest. He gave to a
son-in-law, John Hood, some slaves. To his daughter, Lois, he gave
₵20.

There is a sentence in the will to be noticed, "My Eldor
Children having already had their portions..." From an entry in the
Queen Anne Parish book there is evidence that Robert had a wife, Katurah;
from the Register of Queen Caroline Parish is had the name of his wife,
Elizabeth; the inference is he was married twice. On the other hand
the given name of Robert was often used in the Shipley family so the
above entries may be of two Roberts. In his will Robert mentions,
"to my grandson Robert son of William." His son, William, was born
1729 and if he married at the usual age of twenty-five his son, Robert,
was only about ten years of age when his grandfather made his will.
This is important in order to distinguish him from another Robert Junior,
in Virginia; likely another grandson of old Robert.

Robert Shipley II, the son of Robert and Keturah, was born
October 19, 1713, which includes him as one of the older ones who had
received his portion by gift. He seems to have migrated to southern
Virginia; in 1766, "I, Robert Shipley, of Bedford County in the
Province of Virginia Planter ..."deeded twenty-five acres of land in

---

12
    Liber 31, folio 900, Hall of Record, Annapolis.

Baltimore County, Maryland.[13]

Ten years earlier he had patented 314 acres, granted
September 16, 1756, at which date the area had been set off from
the larger Lunenburg County as Bedford County. This farm was
located in the Hatt Creek community of the Little Falling River water
shed which later became the southeastern part of the newly formed
Campbell County.

The same year he sold the Maryland land he sold off 150 acres
of his patented 314 acres to Robert Irvine, and for ₤47. Five years
later in 1771 he sold the balance of his land, 164 acres, to Daniel
Mitchell. Thereafter, he seems to disappear; the tradition is he
went to Mecklenburg County, North Carolina but his name is not discovered there in the records nor is he listed in the 1790 census;
perhaps he had deceased. The only Shipleys found in that State then
were Eli, Thomas and Richard, and they were "west of Appalatian
Mountain" as a petition reads, dated December 1787.

In Bedford County, Virginia, another Robert Shipley with
Junior attached to his name is of record. The inference is he was
a son of Robert Shipley II. He was plaintiff in a suit at the August
Court of 1761, if of age 21 past, he was born in the late 1730's.
On May 10, 1769, he purchased 262 acres of land from Thomas Daugherty[14]
and, on the same day, Edward Shipley purchased 900 acres from Daugherty.
Both deeds were recorded later the same year, July 27th, and these
acts would seem to indicate close association between Robert Jr. and
Edward. There is no clue to their relationship except a surmise they
were brothers or cousins.

In the 1770's Robert Shipley, Jr. began selling land, disposed
of the Daugherty tract in two parcels and, in addition, sold 250 acres
on both sides of Phelphes Creek, which, from the description, seems
to be a part of the Edward Shipley area.[15] The reason for detailing

[13] Deed Book WG No. H, folio 114.

[14] Deed Book C, p. 350.

[15] Deed Books D, p. 376; E, p. 540; F, p. 569, etc.

these real estate transactions is that the old Harper graveyard
is located on Shipley land. Also, there is the tradition that the
mother of Nancy Hanks Lincoln's mother, or her grandmother, was a
Shipley. In 1782 this whole area of Shipley territory became a part
of Campbell County and thenceforward the name of Robert appears on
the records of the courthouse at Rustville. In April he had business
with John Lane Jr.[16]

In February of 1784 there was some litigation with William
Call.[17] This date is of interest for it was nearby, and that month
Nancy Hanks was born.

By tradition, Robert Shipley, Jr. had sisters, which has been
confirmed.[18] One was Rachel, who married Richard Berry at whose home
Nancy Hanks lived in Kentucky. Another was Naomi, who married Robert
Mitchell. It was their daughter, Sarah, who was captured by the
Indians and returned with other captives after General Wayne's treaty.
She married John Thompson in 1800 and it was her son, Squire Robert
Mitchell Thompson, who knew much of the family history and that his
mother had lived with his Aunt Rachel and Uncle Richard Berry upon
her return. Ann Shipley married David McCord and her descendants
live in Parke County, Indiana.

There is a reference that Marcella Shipley, daughter of Robert
and Rachel Shipley, married Samuel Welch;[19] but whether this is the
same Robert and Rachel is not determined.

Margaret Shipley married (1) Robert Sloan, who was killed in
the Revolutionary War. After the War she married Matthew Armstrong.[20]
There is a tradition in North Carolina that, "...Matthew Armstrong
visited the Shipleys in Kentucky when a young man and told his grandchildren they were related to Abe Lincoln through the Shipleys." Some
of the Shipleys resided in Mason County, Kentucky and "young man"

---

[16] Order Book 1, p. 20

[17] Order Book 1, p. 279.

[18] The Lincoln Kinsman, No. 4, Oct. 1938.

[19] Chancery papers 4820, Ann Arundal County, Maryland.

[20] Puett, History of Gaston County, pp. 151, 152.

Armstrong may have visited his grandchildren of Armstrong or other
names in Kentucky; but he died long before Abraham Lincoln became
widely known. Matthew was born about 1762 and died June 21, 1838.[21]

There seems to be no doubt the early Shipleys were kin to
the ancestors of Nancy Hanks Lincoln; but the connection is obscure.[22]

---

[21]
Tombstone, Smith's Cemetery, Gaston County, North Carolina,
Baber papers.

[22]
The author does not presume that the foregoing chapter about
the Shipley family is definitive. He regrets that more investigation
of the subject is indicated to determine definite connections.

CHAPTER VI

OTHER ALLIED FAMILIES

The Berry Family

According to J. W. S. Clements, the Kentucky line of the Berry family originated in Maryland.[1] Jeremiah Berry died in 1769, owning a large tract of land in Frederick, now Montgomery County, which by will he divided among his sons, including Richard. He gave his widow the home plantation and all the slaves, silver, livestock, furniture, etc., to go to a son and two daughters after her death.

Richard Berry was born in Frederick, now Montgomery County, Maryland and as early as 1750 he was in southern Virginia. He married Rachel Shipley and they resided in Charlotte County, where he owned a farm of 275 acres. In 1780 he sold the farm for an even thousand pounds[2] and the same year entered 600 and 200 acres of land in now Washington County, Kentucky. Nancy Hanks lived in his home for a time. He died in 1798 and the inventory of his estate showed that he owned the 800 acres and listed two slaves, four horses, thirteen head of cattle, and other miscellaneous items.[3]

His son, Richard Berry Junior, whose name is most often associated with Nancy Hanks at the time of her marriage, signed her bond and it was in his home that the wedding and the infare were held. He moved to Montgomery County, Kentucky, where his son, Robert Mitchell Berry was born April 13, 1818. Then, Richard Berry Junior removed to Calloway County, Missouri, where he died prior to 1829. At his death the inventory of his estate listed land, nine slaves, fourteen head of cattle, two yoke of oxen, eighteen head of sheep, twenty-two head of hogs, six horses, a mule, and much other property.[4]

---

[1] Clements-Spaulding & Allied Families, p. 45.

[2] Deed Book 4, p. 210, Charlotte County Courthouse.

[3] Lincoln Kinsman, No. 16, p. 8.

[4] Ibid., p. 3.

His son, Robert Mitchell Berry, died in Missouri in 1913 and in his obituary may be read about his father, "Richard Berry was a man of considerable wealth and while a resident of Kentucky reared Nancy Hanks." It is obvious that both the Richard Berrys, father and son, with whom Nancy lived, were men of property and in comfortable circumstances. If Nancy went to live with the Frances Berry family she was with prosperous people. Nancy Hanks, the orphan, was living in homes of comfort and refinement and the tradition is that she was a very cheerful happy person.

The Mitchell Family

The latest research has revealed that the Mitchell name is quite common in the courthouse records of the Northern Neck of Virginia. Robert Mitchell, who died in 1748 and left a will of record, had a daughter, Judith, who was the wife of George Glascock, an uncle of William Glascock, Junior, who was one time guardian of Abraham Hanks. In addition to Judith, other daughters of Robert and Susannah (Payne) Mitchell were Eliza, who married Moore Fauntleroy; Sarah, who married Thomas Chinn; Frances, who married John Sydnor. Their sons were Richard, who married Ann Sydnor and died in 1781; Dr. John Mitchell; Robert (Jr.), who married Hannah Ball, of a rather noted family.

It is to be recalled that three Hanks men witnessed the will of George Glascock. It is likely that George Glascock's brother-in-law, Robert Mitchell Junior, migrated to Dinwiddie County with William and Richard Hanks, two of the witnesses to the Glascock will. Richard Hanks removed from Dinwiddie to Amelia County and members of the Mitchell family followed, including Robert. Thomas Mitchell of Dinwiddie County purchased a farm from James and Nancy Hanks of Amelia County. Robert and Thomas Mitchell were listed in a local census taken of the Roanoke River country and their names appear as petitioners, with others, to the Court, to permit grist-mills to be built and road repaired. They were neighbors of Robert Shipley. Robert Shipley's daughter, Naomi, married Robert Mitchell. It is not ascertained whose son this younger Robert Mitchell was. An assumption is, he was a son of Robert and Hannah (Ball) Mitchell; but no evidence has been located to sustain it.[5]

---

[5] This researcher is aware that this paragraph is not definitive but the data it contains is placed here for further research.
                                                                A.B.

The Thompson Family

Robert and Naomi Mitchell were the parents of Sarah who married John Thompson, January 17, 1800, at the home of the same Richard Berry, Junior, where Nancy Hanks was married. They had ten children. Among them, "...were born two daughters, named Jane and Patsy; these girls married brothers, Jane married Alexander Noe, and Patsy married Aquilla Noe."[6] Another daughter, Naomi, married John Hobart, January 20, 1825. Their first child, a daughter, the late Charlotte (Hobart) Vawter, was teaching school when the name of Nancy Hanks first became known, and recollected hearing her grandmother, Sarah Mitchell Thompson, tell about Nancy Hanks.

When Lamon's Life of Lincoln was published (1872) with its innuendo that Nancy Hanks was not legally married, Mrs. Vawter who knew better, wrote a letter to the Louisville Courier Journal and repudiated the implications. She, also, had her uncle Squire Robert Mitchell Thompson start a search for the marriage record of Nancy Hanks at the Washington County, Kentucky courthouse, and it was found there, and scotched the imputation.

It was Squire Robert Mitchell Thompson who made affidavit that, "The mother[7] of Nancy (Hanks) Lincoln, who was the mother of Abraham Lincoln, was an own cousin of affiant's mother." A cousin has one parent who is a brother or sister of the parent of the other cousin. Paraphrasing the sworn statement of Squire Robert Mitchell Thompson, it would read, "Sarah Harper Hanks was an own cousin[8] of Sarah Mitchell Thompson."

The parents of Sarah Harper Hanks were George and Elizabeth Harper; the parents of Sarah Mitchell Thompson were Robert and Naomi Shipley.

The presumption is, based upon the tradition in the Vawter family that Nancy's mother was of Shipley descent, and more specifically: from the sworn statement of Squire Robert Mitchell Thompson that the mother of Nancy Hanks Lincoln was the daughter of a Shipley woman, it would indicate that Elizabeth, wife of George Harper, was born Elizabeth Shipley.

---

[6] Wm. B. Noe to Mrs. C. R. Galloway, April 5, 1932, copy Baber papers.

[7] Italics are the author's.

[8] Webster defines "own cousin" as Specif.: Own, first, or full, cousin, or cousin-german.

If Elizabeth Shipley was the sister of Naomi, then she was the daughter of Robert and Sarah Shipley of Maryland and Virginia.*

---

*This researcher is well aware that the Shipley-Hanks connection is not definitely determined for the present purpose. There were ample possibilities for other Hanks-Shipley marriages, and in Virginia. It is probable that the Shipley family was in Virginia before it became established in Maryland. The land grant records of Virginia show that John Shipley patented 430 acres in 1668; his probable son, Richard Shipley, patented 130 acres in 1673. (V, 1, pp. 475-6). Walter Shipley patented 746 acres November 4, 1685 (V, 7, p. 485). Daniel Shipley was in old Rappahannock County in 1685 (Rec. VII, p. 62).

According to the Kingston Parish records Ralph Shipley married Joyce Beard, Feb. 17, 1755, in Gloucester County, where Thomas Hanks resided. Their children were: Joseph, b. Nov. 18, 1764; George, b. Aug. 9, 1767; Richard, b. Oct. 27, 1769; Susannah, died Dec. 5, 1773; and Mildred died Nov. 20, 1776.

Joseph Shipley married Jane, April 16, 1762, in the same parish of Gloucester County. Their children were: George, b. July 1, 1764; May, who died July 5, 1772; Ann, born Dec. 1, 1776.

Dorothy Shipley married Philip Reed, May 6, 1764.

In the First U. S. Census of Virginia, which took over the 1782-3-4 listings were:

					W.	B.
p. 54	John Shipley, Gloucester Co., Kingston Par.,	1783,	4	1
p. 68	John " , " " , 1784	4	
p. 68	Joseph " , " " , 1784	7	
p. 54	Ralph " , ⸬ , 1783	8	
p. 68	Ralph " , " , 1784	7	
p. 25	Richard " , Hampshire Co., 1782	4	
p. 72	Richard " , " 1784	3	

On Nov. 4, 1782 in Hampshire Co. also resided Joseph Hanks with 11 whites and William Lee, his neighbor, with 9 whites. Joseph Hanks is supposed to have married Nannie Shipley or Nannie Lee; which cannot be determined from presently known evidence.

What is obvious from this evidence is that there were opportunities for several Hanks and Shipley family connections.

PART III

GENEALOGIES

PART III

CHAPTER I

G E N E A L O G I C A L   R E C O R D

OF

THE DESCENDANTS OF RECORD

OF

PETER HANKS

OF

Anne Arundal County, Maryland

from

circa 1700 unto circa 1800

and

The Nancys born to them.

CHARTS TO SHOW DESCENDANTS
of
PETER HANKS THE 1st
THE NANCYS BORN INTO THESE FAMILIES
of
MARYLAND & LOUDOUN COUNTY, VIRGINIA

Authorities	Code*	Names, etc.
St. Margaret's Par. rec. (5 mi. North of Annap.)	a	ELIZABETH HANKS[1] b. No record d. Sept. 17, 1702

* * *

| St. Ann's Par. rec.; Hall of Records; Will; Annapolis, Md. | ad | PETER HANKS b. No record m. Aug. 20, 1702; Mary Beeze; in Anne Arundal Co., Md. d. by July 24, 1733. 4 children: ada* Lydia, b. Sept. 25, 1704. adb William, b. July 25, 1707. adc Elinor, b. July 10, 1709 add Peter, b. 1711, baptised, Sept. 20, 1713; d. 1733. |

| Queen Caroline Par. rec. at the Diocesan Library Baltimore, Md. | ada | LYDIA HANKS b. September 25, 1704, in Anne Arundal Co., Md., Bapt. 9/20/1713 m. John Martin, circa 1721. 5 children; 3 sons, 2 daus. a*Joshua, b. Sept. 21, 1723 b John, b. Oct. 21, 1725 c Eunice, b. Feb., 1727 d.Mary, b. Feb. 17, 1729 e William, b. Aug. 2, 1732 |

[1]It is not known that Elizabeth was the mother of Peter; she may have been from Virginia.

* An entire code symbol indicates that the line of that particular individual is continued; a single letter indicates the name is dropped.

adb   **WILLIAM HANKS**
                 b. July 25, 1707; Bapt. Sept. 20,
                    1713; in Anne Arundal Co, Md.
                 m. Ruth Ryan, dau of John Ryan.
                    They resided in Anne Arundal
                    Co. William joined the Friends;
                    "Wm. the Quaker." Migrated
                    to Loudoun Co., Va.
                 d. Circa 1770, in Loudoun Co., Va.
                 Known Children:
                 adba Peter,III, B. c 1737
                 adbb William, b. Apr. 27, 1739
                 adbc Rachel, b. c. 1750
                 adbd Jonathan, b. before 1754.
                 adbe Margaret, m. Thos. Wyatt

adc   **ELINOR HANKS**
                 b. July 10, 1709; Bap. Sept. 20,
                    1713, in Anne Arundal Co., Md.
                 m. Robert Nelson.
                 d. probably before 1733.
                 They acquired land, 100 acres,
                 Anne Arundal Co., Md.

add   **PETER HANKS II**
                 b. 1711; Bapt. Sept. 20, 1713
                 d. 1733; same year as his father.

———O———

adab   **JOHN MARTIN**, son of **Lydia** Hanks.
                 b. Oct. 21, 1725, in Ann Arundal
                    Co., Maryland.
                 m. Ann Dorsey.
                 Children:
                        a Benjamin, **b.** June 6.(page
                        b Tabitha, b. .... 12th, torn)
                        c Joshua, b. ....

a. Archives;
amily records of
iolett Huff; Rev.
eon Marshall.

adba

PETER HANKS III, son of Wm. the
    Quaker.
b.c.1737 in Maryland
Rev. War soldier on Pa. frontier.
Resided in Loudoun Co., Va.
m. Elizabeth Wyatt, dau. of Thomas
    Wyatt of Loudoun Co., Va.
    Moved to Bedford Co., Pa;
    Rostraven Twp.. Removed to
    Salisbury Dist., N.C.; thence
    to Montgomery Co., Kentucky.
    Known children:
adba a Peter IV, killed at Tippe-
        canoe, Nov. 7, 1811
adba b Jonathan, b. Nov. 29, 1767.
adba c William, minister.
adba d Absalom, d. 1827.
adba e Samuel, m. Mar. 16, 1802
adba f Ruth, b. June 13, 1782
adba g Nancy (?)
adba h Savilla b. Jan, 18, 1787.

amily rec.
y Dr. W.J. Lodge;
.H. rec.; Will.
 1, p. 401
 obated July 28,1814
ave much to his
randdaughter, Duanna
see adbbd-a)

adbb

WILLIAM HANKS, son of Wm. the
    Quaker.
b. Apr. 27, 1739, in Anne Arundal
    Co., Md.; d. July 15, 1814.
m. Sarah _____
Resided in Montgomery Co., Md.
Crossed to Loudoun Co., Va.
Removed to Bedford Co., Pa. about
    1800. (Wm. of Bedford)
9 children; 3 sons, 6 daus.
adbb a Rachel, b. Dec. 11, 1761.
adbb b Fleetwood, b. Jan. 19,1764
adbb c John, b. in 1760's.
adbb d Nancy, b. Oct. 4, 1769. twins
adbb e Rosanna, b. Oct. 4, 1769.
adbb f Leah, b. June 22, 1771
adbb g Mary,
adbb h Benjamin, b. June 14, 1797.
adbb i Sarah, b. Oct. 12, 1781.

riends Rec.,
airfax Meeting.
.H. Records, Will.

adbc

RACHEL HANKS, dau. of Wm. the
    Quaker.
b. In Maryland.
Joined the Friends; was put out.
m. Joseph Wilkinson, a widower.
They resided in Loudoun Co., Va.
Children not known; Step-children
though: Sarah, Joseph, and Jesse
Wilkinson.

adbd   JONATHAN HANKS, son of Wm. the
                Quaker.
         b. in Maryland.
         Taxed in Loudoun Co., Va.
         Went south to the James River;
         Thence to Western Kentucky.
         m. Jamima _____.
         He d. circa 1800; she was living,
          a widow, in 1830's.
            Children
                   a John
                   b Jane
                   c Conrad
            adbd d Nancy, m. Peter Jones.

adbe   MARGARET HANKS, Dau. of Wm. the
                Quaker.
         m. Thomas Wyatt, widower.
         They resided in Loudoun Co., Va.
         He died 1772.
         Children of his (1) wife:
                Mary Linn.
                Elizabeth Hanks.
                Sarah Cooper.
                John.
                Edward.

         Children of his (2) wife, Margaret
           Hanks:
                a Thomas Wyatt.
                b Ruth.
                c Abner.
                d Margaret
                e Reuben.

adbaa PETER HANKS IV, son of Peter III.
b. probably in Maryland

Pirtle, p. 122.

d. mortally wounded at the Battle
of Tippecanoe, Nov. 7, 1811.
m. Isabell _____; she b. c 1774;
she m. (2) Calvin Merry.

1810 census.

Resided in N.C.; thence to Mont. Co.
Ky.; thence to Knox Co.,Ind..
Children:

a. Wyatt, b. Nov. 27, 1795.
b. John, b. Oct. 10, 1797.
c. William, b. Nov. 7, 1799.
d. Harriett C., b. Sept. 12,1801
e. Horatio McM., b. Mar. 30,1803

f. Alabama, b. April 18, 1805.
g. James S., b.   1805.
h. Minerva F., b. Aug. 4, 1807.
i. Samuel G., b. June 5, 1810.
j (2) Juliett Merry, b. 1816

adbab JONATHAN HANKS, son of Peter III.
b. Nov. 29, 1767, in Loudoun Co., Va.

Draper Papers
C.H. records

d. after 1838, in Montgomery Co.,Ky.
m. Barbara _____; resided in Montgomery County, Kentucky; taxed 100
acres.
Children:
a. Vancouver
7 daughters (names not known)

adbac WILLIAM HANKS, son of Peter III.
b.

C.H. records
His. of Gibson Co.Ind.

d. Gibson Co., Indiana
m. Mary _____
Was a minister; organized churches in
Gibson Co., Indiana.

Will; Pro. recs.

Eight children:
a. Peter, b. 1794.
b. Ruth, b. 1797.
c. Nicholas, b. 1799.
d. Matilda, b. 1801; m. John Mayhall
e. Elizabeth, m. (1) John Williams
b. 1802;   (2) T. Mayhall
f. Malinda; afflicted.
g. James Stewart, b. 1806
h. Harriett, m. Elijah Lucas.

adbad ABSALOM HANKS, son of Peter III.
b.
d. 1827, in Clark Co., Kentucky.

C. H. Rec.
Clark Co., Ky.
(Absalom Hanks received
Cert. #1786 for campaign
against Wabash Indians)

m. Malinda Tribble
They resided at N. edge of Winchester, Kentucky.
Four children:
a. Absalom, Jr.
b. Mary, m. Tucker Ragland
c. Betsey, m. John D. Weaver
d. Margaret, m. Matthew Markland

(Absalom Hanks Markland was the P.M. of Grant's Army.)

adbae

C.H. Rec.
Mason Co., Ky.
Montgomery Co., Ky.

SAMUEL HANKS, son of Peter III.
b.
d.
m. Nancy Wyatt, March 16, 1802, in Mason
County, Kentucky
Resided in Montgomery Co., Ky. and Powell
Co., Ky. Was agent to sell land.
Children:
a Ackland, d. 1833
b Hannibal D.
c Romulus Lycurgus, had 1 son, 3
daus. (See His. Rome Hanks)
d Castryra, m. John Hon
e Armina Dye Meldia Toris, m. Isaac
Hon
f Laura Sudlett Zellica, m. Moses
Hon
g Cordelia, m. John Miller.
h Adella Woodville, m. Cobb
i Minerva, m. Noland.
j Euphrasia, m. Craig

adbaf

C.H. Rec.
Family Rec.
Letters of Rev.
Leon Marshall &
Judge Marshall.

* Another account says
d. at Murphreysboro, Ill.

RUTH HANKS, dau. of Peter III.
b. June 13, 1782, in Salisbury Dis. N.C.
d. Sept. 25, 1844, in Gibson Co., Ind.*
m. Hubbard Marshall, son of Humphrey
Marshall.
Children:
a Savilla
b Nancy, d. Sept. 1821, aged 21.
c John Hanks, b. Mar. 4, 1804.
d Salina
e Martha, b. June 23, 1813.
f Humphrey, d. inf.
g Hubbard L., killed in Mo.
Civil War.
h Randolph, b. Dec. 24, 1821.
i Frank, killed by horse, age 12.
j Mary, m. Thomas Potter.
k Samuel
l William, d. inf.
m Sarah, m. John Garrison.

adbag

Family tradition; no
records located; Not mentioned
in the correspondence between Rev. Leon
Marshall & Judge Marshall of State of
Kansas in 1895. May have been the Nancy
Hanks who "Went south" from Mt. Sterling, Ky.?
A.B.

NANCY HANKS (?)
b. Between 1782 of Ruth above and
1787 of Savilla following.

adbah   SAVILLA HANKS, probable dau. of Peter **III.**
         b. Jan. 18, 1787
         d. 1853, in Marion Co., Ill.
         m. James Craig; he b. 1784; d. 1843.
         They were married April 21, 1803.
         Children:

                 a William Craig, b. Feb. 14,1804
                 b Absalom, b. Feb. 20, 1806.
                 c **Elizabeth,** b. Jan. 27, 1808.
                 d Samuel H., B. May 22, 1810
                 e John, b. June 9, 1812.
                 f Nancy, b. May 22, 1814.
                 g Ambrose, b. Aug. 18, 1816;
                             d. 1876.
                 h Margaret, b. Aug. 17, 1818.
                 i Sarah Jane, b. Aug. 16, 1821
                 j Martha Ann, b. Aug. 24, 1823
                 k James K., b. Dec. 28, 1824.
                 l Benjamin D., b. Dec. 16, 1826.
                 m Mary, b. March 9, 1828.
                 n Barbara, m. Searcey.

adbba   RACHEL HANKS, dau. of Wm. of Bedford.
      b. Dec. 11, 1761, in Maryland in Ann
           Arundel County, Md.
      d. April 1, 1842, in Bedford Co., Pa.
      m. Ephram Akers Oct. 1784; he b. 1761;
          d. May 14, 1817 and int. Cem. at
          Akersville, Pa.
      Children:
         a Sarah, b. Oct. 14, 1785.
         b Hannah
         c John
         d Rachel
         e Zellah
         f Leah
         g Elizabeth
         h Ephraim, b. Oct. 4, 1798.
            d. Nov. 20, 1868.

adbbb   FLEETWOOD HANKS, son of Wm. of Bedford.
      b. Jan. 19,1764, in Frederick Co., Md.
      d. Jefferson Co., Ky.
      Was taxed in Loudoun County, Va. 1787 to
                 1790.
      m. Ruth (Wyatt?) ~~1790~~;
      Moved to Bedford Co., Va.; thence to
      Kentucky 1802.
      Children:
         a Nancy Hanks, b. 1785 by census
               of 1850 in Arkansas.
               m. Enoch Holdron 1805.
               m. (2) Frank DeMar
               d. Feb.1870 in
               Phillips Co., Ark.
         b Fleetwood, b. May 12, 1797 in Va.
         c William, m. Aug. 21, 1812, Bedford
               county, Virginia.
         d Millander, d. Sept. 25, 1836;
         e John, d. 1834 at Vicksburg, Miss.
         f Mary, m. William DeMar
         g James, d. 1860 at Charleston, Ind.

adbbc   JOHN HANKS, son of Wm. of Bedford.
b. in 1760's in Maryland.
d. 1805, in Loudoun County, Virginia.
    His estate appr. Feb. 2, 1809;
    settled, Aug. 8, 1814.
m. Abigail _____; she m. (2) Howder,
               Hewder, Houser?
Children:
     a Stiles
     b Leah
     c Isaiah
     d Cephas
     e Elizabeth
     f Jeremiah, b. Jan. 19, 1791.

adbbd   NANCY HANKS, dau. of Wm. of Bedford.
b. Oct. 4, 1769, in Loudoun Co., Va.
d. June 17, 1835, in Bedford Co., Pa.
     a Dau. Duanna, b. Dec. 20, 1787,
          in Loudoun Co., Virginia.
          d. May 23, 1850.
m. (1) Nicholas Schooley; he d. July 9,
Children: 1795.
     b Isaac
     c Sarah   twins, b. 1793.
m. (2) Robert Akers, Dec. 24, 1799.
    He b. Sept. 24, 1771;
       d. Dec. 29, 1838, Bedford Co, Pa
Children:
     d John Wesley, b. May 14, 1801;
                d. Oct. 16, 1866.
     e Isreal, b. Feb. 2, 1804;
            d. Feb. 14, 1880.
     f Stephen,   d. Inf.
     g Timothy) twins, b. Aug. 29, 1806
                     d. Feb.21, 1881.
     h Asberry, b. June 25, 1811;
             d. Nov. 3, 1863.
     i Wilson Lee, b. Dec. 28, 1814;
                d. Nov. 6, 1895.

adbbe   ROSANNA HANKS, dau. of Wm. of Bedford.
b. Oct. 4, 1770
d. June 28, 1889 in Bedford Co., Pa.
m. Jacob Lodge, Feb. 9, 1786;
   He b. May 31, 1759, d. May 9, 1851.
Rosanna practiced medicine.
Children:
        a Susanna, b. Nov. 10, 1787;
                d. Jan. 16, 1882.
        b Nathan, b. Aug. 26, 1788;
                d. Nov. 27, 1815.
        c Jacob, b. July 22, 1794;
                d. Aug. 18, 1865.   1867.
        d Wm. Lodge, b. 1796; d. June 20,
        e Aquilla, b. Aug. 30, 1798;
                d. May 17, 1863.
        f. Nancy b. 1803; d. Nov. 29, 1866.
        g Harvey, b. 1804; d. 1806.
        h Mason, b. Oct. 14, 1806;
                d. Oct. 19, 1869.

adbbf   LEAH HANKS, dau. of Wm. of Bedford.
b. June 22, 1771, in Loudoun Co., Va.
d. Sept. 4, 1854, in Bedford Co., Pa.
m. Timothy Hixon, March 20, 1797 in
    Loudoun Co., Virginia. He was born
    May 1, 1775 and died Jan. 15, 1857.
Children:
     a Jabez, b. Aug. 5, 1799; d. Apr 4,1877
     b Benjamin
     c Ephraim, b. Feb. 7, 1802; d.Feb 4,1878
     d Rachel, b. Apr. 28, 1804; d. Oct. 21
                        1857.
     e Mary, b. Nov. 3, 1806; d. Feb. 1,1861
     f Nathan, B. Dec. 15,1809; d.Nov.1,1856
     g Timothy, b. Sept. 2,1812; d. Mar 19,
                      1890.
     h Julia Ann, b. Aug. 5,1815; d. April
                      14,1896.

adbbg   MARY HANKS, dau. of Wm. of **Bedford**
                m. Samuel Jackson
                Children:
                  a John, B. June 30,1800; d. Jul 5, 1871
                  b Stiles, b. Dec.29,1801; d. June 26,
                                            1873.

                  c Fleetwood
                  d **Nathan**, b.
                  e Jeremiah, b. Dec. 5,1811; d. **July 5,**
                                            1838
                  f Jonah, b. Feb. 2, 1814; d. **July 5,**
                                            1838

                  g **Elizabeth**

adbbh   BENJAMIN HANKS, son of Wm. of **Bedford.**
                b. June 14, 1797, in Loudoun Co., Va.
                d. Oct. 28, 1822.
                m. Rebecca **Barton,** Dec. 1803.
                Children:
                  a Sarah, b. Nov. 1, 1804
                  b Lanan, b. Aug. 29, 1805
                  c John, b. Nov. 15, 1806
                  d Elijah, b. July 7, 1809
                  e Candace, b. May 6, 1811
                  f **Bartley,** b. Oct. 20, 1812
                  g Jared, b. June 28, 1814
                  h Fletcher, b. Nov. 23, 1815
                  i William, b. June 18, 1817
                  j Mary, b. Mar. 17, 1819
                  k Jason, b. Nov. 12, 1820
                  l Delilah, b. Dec. 28, 1822.

adbbi   SARAH HANKS, dau. of W$_m$. of **Bedford.**
                b. Oct. 12, 1781, in Loudoun Co., Va.
                d. In Athens Co., Ohio
                m. James James.
                  He was a **tanner by trade.**
                Children::   1826.
                  a **Isaac,** b. Jan. 31, 1801; d. Jan 31,
                  b Asa M.,b. Sept.2,1802; d. Sept. 15,
                                          1887.

                  c William, b. April 9, 1804;
                          d. Feb. 6, 1851.
                  d Anna, b. Jan. 26, 1806; d. **June** 19,1880
                  e Duanna, b. Apr. 1,1808; d. 1858.
                  f Sitha, b. Nov. 28,1811; d.June 9,1864.
                  g Joel, b. May 22,1814; D. Sept. 1855.
                  h Rhoda, b. Mar. 20,1816; d. Jul 19,1869.
                  i Matson, b. March 17, 1819.

adbdd NANCY HANKS, dau. of Jonathan.
b. circa 1784, in the James River Country
of Virginia.
Went with her parents to Western Kentucky.
Resided in Henry County.
m. Peter Jones, April 16, 1804 in Henry
County, Kentucky.
Her mother was Jerima Hanks; her bondsman
was James McKenney and **Abner** Ford, and not
Abner Hanks, as has been erroneously
reported.

No further record located; a Peter Jones
later lived in Gibson County, Indiana near
other Hanks families.

Hitchcock lists this Nancy Hanks as the
daughter of Abraham Hanks; but there is
no record that Abraham had a later wife
than Sarah, who died about 1790; neither
can she be the daughter of Abraham Hanks,
Jr., for he was married in 1792, probably
too early for a daughter to be married by
1804.

Also, she has been named as a daughter of
Abner Hanks, and Abner Hanks did at one
time reside in Henry County. But this
inference comes from an error: in an
early transcribing of marriage records the
name Hanks was inadvertantly substituted
for **Ford**. The original papers in the old
bond box clarifies the record.

A.B.

CHAPTER II

G E N E A L O G I C A L   R E C O R D

OF

THE DESCENDANTS OF RECORD

OF

THOMAS HANKS

OF

VIRGINIA

from

circa 1700 to circa 1800

and

The Nancys Born To Them

THE FIRST HANKS OF RECORD

John Hanks	1623
George Hanks	1633
Enoch Hanks	1653
Thomas Hanks	1653
Robert Hanks & his wife, Margaret	1661

* * *

Shelbourne, _In Freedom's Dawn_ [a]

Patent Book

THOMAS HANKS
b. Probably before 1630; d. circa 1675.
m. Probably Elizabeth_____.
He first acquired land in the area between the Mattapony and the Rappahannock River, in Virginia, February 16, 1653; subsequently continued to patent land including some in now Richmond County.*

Possible children:[**]
aa William, b. circa 1650
ab George, of Richmond County, Va.
ac Robert, of Richmond County, Va.
ad Peter, of Ann Arundal County, Md.

Presumptive
Conjectural

* No records have been located further of Thomas Hanckes or of his estate; it has been conjectured that his name and property disappeared during the turmoil of the Bacon Rebellion. On the route of an antient road from the Rappahannock River to the Falls of the James River, now route 360, near the boundary line of Essex and King and Queen Counties, stands this historical marker:

BACON'S NORTHERN FORCE

At Piscataway, near here, the northern followers of Bacon the rebel assembled in 1676. On July 10, 1676 an action was fought with Governor Berkeley's supporters, some of whom were killed and wounded. Several houses were burned. Passing here the rebels marched south to the Pamunkey River, where they joined their leader, Bacon.

***
There is no direct evidence that these men were sons
of Thomas Hanks but, from the fact, he is the only
one of record then, in that area, who could have been
their father; from proximity; from possibility and
probability, they are so presumed. William, being an
owner of land without record or purchase, is presumed
to have been the eldest son and acquired the land by
inheritance according to the then law of primogeniture.
When his estate was later probated in Richmond County,
the Inventory listed certain assets "from across the
river" which meant south of the Rappahannock. The fact
he had property in that area tends to confirm whence he
came. For a more complete discussion see Barton's
LINEAGE OF LINCOLN.

aa

WILLIAM HANKS I
b. circa 1650; d. 1704, in Rich. Co., Va.
was known as "The Carpenter ".
m. Sarah _____; she m. (2) Richard White.
Children:
aaa William II, b. Feb. 14, 1679.
aab Luke I, b. circa 1685.
aac John,I, b. circa 1690.

aaa

WILLIAM HANKS II.
b. Feb. 14, 1679, in Rich. Co., Va.
d. May 1, 1733, in Rich. Co., Va.
m. Hester C. Mills, dau. of John and
    Hester White Mills.
Was a farmer and carpenter; left instruction in his Will for the oldest son to
teach his brothers the carpenter trade.
Children:
aaaa William III, b. May 26, 1712.
aaab John, b. June 24, 1714.
aaac Hannah, b. Feb. 14, 1717.
aaad Sarah, b. Feb. 20, 1720.
aaae Richard, b. Aug. 14, 1723.
aaaf Susannah, b. Dec. 18, 1725.
        (dau. of Hannah ?)
aaag Thomas, b. July 26, 1728.
aaah James, b. Feb. 12, 1732.

aaa WILLIAM II & HESTER C. MILLS HANKS, their children and grandchildren

	aaaa	WILLIAM HANKS III

Parish records
b. May 26, 1712, in Richmond Co., Va.
d. 1787 in Granville Co., N. C,
m. Sarah Durham, Jan. 26, 1738 in Rich.Co
Was known as "The Carpenter."

Deed Rec.
Moved to Amelia Co.,Va; to Dinwiddie Co.Va
Thence to North Carolina.
Children:

Parish Records and Will
aaaaa Elijah, b. 1740
aaaab Million, b. 1742
aaaac Judith, b. 1744
aaaad Argyle, b. 1746
aaaae Susanna, b. 1749
aaaaf Hannah, b. 1752
aaaag William IV, b. 1755

Par. Rec.   aaab   JOHN HANKS.
b. June 24, 1714
d. in North Carolina
m. Mary Mott, dau. of John & Ann Mott
Will   John Mott dec. in Lancaster Co.
Deed Books   Moved to Hanover Co., Va.; thence to
Halifax Co., N.C. and to Dobbs Co.
Known Children:
aaaba Mott, b. 1742
aaabb John, b. c 1745
aaabc Epiphroditus, b. 1747
Possible Child:
aaabd Moses, b. 1748

Par. Rec.   aaac   HANNAH HANKS
b. Feb. 14, 1717, in Richmond Co., Va.
m. James Webb
Children:
aaaca   James Hanks Webb; d. Nov.30, 1750.

Par. Rec.   aaad   SARAH HANKS
b. Feb. 20, 1720, in Richmond Co., Va.
m. Possibly a Mr. Draper.

aaae   RICHARD HANKS
b. Aug. 14, 1723, in Richmond Co., Va.
d. after 1788, probably in N.C.
m. Mary Hinds, before 1753; she was a
    dau. of James & Patience Hinds; and
    b. May 2, 1734.
Presumed children:
aaaea William, b. 1750's
aaaeb James, b. 1759
aaaec Joshua, b. 1760
aaaed Richard, b. 1762
aaaee Thomas, b. 1763
aaaef David
aaaeg Patience
aaaeh Dicey
aaaei Katy
      Felix (?)
They resided in Amelia Co., Va.: thence
to Guilford and Rowan and Cos. in N.C.

aaaf   SUSANNAH HANKS.
b. Dec. 18, 1725; dau of Wm. & Hannah
    Hanks; (Hannah a supposed error for
    Hester.)
m. William Hightower, Oct. 12, 1743 in
    Richmond County, Virginia.
They resided in Amelia County, Virginia.

aaag   THOMAS HANKS
b. July 26, 1728, in Richmond Co., Va.
d. 1777, in Amelia County, Va.
Bequeathed land in Chesterfield County to
nephew, Thomas Draper.

aaah   JAMES HANKS
b. Feb. 12, 1732, in Richmond Co., Va.
No further record discovered in Rich. Co.
Probably moved to Amelia Co., Va.
May be the James later in Bedford Co., Va.
    (See aabh)

aaaa WILLIAM III & SARAH DURHAM HANKS,
their children and grandchildren

	aaaaa	ELIJAH HANKS.

Par. Rec.
Will
Craft Will
B.B.

D.B.
Will

aaaaa   ELIJAH HANKS.
b. Dec. 17, 1740, in Richmond Co., Va.
d. 1798, in Granville Co., N·C.
m, Ann Craft, dau. of Thomas Craft
As a young man he was in Amelia Co., Va.
Perhaps in Dinwiddie Co., Va.
Thence to North Carolina.
Children:
aaaaa a Samuel
aaaaa b David
aaaaa c Thomas
aaaaa d John, b. 1770
aaaaa e William
aaaaa f Betsey

Par. Rec.

aaaab   MILLION HANKS
b. Aug. 21, 1742, in Richmond Co., Va.
m. Mireman Barnes

aaaac   JUDITH HANKS
b. Dec. 29, 1744 in Richmond Co., Va.
d. before 1787, date of her father's will.

aaaad   ARGYLE HANKS
b. Feb. 2, 1746, in Richmond Co., Va.

Pro. Rec.
Mar. rec.

d. in Granville Co., N.C.
m. (1) Million Hargrave, Dec. 28, 1773
Children:
aaaad a William, b. 1774
aaaad b Milly

Mar. Rec.

m. (2) Francis Hargrave, June 20, 1783.
Children:

Pro. Rec.

aaaad c Nancy, b. 1784.*
aaaad d Mary "Polly"
aaaad e Sarah "Sally"

Guard. Accts.

aaaad f "Ardel"
aaaad g John Durham
aaaad h Willis Mills, b. after 1791
aaaad i Green S., b. 1791

---

* Nancy: (q.v.) Chap. IX, iv.

aaaa WILLIAM III & SARAH DURHAM HANKS,
   their children & Granchildren

aaaae   SUSANNA HANKS
          b. Sept. 19, 1749, in Richmond Co., Va.
          m. Thomas H. Phillips, Dec. 10, 1794, in
             Granville County, North Carolina.

aaaaf   HANNAH HANKS.
          b. Feb. 11, 1752, in Richmond Co., Va.
          m. _____ Moore.

aaaag   WILLIAM HANKS IV.
          b. circa 1755, in Virginia.
          d. after Nov. 8, 1794 and before May 1795.
          In Granville County, North Carolina
          m. Sally _____.
          Child, one only:
             aaaag a William Henry V.

aaab JOHN AND MARY MOTT HANKS, their children
       and grandchildren.

<table>
<tr><td>aaaba</td><td>MOTT HANKS</td></tr>
</table>

                    aaaba   MOTT HANKS
b. April 21, 1742 in Richmond Co., Va.
d. Jan. 3, 1821, in Dobbs Co., N.C.
m. (1) Mary _____.
   (2) Susannah _____.
Was residing in Dobbs Co. in 1790 census

Bible

Children:
aaaba a Nathan, b. Feb. 28, 1774
aaaba b Woodman, b. Nov. 1, 1775
aaaba c Isaac, b. Feb. 22, 1776
aaaba d Lucy, b. Oct. 1, 1778
aaaba e Nancy, b. June 21, 1780
aaaba f Lucky, b. May 17, 1783
aaaba g Cotton, b. Jan. 28. 1786
      h Elijah, b. Dec. 2, 1787

                    aaabb   JOHN HANKS
b. c 1745, in Va.; thence to N.C.
m. Mary Dawson
 Resided in Christian Co., Kentucky

B. papers

Children:
aaabb a Thomas, b. Jan. 24, 1777
aaabb b Joseph
aaabb c Joshua, b. Feb. 17, 1787
aaabb d John
aaabb e Nathan
aaabb f Betsey

                    aaabc   EPIPHRODITUS HANKS
b. Jan. 25, 1747 in Hanover Co., Virginia
d. July 4, 1838, in Sumpter Co., S.C.
m. (1) _____
Children:
aaabc a William , b. after 1774
aaabc b James, b. after 1774

m. (2) _____Lanier.
Child, one only:
aaabc c Stephen, b. April 15, 1786

aaab JOHN AND MARY MOTT HANKS, their children
and grandchildren.

		aaabd	MOSES HANKS [*]
Fam. Rec.			b. July 15, 1746 or 48 in Virginia
Tomb.			d. Aug. 19, 1831 in Maury Co., Tennessee.
			m. Aggatha Dodson
census			Resided in Pitts. Co., Va. 1790.

Removed to Pulaski Co., Ky., c 1800
Thence to Maury Co., Tennessee.
Children:
aaaba a Joiasy, b. 1769
aaabd b Frances, b. 1771
aaabd c George, b. 1773
aaabd d Moses, b. 1779
aaabd e Elizabeth, b. 1782
aaabd f Troy, b. 1784
aaabd g Thomas, b. 1786
aaabd h Idella, b. 1788
aaabd i Sarah, b. 1790
aaabd j Elijah, b. 1793
aaabd' k Mary, m. Lynn.

[*] In an unpublished MS by
Hitchcock. Moses is placed as
a son of John & Mary Mott Hanks;
but the authority is not stated.

After a preliminary edition of this manuscript was mimeographed,
new evidence was received that Moses Hanks was not the son of John
and Mary Mott Hanks.

In a statement made May 1890, by Mr. Hanks Neville Hill, who
was born March 10, 1813, and well knew his grandfather Moses, he
said, "Grandfather Moses' Hanks was born in Virginia, where his
parents died, leaving him an orphan at an early age."

Since John Hanks was alive in North Carolina in 1782, as his
son, Epiphroditus, states in his application for a Revolutionary War
pension, and as John Hanks is listed in the U.S. Census of Wayne County,
North Carolina, 1790, he lived long beyond the childhood of Moses,
who was born on the date above stated.

Please refer to pages 248 and 316.

aaae RICHARD AND MARY HINDS HANKS
their children and grandchildren

             aaaea   WILLIAM HANKS
                           b. in the 1750's.
                           d. in Rutherford Co., N.C.
                           m. Keziah Wright, possibly in S. C.
                           Removed to Rutherford Co., N.C. near Bostic
                             Occupation, shoemaker

Chart, confirmed
by census number

                           Children:
aaaea a Mary
aaaea b Thomas
aaaea c Noah, b. Jan. 1, 1790.
aaaea d John
aaaea e Rachel
aaaea f James
aaaea g Nancy, b. c 1800[*]

             aaaeb   JAMES HANKS
Pension Appl.   b. 1759, in Dinwiddie Co., Virginia.
#4564   d. c 1840-50 in Wilkes Co., N.C.
                           Was in Rev. War; received pension.
Marriage Record   m. Mary Starrett, Aug 26, 1779 in
                             Lincoln County, N.C.
                           Resided a few years in Surry Co., thence
                             to Wilks Co.
                           Children, as known, probably others.
aaaeb a Richard
aaaeb b David
aaaeb c William, "Billy"
aaaeb d Mary "Polly"

[*]Of whom more here, (q.v.) Chapt. V, 111

aaae RICHARD AND MARY HINDS HANKS
their children and grandchildren

aaaec   JOSHUA HANKS

Fam. Rec. by
C.L. Hanks

b. 1760, in Amelia Co., Va.
d. 1854, in Grayson Co.
m. Ruth Bryant, 1784, in Surry Co., N.C.
Thence across line to Piper's Gap, Va.
Children, 16:

aaaec e Zachariah	aaaec i William
aaaec b Richard	aaaec j Mary
aaaec c Thomas, b. 1797.	
aaaec d Ruth	aaaec k Susannah
aaaec a Joshua	aaaec l Rhoda
aaaec f Nancy**	aaaec m Lydia
aaaec g Thursa	aaaec n Patience
aaaec h David	aaaec o James

aaaec p John

aaaed   RICHARD HANKS (JR.)
b. 1762, in Amelia Co., Virginia.
d. in Lincoln Co., N.C.: after 1827.

Appl. #4570

Bible

Was in Revolutionary War; pensioned.
m. Phebe Hayes, Oct. 17, 1785.
Children:
aaaed a John, b. 1786
aaaed b Joshua, b. 1789
aaaed c Martha, b. 1791
aaaed d James, b. 1794
aaaed e Thomas, b. 1797
aaaed f Mary, b. 1799
aaaed g David, b. 1802
aaaed h Nancy, b. 1805***
aaaed i Nathan, b. 1811

** Of whom more here, (q.v.) Chap. VII, vi.

*** Of whom more here, (q.v.) Chap. IV, vii.

aaae RICHARD AND MARY HINDS HANKS
their children and grandchildren

        aaaee   THOMAS HANKS
                      b. 1763, probably in Amelia Co., Va.
                      d. Nov.5, 1851, in Gaston Co., Va.*
                      Interred in Old Goshen Cem.
                      Was a Revolutionary War Soldier.
                      m. Lucretia Hargrave, Mar. 2, 1789.
                      Children as known:
                      aaaee a A son, b. 1789, name unknown.
                      aaaee b Elizabeth, b. April 29, 1791;
                                    d. Feb. 16, 1875.
                      aaaee c William, b. 1798; d. Dec. 13.1865.
                                m. Lucy Jane,
                                      b. Dec. 16, 1814
                                      d. June 4, 1900

        aaaef   DAVID HANKS
                      b.
                      d.
C.H. Rec.   m. Elizabeth Hoyle, Oct. 31, 1783 in
                          Lincoln County, N.C. Their bond was
                          signed by Frederick Bess, a bro-in-law.

        aaaeg   PATIENCE HANKS
                      b.
                      m. Frederick Bess.
                      d. in North Carolina.

        aaaeh   DICEY HANKS
                      b.
Par. Rec.   m. Zacariah Hampton, Dec. 27, 1803 in
                        Lunenburg Co., Cumberland Parish, Va.
                      d.

* Hitchcock list the Thomas Hanks, son of Richard Hanks, Sr., as
deceased, March 28, 1797, and gives no authority. It seems more likely,
to this researcher, that this Thomas of Rowan Co., N.C. where Richard
Hanks Sr. lived, and by his proximity to other known sons of Richard,
was also his son. In addition there were five Hanks brothers in the
Revolutionary War and it takes Thomas to make five.
                                          A.B.

aaae RICHARD AND MARY HINDS HANKS,
their children and grandchildren

                                 aaaei   KATY HANKS
                                            b.

Mar. Rec.   m. John Hammock, March 31, 1791 in
                                           Lunenburg Co., Cumberland Parish, Va.
                                          d.

Presumptive
from Proximity   aaaej   FELIX HANKS
to Richard in   b. circa 1765; for bought land in 1790.
Rowan Co., N.C.   from John Lopp, who was Richard Hanks,
                                           Jr.'s Capt. in the Revolutionary War.

aaag   THOMAS HANKS

Will; C.H. Rec.   No children mentinned in Will;
Amelia Co., Va.   but a nephew, Thomas Draper.
                               For interest the Inventory is listed:
                               Appraisal May 22, 1777.

                               Negro Ned   Ł100
                               2 beds & Furn.   12
                               Wearing Appl.   8 6
                               Saddle & Bridle   1 10
                               Pot Hooks   0 10 0
                               Pewter   1 4 6
                               Chest   1 10 0
                               Fiddle, parcel books 3 9 0
                               Looking glass   0 5 0

aaaaa ELIJAH AND ANN CRAFT HANKS
their children and grandchildren

aaaaa a . SAMUEL HANKS
b.
ed
Resided in Orange Co., N.C.
d.

aaaaa b DAVID HANKS
b.
d.

aaaaa c THOMAS HANKS
b.
m. Margaret Clements, Dec. 23,1784 of
Dinwiddie Co., Va. Taxed 1785, 1,
1 horse, 1 cattle.
Probably resided in Lunenburg Co., Va.
d.
Children:
Possibly Thomas, who m. Ann Reece dau.
of Robert Reece, April 26, 1831 in
Brunswick Co., Va.

aaaaa d JOHN HANKS
b. 1770
d. 1839, in Chatham Co., N.C.
m. Jane Armstrong, dau. of John Armstrong,
Oct. 8, 1795, in Orange Co., N.C.
Children:
a Jane, m. John M. Ray,2/3/1826
b Nancy, m. John Holt, 4/6/1828
c John A.,b. April 19, 1812;
m. Euphemia Morris
(2) Catharine
d Martin, named for Martin Armstrong.
e Wesley, bachelor; sheriff of
Chatham Co., N.C.

aaaaa e WILLIAM HANKS
b.
d.

aaaaa f BETSEY HANKS
b.
d.

aaaad ARGYLE & MILLION HARGRAVE HANKS
    their children and grandchildren

        aaaad a   WILLIAM HANKS
                        b. 1774

        aaaad b   MILLIE HANKS
                        b.
                        m. Doke Prewett, Sept. 27, 1799, in
                           Granville County, N. C.

aaaad ARGYLE & FRANCES HARGRAVE HANKS

        aaaad c   NANCY HANKS*
                        b. 1784, in Granville Co., N.C.
Probate records   d. 1804; estate probated.

        aaaad d   SALLY HANKS
                        b.
                        m. James Monroe, Dec. 28, 1803 in
                           Granville County, N. C.

        aaaad e   MARY "POLLY" HANKS
                        b.
                        m. Benjamin Heflin, Dec. 3, 1806 in
                           Granville County, N.C.

        aaaad f   ARGYLE "ARDIL" HANKS
                        b. 1791.
                        Bachelor.
                        d. 1865; inter. under a large oak tree
                           on Hanks farm.

        aaaad g   JOHN DURHAM HANKS
                        b.
                        Bachelor
                        d. 1865; left estate to bro. Argyle, with
                           exceptions. Buried under same oak
                           tree on Hanks farm.

        aaaad h   WILLIS MILLS HANKS
                        b. after 1791
                        d. 1817, in Greenville, S.C.
                        Left a Will, probated Granv. Co.May 1817.

        aaaad i   GREEN S. HANKS
                        b. 1791
                        Was living in 1829

* See Chap. V, iv.

aaaag WILLIAM IV & SALLY HANKS,
         their children

    aaaag a   WILLIAM HENRY V.
               b. before 1795, in Granville Co., N.C.

aaaba MOTT AND (1) MARY HANKS (2) SUSANNA HANKS
       their children

    aaaba a   NATHAN HANKS
                  b. Feb. 28, 1774
                  m. Elizabeth Hood, March 14, 1799;
                     she was the dau. of Nathaniel Hood.

    aaaba b   WOODHAM HANKS
                  b. November 1, 1775.

    aaaba c   ISAAC HANKS
                  b. Feb. 22, 1776

    aaaba d   LUCY HANKS
                  b. Oct. 1, 1778
                  No further record located

    aaaba e   NANCY HANKS*
                  b. June 21, 1780
                  No further record located.

    aaaba f   LUCKY HANKS
                  b. March 17, 1783

    aaaba g   COTTON HANKS.
                  b. January 28, 1786

          h   ELIJAH HANKS
                  b. December 2, 1787

* See Chapter V, v1.

aaabb   JOHN AND MARY DAWSON HANKS, THEIR CHILDREN
and GRANDCHILDREN.

C.H. Notes   aaabb a   THOMAS HANKS
                                 b. Jan. 24, 1777
                                 d. c. 1826, in Hopkins Co., Ky.
                                 m. Catharine C. Beck, Aug. 5, 1812, in
                                    Hopkins County. She was born August
                                    8, 1796; d. Oct. 1, 1857, in Sang. Co.,
                                    Illinois.
                                 Nine children
                                         a Harriett E., b. 1813
                                         b William W.
                                         c Thomas W.
                                         d Stephen Beck
                                         e Mary Ann
                                         f David C.
                                         g Samuel S.
                                         h Elizabeth
                                         i Pembroke

                    aaabb b   JOSEPH HANKS
                                 b.
                                 m.
                                 Children--Five, 1810 census

                    aaabb c   JOSHUA HANKS
                                 b. Feb. 17, 1787
                                 d.
C.H. NOTES   m. Easter Gatlin, Nov. 23, 1817 in
                                    Hopkins County, Kentucky.
                                 Children (Nine)
                                         a Mary D. b. 1818
                                         b William C.
                                         c Mahala
                                         d Nancy
                                         e Stewart C.
                                         f Elizabeth
                                         g Caroline
                                         h Robert Mansfield
                                         i Martha

aaabb JOHN AND MARY DAWSON HANKS
their children and grandchildren

<table>
<tr><td></td><td>aaabb d</td><td>JOHN HANKS, JR.
b.</td></tr>
</table>

       aaabb d   JOHN HANKS, JR.
                           b.
C.H. notes   m. Charity _____
                           Children:

       aaabb e   NATHAN HANKS
                           b.
Mar. Rec.   m. Sinea Henry, March 14, 1822.

       aaabb f   BETSEY HANKS
                           b.
Mar. Rec.   m. Russell Gray, August 16, 1809 in
                                Hopkins County, Kentucky.

aaabc   EPIPHRODITUS AND (1) Wife HANKS
   Their children and grandchildren

      aaabca   WILLIAM HANKS
                 b. Dobbs County, N. C.
                 d.
                 m. Sophie Reams, circa 1800; she died
                    August 23, 1830.
                 Resided in Montgomery & Wilcox Cos. Ala.
                 Children:
                          a Howell G., b. 1802.
                          b Elizabeth
                          c Mary
                          d Phodea Ann
                          e Lemuel
                          f William
                          g Stephen
                          h Sarah
                          i Hezekiah
                          j Ira,
                          k John Wesley
                          l Sophie Allen.

      aaabcb   JAMES HANKS
                 b. Dobbs Co., N. C.
                 m.
                 d.

   EPIPHRODITUS & (2) _____LANIER HANKS
      Their only child and grandchildren

      aaabcc   STEPHEN HANKS
                 b. April 15, 1786 in LaNoir Co., N.C.
                 d. Sept. 1853, in Harris Co., Ga.
                 m. Elizabeth Corbett, 1814; she died
                    Dec,, 1843.
                 Stephen became a physician and surgeon;
                 went to Harris County, Georgia in 1843.
                 Children-13:
                          a Sarah E.
                          b Mary A.
                          c Frances M., b. 1821
                          d Stephen L.
                          e Louisa R.
                          f Ellen
                          g Martha
                          h Harriett
                          i George McD.
                          j James M.
                          k Hampton H.
                          l Thomas.

aaabd MOSES AND AGGATHA DODSON HANKS
         THEIR CHILDREN

aaabd a   JOIASY HANKS
           b. July 13, 1769, in Virginia
           d. 1847 in Missouri.
           m. Reuben Hill; he was born June 17, 1761;
              d. Jan. 16, 1833. Was a Baptist
              Minister; hatter by trade.
           Children:
              14, incl. Gen. George Hill.

aaabd b   FRANCES HANKS
           b. Sept. 6, 1771, in Virginia
           m. Fortunatus Dodson, Sept. 23, 1793 in
              Halifax Co., Virginia.

aaabd c   GEORGE HANKS
           b. June 6, 1773, in Virginia.
           d. Sept. 1859 in Anderson Co., Texas.
           m. Lurane Hill, Oct. 29, 1791 in Pitts. Co.
              Virginia.
           They moved to Pulaski Co., Ky.; to Maury
              Co., Tenn.; to DeSota Co., Miss.; to
              Texas.
           m. (2)._____

aaabd d   MOSES HANKS
           b. Jan. 6, 1779 in Pitts. Co., Va.
           Went to Texas.

aaabd e   ELIZABETH HANKS
           b. Sept. 9, 1782, in Pitts.Co., Va.
           m. Robert Williams, June 1, 1799, in
              Lincoln County, Kentucky.

aaabd f   TROY HANKS
           b. May 2, 1784 in Pitts. Co., Va.
           May have gone to Illinois.

aaabd g   THOMAS HANKS
           b. Apr. 30, 1786, in Pitts. Co., Va.
           d. Nov. 28, 1857, in Anderson Co. Tex.
           m. Sarah "Sally" Hill, Sept. 8, 1804
           Was Baptist Min. in Tenn. & Tex.
           Organized a wagon train from Nashville,
            Tenn. to join the Austin Colony.
           Children: 9 named in his will.

aaabd MOSES AND AGGATHA DODSON HANKS
      THEIR CHILDREN

aaabd h   IDELLA HANKS
             b. Jan. 5, 1788 in Pitts. Co., Va.
             m. _____ Dodson.

aaabd i   SARAH HANKS "Sary"
             b. Mar. 15, 1790 in Pitts. Co., Va.
             In late life lived with her bro. George.

aaabd j   ELIJAH HANKS
             b. Dec. 16, 1793 in Pitts. Co., Va.
             d. Aug. 12, 1871 in Maury Co., Tenn.
             m. (1) Mary Woolverton; she was born
                Dec. 24, 1795; d. July 31, 1854.
             Children: Nine
             m. (2) Mrs. Esther L. Miller
             Elijah got religion at the time of the
             earthquake, 1812, became a minister.

aaabd k   MARY HANKS
             m. _____ Gyn.

aaaea WILLIAM AND KEZIAH HANKS
Their children

a MARY HANKS

b THOMAS HANKS

Harriett Sisco, aaaea c NOAH HANKS
Dau.-in-law.
b. Jan. 1, 1790, in South Carolina
d. Apr. 5, 1853; Salem, Henry Co., Iowa
m. Sophia Kendall; she was born Nov. 73, 1798.
Milton, Mahoning Co., d. Feb. 1, 1876, Ohio.

d JOHN HANKS

e RACHEL HANKS

f JAMES HANKS

g NANCY HANKS*
b. circa 1800

Birth date from
testimony of Nancy
Hollifield and Berry
H. Melton.

*See Chap. V, 111.

aaaeb JAMES AND MARY STARRETT HANKS
    Their known children

aaaeb a   RICHARD HANKS
            b. after circa 1780.
            (Possibly the Richard to Christian Co.,Ky.,
             and to Nashville; reason: not many
             Richards)

aaaeb b   DAVID HANKS
            b. in 1780's.
            Was a minister and soldier.

aaaeb c   WILLIAM "BILLY" HANKS.
            b.
            m. _____ Lyons.
            Children:
            aaaebc a Jacob, b. Aug. 15, 1811.
                    b James, b. July 4, 1813;
                      m. Lucinda Sparks, Jan 13, 1838.
                    c Mary, b. Mar. 26, 1816
                    d Samuel, b. Mar. 28, 1818
                      m. Lettie D. Cockerham,
                        Jan. 12, 1860.
                    e William, b. Aug. 3, 1820;
                      m. Nancy McCann, Mar. 16,1845.
                      They had a dau. Jane, m. W.F.
                      Cockerham, Nov. 22, 1867.
                    f David, b. Feb. 22, 1823.
                    g Frances, b. Apr. 26, 1825.
                    h Jennie, b. Feb. 18, 1828.
                    i Dr. Hugh, b. July 15, 1832;
                      m. Martha Stergill; she was
                      born 1835.

aaaeb d   MARY "POLLY" HANKS
            b.
            m. Isaac Swann, Aug. 18, 1804 in
               Lincoln County, North Carolina.

aaaec   JOSHUA AND RUTH BRYANT HANKS
            Their children

aaaec e   ZACHARIAH HANKS
                b.
                m. Susan Rector.
                Went to Missouri.
                Children:
                    Andrew Jackson; Benjamin Franklin;
                    David; Elizabeth; Jessie; Ruth; and
                    William.

aaaec b   RICHARD HANKS
                b. d. inf.

aaaec c   THOMAS HANKS
                b. Oct. 28, 1797.
                d. Feb. 13, 1840, at Nebraska City, Neb.
                m. Jane Moore.
                Children:
                    David; Edward; Mahala; Leroy; Cannoy;
                    Hugh; Thomas; Susan.

aaaec d   RUTH HANKS
                b. May 24, 1797; d. Feb. 15, 1879
                m. J. Vaughn.

aaaec a   JOSHUA (JR.) HANKS.
                b. May 1, 1782
                m. Rosamond Carrico
                Children: Known only:
                    Creed L. Hanks, m. Minerva Moore.

aaaec f   NANCY HANKS*
                b.
                m. George Moore.
aaaec g   THURSA HANKS, m. Henry Mallory
        h   DAVID HANKS, D. inf.
        i   WILLIAM HANKS, m. (1) Nancy Carrico;
                            (2) (3) (4).
        j   MARY HANKS, m. Peter Cooley
        k   SUSANNA HANKS, m. John Mooney, 1829.
        l   RHODA HANKS, m. Enoch Moore.
        m   LYDIA HANKS, m. James Moore.
        n   PATIENCE HANKS, m. William Davis
        o   JAMES HANKS, bachelor.
        p   JOHN HANKS, m. Della Carrico.

* It is to be observed that this Nancy Hanks married George Moore.

aaaed RICHARD JR. AND PHOEBE HAYES HANKS
       Their children

aaaed a   JOHN HANKS
           b. Aug. 31, 1786; m. Elizabeth Weathers,
           Aug. 14, 1810. They moved to McMinn Co.,
           Tenn., where they reared a family. The
           1830 census shows 3 sons, 4 daus.
           Known Children:
               Alford, b. 1815; m. Sally_____
               John M., m. Mary Bell Dixon.

aaaed b   JOSHUA HANKS
           b. May 1, 1789; m. (1) Mary "Polly"
               Rennick, Feb. 13, 1812.
           To Morgan and Scott Counties, Tenn.
           3 Daughters:
               Mary Ann, Martha, Nancy, b. Dec.30,1812
           Joshua left there and
           m. Amelia Rape of Nashville, Tenn. Then
               to Alton, Illinois.
           Children:
               John Lawson Pope, Louisiana, Indiana,
               Caroline, Peter, Frances, Clark J.,
               Benjamin, Richard, Hardin, Thomas.

aaaed c   MARTHA HANKS
           b. Sept. 21, 1791; m. Dr. Jesse Holland
               of Gastonia, N. Carolina.

aaaed d   JAMES HANKS
           b. Mar. 8, 1794; d. inf.

aaaed e   THOMAS HANKS
           b. Mar. 28, 1797; m. Elizabeth Tunderbrink
               They went to Western Illinois; to Greene
               Co.

aaaed f   MARY HANKS
           b. Oct. 10, 1799; m. Eli Bigham. He died
               Oct. 17, 1853, aged 58.
           She died Aug 4, 1884; int. Patterson, Ill.

aaaed g   DAVID HANKS
           b. July 17, 1802.

aaaed RICHARD JR AND PHOEBE HAYES HANKS
Their Children.

<table>
<tr><td></td><td>aaaed h</td><td>ANN "NAN" HANKS*</td></tr>
</table>

	aaaed h	ANN "NAN" HANKS*
Bible Rec.		b. July 25, 1805; m. Luke Brown,
C.H. Rec.		Sept. 12, 1821.
	aaaed 1	NATHAN HANKS
		b. Feb. 6, 1811; went to Cane Hill, Ark.;
		Operated a wagon factory.

* This is the Nancy Hanks who is named in Western Illinois tradition,
as the sister of Joshua and one who married Tom Lincoln; it is
obvious she was born too late. (q.v.) Chapt. IV, v.

* * * * *

END OF THE SIXTH GENERATION OF THE DESCENDANTS

OF

WILLIAM HANKS II.

CHAPTER III

G E N E A L O G I C A L   R E C O R D

OF

THE DESCENDANTS OF RECORD

OF

THOMAS HANKS

OF

VIRGINIA

from

cira 1700 to circa 1800

and

The Nancys Born To Them

THE FIRST HANKS OF RECORD

John Hanks	1623.
George Hanks	1633.
Enoch Hanks	1653.
Thomas Hanks	1653.
Robert Hanks & his wife, Margaret	1661.

* * *

Authorities	Code	Names
	a	THOMAS HANKS

THOMAS HANKS
b. Probably before 1630; d. circa 1675
m. Probably Elizabeth _____.

Patent Book
He first acquired land in the area
between the Mattapony and the Rappahannock
Rivers, in Virginia, Feb. 16, 1653; subsequently continued to patent land including some in now Richmond County. No
probate record of his estate has been
located.

Possible Children:*
aa William, b. circa 1650.

Presumptive &
Conjectural
ab George, of Richmond Co., Va.
ac Robert of Richmond Co., Va.
ad Peter, of Ann Arundal Co., Md.

* There is no direct evidence that these men were sons of Thomas Hanks,
but from the fact, he is the only one of record then, in that area,
who could have been their father; from proximity; from possibility and
probability, they are so presumed. William, being an owner of land
without record of purchase, is presumed to have been the oldest son
and acquired the land by inheritance according to the then law of
primogeniture. When his estate was later probated in Richmond County
the Inventory listed certain assets "from across the river" which meant
south of the Rappahannock. The fact he had property in that area tends
to confirm whence he came. For a more complete discussion see Barton's
LINEAGE OF LINCOLN.

| | aa | WILLIAM HANKS I. |

WILLIAM HANKS I.
b. circa 1650; d.1704, in Richmond Co.,Va.
Was known as "The Carpenter,"
m. Sarah _____; she m.(2) Richard White
Children:
aaa William II, b. Feb. 14, 1679.
aab Luke I, b. circa 1685.
aac John, b. circa 1690.

aac   JOHN HANKS I

                b. circa 1690
                d. 1740 in Richmond Co., Va.
                m. Catharine _____.
                Children:
                aaca William of John, b. Mar. 9, 1715.
                aacb Eleanor, b. March 18, 1717
                aacc Elizabeth, b. Oct. 18, 1720.
                aacd Catharine, b. Apr. 7, 1723; d. inf.
                aace Sarah, b. Apr. 7, 1723; survived.
               ·aacf Joseph, b. Dec. 20, 1725.
                aacg Catharine, b. Dec. 20,1725, twin
                aach John, b. May 4, 1728.
                aaci Thomas, b. July 1, 1732.
                aacj Alexander, b. Dec. 2, 1734.

aaca   WILLIAM HANKS
        b. Mar. 8, 1715, in Richmond Co., Va.
        m. Winifred _____.
        Lived in Caroline Co., 1747; in Lancaster
        County, 1782; tithed.
        Probably died in Lancaster Co.
        Children: Record of one only: probably
                   others.
                a Mary Ann, b. Apr. 16, 1737 in
                   Richmond County, Va.

aacb   ELEANOR HANKS
        B. Mar. 18, 1717 in Richmond Co., Va.
        m. _____ Dodson
        d. after 1782.

aacc   ELIZABETH HANKS
        b. Oct. 18, 1720, in Richmond Co., Va.
        m. _____ Woolard
        d. after 1782.

aacd   CATHARINE HANKS
        b. 1721; d. in inf.

aace   SARAH HANKS
        b. Apr. 7, 1723, in Richmond Co., Va.
        d. before 1782.

aacf   JOSEPH HANKS
        b. Dec. 20, 1725 in Richmond Co., Va.
        d. after 1785
        m. Ann Lee
        Lived in Richmond Co. Va.; road surveyor;
           adm. of his Mother's estate, 1782.
        Children: Rec. of one only.
                a Betty, b. Mar. 4, 1771 in Richmond
                   County, Va.

aacg   CATHERINE HANKS
        b. Dec. 20, 1725, twin of Joseph
        d. after 1782.
        Spinster.

aach   JOHN HANKS
        b. May 4, 1728 in Richmond Co., Va.
        d. after 1810 in Woodford Co., Ky.
        Was Rev. War Soldier; drew pension.
          m. Susannah
          Children:
          aach a George   aach c John
          aach b Abner   aach d Elijah

aac   JOHN AND CATHARINE HANKS
Their children & grandchildren

aaci   THOMAS HANKS
              b. July 1, 1732, in Richmond Co., Va.
              d. after 1784 tithe rec.
              m. Betty Lee
              Appears on 1782, 1783, 1784 tax record
              as "T" Hanks. (T can stand for only
              Thomas, Turner's name is written in full)
              They received £9 11s 9p from the estate
              of the Grandfather of Betty Lee, 1769.
              Children:
              aacia Joseph, b. Feb. 21, 1764.
              aacib Nansy, b. Sept. 15, 1766*

              *The date of birth eliminates this
               Nancy from consideration.

aacj   ALEXANDER HANKS.
              b. Dec. 2, 1734 in Richmond Co., Va.
              d. Sept. 16, 1776 as a Revolutionary
                 Soldier. Was private in Capt. Burges
                 Ball's Co. of 5th Va. Reg. of Foot.
                 under Lt. Col. Josiah Parker.
                 There were no children listed as his
                 heirs when his brother, Joseph, settled
                 their mother's estate, 1782.

aach   JOHN AND SUSANNAH HANKS
Their children

aacha   GEORGE HANKS
b. before 1762 in Richmond Co., Va.

Pro. Rec.
Alse Dale Will
d. 1824 in Woodford Co., Ky.
m. Elizabeth Dale, dau of Thomas & Alse
Dale. She was born January 6, 1758,
in Richmond County, Virginia.
Children:
aacha a Winifred, b. Oct.27, 1791
aacha b Alse, m. Mar. 15, 1799.
aacha c Fanny.

aachb   ABNER HANKS
b. 1763 in Richmond County, Virginia

Family Rec.
Pension Application
Alse Dale Will
d. Sept. 5, 1846, in Johnson Co., Ind.
Was a soldier of the Rev. War.
m. (1) Mary Dale, dau of Thos. & Alse Dale
(2) Elizabeth "Becky" Goodwin,
May 9, 1806.
(3) Frances McEndre, Mar. 3, 1812, in
Gallatin Co., Kentucky
(4) Sarah Goodman, 1821.
(5) Sallie Shouse, Aug. 20, 1832, in
Johnson Co., Indiana.

ABNER & MARY DALE HANKS
*** aachb a Matilda, b. Dec. 10, 1788; m.
Benj. Utterback; 15 children.
b Thomas, b. Mar. 11, 1791; m. Sally
Tandy, Dec. 22, 1812.
c Susan, b. Aug. 22, 1793; m. Jas.
Smith; (2) Graddy.
d Mary, b. Mar. 5, 1796; m. Elisha
Mills.
e Elizabeth, b. Jul. 6, 1798;
m. John Utterback.
f Ailsie, b. Feb. 15, 1800; m.
John Utterback, his 1st.
g John Dale, b. Apr. 20,1802; m.
Franc McAndrew
h Maria, b. Aug. 4,1804; m. J.Smith;
(2) Mott; (3) Kiphart.

*** It is obvious that Abner's first child was born four years after the
birth of Nancy Hanks Lincoln.

aach   JOHN AND SUSANNAH HANKS
        Their children

aachb   ABNER & **BECKY GOODWIN HANKS**
            aachb ı Sarah, b. Apr. 1,1808; m. Corbin
                        Utterback.
                  j Sydnor, b. April 11, 1811.

            ABNER & **FRANCES** McENDRE HANKS
                  k Milton, b. Feb. 15, 1813; m.
                        Rebecca Utterback.
                  l Washington, b. Mar. 20,1814;
                        Entered land in Indiana.
                  m Martha, b. Aug. 31,1815; m. Elisha
                        Dehart.
                  n Caroline, b. Jan. 5, 1817; m.
                        Hezekiah Utterback
                  o Grace, b. **July** 22, 1818; m.
                        Willis Deer,Sr. to Md.

            ABNER & SARAH GOODMAN HANKS

                  p Amanda
                  q America, m. David **Byers.**

            ABNER & SALLIE SHOUSE HANKS

                  r David
                  s Cynthia
                  t Jack

aachc   JOHN HANKS.
            b. Oct. 20,1765, in Richmond Co., Va.
            m. Susan _____(Sydnor)
            Went to Kentucky.
            Children: one only, a son:
            aachc a Sydnor Dale, b. Dec. 29, 1793.

aachd   ELIJAH HANKS.
            b. Oct. 19, 1766, in Richmond Co., Va.
            m. Widow, Winnie Dale Bryant, dau of Thos.
                        and Alse Dale.
            Resided in Mercer and Woodford Cos., Ky.
            They donated church site; were anti-
                slavery.
            Elijah took a flat-boat to New Orleans;
                was killed and robbed.
            Children: None; but there were Bryant
                step-children of Elijah's.

aac1   THOMAS AND BETTY LEE HANKS
       Their children

aac1a   JOSEPH HANKS.
           b. Feb. 21, 1764 in Richard Co., Va.
           No further record discovered;
           Not identified later.

aac1b   NANSY HANKS (sic)
           b. Sept. 15, 1766, in Richmond Co., Va.
           (Probably named for her aunt Ann Lee Hanks,
             wife of her Uncle Joseph Hanks)

* * *

END OF THE FIFTH GENERATION OF THE DESCENDANTS

OF

JOHN HANKS I.

CHAPTER IV

G E N E A L O G I C A L   R E C O R D S

OF

THE DESCENDANTS OF RECORD

OF

THOMAS HANKS

OF

VIRGINIA

from

circa 1700 to circa 1800

and

The Nancys Born To Them

THE FIRST HANKS OF RECORD

John Hanks	1623.
George Hanks	1633.
Enoch Hanks	1653.
Thomas Hanks	1653.
Robert Hanks & his	1661.
wife, Margaret	

* * *

Authorities	Code	Name
	a	THOMAS HANKS

THOMAS HANKS
b. Probably before 1630; d. circa 1675.
m. Probably Elizabeth _____.

Patent Book

He first acquired land in the area between the Mattapony and the Rappahannock Rivers, in Virginia, Feb. 16, 1653; subsequently continued to patent land including some in now Richmond County. No probate record of his estate has been located.

Possible children:*
  aa William, b. circa 1650.

Presumptive &
Conjectural

  ab George, of Richmond Co., Va.
  ac Robert, of Richmond Co., Va.
  ad Peter, of Ann Arundal Co., Md.

*there is no direct evidence that these men were sons of Thomas Hanks, but from the fact, he is the only one of record then, in that area, who could have been their father; from proximity; from possibility and probability, they are so presumed. William, being an owner of land without record of purchase, is presumed to have been the oldest son and acquired the land by inheritance according to the then law of primogeniture. When his estate was later probated in Richmond County, the Inventory listed certain assets "from across the river" which meant south of the Rappahannock. The fact he had property in that area tends to confirm whence he came. For a more complete discussion see Barton's LINEAGE OF LINCOLN.

                         aa   WILLIAM HANKS I
b. circa 1650; d. 1704, in Rich. Co., Va.
Was known as "The Carpenter."
m. Sarah_____: she m. (2) Richard White
Children:
  aaa William II, b. Feb. 14, 1679.
  aab Luke I, b. circa 1685
  aac John, b. circa 1690

| | aab | LUKE HANKS I, son of William I. |

aab   LUKE HANKS I, son of William I.
b. circa 1685, and before 1687, in Rich.
    County, Virginia
d. before Feb. 1757 in Lancaster Co., Va.

b. after birth of
William & was 21 by
1708.
Probate recs.

His estate indicated he was a farmer and
    tobacco grower.
m. (1) Elizabeth _____.
Children:

Surmise*

  ? William, d. circa 1756 in Lancaster
    Co.; left son, John.

Presumptive**
    "
N.Farnham Par. Rec.
    "   "   "
Possible;
Ky & S.C. Fam. Trad.
S.C. Fam. Tra.***
Possible:
N. Farnham Par. Rec.
S.C. tradition
Evidential:

aaba Luke Junr., b. c 1715 (Luke II herein)
aabb Dawson, c. 1717.
aabc Alexander, b. Oct. 21, 1719.
aabd Lucretia, b. June 1, 1722.
  ? Ann, b. c. 1725.
aabe George
aabf Joseph
  ? Sarah, b. c 1735.
aabg Turner, b. June 18, 1737.
aabh James, b. c. 1739
aabi Abraham, b. after 1743 and before 1750
aabj Moses

Probate Rec. and
N. Farnham Par. Rec.

m. (2) Sarah _____.
aabk Martha, b. May 26, 1752.

*No clue to place this Wm., but both bros. of Luke I named first sons
William.

**Records refer to Luke Hanks Junr., who could have been a son of no
one else than Luke I.

***Knotts of S.C. interviewed Mrs. Laura Hanks, Mrs. Jane Drake, and
Matthew E. Hanks; received from them family traditions that seem to include George, Joseph, James, and Abraham as brothers of Luke Hanks II.

RESEARCHERS NOTE: Of all the lists of children of Hanks families, the
determination of the children of Luke Hanks I is the most difficult and
probably the most important for historical purpose. If he married at the
usual age of twenty-five, or about 1710, his first children should have
been born in due course; but the first birth dates of record are of
Alexander and Lucretia. Both of Luke I's brothers named their sons
William, for their father; perhaps Luke I did. William, who d. 1756 is
unplaced; it is a surmise he was a first son of Luke I, but there is no
clue.
There is no doubt that George was a son. The tradition is clear in Ky.
and in S.Carolina. There are no records of him later than the Battle of
Yorktown so he undoubtedly was killed there.

Knotts does not specifically list Joseph as a son but indirectly as a
brother of Abraham, who was a son. The family traditions in Kentucky
and in Illinois are that they were brothers, which makes this unplaced
Joseph a son of Luke Hanks I. Joseph was probably born of Elizabeth for

he named his first daughter Elizabeth.

Indirect evidence indicates that Abraham was a son of Luke I, and fits no other case. Abraham named a daughter Sarah, which may have been for his wife or his father's wife, Sarah, his mother or step-mother.

For more detailed information please refer to Part II, Chapter IV, iv.

Adin Baber

February 19, 1960

The circumspect student of Hanksiana, and of the ancestry of Nancy Hanks Lincoln, is respectfully referred to the chart of names on page 248, and to the frontispiece.

Melda (Mrs. C.W.) Waldrop first sent a copy of these names, in a letter to the writer, February 10, 1960. In it she wrote, "Here is what was on a little scrap of paper in the Bible, afraid it does not help." She is mistaken in her mild surmise, -- it does help -- and exceedingly so.

For she further writes, "The only thing it could be is the Hanks' under Luke, and the other names could have been Hills.* I do remember hearing in our family that both sides of the family had Bible names."

These two lists of names, put down by some one long since dead, and probably from memory, although apparently for a Biblical study of origins of names of ancestors, are so much in agreement with the names of known children of both Luke Hanks and of Thomas Hill, that they are more than a coincidence.

It is the considered judgment of this writer and the compiler of Hanks family genealogies, that the names listed under the name of Luke are names of his children. That it is only a partial list is known by the omission of other names that are recorded as children of Luke in the Register of North Farnham Parish of Richmond County, Virginia.

Therefore this list of names confirms a part of the list of names of children of Luke Hanks I, as set out on the previous page 315.

It can now be stated categorically that the grandfather Hanks of Nancy Hanks Lincoln was Luke Hanks I, of Virginia.

Adin Baber

* Also repeated in a long-distance telephone conversation this same day.

317

aab LUKE I AND **ELIZABETH HANKS**
Their children & grandchildren

<table>
<tr><td></td><td>aaba</td><td>LUKE HANKS II</td></tr>
<tr><td>Calculated</td><td></td><td>b. c 1715 in Richmond Co., Va.</td></tr>
<tr><td>Pro. Rec.</td><td></td><td>d. 1789, in Anderson Co., S. C.</td></tr>
<tr><td>Will of Dale</td><td></td><td>m. Nancy Dale, kinswoman of Thos. &
Elizabeth Dale of Prince William Co.,Va.</td></tr>
<tr><td></td><td></td><td>They resided in Fauquier Co., Va. in 1770s</td></tr>
<tr><td>O.B.</td><td></td><td>where Luke was sued for debt and admitted
it, Mar. Ct. 1773.</td></tr>
<tr><td>Ch. rec.</td><td></td><td>His wife, Nancy, joined Broad Run Church,
1778;</td></tr>
<tr><td>Ch. rec.</td><td></td><td>Luke joined the same, 1779.</td></tr>
<tr><td>will</td><td></td><td>He inherited from Thos. Dale, 1779.</td></tr>
<tr><td>Tax List</td><td></td><td>Moved to Prince Wm. Co.,Va by 1782; taxed
there, 1783.</td></tr>
<tr><td>D.B.</td><td></td><td>Sold his remaining interest in real estate
in 1784. Migrated to Southern Va.;
thence to S.C.</td></tr>
<tr><td>Census</td><td></td><td>His wife, a widow in Pendleton Co.,by 1790</td></tr>
<tr><td>Pro. rec.</td><td></td><td>Children:</td></tr>
</table>

aabaa Thomas
aabab Luke III, b. 1784
aabac John
aabad Robert
aabae George
aabaf Elizabeth
aabag Lucretia
aabah Priscilla
aabai Martha
aabaj Susan
aabak Judith
aabal Nancy*

<table>
<tr><td></td><td>aabb</td><td>DAWSON HANKS</td></tr>
<tr><td></td><td></td><td>b. c 1717, in Richmond Co., Va.</td></tr>
<tr><td>O.B. 11 574</td><td></td><td>Living in Richmond Co., Va., 1746</td></tr>
<tr><td>Acct. B</td><td></td><td>Attended Luke Hanks I estate sale in
Lancaster Co., 1757.</td></tr>
<tr><td></td><td></td><td>No rec. or clue of wife or children</td></tr>
</table>

*Cf: Chap. V, ii.

aab LUKE I AND ELIZABETH HANKS
Their children and Grandchildren

	aabc	ALEXANDER HANKS
Par. Rec.		b. Oct. 21, 1719, in Richmond Co., Va.
O.B.		Was in Lancaster Co., 1746
O.B.		Henry Tabscott granted judg. vs his estate, 1750.
		No rec. or clue of wife or children.

	aabd	LUCRETIA HANKS
Par. Rec.		b. June 1, 1722 in Richmond Co., Va.
		No further record.

		ANN HANKS
		b. c 1725
Presumptive		Possible, even probable, dau of Luke I, Her dau. Charlotte, b. Dec. 25, 1740; Christmas.

	aabe	GEORGE HANKS*
		b. c 1728 in Richmond Co., Va.
Fam. Rec.		d. Killed in the Battle of Yorktown.
		m. Possibly: Elizabeth_____.
		Children: Probably
Conjectural		aabea George, m, Mary Toggle.

* A History of Kentucky, in reference to Thomas H. Hanks reads, "...his grandfather was George Hanks, resided on the Potomac River in Virginia, prior to the Revolutionary War -killed at Yorktown..." But by positive evidence, the grandfather of said Thomas H. Hanks, was Turner Hanks, son of Luke I. It is therefore, the inference that George was a brother of Turner and son of Luke Hanks I.

aab LUKE I AND ELIZABETH HANKS
their children and grandchildren

aabf   **JOSEPH HANKS***

Apprx.   b. c 1730's in Virginia.
Will   d. 1793, in Nelson Co., Kentucky
Will   m. Nannie _____. (She may have been a
           Lee or Shipley.)
D.B. Tax List   They resided in Hampshire Co., Va.,
           1782-4
D.B.   Sold option in land there, Nov. 9, 1784.
D.F. Hanks   Thence to Halifax Co., Va.; thence to Ky,
Will   Children:
    aabfa **Thomas**, b. c 1759
    aabfb **Joshua**
    aabfc **William**, b. 1766
    aabfd **Charles**
    aabfe **Joseph Jr.**, b. 1781.
    aabff **Mary "Polly"**
    aabfg **Elizabeth**
    aabfh **Nancy****

aabg   **TURNER HANKS**

Par. rec.   b. June 18, 1737, in Richmond Co., Va.
    d. Oct. 6, 1794, in Richmond Co., Va.
    m. (1) Million ____; they resided in
         Richmond Co. Purchased 105 acres
         land from Thos. Durham, 1764; this
         farm later owned by their son, Luke.
    Children:
    aabga **Mary "Molly"** b. 1761
    aabgb **Hannah**, b. 1767.
    m. (2) Sarah _____.
    Children:

aabgc **George**, b. 1769	aabgf **Pitman**, b1776
aabgd **Luke**, b. 1771	aabgg **Chichester**
aabge **Raleigh**, b. 1773	b. 1781
	aabgh **Turner**, b 1784

*There is no proof that Joseph was a son of Luke I. The premise is, he is
unplaced: (Cf: Chap. VII, vii, xiv) If he is a brother of Abraham Hanks, as
tradition and evidence seems to place him: he is a son of Luke I.

** Of this Nancy, see Chap. V, v.

aab LUKE I AND ELIZABETH HANKS
Their children and Grandchildren

	aabh

JAMES HANKS, probable son of Luke.
b. c. 1739; d. after 1800 in Pitts. Co.Va.
m. Nancy (Hamlin or Homlin ?) probably in
    Loudoun County, Virginia.

D.B. 10, p. 228   In Amelia County, 1763.
D.B. 6, p. 406   To Bedford Co., 1780.

Children:
aabha   Abram, b. Apr. 2, 1759.
aabhb   Thomas, b. 1766.
aabhc   James,Jr., b. c 1770.
aabcd   Tabitha, b. c 1773.

aab LUKE I AND ELIZABETH HANKS
their children & grandchildren

Authorities	Code	Name
	aabi	ABRAHAM HANKS
Bound 1763		b. circa 1745; after 1742 and before 1750. in the Northern Neck of Virginia.
Tradition Plausable		d. circa 1790, in Campbell Co., Va. Probably buried in the old Harper Grave-yard, near Hatt Creek Church.
Family Rec.		m. Sarah Harper, probable dau. of George & Elizabeth (Shipley) Harper of Prince William Co., Virginia
Order Book		Resided in Fauquier Co,Va. 1773; sued for debt.
Calk's Journal Tra. Calk's Descend.		Accompanied William Calk to Boonesborough, Ky. (Va. then); helped survey the town; worked for Calk. Returned to Virginia, Autumn 1775.
Order Book, Deed Book C.H. Rec.		Witnessed apprenticeship paper, Brown to Calk, in Prince Wm. Co. Tithed in Pr. Wm. Co., years 1782 and 1783.
Early,Campbell Chronicles Tradition of Fam.		Removed to Campbell Co., Va. 1783. Probably Associated with James Hanks Sr. Occupation: blacksmith & mechanic.
Fam. Tradition Mrs. Steube, Danv.Ill.		Sarah, the wife, deceased, circa 1790 at the birth of a dau, probably Polly. Younger children "farmed out."
Presumed from all available evidence. Evidence of birthdates. From Ada Hanks census; none agree first taxed 1803; was probably 21. Vital Statistics of Ky. Bible First taxed 1807 Died, 1876, aged "almost 90" by family tradition Census and her grandson Dr. James LeGrand		Children: aabia Abraham Jr., b. c 1770; m. Mary "Polly" Combs, 1792. aabib Luke, b. 1771. aabic William, b. 1772 or 75. aabid George, b. 1782. aabie Fielding, b. 1783. aabif Nancy, b. 1784, in Va.* aabig John, b. 1786. aabih Sarah, b. 1788. aabii Polly "Sarah" b. 1790 or 92.

*Confer Chap. V,x; Chap. XIV.

I hereby affirm that the foregoing is true and correct; based on conclusions from the evidence and to the best of my ability.
Adin Baber.

aaba LUKE II AND NANCY DALE HANKS
       Their sons

aaba a   THOMAS HANKS
            b. in Va.
            m. Elizabeth Orr. To Anderson Co.,S.C.,
               1778.

aaba b   LUKE HANKS III
            b. Oct. 15, 1774, in Virginia
            d. Apr. 25, 1856, in S.Carolina
            m. Elizabeth Hanie; she d. July 25, 1856,
               aged 74.
            Children: 9 sons, 1 dau.
                  a Tillman; went to Ala.
                  b John
                  c Thomas
                  d George
                  e Anthony; went to Galveston, Tex.
                  f Stephan, m. Laura_____, 1841.
                  g William
                  h Nimrod,
                  i James
                  j Luke IV, b. Nov. 15, 1828;
                        m. Martha _____.
                  k Rachel, m. _____ Cobb.

aaba c   JOHN HANKS
            b. in Virginia -- Went to Tennessee.

aaba d   ROBERT HANKS
            b. in Virginia.

aaba e   GEORGE HANKS.
            b. in Virginia. Went to South Carolina.
            m. "Polly" Mary, _____.
            Removed to Pendleton Dis. S. Carolina 1819
            Known Children:
            aabde a James R., Crittendon Co.,Ky.1843.
                   b Matthew E., Gum Log, Pope Co.,Ark.

aabea **GEORGE** AND MARY TOGGLE HANKS
Their children

a   **CATHARINE HANKS**
        b. prior to 1782.
        d.

b   **WILLIAM HANKS**
        b. prior to 1782.

        JACK HANKS
        b. prior to 1782.
        d

aabf JOSEPH AND NANNIE HANKS
     Their Children

    aabf a   THOMAS HANKS
                  b. circa 1759 in Virginia

    aabf b   JOSHUA HANKS
                  b. circa 1763, in Virginia
                  Served in the Wabash Indian War, 1787;
                  received Cert. #762 for $7.33, Aug. 10,
                  1787.
                  d.

    aabf c   WILLIAM HANKS
                  b. 1766, in the Rappahannock River Country
                    of Virginia.
                  d. after 1850 in Macon Co.,Ill. Int. Gouge
                    cemetery.
                  m. Elizabeth Hall, Sept. 12, 1793 in Ky.
                  They resided near Falls of Rough in Gray-
                    son County, Kentucky.
                  Removed to Illinois about 1830.
                  Children:
                  aabfc a <u>Nancy</u>   g Joseph
                          b James   h Ceclia
                          c William   i .Lucinda
                          d Elizabeth   j Andrew
                          e John   Jackson
                          f Charles   k Sarah

    aabf d   CHARLES HANKS
                  b. In Virginia.

aabf JOSEPH AND NANNIE HANKS
       Their Children

        aabf e   JOSEPH HANKS, JR.
                      b. 1781 in Virginia
                      Taken by his parents to Kentucky; went
                            back to Virginia, after 1793; returned
                            to Kentucky and became a Carpenter at
                            Elizabethtown.
                      m. Mary Young, Nov. 10, 1810 at Elizabeth-
                            town.
                      Migrated to Adams Co., Ill. where he died
                            April 4, 1856.
                      Children:

aabfe	a Jacob Vertrees	aabfe	h Ann
	b Elizabeth		i Amaltha
	c Susannah		j Caroline
	d Nancy		k Isabell
	e John		l _____
	f Joseph		m _____
	g Mary		

        aabf f   MARY "POLLY" HANKS
                      b. in Virginia
                      m. Jesse Friend, in Hardin Co., Ky,
                            December 10, 1795.
                      d. in Edgar Co., Illinois after 1830.

        aabf g   ELIZABETH HANKS.
                      b. 1776 in Virginia
by Mar. License   m. Thomas Sparrow, Oct. 17, 1796 in
                          Mercer County, Kentucky
                      d. October 1818, in Spencer County, Ind.

        aabf h   NANCY HANKS*
                      b. in Hampshire Co., Va (W.Va.) in 1784
                      d. Spencer Co., Ind. about 1824; buried at
                          side of Nancy Hanks Lincoln
                      m. Levi Hall about 1800
                      Child: aabfh a Dennis Friend Hanks
                      Children:

	b Squire	f	Joseph
	c Lydia	g	Mahala
	d William	h	Letitia
	e Alfred		

* This is the Nancy so often mistaken to have married Thomas Lincoln.
She was born June 13, 1794, in Kentucky. See Chapt. V,v.

aabg TURNER AND (2) SARAH HANKS*
      Their sons

<table>
<tr><td></td><td>aabgc</td><td>GEORGE HANKS</td></tr>
</table>

Par. Rec.
Pro. Rec.
Mar. Rec.

aabgc GEORGE HANKS
       b. June 22, 1769, in Richmond Co., Va.
       d. 1847 in Franklin County, Kentucky
       m. Lucy Mildred Mitchell, Oct. 6, 1791 in
          Woodford County, Kentucky.
       Children: Seven.
            a George   e Turner
            b Edmond   f Elizabeth
            c Milton   g Nancy Ann
            d Jeremiah

aabgd LUKE HANKS.
       b. May 17, 1771, in Richmond Co., Va.
          First taxed 1792.
       d. 1817, in Richmond County, Virginia.
       m. (1) Levina Stott, Jan. 4, 1792; dau.
             John and Lucy M. Stott
       Children:
            a Ewell   c Turner
            b John   d Sallie

aabge RALEIGH HANKS
       b. April 1, 1773.

aabgf PITMAN HANKS
       b. Dec. 3, 1776 in Richmond Co., Va.
          (another date 1775)
       d. in Clay Co., Missouri
       m. Eliza Mitchell, Jan. 1, 1797. Six sons
          in Confederate Army.
       Children:
            a George   e Turner
            b John   f Gallatin
            c Jeremiah   g Sally Ann
            d Hickman   Lucy(?)

* It is to be observed by the marriage dates that the
  members of this generation were all born after 1784.

aabg TURNER AND (2) SARAH HANKS*
      Their Sons

    aabgg   CHICHESTER HANKS
                b. May 31, 1781, in Richmond Co. Va.
                   (Another date 1778)
                d. July 12, 1868, in Anderson County, Ky.
                   Int. Salt R. Ch.
                m. Mrs. Elizabeth Penny, July 15, 1823,
                   Franklin County, Kentucky. She died
                   June 27, 1862, age 92.
                Children:

a Thomas	d Susan
b Joseph	e Mary
c Frankie	f Helen.

    aabgh   TURNER HANKS
                b. Mar. 5, 1784. Bible date: 1781. In
                   Richmond County, Virginia (?)
                d. July 29, 1858, in Anderson Co., Ky.
                m. Nancy Holman, December 28, 1820
                Children
                   a William Taylor
                   b Thomas Holman
                   c Sarah Ann
                   d Mary Jane
                   e Reuben Anderson
                   f Frances Marian
                   g Turner Bond (?)

* It is to be observed by the marriage dates that the members of this generation were all born after 1784.

aabh or possible aaah JAMES HANKS
His children

Pension Appl 4569, Archives	aabha	ABRAM HANKS b. April 2, 1759 in Amelia Co., Virginia d. July 10, 1833, in Lincoln Co., Tenn. In Rev. War; enlisted Aug. 1777, in Bedford Co.; Volunteered April 2, 1779, from Charlotte C.H., Va.
C.H. Rec.		m. Lucy Jennings; got bond Mar. 30,1799; and married April 2, 1799 in Campbell County, Virginia. Children:

Stone at
Hatt Creek
		a I.J., b. Jan 19, 1800
		             d. May 2, 1810.
		    b John, to Tenn.

census
1854, age 84
	aabhb	THOMAS HANKS
		b. 1766
		d. After 1850, in Pitts. Co., Va.
		m. Nancy Brooks, Oct. 23, 1792, Friend's
		ritual. She dau. of James Brooks of
		Brookneal.
		Several children:
		    a Sarah, m. Dabney Clark Nov. 21
		                         1812.
		    b William
		    c James
		    d John

	aabhc	JAMES HANKS, JR.
		b. circa 1770
		Resided in Campbell Co., Va.
		Purchased land, 150 acres June 5, 1795,
		from Abrm Hanks
		Sold the land, Sept. 9, 1799, to James
		Hood.
		No further record of James.
		(May have been "The Mighty Hunter" of Ky.,
		and at the Battle of Tippecanoe.)
		m. Sarah Hanks --aabih
		Children:
		    a William, b. April 30, 1807
		    b Permelia, b. 1809.

	aabhd	TABITHA HANKS
		b. 1770's
		m. Samuel Barnes, Nov. 1, 1793, in Camp-
		bell County, Virginia.
		    Bond signed by James Hanks <u>Sr.</u>
		        Chas. Cobb, Min.

aab1 ABRAHAM AND SARAH HARPER HANKS
Their children and grandchildren

aab1a ABRAHAM HANKS, JR.
Est. b. c. 1770 in Virginia
Last son b. d. after 1814 in Kentucky
Rec. Taxed in Caswell Co., N.C. 1791-2-3
Mar. Rec. m. Mary "Polly" Combs, Jan. 12, 1792 in
  Caswell County, N.C.
Rec. They moved to Montgomery Co., Ky by 1800
  Children (Known and Presumptive):
Hardin Co., Rec. a Mary "Polly" m. Richard Rogers
  b Abraham, m. Mary Ann Wigglesworth
  c Thomas Jefferson, b. c 1805
  a Dau.
  d Dulcena, m. Lewis Ringo
  e Andrew Jackson, b. 1814
  f Elza, b. 1815; d. Feb. 19, 1866.

aab1b LUKE HANKS
Ada Hanks b. c 1771 or 72, in Virginia
"   " d. c 1855, in Brec. Co.,Ky. aged abt 83
Census 1890 Lived in N.C. Thence to Knox Co., Tenn.
  m. (1) _____
  Child:
Fam. Rec. a Nancy m. Peter French in Brec. Co.,Ky
D.B. m. (2) Celia_____
  Children:
  b Henry, his son, Willis.
  c Winifred
  d John Wesley, b. 1813, in Knox Co.Tenn
  e Stephen, D. Oct 28,1877; Union Star,
  Kentucky.

aab1c WILLIAM HANKS
Census disagree b. c 1775, in Va; d 1857 in Brec.Co.,Ky.
  Buried at Horsley Chapel
Mar. Rec. m. (1) Margaret Wilson, Dec. 28, 1797.
  Madison County, Kentucky
  Children:
  a John, b. 1801, in Kentucky
Fam. Rec. Mar. Rec. b Polly, m. John Wood, Dec. 21, 1815 in
  Hardin County, Kentucky
Fam. Rec. c Elizabeth, m. Jubel Meador, May 10,
  1821.
Fam. Rec. d William, b. Jan. 1,1804 in Hardin Co.,
  Kentucky
Mar. Rec. e Margaret, m. Thos. Courtney,
  Aug. 4, 1830
Mar. Rec. f Permelia, m. Jowell Faquay, April
  14, 1828.

aab1   ABRAHAM AND SARAH HARPER HANKS
Their children and grandchildren

	aab1c	WILLIAM HANKS

Mar. Rec.   aab1c   WILLIAM HANKS
   m. (2) Elizabeth Loyd, July 9, 1811.
   Children:
Rec.   g James, d. April 13, 1841.
Mar. Rec.   h Jemima, m. Dec. 31, 1831, Absalom
                 Robbins.

          aab1d   GEORGE HANKS
Pd. 1st tax 1803   b. c 1782 in Prince William Co., Va.
Family Rec.   d. 1814, in Montgomery Co., Ky.
   m. Sibby Harper, dau. of John Harper
Pro. Rec.   Children:
Tombs   a Fielden, b. Jan 16,1812 in Mont.Co.Ky.
     b Fidelia, twin, b. " " " " " "
Family Rec.   c Stephen England, b. Aug 29, 1813 in
               Montgomery County, Kentucky.

          aab1e   FIELDING HANKS
   b. 1783 (V.S.) or 1785 (census) in Va.
V.S. of Ky.   d. Aug. 13, 1861 in Morgan, now Wolfe
            County, Kentucky.
Fam. Rec. and   m. Lydia Harper, dau of John Harper; she
Mar. Rec.   was b. in the Fort of Boonesborough.
V.S.   She died Oct. 12, 1861; both int. at
            Campton, Kentucky.
   Children:
Chart by G'son   a Jordan, b. 1804
Chris. Col. Hanks   b William, b. 1806
     &   c Lucinda "Lucy" b. 1808
from Mrs. W.E. Bach   d Annie, b. 1810
     e Cuthbert Million, b. Sept. 8, 1814
     f Andrew Jackson, b. 1816
     g Nancy, b. 1818
     h George S., b. 1820
     i Louisa, b. 1822
     j Lydia, b.

          aab1f   NANCY HANKS
Bible   b. Feb. 5, 1784** in Campbell Co., Va.
Tombs   d. Oct. 5, 1818, in Spencer Co., Ind.
Mar. Rec.   m. Thomas Lincoln, June 12, 1806 in
            Washington County, Kentucky
   Children:
Fam. Rec.   a Sarah, b. Feb. 10, 1807
     b Abraham, b. Feb. 12, 1809
A.L.   c Thomas, d. in inf., 1811.

** It is to be noted that Nancy Hanks was born in becoming order among
siblings.

aab1   ABRAHAM AND SARAH HARPER HANKS
       Their children and grandchildren

aab1g   JOHN HANKS
Tax   b. c 1786, in Virginia
Pro. Rec.   d. before 1838, in Henry Co., Kentucky.
Mar. Rec.   m. Amy Swift, Nov. 11, 1814 in Henry
                    County, Kentucky. She dau of Thomas
                    Swift.
                 Children:
Fam. Rec.   a Marion, d. Sept. 1852.
                 b Thomas, b. Feb. 27, 1822
                 c Louisa, m. Will J. Baugh
                 d Mary, m. David Harris
                 e Elizabeth, m. Thomas Harris

aab1h   SARAH HANKS
Mrs. Steube   b. c 1788, in Virginia or N. Carolina
Fam. Know.   d. 1876, in Edgar Co., Ill. "aged almost
                    90"
Tra.   m. (1) James Hanks.
                 Children:
Fam. Rec.   a William, b. Apr. 30, 1807 in Montgomery
                    County, Kentucky
Fam. Rec.   b Permelia, b. 1809 in Mont. Co.,Ky.
  "   "   m. (2) Andrew Varvell

aab1i   POLLY HANKS
                 b. c 1790 (Fam. Rec.) 1792 (1850 Census)
                 d. Sept 9, 1854 in St. Francois Co., Mo.
                 Children:
Fam. Rec.   a Sophie, b. Mar. 1809 in Kentucky.
Dr. A.E. Morgan b Greenberry, d. in Indiana
Dr. J. LeGrand   c James Anderson, d. in Mississippi.
Fam. Rec.   d Creed Harris, d. in California.
Mar. rec.   f Margaret, d. Sept. 8, 1877 in Missouri.
Tombs.   e Samuel, b. Jan. 1, 1820; d. Sept 9,
                    1854 in Missouri.

CHAPTER V

HANKS FAMILY OF NEW BERN

Charts to show Hanks families that entered North Carolina after
1800. (Although Horatio was born after the birth of Nancy Hanks
Lincoln, his record is placed here for the benefit of future
research.

abfag HORATIO HANKS, son of (abfa) Benjamin*
      b. Oct. 1790, in Mannsfield, Conn., and with a twin
         sister, Marcia.
      d. in Washington Co., N.C., and is buried in the
         Methodist Cemetery at Plymouth.
      m. Jerusha Freeman, dau. of Frederick Freeman; after
         becoming a widow, she returned to the North; to
         Wymouth, Mass.
      CHILDREN:

      abfag a Benjamin Franklin, b. Jan. 16, 1812.
            b Charlotte Sophronia, b. Aug. 10, 1813; m. Orin
               Trufant.
      abfag c Horatio Ellsworth, b. July 8/10, 1815
            d Charles (Frederick), b. Aug. 30, 1817;
                d. Young.
      abfag e Edgar, b. Aug. 25, 1819.
      abfag f Ossian, b. July 8, 1821.
            g. Cornelia Sophia, b. July 21, 1823; m. Stephen
               L. Arents.
            h. Sylvia Augusta, b. July 7, 1825; m. James
               Swimmerton.
            i. Frances Elizabeth, b. Oct. 25, 1827; m. Silas Binny.
            j Junius, b. Dec. 31, 1829; m. Mary Bogart.
            k Frederick Freeman, b. April 14, 1832.

abfag a BENJAMIN FRANKLIN HANKS, son of Horatio.
      b. January 16, 1812.
      d.
      m. (1) Harriett C. Wallace, July 21, 1834, in Craven Co.,
         North Carolina; she b. Feb. 8, 1818; d. Nov. 11, 1840;
         buried in Maple Grove Cem., Craven Co., N.C.
      Child:
          a William H. Hanks, b. Feb. 19, 1837.

      m. (2) Jane Whitehurst, Aug. 30, 1841, in Carterret Co.,N.C.
      Children:
          b John B. Hanks, m. Emma; was a druggist.

* See page 338 for abfa BENJAMIN HANKS.

abfag c HORATIO ELLSWORTH HANKS, son of Horatio.
      b. July 8/10, 1815.
      d.
      m. Mary Bruce or Gould; she b. 1819; died Jan. 19, 1843;
         buried at Cedar Grove Cem. at New Bern, N.C., where they
         resided.
      Children:
          a Benjamin, b. 1839; d. Aug. 22, 1846.
          b James Bruce, m. Emma J. Matthews,
            March 29, 1860; she b. Dec. 3, 1840; died
            Nov. 26, 1886, in Craven Co., N.C.
            A daughter, Mrs. Jordon, Marshall, Texas.
      m (2) Clarisse Phelps, Oct. 31, 1844.

abfag e EDGAR HANKS, son of Horatio.
      b. Aug. 25, 1819.
      d.
      m. Sophia Cornell, in New Bern;
      They to Little Washington; to Edenton, N.C.
      Children:
         a. Lenora
         b. Carthene
         c. Georgiana
         d. John, a dentist in Jersey City.
         e. Edgar, a dentist in New York City.

abfag f OSSIAN HANKS, son of Horatio
      b. July 8, 1821
      d. April 8, 1890, in Jersey City
      m. (1) Frances Chadwick; she died May 2, 1845;
         aged 22 y, 2 m, 21 d.
      Resided at New Bern, N.C.
      m. (2) Mary Ann Wood; she died Dec. 17, 1870.
      Children: 7
         a Edgar, b. May 9, 1845; d. May 21, 1845.
         b Cornelia Augusta, b. Apr. 19, 1846
         c Mary Frances, b. Jan. 15, 1848;
                m. William H. Crosby.
         d George Henry, b. April 11, 1850.
         e Sarah Elizabeth, b. Dec. 27, 1851;
                d. July 27, 1854.
         f Susan Ann, b. Dec. 19, 1853.
         g. Benjamin F., b. March 5, 1855
              d. May 10, 1855,
                buried at Cedar Grove.

CHAPTER VI

HANKS FAMILY OF NEW ENGLAND

FIRST GENERATION

a   BENJAMIN HANKS 1665-1755[1]
        m. (1) Abigail
           (2) Mary Ripley

SECOND GENERATION

a   BENJAMIN AND ABIGAIL
        aa Abigail, June 8, 1701
        ab Benjamin, July 16, 1702-1787
           m. Mary White

NB#16 of Va.   ac <u>William</u>, b. Feb. 11, 1704*
           <u>tradition to Virginia</u>.
        ad Nathaniel, b. April 15, 1704
        ae Annah, Nov. 14, 1706 m. John Norris
        af Mary, Feb. 14, 1707/8 m. John Simmons
        ag John, Oct. 22, 1709-1742 m. Mary
           Delano
        ah Elizabeth, Mar. 5, 1711 m. Nehemiah
           Pearce
        ai Rachel, May 2, 1712, m. James Bumpas
        aj Joannah, Oct. 9, 1713 m. Beriah Curtis
        ak James, Feb. 24, 1714/15-1756
           m. Abigail Philips.
        al Jacob, 1717-1799, m. Sarah Bruce.

[1] Data from Hitchcock Charts, Lincoln Library, Fort Wayne, Indiana.

*Tradition:-- Went to Virginia, but this researcher thinks it more
likely that Benjamin Hanks was a son of Thomas of Virginia and
migrated to New England. But the question is moot.

THIRD GENERATION

ab   BENJAMIN AND MARY WHITE HANKS
          aba Isaac, June 1, 1725
            b Abigail, Aug 28, 1726-1780
            c William, Oct. 23, 1728-1807
              m. Hannah Sargent
            d John, Oct. 5, 1730-1815
              m. (1) Tabitha Hall
                 (2) Martha Huntington
            e Richard White, Nov. 8, 1734-1810
              m. Hannah Barrows
            f Uriah, May 4, 1736-1809 m. Irene Cass
            g Benjamin, Aug 20, 1738-1810
              m. Ruth Brewster
            h Mary, June 7, 1741 m. Gershom Hall
            i Silas, May 20, 1744-1828
              m. Sarah Webber

ag   JOHN AND MARY DELANO HANKS
          aga Nathaniel, 1737
            b Chloe, August 27, 1737
            c Sergt John, Dec. 25, 1739-1804
            d Nathaniel, Aug. 21, 1741.

ak   JAMES AND ABIGAIL PHILLIPS HANKS
          aka Joseph, Oct. 30, 1743-1775
                m. Elizabeth _____.
            b Hannah, Mar. 3, 1744/5
              m. Nathaniel Gilbert
            c Sarah, 17 ; m. ___ Lathrop
            d Huldah, 1747-1829; m. Joseph Bates.

al   JACOB AND SARAH BRUCE HANKS
          ala Benjamin, Oct. 21, 1754
            b William, July 3, 1757-1826
            c Benjamin, Feb. 6, 1758-1813
              m. (1) Ann Edson
                 (2) Hannah Pope
            d Ebenezer, July 24, 1759-1850
              m. (1) Hepzibah Ward
                 (2) Hulda Jacobs
                 (3) Abigail _____.
            e Rachel, Oct. 21, 1761.
            f James, May 30, 1764-1765.
            g James, June 7, 1766-1834
              m. Polly Ward
            h Rebecca, June 8, 1768
            i John

FOURTH GENERATION

abc   WILLIAM & HANNAH SARGEANT HANKS
             abca Sarah, b. July 8, 1759; d. inf.
               b Levi, b. May 28, 1761
               c Sarah, b. Nov. 22, 1762.
               d Jerusha, b. Dec. 3, 1764.
               e Eleazer, b. July 9, 1766
               f Eleazer, b. Jan 5, 1768
               g Arunah, b. Mar. 24, 1770.
               h Joseph, b. June 14, 1772.
               i Oliver, b. Dec. 31, 1774
               j Jarvis, b. Dec. 10, 1776
               k Oliver, b. Dec. 7, 1778.

abd   JOHN & TABITHA HALL HANKS
             abda Abigail, b. July 6, 1750
               b Isaac, b. Jan 15, 1752
               c Tabitha, b. April 10, 1754
               d Ann, B. Feb. 25, 1756
               e John W., b. Jan. 23, 1758
               f Ruth, b. Dec. 17, 1759
               g Elijah, b. Aug. 30, 1761
               h Mary, b. Nov. 12, 1764
               i Elizabeth, b. Nov. 9, 1767
               j Theophilus, Mar 1, 1769
               k Azariah, b. Sept. 20, 1774
               l Diadema, b. June 25, 1776
               m Enoch, b. Jan 9, 1779

abe   RICHARD WHITE AND HANNAH HARROWS HANKS
             abea Catharine, b. Oct. 12, 1755
               b Esther, b. Aug. 19, 1757
               c Richard, b. Oct. 25, 1759
               d Hannah, b. June 4, 1761
               e Asa, b. Aug. 20, 1764
               f Rachel
               g Thomas, b. June 21, 1772
               h Richard, b. June 18, 1774
               i Jerima, b. April 3, 1775

abf   URIAH AND IRENE CASE HANKS
         abfa   Benjamin, Oct. 29, 1755
           b   Irene ⎞
                    ⎟ Dec. 28, 1757
           c   Zelpha⎠
           d   Uriah, Oct. 19, 1760
           e   Lurancy, Feb. 26, 1764
           f   Philena, b. Feb. 4, 1765
           g   Libbeus, Oct. 20, 1771
           h   Alpheus, Oct. 7, 1777
           i   Marilla
           j   Rodney, Jan. 4, 1782

abg   BENJAMIN AND RUTH BREWSTER HANKS
         abga   Benjamin, Feb. 6, 1758
           b   Lydia, b. Dec. 24, 1759
           c   Lucy, Sept. 29, 1761
           d   Eunice, Jan. 16, 1764
           e   Celinda, Mar. 9, 1766
           f   Lydia, Mar. 9, 1768
           g   Ruth, June 26, 1770
           h   Zebalena, Feb. 2, 1773
           i   Ariel, Oct. 10, 1775
           j   Azel, Nov. 5, 1787

abi   SILAS AND SARAH WEBBER HANKS
         abia   Consider, b. April 29, 1754
           b   Cynthia, b. Feb. 21, 1756
           c   Silas, b. April 27, 1768
           d   Sarah, b. Nov. 20, 1770
           e   Mary, b. Mar. 21, 1773
           f   Phebe, b. Oct. 10, 1775
           g   Philomela, b. July 1, 1778
           h   Percy, b. July 29, 1780
           i   Philarmon, b. Mar. 31, 1784
           j   Polly, b. April 16, 1786
           k   Zebina, b. Sept. 28, 1791

aka   JOSEPH AND ELIZABETH HANKS
         akaa   Rachel, b. Aug. 13, 1775

alb   WILLIAM AND (1) (2) HANKS
         alba   Jacob
           b   Polly
           c   Enos, b. May 20, 1793
           d   Ebenezer

alc BENJAMIN AND (1) ANNE EDSON
(2) ? HANNAH POPE
   alca Jacob, b. Mar. 8, 1791
     b Reuel, 1796
     c Arza , Jan. 1, 1799
     d Alvin, May 5, 1802
     e _____ Hayden

ald EBENEZER AND (1) HEPZIBAH WARD
(2) HULDAH JACOBS (3) ABIGAIL _____
   alda Isaac, b. Nov. 24, 1785
     b Abigail, b. Oct. 11, 1787
     c Sylvia, b. Dec. 16, 1789
     d Esther, b. Nov. 7, 1792.
     e Ocran, b. Aug. 15, 1795
     f Moses)
             b. April 7, 1798
     g Aaron)
     h Zerah, b. Oct. 15, 1801

alg JAMES AND POLLY WARD HANKS
   alga John, b. April 23, 1787
     b Bethia, b. Jan. 25, 1789
     c Hannah, b. Nov. 25, 1790
     d Melinda, b. July 2, 1792
     e Bethia, b. Aug. 17, 1794
     f Nathaniel, b. July 2, 1796
     g William, b. Mar. 26, 1798
     h Sarah, b. April 13, 1800
     i Ira, b. March 24, 1802
     j Jacob, b. Feb. 10, 1804
     k Elizabeth, b. June 1, 1806
     l Daniel, b. Dec. 24, 1808
     m Melinda, b. Aug 10, 1810; d. inf.
     n Benjamin, b. April 14, 1812
     o Melinda, b. Feb. 13, 1814.

This is the end of the fourth generation of the New England
Hanks family and it is to be noted that there is not a single,
solitary daughter named Nancy.

abfa BENJAMIN and ALICE HOVEY HANKS.
     a. Sophia, b. Dec. 1776.
     b. Fanny, b. July 28, 1778.
     c. Horace, b. Nov. 1780.
     d. Truman, b. June 11, 1782.
     e. Julius, b. 1784.
     f. Charlotte, b. 1788.
  abfag. Horatio, b. Oct. 1790 (twin)*
     h. Marcia, b. Oct. 1790.

*See page 332.

CHAPTER VII

SOME UNPLACED HANKS FAMILIES

In Orange County, Virginia, Rodney Hanks obtained license
to marry Alice Chandler, March 26, 1803. The parents of Rodney
were Reuben and Elizabeth Hanks. Assuming that Rodney was about
twenty-five years of age then, his father would have been born in
the 1750's or earlier.

It is of interest that Thomas Wyatt, of Loudoun County,
Virginia, who died in 1772 and left a will, had a daughter, Elizabeth
Hanks, by a first wife. It is to be noted that his second wife, who
was Margaret Hanks, daughter of William the Quaker, named a son
Reuben Wyatt. The significance of these items has not been connected.

* * * *

The Ivy family, of which Andrew C. Ivy, Ph. D., M.D., of
Chicago, is a prominent member, trace their lineage from Susan Hanks,
born 1769, the daughter of William Hanks. He has not been identified.
Susan married Charles Tankersley, who was born 1765, the son of William
and Margaret (Nelson) Tankersley. The Tankersleys were in Charlotte
County, Virginia, and in Lincoln County, North Carolina.

* * * *

Sampson Hanks married Ellender Stockstill, September 23, 1793,
in Madison County, Kentucky.

* * * *

Joseph Hanks of Texas, born 1808, in South Carolina, was the
son of James Hanks, born 1770, in the same state. James was the son
of William Hanks.

* * * *

The foregoing names the only Hanks so far discovered who
lived before the birth of Nancy Hanks Lincoln, and who have not been
identified and placed for this purpose.

CHAPTER VIII

THE HANK FAMILY OF PENNSYLVANIA
Genealogy

Friends Rec.

a   JOHN HANK, of Ilkston, Derbyshire, England
d. 10 mo. 8, 1679
two sons:
aa   Luke, b. 6 mo. 14, 1673
ab   John, b. 5 mo. 21, 1676

aa   LUKE HANK of Sawley, Derbyshire, England
b. 6 mo. 14, 1673; d.
m. Hannah Brown 2 mo 8, 1702 , dau of
     Richard Brown. She died 11 mo 25,
     1708/9
son:
aaa   John

ab   JOHN HANK
b. 5 mo 21, 1676
Went to the Colony of Pa. by 1698
m. Sarah Evans, 10 mo. 11, 1711, dau. of
     Cadwallader Evans.
John on road commission 1716

Will, Dec 12,1730
Pro. May 3?, 1731

Seven Children:
aba   John, b. 9 mo 20, 1712
  b   Jane, b. 8 mo 12, 1714
  c   Elizabeth, 11 mo 28, 1716
  d   William   1719
  e   William, 9 mo, 12, 1720
  f   Samuel, 1 mo 15, 1723
  g   Joseph,   1725
  h   Sarah, 8 mo, 8, 1728

aaa   JOHN HANK, son of Luke
b.   d. 1772
Sojourn in England 1744 to 1753
m. Rebecca Brian, 7 mo 22, 1737
    She, dau. of Thomas Brian of Burling-
    ton, Co., N.J.
Children:
aaaa   Hannah, b. 1 mo 14, 1738/9
aaab   John, b.   1749

aba	**JOHN HANK**

Friends Rec.
Gwynedd

Hopewell
Meeting

aba   **JOHN HANK**
b. 9 mo 20, 1712; d. by 1781*
m. Margaret Williams, 2 mo 1737
   She b. 4 mo 25, 1721;
   to Augusta Co., Va. 1774;
   Created Rockingham Co., 1777
Children:
abaa   John, b. 1738
   b   Caleb, d. 1770
   c   Jane, d. 6 mo 9, 1745
   d   Joshua, d. 5 mo 31, 1758
   e   Susannah
   f   Elennor
   g   Williams, b. 1754
   h   Margaret, b. April 10, 1755
   i   Hannah, b. 1760.

abb   **JANE HANK**
b. 8 mo 12, 1714; d 1762
m. John Roberts, 3 mo 13, 1736
12 children: Job Roberts

abc   **ELIZABETH HANK**
b. 11 mo 28, 1716
m. John Evans

abd   **WILLIAM HANK**
b. 1719; d. in infancy

abe   **WILLIAM HANK**
b. 9 mo 12, 1720; d. 1796
taxed Berks Co., Pa., 1754.

abf   **SAMUEL HANK**
b 1 mo 15, 1723
disowned by Friends, 7 mo 28, 1752.
Went to New Jersey.
m. Sarah Going, Burlington Co., N.J.
   October 26, 1758.

abg   **JOSEPH HANK**
b. 1725
Resided in Berks Co., Pa.
Disowned by Friends, 26 da 9 mo, 1754.
taxed from 1754-1758-1780

abh   **SARAH HANK**
b. 8 mo 8, 1728, in Berks Co., Pa.
To Burlington, N.J. 3 mo 31, 1752.

*Therefore, Margaret Williams
Hank was a widow by 1784.
     A.B.

aaaa   HANNAH HANK
b. 1 mo 14, 1738/9 in Burlington County,
New Jersey.

aaab   JOHN HANK
b. 1749, son of John of Burlington, N.J.
in Burlington County, N.J.

abaa

JOHN HANK
b. 1738, son of John Hank of Gwynedd
Enlisted in Provincial Service of Pa.,
    May 21, 1759
Enlisted in 8th Va. Reg. Mar. 22, 1776;
Re-enlisted, 1779;
Captured at Charleston, S.C. 1780;
Fought at Trenton & Brandywine,
Ill at Valley Forge
Never married.
resided in Monroe Co., Va. (W.Va.)
Applied for Rev. War Pension 1818.

abab

CALEB HANK
m. but no children
d. 1770

abae

SUSANNAH HANK
b.   d.
m. Thomas Bryan
Disowned by Friends 2 mo 2, 1778

abaf

ELEANOR
disowned.

abag

Williams Hank
b. 1754 in Pa; d. Sept. 3, 1823.
m. Susannah Berry in Rockingham Co., Va.
    She died July 23, 1837
They moved to Greenbrier, which became
    Monroe County, Virginia.
Purchased 276 acres at foot Little Mt.1789
    "   80 "   "   "   "   " ".1797
Children: (No Nancy)
abaga David, b. Mar. 5,1788 in Rocking-
                ham Co., Va.
     b Caleb, b. Sept. 1, 1789, in Rock-
                ingham Co., Va.
     c Margaret, b. 1792, in Greenbrier
                County, Virginia
     d John, b. 1794, in Greenbrier Co,Va.
     e William, b. Aug 31, 1796 in Green-
                brier Co., Va.
     f Mary, b. 1798, in Greenbrier Co.Va.
     g Jehu, b. May 24, 1801, Monroe Co.Va

abah   MARGARET HANK
            b. April 10, 1755; d. Sept. 22, 1797 in
               Greenbrier Co., Va.
            m. William Cherrington

abai   HANNAH HANK
            b. 1760
            m. Asa Luphin, July 17, 1787
               He was born 3 mo 16, 1757.

It is obvious that no Nancy Hanks was born into this family in 1784.
            A.B.

PART IV

APPENDAGE

PART IV

CHAPTER I

HERNDON'S IDIOSYNCRACIES

If Herndon was not the instigator, he was the chief propagator of the theory that Nancy Hanks Lincoln was an illegitimate. However, he seemed to vacillate between belief and non-belief of the charge he himself had made, same as he, for years previously, argued the similar question as to Lincoln. What is the explanation of his insistence upon discussing this "tiresome question" as it has been called.[1]

Was he a sensationalist; or suffering from confusion and commingling gossip and forgetfulness; or did he fabricate to justify his theory that Lincoln's genesis was from a "Putrid Pool" of low Hankses?[2] When he unfolded to Hart about the buggy ride and repeated, "It is true"[3] did he feel a compulsion to narrate imagination, first registering an escape clause "As I understand the facts"; and is not this another case of "fabricated minuteness"?[4] If his knowledge was, as he often affirmed, factual, why did he spend any time soliloquizing on the misinformation he thought Dennis Hanks had given?[5]

That Herndon intended to be dramatic is amply indicated by the abrupt manner with which he expressed what he knew to be sensational, such as his announcement of the Ann Rutledge incident as a phase of an awful moment in the life of Lincoln; and his startling exposure of the alleged buggy ride tale to Hart and to Lamon. Then he qualified his statement to Lamon by admitting, "Human memory is uncertain and it is possible somewhat of my ideas are made up of rumor and rumor alone".[6] Thusly, did not Herndon confirm the unreliability of his own testimony?

---

[1] Donald, Lincoln's Herndon, p. 307.

[2] Herndon, Herndon's Lincoln, Preface.

[3] Herndon to Hart, Dec. 28, 1866, Herndon-Weik Coll.; also Hertz, The Hidden Lincoln, p. 51.

[4] Randall, Lincoln the President, p. 55.

[5] Herndon's Soliloquy, MSS; Hertz, The Hidden Lincoln, p. 410; Barton, The Paternity of Abraham Lincoln, p. 52.

[6] Herndon to Lamon, March 6, 1870, Herndon-Weik Coll.

Again he said to Lamon, "My opinions are formed from the
evidence... some of which I heard from Lincoln, others are references
springing from his acts, from which he said, and from what he didn't
say"[7](Italics mine). To another he wrote "I knew the man so well that
I think I could read his secrets and ambitions."[8] But then he admitted
to Lamon how it was done, "I know he scarcely trusted any man with his
more profound secrets, I had to read them in his facts, acts, hints,
face, as well as what he did not do or say.(Italics Herndon)[9]

What Lincoln did not say was no handicap to Herndon, for, as
he told Weik, "I am somehow or other quite intuitive",[10] and to Remsburg,
"You had to take some leading - great leading and well established fact
of Lincoln's nature and then follow it by accurate and close analysis
wherever it went. This process would lead you correctly, if you knew
human nature and its laws."[11] Is it possible that in this method
Herndon evolved what he thought was the truth of the buggy ride?

One instance: Herndon wrote to Weik and recommended he "put the
speech in Jeff Davis' mouth" and suggested, "Here are two good ideas
which you can elaborate...."[12]

On another occasion, he wrote, "You might put the following
words in Lincoln's mouth and they would be substantially true", then,
pretending to quote Lincoln, "What can I do, what can any man do...
No, I cannot even think against it!"[13] All this and more too, Herndon
put into Lincoln's mouth. Since he himself elected to put words into

---

[7]Herndon to Lamon, Feb. 25, 1870, Herndon-Weik Coll.

[8]Herndon to Keys, Apr. 14, 1866, Herndon-Weik Coll.

[9]Herndon to Lamon, Mar. 6, 1870, Herndon-Weik Coll.

[10]Herndon to Weik, Nov. 29, 1890, Herndon-Weik Coll.

[11]Herndon to Remsburg, Sept. 10, 1887, Herndon-Weik Coll.

[12]Herndon to Weik, Jan. 27, 1888, Herndon-Weik Coll.

[13]Herndon to Weik, Feb. 7, 1887, Herndon-Weik Coll.

Lincoln's mouth, how are we to know what part of the reported buggy ride converation is actually by Lincoln, and what part was "put in Lincoln's mouth"?

It is notable and may be significant that Herndon was constantly asserting and repeating that he was always telling the truth. Many have literally accepted this as sincerity, and passed it on in their writings as proof that what they were repeating after Herndon was true. This, in my opinion, needs qualification.[14]

Usually, when a man begins to remark and affirm as to his own honesty, he may be in a shadow land of doubt about his ability to remain honest, and is attempting to reassure his confidence in himself. It does not seem to occur to a strictly honest man to refer to the subject of honest in himself at all. This observation is not so much to impugn Herndon, but to question his faith in his own assertions, as he questioned them himself in his soliloquy.[15]

In this, dated 1887, he observed in the first line, "Dennis Hanks and all the other Hankses, their cousins and relatives, call Nancy Hanks, Nancy Sparrow. Lucy Hanks was her mother." This is, Lucy Hanks Sparrow, was the mother of Nancy Sparrow, who was thought to be Nancy Hanks Lincoln. In his next line, he says, "Nancy Hanks was taken and raised by Thomas and Betsey Sparrow". Then he goes on to say Lincoln told him, "My mother's name is Nancy Hanks." Herndon's query was "will some gentleman or lady kindly help me?" Of course, he was confused - we now know he was dealing with more than one Nancy. With such a defective and erroneous premise, he may be forgiven for his incorrect deductions; but why does he apologize at the end by saying, "However the record tells its own story, and speaks for itself; and had not the record spoken out, it is more than probable that I should have kept the secret forever, though I was not forbidden to reveal the fact after Lincoln's death."[16]

It is to be observed and remarked that Herndon has dated this self-examination 1887, which was twenty years after he began to collect information about Nancy Hanks Lincoln and her mother. Is it not odd he had not made up his mind in such a long time?[17] Here he refers to a record, as also he does in a letter to Bartlett. To what record he subsumes is not clear. If, by record he meant reputation, he was speaking of a woman dead and gone for fifty years, who had been such

[14] Warren, Sifting the Herndon Sources.

[15] Herndon, Herndon's Soliloquy: Hertz, The Hidden Lincoln, p.410.

[16] Ibid.

[17] Ibid.

a nonetity that no one would have remembered her more than casually.
If any record of her existed at the time of the buggy ride, an admonition
to silence would have been futile, as Lincoln would have known. There
is no record. The only reputation she had was improvised by Herndon,
and from hearsay in Illinois and reminiscences in Indiana. Also, the
assumption that Herndon would outlive Lincoln and be able to communicate
such alleged secrets, probably arose from the fact it had happened.
The record is of Herndon, and not of Nancy, and has a connotation of
mild guilt.

On the theory that the faults of our own are most easily,
even agreeably, recognized in others, attention is called to Herndon's
adverse criticism of Dennis Hanks, "Dennis, sly, shrewd Dennis."[18]

When Herndon galloped posthaste to inform Bartlett on the
subject,[19] he omitted to recur to the buggy ride, as he had twenty
years previously, and used what he termed "the record of the woman
bears out her son's statement", as if Lincoln's statement, if he made
such, needed confirmation. Only five days later Herndon admitted to
Bartlett that "There appear to have been two Nancy Hankses - one the
mother of Abraham and the other the mother of Dennis Hanks....now at
this late date...can there not be a mistake in the identity of persons?"
Was Herndon haunted by the ghost of scandal he had conjured?

Another example of aberration on Herdon's part was his inclination to dissimulation by omitting to quote others in full - a case in
point is a letter to Lamon in which he quoted only part of a specific
statement Lincoln had written to Samuel Haycraft, "You are mistaken
about my mother...", and left off the very explanatory ending, "Her
maiden name was Nancy Hanks."[20]

By evasion, Herndon was remiss in presenting to the public
that was expected to read his book much about the Hanks family that
Lincoln had seen fit to include in his autobiographical notes. As he
explained to Hart, "Have faith in the only man who knows what to do to

[18] Herndon, Herndon's Soliloquy; Hertz, The Hidden Lincoln, p. 110.

[19] Herndon to Bartlett, Sept. 25, 1877, Herndon-Weik Coll.

[20] Lincoln to Haycraft, May 28, 1860, Haycraft Coll.

hedge, dodge, explain, modify, or deny, etc."[21] So succinctly does not Herndon ascribe his own attributes?

It has been conjectured by some students of Lincoln that Herndon was disappointed in that he had not received a job in the Lincoln administration; and that may have been the symptom of a displeasure that was deeper.

That Herndon was a vindictive man, there is not a doubt – it is indicated by the way he treated Mary Lincoln, even after she wrote to him a kindly letter.

The wedding of Abraham Lincoln and Mary Todd is one of the great personal interest items of Lincoln's life for most readers. Here Herndon surely spread himself to build up a sensational story of deserted bride bereaved by an absconded bridegroom, all of which is not supported by any evidence in fact. There seems to have been a troubled courtship and a postponed wedding, but those who pursue the subject, learn that Herndon's report of the affair is dismayingly distorted, and there is no reliance as to its being historically correct.[22]

Adding to this characterization of Herndon, that of an apparent lack of consideration for the feelings of others, his low regard for everyone by the name of Hanks, and his castigation of all Hanks women, including Mary Todd, it is doubtful if he gave sympathetic consideration to the subject of Lincoln's maternal ancestry, but wrote with a whoop to emphasize an opaque origin of Lincoln.

Perhaps it is that Herndon had had his feelings hurt for the reason he had been unable to impress Lincoln and convince him of the supposed fact of his own great intellectual capacity. Perhaps Lincoln's last words to Herndon, which may have been intended estoppal to an application for a high office, still rankled, "Billy, how many times you been drunk?"

He sums it up very well in a letter he wrote to Weik (Aug. 16, 1887, Hertz, p. 199)[23]he said,"In a late letter to you, the one enclosed..., I made a fool of myself."

[21]Herndon to Hart, Dec. 28, 1866, Herndon-Weik Coll.

[22]Randall, Lincoln the President, pp. 57-61.

[23]Herndon to Weik, Aug. 16, 1887, Herndon-Weik Coll.

CHAPTER II

JOHN LOCKE SCRIPPS

It would seem, from a study of available evidence, that Herndon and his followers have placed undue emphasis on the reticence of Lincoln to tell his Hanks family history. In his book, Herndon made a special reference to what he specified "a great reluctance and a significant reserve".[1]

In the following paragraph, Herndon leads his reader up to learn what he asserts was told by Lincoln on the only "one time when Mr. Lincoln ever referred to it."[2]

Associates of Lincoln have left reminiscenses in which are references to his family and his mother,[3] which indicate that conversation with him was had on the subject. In the few autobiographies, both the paternal and maternal sides of his ancestry are brought out, and his mother is mentioned and named, but neither grandmother. It is thought he surely must have seen and known his grandmother, Bathsheba, yet she is not mentioned among the Lincoln relatives.[4]

In several instances, as reported, he remarked upon the intellectual capacity of his mother, and he stressed that point when interviewed by John Locke Scripps, the newspaper man, for the purpose of composing a campaign biography.[5] Scripps later incorporated into the biography all that was sufficient for political expediency. He was writing about Lincoln, and not Lincoln's families. Shortly after the death of Lincoln, Herndon began a correspondence with Mr. Scripps, and the first letter he received was a rather conventional reply dealing with the character of Lincoln.[6] In a second letter, Herndon was

---

[1] Herndon and Weik, Herndon's Lincoln, p. 1

[2] Herndon and Weik, Herndon's Lincoln, p. 3

[3] Confer Chapter I.

[4] McMurtry,

[5] Scripps, Life of Abraham Lincoln, Chicago Press & Tribune Co., 1860.

[6] Scripps to Herndon, May 9, 1865, See Publication of the Illinois Historical Society, No. 31, p. 107.

told that, "The statements therein contained (in the Campaign Life) as respects to facts and antecedents of the early life of Lincoln are substantially as communicated by him to me."[7]

Herndon was persistent, and received a third and longer letter from Mr. Scripps, which was duly and carefully filed away. Twenty years later it went to Weik, who inserted a part of it in the book Herndon's Lincoln, in order to confirm their intimation of Lincoln's "great reluctance and significant reserve" to talk about his mother's family.

They quoted, "Lincoln seemed to be painfully impressed," he wrote, "with the extreme poverty of his early surroundings, and the utter absence of all romantic and heroic elements. He communicated some facts to me concerning his ancestry, which he did not wish to have published then (italics mine) which I have never spoken of or alluded to before (italics mine)."[8] The use of the word "before" in ending the sentence, Scripps, an expert in the semantic use of words, would seem to merely indicate a lack of occasion to reveal the subject which he is now discussing with Herndon, rather than to have held inviolate some great and scandalous secret.

In the phase "published then", the "then" as quoted, does not appear in the original letter, and is an interpolation. It may have been used inadvertently, but its connotation does seem to imply a suspicion of design that Herndon is now revealing to the world in a following paragraph of his book[9] what was hidden by the "significant reserve" that might have been fatal to the success of the campaign.

That Scripps, with reportorial ability, did not permit much to be reserved, was communicated to Herndon, as follows:

> "Yours of yesterday at hand and its tenor induces me to reply more specificcally to your previous note of enquiry respecting my little campaign life of Lincoln. I believe I try to satisfy my conscience in whatever I do; and I assure you, I never performed a work more con- scientiously in my life than the production of that biographical sketch."

---

[7] Scripps to Herndon, May 9, 1865, See Publication of the Illinois State Historical Society, No. 31, p. 107.

[8] Herndon & Weik, Herndon's Lincoln, p. 2.

[9] Herndon & Weik, Herndon's Lincoln, p. 3.

Here is an assurance that Scripps gathered correct information from Lincoln, and now follows testimony that it was wholly and freely given:[10]

"I am also very sure that Mr. Lincoln was equally sincere and conscientious in furnishing me with the facts connected with his own and his family's history."

Confirming this, Scripps had written in the campaign biography:

"In the autumn of 1818, Abraham, in the loss of his mother, experienced the first great sorrow of his life. Facts in the possession of the writer.(Italics those of another)[11] have impressed him with the belief that, although of but limited education she was a woman of great native strength of intellect and force of character."

Scripps continued further, but this is sufficient to show that Lincoln did tell Scripps about his Hanks family, Mr. Scripps did inform Herndon, and Herndon did ignore much of the substance of Scripps' letters to him.

There is no loss of what idea Mr. Lincoln "did not wish published". From Scripps' third letter[12] it would seem that Mr. Lincoln did not wish to invite the sympathy of the public for his early poverty and the abject misery of losing his mother. We are not left in doubt about this, for Mr. Joseph Medill reported to Scripps' daughter years later.

"I remember the pamphlet, The Campaign Biography, very well... your father was not satisfied with the pamphlet because Mr. Lincoln insisted on pruning out of it many of the most readable and interesting passages in regard to Lincoln's early life and other matters."[13]

Was not Herndon guilty of dissimulation by omission of words and ignoring portions of the letters and quoting part of one only? To indicate guilt, there must be intent - was there not intent on the part of Herndon to belittle the Hanks family?

---

[10] Scripps to Herndon, June 24, 1865, Herndon-Weik Coll., Group IV #198.

[11] Gilchrist, Joy Foundation MSS, Thomas Starr, Detroit.

[12] Scripps to Herndon, June 24, 1865, Herndon-Weik Coll., Group IV,#198.

[13] Medill to Dyche, Feb. 13, 1895, See Publication of the Illinois State Historical Society, No. 31, p. 107.

CHAPTER III

DENNIS FRIEND HANKS

The qualification of Dennis Hanks to speak with the authority of an expert genealogist on the maternal ancestry of Abraham Lincoln has been questioned: Herndon himself expressed no confidence in him;[1] Lamon ridiculed his statements;[2] Lea and Hutchison dismissed him as "irresponsible and unreliable";[3] Warren devotes a pamphlet on a critical consideration and analysis of his source materials;[4] but many have accepted all he said as true and correct; Barton thought he "was rather a competent genealogist in his way";[5] and Beveridge explained he could sort out the truth - how, he does not say.[6]

These diverse criticisms are based upon about the same material, with the exception that Herndon and Weik had personal interviews with Dennis. In fact, the information from them is written in Herndon's own script, with his characteristic staccato style, and signed by Dennis.[7]

The first talk occurred at the Sanitary Fair in Chicago in June and Herndon began to collect Hanks family data. He already had conflicting testimony: he had from John Miles that the mother of Lincoln was Nancy Sparrow;[8] and he had from William Greene that the mother of Lincoln was Lucy Hanks.[9]

---

[1] Herndon to Lamon, February 24, 1869.

[2] Lamon, Life of Abraham Lincoln

[3] Lea and Hutchison, Ancestry of Abraham Lincoln, p. 108.

[4] Warren, Lincoln Kinsman, No. 45.

[5] Barton, Lineage of Lincoln, p. 215, 222.

[6] Beveridge, Lincoln.

[7] Interview, Hidden Lincoln, p.

[8] Miles to Herndon, May 25, 1865, Herndon-Weik Coll.

[9] Green to Herndon, May 29, 1865, Herndon-Weik Coll.

It makes one wonder if Herndon did not try to reconcile this initial descrepancy by suggestive interrogatories. However it was, Dennis promptly concurred that Nancy Sparrow was the mother, and named Lucy Hanks as the grandmother, and who "was my own aunt".

By the time of the interview the following week, he was committed to the name, Nancy Sparrow, which was contrary to the biographies of the day. Further, he named Henry Sparrow as the husband of Lucy Hanks and the father of Nancy. He affected to give some information about the Lincoln family history, much of which was erroneous, but could have been used as clues for further research. So could have been used the little he knew about the Hanks ancestry.

The following fall Dennis was again interviewed by Herndon who went to Charleston, Illinois, the home town of Dennis. There, by Mr. O. B. Ficklin, he was "told to be careful about what Hanks said". So, having been put on his guard, he "closely and critically examined Hanks and he confessed he knew nothing - except as abm (sic) stated."[10]

If all that Dennis knew about Lincoln's Hanks family history was only what "Abraham had stated" and if no more was told to Dennis than the reporters for the Campaign biography writers have said was stated to them by Mr. Lincoln, then, indeed, Dennis did not have much information.

Notwithstanding, Herndon's professed lack of confidence in Dennis' veracity, they carried on an extended correspondence until, according to Weik, at least fifty pages of information had been provided by Dennis.[11]

About twenty-five years ago, the writer discussed the character of Dennis Hanks with elderly people and his connection with the Charleston, Illinois affray of Civil War Days. Among those interviewed were, the lates, Mr. Ike Miles of Charleston, Mr. William Slemmons of Paris, and the two Shoaf brothers, grandsons of Dennis, and at Paris.

Previously, Dr. Barton was overheard discussing various subjects with the late Mrs. Lucy Lamon, of Paris, including the character and reliability of Dennis, and there was nothing so untoward as to be recollected.

---

[10]Herndon Interviews Dennis, Charleston, Illinois, Sept. 8, 1865, Herndon-Weik Coll.

[11]
Warren, Lincoln Kinsman, No. 45, p. 1

Judge Walter Lamon, the son of Mrs. Lucy, above, as a young man knew Dennis and would, in passing by, see him sitting on the Shoaf front porch reading. He stated "Dennis had a good mind, was quite a reader, minded his own business and would carry on a conversation with any passer-by."[12]

My father, Dexter Baber, when a boy and young man, knew Dennis in a casual way, that is, as well as young people may know older people. He has told me that Dennis would come into the butcher shop of Berry Hanks but he doesn't recollect that Dennis ever purchased meat. He states, "Dennis was courteous, quiet and well dressed, wore black clothes and a 'billy-cock' hat. He would start home and did not stop on the street to talk like Willis Hanks, who would 'hold out' on the east side of the square."

It is a concensus of agreement that Dennis had a good mind and memory and could have repeated verbatim what he may have heard about the Hanks family, and that he was honest enough to tell what he knew of his own family and parentage.

Certainly, as Barton has said, in his discussion about Dennis and his family, "is that he should have known his own mother", and Dennis said that his own mother was Nancy Hanks, wife of Levi Hall, and he recognized the Hall boys as half-brothers. He named Charles Friend to be his father, and wrote, "This don't doubt."[13] He did not know his own grandfather on his mother's side. He asserted that Lucy Sparrow was his aunt, and Abe Lincoln's grandmother, and insisted that she was a sister of his mother, Nancy, and her two sisters, Polly Friend and Elizabeth Sparrow.[14]

However, to justify Dennis' conclusions - Lucy was his aunt, and in this relationship, Dennis was the natural nephew of his aunt, Elizabeth Sparrow; and also by informal adoption, the foster son of his aunt Elizabeth, and Thomas Sparrow, her husband. Thomas moved his family back to Mercer County for a period of three years, and into the neighborhood of Henry Sparrow, his wife, Lucy, and their children. Henry and Thomas being brothers, and their wives, Lucy and Elizabeth, sisters-in-law respectively, all the Henry Sparrow children would have called Thomas and Elizabeth "Uncle" and "Aunt", which was correct. No doubt, in my mind, this three to six year old boy, Dennis, called Henry Sparrow and wife "Uncle Hendry" and "Aunt Lucy". To sum up: they were his foster uncle and aunt.

---

[12] Lamon to Baber, March 23, 1951, Baber papers.

[13] Hanks to Friend, March 25, 1866.

[14] Hanks-Herndon correspondence, Herndon-Weik Coll.

The point of issue is that Dennis never would admit that the maiden name of Nancy Lincoln was other than Nancy Sparrow, and this contradiction with what Lincoln had said that his mother's maiden name was Hanks, has occasioned several explanations, all conjectural - one is that Dennis plainly lied from hesitation to admit ignorance of the case;[15] another, that he lied to cover family irregularities;[16] and which has been repeated more suavely, "he waded knee deep in falsehood as a gentleman to save his cousin from opprobrium."[17] Another theory is that Dennis, being a bastard himself, with some odd quirk, perversely prevaricated.[18]

It is doubtful that Dennis lied, or lied intentionally to cover up and be a gentleman, or lied to be malicious and spiteful. In the first place, the general reputation of Hankses is, and was, that of honesty. Being rather easy-going, casual, and unimaginative, they are apt to accept the true status from a lack of inclination to bother about bolstering up a better tale. Perhaps Dennis was like that.

Now as to the lying in order to save the good name of a lady? Certainly, any gentleman would do so, and Dennis was a gentleman - perhaps unpolished, but innately courtly, but there was no incentive to lie to save anyone. Neither he nor John Hanks admitted irregularities, or that Nancy Lincoln was base born. Herndon originated that one with his buggy ride. That Dennis perversely lied maliciously is refuted by his reputation for kindness. As an example - my father,[19] a matter-of-fact man, has told that when he was a boy, and Dennis was gatekeeper at the local county fair, (a job he had annually) a group of boys, knowing Dennis, would go early to the fair and congregate at his gate. At an opportune time, he would exclaim to them, "What! Get out of my way, get in here." and shove them into the fair grounds.

A few years ago, one of my daughters, working for the press, had an interview with an old lady who had not missed the annual county fair in 75 years. She told how her father would take the family and

15 Lamon, *Life of Lincoln*.
16 Herndon to Weik, April 14, 1885, Herndon's Soliloquy.
17 Barton, *Lineage of Lincoln*, p. 215.
18 Waldo Lincoln, *History of the Lincoln Family*, p. 338.
19 Dexter D. Baber, born 1867.
20 Paris, Illinois.

a wagon load of children. The admission fees for all would have totaled a tidy sum. The "old man at the gate" would say, "Oh my, I can't count so many - drive in." That old man was Dennis.

Did such a kind-hearted man lie to injure a woman, dead and gone? The ones who thought of that one had better be psycho-analyzed themselves! Dennis had written of Nancy Lincoln, "...if you call hir Hanks you make hir a Baseborn child, which is not trew."[21] An author, who charges lying, says this last phrase shows motive. What it shows is that Dennis was trying to point out to Herndon the latter's lack of logic. Finally Dennis grew impatient of the gamon and asked some questions in turn, rather pertinently, "Billy, it seems to me... that you ask the same questions over several times how is this Do you forget or are you like the Lawyer trying to make me cross my path or not."[22]

Dennis seems never to have gotten his exact relationship to Abraham Lincoln clear in his own mind. For instance - Polly Hanks and Elizabeth Hanks were sisters, as Dennis had asserted, but in a single paragraph in a letter, he said, "..Polly Hanks Abe's mothers ant," and, "Elizabeth Hanks A Lincoln's ant." As these two women were sisters, it is obvious that these sentences are not consistent, but perhaps these statements were made inadvertently.[23]

Sometimes Dennis thought that he was a first cousin to Abe's mother, (Nancy) as indicated when he wrote, "My mother and Abes mothers mother was sisters."[24] Other times he thought he was a first cousin to Abe, as he wrote in a "Biographical Sketch for an old friend," "I Dennis F. Hanks and A Lincoln ar cousins..."[25]

Of course, some degree of cousin-ship was a fact.

Dennis did not know just where he had been born, but that can be overlooked. In an autobiography, he stated that he was born in an old peach orchard near the South Fork of Nolin.[26] Again he said he was born in Elizabethtown.[27]

---

[21] Hanks to Herndon, Feb. 10, 1866, Herndon-Weik Coll.

[22] Hanks to Herndon, Mar. 7, 1866, Herndon-Weik Coll.

[23] Hanks to Herndon, Mar. 7, 1866, Herndon-Weik Coll.

[24] Hanks to Herndon, April 2, 1866, Herndon-Weik Coll.

[25] Dennis Hanks, Autobiography, Paris, Illinois, 1877.

[26] Hanks to Herndon, April 2, 1866, Herndon-Weik Coll.

[27] Hanks, Interview by Weik, March 26, 1885, Paris, Illinois.

He did not know his grandfather on his mother's side.

Dennis died October 21, 1892,[28] and is buried in the old cemetery at Charleston, Illinois.

What Dennis knew of his own observation and personal knowledge and immediate family is of high value to students of Lincoln, and what he has told of such can be depended upon. The traditional information he gave is equal to, and not superior to, other traditions from other sources, and may be accepted as clues to be checked, and used or rejected.

----

[28] Tombstone inscription.

CHAPTER IV

LUCEY HANKS SPARROW

The **first** instance of the use of the name Lucy, in connection with the family of Lincoln I have been able to locate, was in the Howell Campaign biography, where it was given as the name of Lincoln's own mother. In a copy of that book, which Lincoln read and corrected for Samuel C. Parks, he crossed out the word 'Lucy', and on the margin of the page, wrote 'Nancy' as his mother's first name, but there was no further notation. There is no evidence whatso-- ever that Lincoln ever wrote or used the name of Lucy as that of his mother's mother, particularly to the early biographers. Herndon asserted later in correspondence with Hart and Lamon that he had first heard the name on the famous infamous buggy ride in 1851; but it has been doubted by contemporary associates of Lincoln that he vouchsafed such to Herndon.

There is no certainty, no proof, nor even evidence, beyond tradition of only one source, that the first name of Nancy Lincoln's mother was Lucy, though it verily was a fair assumption, Lucy being a common name in the Hanks family, usually from Lucinda, sometimes Lucretia. There were several Lucy Hanks either born or married into the early Hanks families of Virginia and Kentucky.

There was Lucy Mitchell, who married a George Hanks;[1] Lewsee, daughter of Joshua Hawks or Hanks, and probably named for an aunt Lucy, wife of an early Abraham Hawks or Hanks;[2] Lucy, daughter of Mott Hanks;[3] some Lucy Hanks slaves, one named in the will of Alse Dale;[4] Lucy Jennings who married Abraham Hanks, the Revolutionary soldier,[5]

---

[1] Marriage record, Courthouse, Woodford County, Kentucky.

[2] Will Book 2, p. 151, Courthouse, Amelia County, Virginia.

[3] Hanks Family records.

[4] Probate Records, Dec. Court 1802, Courthouse, Woodford Co., Ky.

[5] Marriage Record, p. 71, Courthouse, Campbell Co., Virginia.

Lucy or Lucretia Hargrave, who married Thomas Hanks in North
Carolina, and a Lucey Hanks, who married Henry Sparrow.[6] Warren
has demonstrated that this latter Lucey was the one that Dennis
Hanks had in mind when he discussed the subject of the mother of
Nancy Sparrow in his correspondence with Herndon.[7]

The courthouse records do indicate that there was a Lucey
Hanks in Mercer County, Kentucky, and that she married Henry Sparrow.
To them were born eight children, as named by a granddaughter, Amanda
Pilcher,[8] and the correctness of the list is confirmed by courthouse
records of their marriages. She does not name a Nancy, nor mention
a half-sister of her uncles and aunts, as has been the accepted implication.

Dennis named only three daughters in his list to Herndon,[9]
and two of his names, Nancy and Sally, are not in the Pilcher list.

In his letter to Sophie Hanks LeGrand,[10] he named four
daughters, including Nancy and Sally, and left off the names Margaret
(Peggy) and Polly. Of course, if Lucey had had two daughters prior
to her marriage to Sparrow, their surnames would have been Hanks; and
their given names could have been Nancy and Polly.

Since Howell used the name Lucy in his write-up, it was no
doubt furnished to him by Howard, his reporter he had sent to Springfield to interview Lincoln and gather information. Howard was the
only reporter who ventured from Springfield to New Salem for additional
news about Lincoln.[11]

He may have gotten the name Lucy as Lincoln's mother from some
of the associates of Lincoln who had come from Kentucky, but it is
more probable that he had it from one William G. Greene, who had known
Lincoln at New Salem, 1830, and was commonly known locally as 'Slippery
Bill' Greene. Certainly, it was Green who first offered the name Lucy
Hanks, in the same way, as the mother of Lincoln, to Herndon in a
letter wherein he said, "Yours of the 20 inst...Mr. Lincoln's mothers
maiden name was Lucy Hanks she was native of State of Virginia I have

[6] Marriage record, p. 16, Courthouse, Mercer County, Kentucky

[7] Dennis Hanks, Herndon Letters of 1866, Herndon-Weik Coll.

[8] Amanda Pilcher to Barton, Aug. 6, 1922.

[9] Hanks to Herndon, Feb. 28, 1866.

[10] Hanks to LeGrand, Feb. 5, 1887.

[11] Howell, Life of Lincoln, p. 18.

understood she was rather above the average size for women but
know nothing further of her..."12

    The same week Herndon heard from Green, in answer to another
letter of inquiry from Herndon, he received a letter from one John
Miles, who Herndon had, "desired him to go down and see Jno. Hanks."
Miles did so, and his reply stated that Nancy Sparrow was the mother
of Lincoln, and "that her mother's maiden name was Lucy Hank, and was
born in Virginia."13 This rather meagre and conflicting information
from the two men was received by Herndon just a few days before he
interviewed Dennis and John Hanks at the Sanitary Fair in Chicago,
June 1865.

    The reports of these interviews are written down in Herndon's
handwriting, and the phraseology is in his own staccato style, and not
in the usual and unique diction found in the bona fide letters of Dennis
Hanks, nor in the common parlance of the reported remarks of rough
old John Hanks. The question is, how much editing did Herndon do? Is
it possible that he inadvertantly suggested the word-name 'Lucy', and
Dennis, having known and lived near Lucey Hanks Sparrow for three years
in his early boyhood, being Dennis-like, was reluctant to admit ignorance,
and accepted the name?

    Lucey Hanks had married the brother, Henry, of Dennis' foster
father, Thomas, whose wife, Elizabeth, was Dennis' true aunt, and
thusly was created a relationship that Dennis later mistakenly inferred
made Lucey a sister to his mother and her two sisters.

    In a series of letters to Herndon, Dennis insisted that there
were four Hanks sisters, including Lucy. However, the will of Joseph
Hanks, which names five sons, and does specifically name three daughters,
including a Nancy, the mother of Dennis, does not name a daughter, Lucy,
nor heirs of a deceased son. Dennis did not know the name of his grandfather, Joseph.14 Fish, the distinguished attorney and student of
Lincolniana, taking cognizance of the omission of the name Lucy from
the will, discounted the suggestion she was a daughter, and wrote a

---

12Green to Herndon, May 28, 1865, Herndon-Weik Coll.

13Miles to Herndon, May 25, 1865, Herndon-Weik Coll.

14Hanks to Herndon, Feb. 25, 1866, Herndon-Weik Coll.

long letter to Barton, (Barton followed Dennis and with fatuous reasoning,) to dissuade him from using the name as a daughter, but failed. [15]

Whatever the source of the name Lucy, Herndon had accepted it, and passed in on to Charles Friend of Kentucky.[16] Several years later it came back, like a boomerang, in a letter from Friend to Dennis.[17] Dennis, in turn, sent the Friend letter on to Robert Lincoln.

Robert showed the letter to Jno. G. Nicolay, who, with Hay, was preparing to write a history of Robert's father. They in turn corresponded with Friend,[18] and accepted the name of Lucy as information that came from Kentucky, when in fact it had originated as almost a conjecture in Illinois! They incorporated it as the name of the mother of Nancy, but had some difficulty in fitting a Lucy into the Hanks family group she was supposed to be in. They did so by composing an ambiguous paragraph wherein was committed literary bigamy by lumping four Hanks women with miscellaneous husbands![19]

The works of Nicolay and Hay were widely read, and the name Lucy passed into general acceptance as the name of one of Lincoln's grandmothers. Ironically, years later, Charles Friend was to state, and under oath, "Neither have I heard the name of Lucy Hanks mentioned by the old people whom some say was the sister of Elizabeth, Polly or Mary, and Nancy Hanks, and the mother of another Nancy Hanks who married Thomas Lincoln."[20]

Another source that has been quoted as an authority for the use of the name Lucy, is the Rev. Mr. Murr of southern Indiana, who knew personally some of the people who knew the Lincolns there. But when it comes to examining his evidence, it is that he had it rather surreptitiously from an elderly lady who had it from her mother and her grandmother back in Kentucky, and no one ever said anything to the contrary. This sort of information is rank hearsay, and as such, is not acceptable.[21]

---

[15] Fish to Barton, Library, Chicago University.

[16] Herndon to Friend, Feb. 15, 1866, L-K No. 46.

[17] Friend to Hanks, June 26, 1873, L-K No. 46.

[18] Nicolay to Friend, July 26, 1873, L-K No. 46.

[19] Abraham Lincoln a History.

[20] Affidavit, Charles Friend, Nov. 26, 1921, Warren Papers, Ft. Wayne, Indiana.

[21] Murr, Indiana Magazine of History, Dec. 1917, p. 333.

It may be of significance that Squire Robert Mitchell
Thompson, who stated that his mother, Sarah, was a first cousin
of the mother of Nancy Hanks, never mentioned the name Lucy in
any interview previous to his last one just before his death, 1895.

A niece of Squire Robert, and a granddaughter of his mother,
Sarah, born Charlotte Hobert, who first gave much information leading
to locating records of the marriage of Nancy Hanks to Thomas Lincoln,
and a descendant of the Shipley family, did not use the name Lucy.

One of the Macon County, Illinois, Hanks men, whom Lincoln
recognized as kindred of his mother, Andrew Jackson Hanks, a descendant
of Joseph of Nelson, through his son, William, wrote,[22] "I have no
reason to think that Lucinda was the name of Nancy Hanks' mother but
in ancering (sic) the question you asked: from the statement that
Uncle Johnny made you...I think the parties that done Uncle John's
writing made the mistake and did not make it mean as he understood it
to."

The declination to accept Lucey Hanks, single or married to
Henry Sparrow, as the mother of Nancy Hanks Lincoln, is to fly into a
veritable literary shower of the tradition that she was; it is even
contrary to the conclusions of some rather eminant authors. There is
no proof that Lucey was not the mother of a daughter, Nancy; but there
is not a scintilla of evidence that her Nancy became the mother of
Abraham Lincoln, save the testimony of one man, Dennis Hanks; which is
offset by a preponderance of presumptive evidence of others, who were
in equal standing to have known whereof they spoke.[23]

---

[22]
Hanks to Hitchcock, October 7, 1894, Lincoln Foundation,
Fort Wayne, Indiana.

[23]See next page.

CHAPTER IV

NANCY SPARROW

Nancy Sparrow was the name agreed to by Dennis and John Hanks
as the maiden name of Lincoln's mother, and asserted as such to
Herndon; but Lincoln,himself, had told his early campaign biographers
that his mother was Nancy Hanks. Herndon, faced with these conflicting
statements, naturally accepted what Lincoln had said, and declared
that Dennis lied, and that John, the honest one, just did not know.[1]
Several explanations have been attempted and offered for this confusion,
and all conjectural. The most likely excuse is that the two Hanks men
were mistaken. Both were boys under school age when Nancy married,
and lived many miles from her. There were at least three women in
Kentucky who have been called "Nancy Sparrow," and at various times;
the Nancy who married Tom Lincoln, the Nancy who married Levi Hall,
and the Nancy who married Richard Elliott.

Nicolay and Hay thought that they were referring to the Nancy
who married Tom Lincoln when they wrote, "The childhood of Nancy
was passed with the Sparrows and she was oftener called by their name
than her own."[2] But Mrs. Hitchcock learned that that Nancy had resided
in the Berry home in Washington County, that another Nancy had resided
in the Sparrow home, and of the latter she wrote, that Charles Friend
married Nancy Sparrow, and had a son named Dennis, who has been often
mentioned as one of the Hanks family.[3]

Then Lea and Hutchison repeated, "Charles and Nancy (Sparrow)
Fried (sic) were the parents of the irrespressible and unreliable
Dennis Friend, one of the President's youthful associates, who
assuming the name of Dennis Hanks, did much to complicate the already
difficult problems of the Hanks genealogy, which the mendacity of his
declining years still further confused."[4]

---

[1] Herndon to Lamon, Feb. 24, 1869.

[2] Nicholay & Hay, Lincoln, A History, Vol. I, p. 24, 84.

[3] Hitchcock, Nancy Hanks, p. 50.

[4] Lea & Hutchison, Ancestry of Lincoln, p. 108.

But Dennis had resolved the matter, so far as his birth was concerned. He explained to Herndon that his own mother was a Nancy Hanks, who had married Levi Hall, and mentioned the Hall boys as his half-brothers. He wrote to a nephew, Charles Friend, Jr., that his mother, Nancy, had told him his father was Charles Friend, "This don't doubt."[5]

As Dennis' mother lived with the Thomas Sparrows, after her father's death, and when Dennis was born, the child may have been called by the names of Sparrow or Friend, but in conformity with the custom that a child takes the surname of its unmarried mother, it was quite right and proper that Dennis had the name Dennis Friend Hanks. So we learn that Dennis' mother was one of the evanescent Nancy Sparrows of Kentucky.

There is a legend that the Nancy Hanks, who was the mother of Lincoln, also lived for a time with the Thomas Sparrows. This would seem to have been entirely plausible. Lincoln has said that his mother was kin to the Hankses of Illinois, and Thomas Sparrow's wife, Elizabeth, the daughter of Joseph Hanks, certainly was of close kin. Nancy Hanks Lincoln, having been an orphan, quite likely resided with the Joseph Hanks family for a time, then the Sparrows, and was "oftener called Sparrow than Hanks". It could have been that Dennis really thought her name was Sparrow, and that she was a daughter of his own Aunt Lucy Sparrow.

A third Nancy Sparrow is of record in the Nelson County courthouse. She married Richard Elliott, May 27, 1800, and the bond is joined by Benjamin Elliott,[6] and the return is signed by W. W. Hays, the same minister who married some of the Hankses. On the original paper is the word 'widow'. No parent or guardian or kinsman named Sparrow gave consent, which probably was not necessary since she was a widow. Whether she was a grass or sod, common law or legal widow, is not known.

In a rather ambiguous paragraph, Barton infers some connection of this Nancy Sparrow, widow, to a Nancy Elliock, who married James Bolin at an earlier date in Mercer County - then he conjectures that this Nancy Sparrow may have been the widow of a James Sparrow, deceased.[7] There is nothing found in the records to confirm such conjecture.

_____

[5] Hanks to Friend, March 26, 1866.

[6] Marriage record, Courthouse (attic) Nelson County, Kentucky, Bond Box E. (The Elliott family probably were from Richmond County, Va. In 1737, John Hanks, Richard Elliott and John Dodson, were cited for not attending church.)

[7] Barton, Lineage of Lincoln, p.

That she was of some interest in and to the Hanks family is indicated by Dennis Hanks in a letter to Charles Friend, wherein he asks, "How many of the Elliotts is a living?"[8] A mild surmise could be that if Lucy Hanks Sparrow had a daughter Nancy, as Dennis thought, this Nancy Sparrow, widow, was first Nancy Hanks, took the name of Sparrow, and later married Elliott. The implications of the widowhood shall not be dwelled upon for the reason that such inquiry is out of this line. Nancy Sparrow of Kentucky, singular and plural, can be eliminated as a possible mother of Lincoln.

---

[8] Hanks to Friend, March 26, 1866.

See Sparrow connections, in Appendix.

INDEX

Hanks, George (aaabdc), 285, 298
" , George McDuffie (aaabc ci), 297
" , George S., (aabie h), 330
" , Grace (aachb o), 311
" , Greenberry (aabii b), 179,331
" , Green S., (aaaad i), 282, 292
" , Hampton H. (aaabc ck) 297
" , Hannah (Hester ?), 281
" , Hannah (aaaaf), 280, 283
" , Hannah (aaac), 279, 280
" , Hannah (aabgb), 319
" , Hannibal D. (adbae b), 269
" , Hardin (aaaed bj), 303
" , Harriett E. (aaabb aa), 295
" , Harriett (aaabc ch), 297
" , Harriett (adbac h), 268
" , Harriett C. (adbaa d) 268
" , Helen (aabgg f), 326
" , Henry (aabib b), 329
" , Hezekiah (aaabc ai), 297
" , Hickman (aabgfd) 326
" , Horatio McMullen (adbaa e), 268
" , Howell G. (aaabc aa), 297
" , Dr. Hugh (aaaeb ci), 301
" , Hugh, (aaaec cf), 302
" , Idella (aaabd h), 285, 299
" , I. J. (aabha a), 328
" , Indiana (aaaed bc) 303
" , Ira, (aaabc aj), 297
" , Isaac (aaaba c), 284, 294
" , Isabell (aabfek), 325
" , Isabell, wife of Peter IV, adbaa, 268
" , Isiaah, (adbbcc), 272
" , Jack (aabea c), 323
" , Jack (aachb t), 311
" , Jacob (aaaeb ca), 301
" , Jacob Vertrees (aabfea), 325
" , James (aabab i), 322
" , James (aabfc b), 324
" , James (aaabc b), 284, 297
" , James (aaaea f), 286, 300
" , James (aaaeb), 281, 286, 301
" , James (aaaeb cb), 301
" , James (aaaec o), 287, 302
" , James (aaaed d), 287, 303
" , James (aaah)(see aabh), 91, 92, 97, 98, 279, 281
" , James (Sr.),(aabh) (see aaah), 97, 98, 99, 315, 320, 328
" , James (Jr.) (aabhc), 33, 35, 100, 320, 328
" , James (aabhb c), 328

Hanks, James (aabicg), 330
" , James (adbbb g), 271
" , James Anderson, (aabii c), 180, 331
" , James M. (aaabc cj), 297
" , James R. (aabae a), 322
" , James Stewart (adbaa g), 268
" , Jane (aaaaa da), 291
" , Jane (aaaeb cea), 301
" , Jane (adbdb), 267
" , Jared (adbbh g), 274
" , Jason (adbbh k), 274
" , Jemima,wife of Jonathan adbd, 267, 275
" , Jemima (aabich), 330
" , Jennie (aaaeb ch), 301
" , Jeremiah (aabgcd), 326
" , Jeremiah (aabgfc), 326
" , Jeremiah (adbbc f), 272
" , Jessie (aaaec e) 302
" , John, the immigrant, 277, 306, 314
" , John (Delaware Co., Pa.) 40
" , John (aaaaa d) 282, 291 (married Jane Armstrong)
" , John (aaaaad c), 291
" , John (aaab) 279, 280, 284, 285. Married Mary Mott
" , John (aaabb) 280, 284, 295, 296. Son of John.
" , John (aaabb d), 284, 296
" , John (aaaec p), 287, 302
" , John (aaaea d), 286, 300
" , John (aaaed a), 25, 287, 303
" , John (aabab b), 322
" , John (aabfe e), 325
" , John (aabic a), 329
" , John (aabig), son of Abraham, 29, 168, 174, 321, 331
" , John "The Railsplitter" (aabfc e) 2, 4, 159, 208, 209, 324
" , John (aabha b), 328
" , John (aabhb d), 328
" , John (aac), 279, 306, .307, 308, 309, 314
" , John (aabac), 317, 322
" , John (aach), 307, 308, 310, 311
" , John (adbaab), 268
¥ , John (aabgd b), 326
ⁿ , John (aabgf b), 326
" , John (adbbb e), died at Vicksburg, 271